Imperial Germany's
"Iron Regi
of the First W

War Memories of Service with
Infantry Regiment 169
1914 -1918

Second Edition

by

John K. Rieth

Badgley Publishing Company

ISBN 978-0-9988045-0-7

IMPERIAL GERMANY'S
"IRON REGIMENT"
OF THE FIRST WORLD WAR
Table of Contents

Notes on Maps

Online Map:

In the period between August 1914 through November 1918, Infantry Regiment 169 operated across the span of the entire Western Front; an enormous amount of territory. To best understand these operations in topographical form, readers are invited to visit the Map Page of this book's website: www.ironregiment169.com. A Google Earth map marks over 150 locations associated with IR 169's wartime journey, with trench locations and battle lines provided for the more significant campaigns. The Google Earth imagery allows the reader to see the actual terrain, with most of the locations still untouched by urban sprawl. This function also can be used in battlefield visits to pinpoint the exact locations where these dramatic struggles took place.

General Orientation Maps:

In the three pages that follow, maps are provided that depict IR 169's prewar, garrison basing; the early 1914 battles along the southern portion of the Western Front; and the 1915 – 1918 battlefields in the central and northern Western Front. These maps are useful to orient readers to the general sectors of operations.

Battle Maps:

Throughout the book, maps are included to detail specific battles and campaigns, and the ground won or lost. While some of the maps have German text, they will still give readers a clearer understanding of the flow of battle. Many of the maps included are periodic in nature and are available in the public domain. A complete listing of map sources is found in the bibliography section.

Map Index

Albert Rieth, Bugler, 9th Company, Infantry Regiment 169, as depicted in this 1915 sketch drawn by his father, Gustav.

Farewell my house on the ridge in the upland forest.

Do you hear the lament of the storm and the waves?

Tell me! Whisper in my heart.

Whether we will meet again.

And whether I come back or fail to return,

As may be allotted fate.

What you gave me my house of green,

I will never forget.

Albert Rieth
March 7, 1915

~ x ~

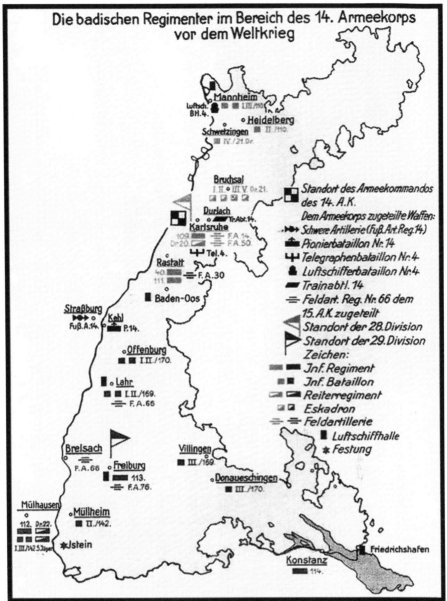

Map depicting the pre-war garrison locations of Baden regiments. IR169's headquarters and 1st and 2nd Battalions were in Lahr, with 3rd Battalion in Villingen.

(BIWW)

Southern Portion of Western Front

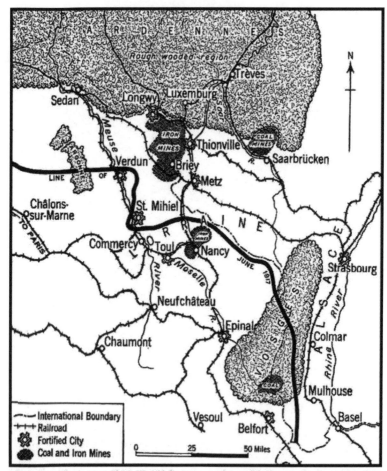

1914: In early August 1914, IR 169 first saw action at Mulhouse. In the mid-to-late August Battle of the Frontiers, the regiment fought a series of engagements centered 40 miles west of Strasbourg. In September, IR 169 took part in the offensive that created the center, lower portion of the St. Mihiel Salient.

1917: In early 1917, IR 169 returned to the Alsace to serve in the trenches by Altkirch, between Belfort and Mulhouse.

1918: IR 169 wintered in the Argonne Forest prior to deploying for the Spring Offensives to the north. The regiment returned to the Argonne in late September, where it fought to its destruction on 1 November.

(AABE)

Central and Northern Portions of Western Front

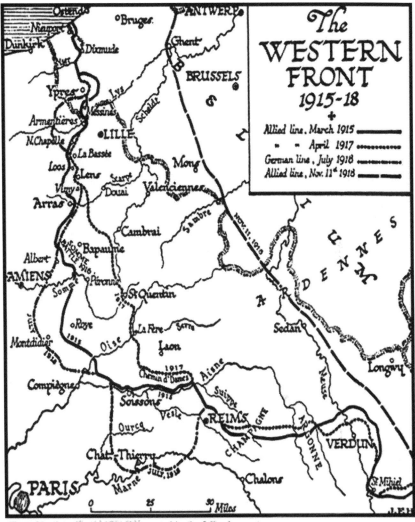

From North to South, IR 169 operated in the following sectors:

- 15 miles southeast of Ypres, 1918
- La Bassee, 1914
- Arras/Vimy, 1918
- Somme Battlefront (Bapaume area), 1915-1916, 1918
- Montdidier, 1918
- Chemin des Dames, 1917, 1918
- Marne, 1918
- Argonne, 1918

(AABE)

Author's Notes

"We took the first enemy trench to rest up before taking the second trench, when the enemy artillery suddenly started to fire upon us. They knew the distance very well, and we laid flat into the trench, but were nearly buried alive.

The shells and shrapnel so often burst in the trench that I thought the 3rd Battalion, Regiment 169 had ceased to fight. A piece of shrapnel took the drum out of the drummer's hands without injuring him. But meanwhile we had dead and wounded. Next to me someone shouted, "Help, help me, I am wounded!" I wondered how one could best take him out of this witches' cauldron, because if we both exposed ourselves in full size we would have been easy targets for the French infantry. "

Albert Rieth, Bugler, Infantry Regiment 169: Battle of the Frontiers, Hochweiller, Lorraine Province, August 20, 1914.

"Still the English attack; even though hundreds of them are shot down in front of our lines, fresh waves continue to pour over from their jumping-off positions. We have to shoot!

The English are already in hand-grenade range; grenades fly to and fro. The machine gun's barrel's been changed and the gun jacket filled - load! Hand-grenades and rifle-grenades explode violently in front of the gun – the loading begins to tangle! You recite loudly, slowly and clearly saying to yourself: "forward - feed - back!"....tack-tack-tack-tack....a furious sustained fire once more strikes the "khakis" in front of us!"

Otto Lais, Machine Gunner, Infantry Regiment 169: Battle of the Somme (Serre Sector), July 1, 1916.

These are the words of two German soldiers who served with Infantry Regiment 169 (IR 169) in two very different periods of World War I. The first hand accounts of such men, combined with the voices of other opponents, unit journals and other rare sources, provides a unique telling of a German regiment's journey through the entire Great War.

This second edition version of *"The Imperial Germany's Iron Regiment of the First World War,"* adds a significant amount of new content - over 100 pages of text - that was not available when I released my first effort in 2014. Publication of the first edition provided a forum for those with further interest in IR 169, which in turn generated a rich collection of additional source material. Armed with this wealth of new information, I had the opportunity to provide a more complete telling of IR 169's story.

My direct link to IR 169's history comes through a veteran of this unit, my grandfather Albert Rieth. His story lives in my memories, and more specifically, in his war-time journal that my family uncovered years after his death.

In the late 1920s, Albert Rieth immigrated to the United States from his home in Pforzheim, in the state of Baden, to escape the economic chaos of post-war Germany. A master toolmaker, Albert established residence in Providence, Rhode Island where he raised his family and established a lifelong career in the jewelry industry. Known to my sisters and I as 'Opa,' Albert was a perfect grandfather. He enjoyed a zest for life, possessed a keen sense of humor and retained a sharp mind through the time of his death, at age 79, in 1970. Although I was only 10 years old when he passed away, he left a strong imprint on my youth.

As a young boy, I began to develop a deep and lifelong interest in military history. I was fascinated by the fact that my kindly old grandfather had once served with the Kaiser's Army. These were days when World War I veterans, most in their 70s and 80s, could still be found marching in local Veterans Day parades. From an American perspective, any local reference to the Great War was understandably Doughboy-centric. That seemed fine with Albert, who had little interest in reliving the war. Still, I did what I could to pry out any stories from his time in the German Army.

Albert, for his part, always downplayed his wartime experiences. He took a certain pride in considering himself as one of the Kaiser's less motivated soldiers. When pressed for details, he would be willing to recount a number of rather humorous tales common to any soldier of any army. As I recall, the more often-told stories, most of the pre-war era, seemed to center on his acts of discreet subversion against a particularly toxic non-commissioned officer. Albert held little fondness for military life and used a German vernacular for describing the uselessness of his officers.

While I was certainly amused by Albert's funnier tales, I would often press him for accounts about the war. Although he would occasionally share a fragmented battle scene, he seldom went into great detail, and certainly never left anyone in his circle of family and friends with an overall understanding of his service. We knew that he was wounded fairly early in the war, with my later research confirming his being wounded in late August 1914 and again in January 1915.

Still, there were a few select combat memories that seemed to endure. Perhaps he selected these vignettes to illustrate the waste and tragedy of war. Those stories that resonated most were descriptions of massed ranks of attacking French infantry, conspicuous in their blue coats and red kepis and pants, being blown apart by German artillery and machine gun fire. Another instance (where my research for this book would enable me to pinpoint the specific location and time) was of an ambush of a French artillery battery. In this action, Albert spoke of how, at close range, his unit's machine gun and rifle fire slaughtered scores of French gunners and horses. A final story defined his hatred of war. It was about a battle where his unit was overrunning a French position. In the course of the attack, Albert jumped in a ditch to find a dying French soldier, lying in agony with a grievous stomach wound as he spent his last moments gazing at a picture of his family. Looking at Albert, the Frenchman's expression suggested that he expected to be bayoneted. Instead, Albert dropped his rifle and tried to give some comfort to this dying man. This incident must have had a significant impact on Albert, as it transformed his foe into a fellow victim of war.

Albert's wartime journal became known to me during my teenage years. To my disappointment, the text was hastily written in old script German, a form of writing almost illegible to many Germans educated after the 1930s. Even my father, who spoke and read native-level German, was unable to decipher the content. Years went by and my own path took me on a career as a U.S. Army officer. For decades, the journal was essentially forgotten, along with any hope of getting it translated into English. My 1995 assignment to the U.S. Embassy in Bonn, Germany, provided the opportunity to resurrect my interest in its content. I found that an associate at the Embassy, Walter Mueller, who was schooled in Germany in the 1930s, was able and willing to read Albert's script. After the period of a few months, Walt presented me with a superb English translation.

Albert titled his journal "*Kriegserinnernungen*" (War Memories).

It was written in March 1915 while he was recovering in a German military hospital from a foot wound received on a Flanders battlefield. The story details his experiences as a German infantry bugler in IR 169 during the first three weeks of the war.

My tour of duty to Germany put me in proximity to rare sources on the regiment that would have otherwise been impossible to find. With this growing information in hand, I was able to wander across the battlefields described by Albert. The resulting research accumulated from this period led to my writing a short, book-form paper intended for various family members. With my initial project completed in 2000, my interest in the regiment lived on and I continued to collect emerging information. With the arrival of the war's centennial in 2014, it seemed appropriate to expand my earlier research and publish a complete account of IR 169's history.

The more I dug into IR 169's history, the more I came to appreciate the extraordinary scope of the regiment's service. My grandfather's account was only a brief, but important view of the month-long maneuver phase of the war. In examining the broad perspective, we see how IR 169 served in every sector of the Western Front and fought in its most tumultuous battles.

To the extent possible, this book seeks to have the story told from the perspective of the combatants. To that end, we are fortunate to have the recollections of Otto Lais, who served in IR 169 from its posting in the Somme trenches in 1916 through its very end at the Argonne Forest in November 1918. Lais was a remarkable man. After surviving some of the Great War's most terrible battles, he returned to Karlsruhe to become a noted artist. In this second edition, we learn that Lais was recalled to duty in World War II, where he commanded a grenadier regiment in Normandy and the Netherlands and was awarded Germany's highest honors for valor. He again returned home where he quietly spent his later years as an art teacher. There is no doubt this complicated artist was a fierce warrior and skilled combat leader.

In the postwar period, many German regiments published their own official histories. Unfortunately, IR 169 was not among this list, and left future generations with no formal, archived narrative. This shortfall apparently rankled Lais, who in the period 1935-1942, authored three works, all published by G. Braun, Karlsruhe, on his IR

169 wartime experiences. Among his talents as an artist and combat leader, Lais was also a gifted writer. His descriptions of World War I battlefield horrors rival the best of the war's better-known first person accounts. In my first edition, I presented selections from his 1935 pamphlet, *Experiences of Baden Soldiers at the Front, Volume 1: A Machine Gunner in the Iron Regiment (8th Baden Infantry Regiment No. 169)*. This piece covers IR 169's service in the 1916 Battle of the Somme in 1916, and the regiment's return to the same battlefields in August 1918.

For this second edition, I was able to acquire and translate selections from Lais' other two books. Lais' 1936 *A Regiment Dies a Hero's Death,* describes IR 169's participation in the German Spring 1918 Offensives and its destruction in Meuse-Argonne Campaign. Lais' final work, *The Battle in the Limestone Chalk,* was published in 1942. This book dovetails a general history of the war with Lais' experiences with IR 169 in the 1917 French Aisne Offensive. The inclusion of these two books as primary source material affords us a much more detailed accounting of IR 169's experiences in the final two years of the war. Lais introduces to a number of colorful characters, given additional texture and humanity to our understanding of IR 169.

In the course of my research, I was fortunate to obtain rare source material specific to IR 169. The first is the book *Baden in the World War*, (G. Braun, 1935), which provides a collection of short stories by veterans of Baden units including accounts of IR 169's battles. Another rare source is the IR 169 Field Journal (*Feltschrift*), with an accompanying short history of the regiment's origin and account of the 1916 Battle of the Somme. This material was assembled for an IR 169 reunion in August 1924 and is titled *Commemorative Publication for the 1st Regimental Day of the former 8th Baden Infantry Regiment 169 on 30 and 31 August 1924.* The field journal contains nearly 50 entries that mark each significant movement, engagement and casualty reports from the war's start in August 1914 through the regiment's demobilization in May 1919.

Other valuable source material added to the second edition are recent additions to the study of the German Army in World War I. Most notable are those including Ralph Whitehead's volumes I and II of *The Other Side of the Wire, With the German XIV Reserve Corps on the Somme,* Helion & Company Ltd, UK, 2013; Frank Bucholz and

Frank and Janet Robinson *The Great War Dawning; Germany and its Army at the Start of World War I,* Verlag Militaria, Vienna, Austria, 2013, and Jack Sheldon's *The German Army in the Spring Offensives 1917; Arras, Aisne & Champagne*, Pen and Sword Military, 2015. Inclusion of these new sources certainly added to the depth and accuracy of understanding the men who made up IR 169 and the battles that they fought in.

Much of the primary source material exists only in German language. The challenge of translating these sources was compounded as most of it was printed in the dated, hard-to-read 'Fractur' font. In both editions of the book, my work in translating and editing the sources were augmented by a team of loyal friends, whose efforts were essential in completing the project. Their efforts are more thoroughly described in the acknowledgements section of the book. Briefly I want to highlight the background of several members of this team to include M. Allen Saunders, Tom Bierchenk, Crad Kennedy, Dr. (PhD) Les Cullen, Colonel Patrick K. Keough (U.S. Army, Ret.), Lieutenant Colonel David Moore (U.S. Army, Ret.). Al, Tom, Crad, Les, Pat, Dave and myself, albeit in profoundly different circumstances from those who fought in the Great War, have all in served the United States in various war zones over the years. [Interestingly, the genesis of these recent Balkan, Middle East and Afghanistan conflicts can be directly traced to the lingering aftermath of World War I.] Collectively, I think these experiences help connect us to soldiers of past, and compels us to provide them a voice so their sacrifices will not be forgotten. Our translations have attempted to preserve the voice and style that their authors intended, while also being edited for clarity in a modern, English-language presentation.

Dr. Jack Sheldon, a career veteran of the British Army, stands among the top English-speaking authorities of the German Army of World War I. Dr. Sheldon makes extensive use of first-person soldier accounts as a cornerstone to his books. In the below, abridged introduction to Sheldon's *The German Army at Ypres, 1914*; Oxford Professor of the History of War, Hew Strachan, provides these apt reflections of the use of German accounts in the First World War:

"First-hand German accounts of the fighting on the Western Front of the First World War are dramatically different from those written by British participants. Very often conveyed in the historic present tense, their sentences are short and direct. Using pathos, they cast the dead as heroes, putting direct speech into their mouths and not infrequently closing their observations with an exclamation mark for added and rhetorical effect. For English readers, these German accounts can seem 'over the top,' or tainted with the fascism movement zeal. But the consequence of such superciliousness has been to rob us of an enormously rich and extensive primary source." [1]

The use of German accounts do indeed come with a unique literary style that defines the writing of this era. I think most readers will agree that their words provide a powerful image of the terror in the battlefields, both above and within the trenches where they fought.

As the narrative of this book was coming together, I was struck by the 'Zelig-like' quality of Infantry Regiment 169's wartime experience. At one point or another, IR 169 served in every sector of the Western Front. Throughout the war, IR 169 battled troops from France, Britain, India and French colonial divisions from central Africa. Towards the war's end, it also fought Kiwis from New Zealand as well as American soldiers and marines.

Beginning with the Battle of Mulhouse in August 9, IR 169 was in the midst of the war's brief maneuver phase that continued through the extremely bloody Battle of the Frontiers. The regiment marched in the 'Race to the Sea' and suffered terrible losses in Flanders. In 1915, the regiment moved into the then 'quiet' trenches of the Somme, which became one of the war's worst killing grounds when the British launched their disastrous Somme Offensive in July 1916. In 1917, the regiment saw service that ranged from the trenches of the southern Alsace to pitched battles along the Aisne. In 1918, IR 169 participated in the major spring offensives that pushed the Allied lines far back, and then returned to Flanders and the Somme to face the ensuing Allied counterattacks. Finally, the regiment met its destruction at the hands of United States Marines and Army tanks in the Meuse-Argonne at the very end of the war.

It comes as no surprise that this tempo of intensive combat left IR 169 with appalling casualties. At full strength, IR 169's manning tables called for a complement of 3,500 officers and men. In four years of war, 22,540 German soldiers cycled through the IR 169 ranks. Of these men, over 12,000 were counted as casualties. For those men serving in the ranks at the beginning of August 1914, there was a 400% probability that they would be killed, wounded or captured before the war's end. On multiple occasions, IR 169 battled to the verge of destruction, only to regenerate and be sent back in action within short periods of time.

This book is intended as a tactical history of a specific unit. In doing so, I have tried to provide some degree of operational and strategic context. This helps us understand what greater decisions and events led IR 169 to otherwise insignificant villages and towns; places where men were slaughtered in such numbers that it defies our imagination today. I've attempted to stay clear of making judgments on the causes, atrocities and outcomes of the war. It is safe to say that none of the combatant forces, be they German or Allied, depicted in these pages lacked any measure of deep courage, fortitude and patriotism for their cause.

I have done my best to list specific citations taken from all sources, which I hope at very least, will give credit where it is due and build upon their efforts to illuminate the story of the First World War. For practical purposes, I have omitted references to general information that has been long established in the public domain. In describing measures of distance, I have made use of both metric (meters and kilometers) and Imperial Systems (yards and miles), given the varied use by sources. Likewise, I also mix the title of the German Army rank system in both German and English terms.

With this second edition, I augmented the book's maps with an online version of a Google Earth map that graphically depicts IR 169's battles and travels across the Western Front. Readers can access the map through the website www.ironregiment169.com. The website also includes additional background on the book, a photographic gallery of IR 169 soldiers, and description of my visit to IR 169's August 1914 battlefields.

Prologue

Lahr, Germany; September 30, 1898

The town's citizens began crowding the decorated streets two hours before the event began. Eager faces craned from open windows to gain a first glimpse of the new regiment's arrival. The best viewing would be in the *Urteilsplatz*, the town square, where city officials and senior military leaders would present their speeches. The regimental choir, which arrived some hours earlier, were joined by local singing groups as they took their positions by the reviewing stand.

The citizens of Lahr had good reason for the excitement; this joyous day announced to Germany that Lahr had finally become a garrison town. The town had spent years lobbying for the privilege of hosting a line infantry regiment, a commitment evidenced by their funding the construction of the new *Kaserne,* a barracks complex just under a mile south of the city center. Lahr, with its population of 15,000 residents, was an industrial and trade city on the western edge of the Black Forest. The addition of 2,000 soldiers, comprising two line battalions and a regimental staff, would bring a big boost to the town's economy, prestige and protection. The provision of security was an important consideration, for only 28 years earlier the Franco-Prussian War raged along the nearby Alsace border. Indeed, all residents over the age 40 could well remember the nights of August 1870, when the northwest sky glowed from the burning of the besieged city of Strasbourg, barely 15 miles away.

The crowds cheered a spontaneous 'Hurrah' when the first drumbeats of the nearing 1st Battalion came within earshot. Led by Herr Oberst (Colonel) von Krogh, and followed by the regimental and Imperial German colors, the troops marched into the Urteilsplatz. The battalions had just come off of their summer maneuvers, and the soldiers, with well-tanned faces beneath their black pickelhaube helmets, looked resplendent in dress blue uniforms. The crowd went wild with jubilation and showered the men with flowers as the regimental band played and the choral groups sang. Colonel von Krogh saluted the tribunal, it was then time for the speeches. Lahr's mayor, Oberburgermeister Herr Dr. Schlusser presented his greeting:

"Many greetings from the flags that blow in the wind. Today the problems and worries of which there were many in the last years are forgotten, and the hearts of all "Lahrer" are filled with joy. Today we have a changing point for the history of our city. Smart looking uniforms will now liven up our city, and in the streets that up until now saw busy workers and shopkeepers, we will now hear the sounds of drums and whistles as military music will come into our lives.

Our city, which for hundreds of years has had to tolerate the horrors of disunity, knows what the protection of a mighty united country means. Our city, welcomes, with jubilee, the regiment which will take part of the watch of the Rhine. Let our regiment feel at home.... Let it be an example of what our war commander shall say – with God for the protection of the Fatherland."

Colonel von Krogh, for his part, responded with rather stiff, but still heartfelt thanks as he spoke for a comfortable existence between the regiment and the people of Lahr. Von Krogh then gave the order "*Stand at attention, weapons at attention.*" The battalions moved into a parade formation for the short march to their new home – the Lahr Kaserne. There, Colonel von Krogh addressed just his command, stressing his expectations for the men to respect and get along with the citizens of Lahr. As the noncommissioned officers settled the men into the barracks, the senior officers returned to the town to meet with town officials in the Sonne Gasthaus as the younger officers joined the lower governmental officials in various taverns. That night, the entire officer corps hosted the town elders at the Hotel Kraus for a celebratory dinner, replete with many toasts. Congratulatory telegrams came in from Grand Duke Friedrich, Baden's Regent who ruled from the Karlsruhe Palace, as well as from the Kaiser's Minister of War in Berlin.

The town's newspaper's account of the day closed with the words – "The citizens of Lahr can look back to this day, and can be proud that the majority of the citizens gave their best so that the protection of the Reich can take place! That is an honor!" [2] Baden's 8th *Badische* Infantry Regiment (Imperial German designation IR 169), had arrived.

Meuse-Argonne Battlefront
Landres Sector, 3:59 am, November 1, 1918

In four years of war, IR 169 had faced many desperate circumstances, but none as dire as this one.

Events leading to this last stand began four weeks earlier, when the regiment was rushed to the front to stem the American First Army's fracture of German lines at the Argonne Forest. In 17 days of continuous combat, IR 169, along with its two sister regiments of the 52nd Infantry Division and other German units, repulsed attacks of three large American divisions. The intensity of the fighting was such that the Germans inflicted over 16,000 enemy casualties, with IR 169 losing nearly 700 of the 1,500 men they entered the battle with.

Following a five day rest period, IR 169 was back at the front on October 21. The ceaseless pounding of enemy artillery was a misery, but true disaster first struck on October 28, when an American phosgene chemical attack all but annihilated the 1st Battalion. The second act of the catastrophe occurred during the early morning hours of November 1, when the 2nd and 3rd Battalions moved from a forward reserve position to replace a unit rotating out of the Landres Sector trenches. Of the few hundred men left remaining in ranks, many were replacements who only joined IR 169 a few days earlier.

On the other side of the no-man's-land, the American First Army was about to launch its knock-out blow. Frustrated by weeks of stout German defenses, the Americans assembled the largest attack force they committed in the war. Artillery firepower came from 1,500 guns, with 300 of those targeting the Landres area defenses. The task of eliminating the Landres strong-point was assigned to the Marine Brigade of the battle-tested 2nd Infantry Division, who assaulted alongside a large concentration of heavy and light tanks.

Zero hour of the attack was 4:00 am. Some of IR 169's infantry had yet to enter their new trenches when one of the great barrages of World War I exploded upon them. The furious three-hour bombardment mixed chemical munitions among high explosive shells. A marine officer later remarked how every square foot of the enemy's front line area was struck by shell fire. The ground attack began at

7:00 am. Under the cover of a rolling artillery barrage, the tanks easily churned over the barbed wire entanglements as waves of marines followed closely behind. Within minutes, the attackers set upon those shell-shocked Germans who had survived the bombardment.

Otto Lais' memoirs recorded the final moments of IR 169's destruction:

> "In the night of October 31 - November 1, the regiment marched quickly out of the forested Argonne region into the open fields of Landres and Landreville. During a pitch-black, rainy night, the regiment arrived and began to dig into the open fields and meadows. No sooner had they started to dig when a storm of heavy artillery fire descended upon them. Within two hours, over 100 American heavy tanks and countless light tanks emerged to roll over, crush, and completely wipe out the regiment.
>
> The majority of the officers are dead or severely wounded. The machine gun crews, the anti-tank crews, and the hand grenade troop of the infantry have all been eliminated after a brave defense. Superiority of force has prevailed. Out of the pale gray mist of the dawn come row upon row of gray monsters with the rumbling of motors towards us. The heavy tanks move up one and two meters to the machine-gun nests and the anti-tank guns. The turret gun is lowered - there is a flash of fire and a report.
>
> The defenders are swimming in their blood. 'Move out!'
>
> The tank rattles on. Not one soul returns from the companies deployed to these forward positions. Only one officer, a courier, and three NCO's make it back. These five men, who had a special mission, were captured but were later able to escape.
>
> In the gray dawn of November 1, 1918, the Iron Regiment is no more."

Chapter 1
Prelude to War

Imperial Germany's 8th *Badische* Infantry Regiment, Number 169, (IR 169) existed in the time between 1897 – 1919. The origin, lineage and service of this proud regiment are closely intertwined with the citizens and events of greater Imperial Germany, and in particular, service to its regent state of Baden.

The Imperial German Empire was established in 1871 and lasted until the end of World War I. Under the rule of the Kaiser in Berlin, the German Empire unified a collection of 27 constituent states comprised of a series of kingdoms, grand duchies, duchies, principalities, free Hanseatic cities and one imperial territory. Baden was one of the six grand duchies, and was ruled by the Grand Duke Herzog. Infantry Regiment 169 was created to serve the Grand Duke and state of Baden in times of peace, and the Emperor in Berlin in the event of war.

Baden was a sovereign country from the days of the 12th Century up to the time of joining the Imperial German Empire in 1871. By annexing with the German Empire, Friedrich I retained his royal status and much of the exclusive economic and administrative control of his regency. From the capital city of Karlsruhe, the Grand Duchy of Baden had an area of 5,823 square miles and occupied a large swath of southwestern Germany. This included much of the eastern half of the fertile valley of the Rhine River and the expansive Black Forest. From north to south, and ranging along the Rhine River's west bank, a list of Baden's cities and towns included Mannheim, Heidelberg, Karlsruhe, Pforzheim, Baden-Baden, Offenburg, Freiburg, Lahr, and Villingen. Lahr and Villingen stand out in IR 169's history, with Lahr serving as the regimental headquarters and home for the 1st and 2nd Battalions, and much later, Villingen as the garrison of the 3rd Battalion.

The Imperial German government and its states had dual roles for maintaining the military forces. This system, supported by a vast personnel and industrial infrastructure, served the purposes of both the Kaiser and the state rulers. The royal regent of each of the eight primary Germanic states was responsible for the peacetime manning, training, and fielding of a certain number of military regiments. In the event of war and general mobilization, the state troops fell under the control of the Emperor in Berlin. As such, all the state troops were equipped and trained to a common standard that would ensure effective integration in the event of full mobilization. As part of this scheme, German units at the time had two separate designations, one for the state and the other for imperial service. For IR 169, the '169' served as the regiment's imperial number with '8' as its Baden numeration. In 1914, the Regent of Baden was responsible for maintaining 10 active infantry regiments, one cavalry *Dragoner* regiment, four field artillery regiments, and assorted pioneer, aviation, communications and logistics units.

IR 169's existence resulted from Imperial Germany's policy of building up its army through the years 1898 to 1914. Officially inaugurated on 31 March 1897, Infantry Regiment 169 was created by an amalgamation of existing battalions and companies from the 4th Battalions of the 109th (Baden) Grenadier Life-Guards Regiment, the 110th Grenadier Regiment and the 25th and 111th Infantry Regiments. Immediately after the fall maneuvers of 1898, the 1st Battalion in Karlsruhe and the 2nd Battalion in Rastatt were joined to form the core of IR 169. The regiment was based in the newly designated garrison in Lahr, a town located on the western edge of the Black Forest and 60 miles southwest of Karlsruhe. The regiment's barracks, administrative buildings and training centers were built and donated by the city. Lahr was a classic example of a pre-war German garrison town. In 1913, fifteen years after the regiment's inception, IR 169's 3rd Battalion was created by transferring the 4th Battalion of the 109th Leib Grenadier Regiment from Karlsruhe to Villingen.

German Army regiments reflected the fabric of their society and regions. In the pre-war years, IR 169 had the nickname of the *Handwerksburschen* (Craftsmen) Regiment. In 1916, following the regiment's crucible at the Battle of the Somme, IR 169 adopted the more warrior-like moniker of the *Eisernen* (Iron) Regiment. The term craftsmen was an appropriate prewar description of the skilled pool of artisans that made up the populace, economy and character of greater Baden. Between Baden's capital seat in Karlsruhe and the Wurttemberg city of Stuttgart, stands Pforzheim. A glimpse of Pforzheim, and the childhood of Albert Rieth, one man destined for IR 169's first days of combat, provides an example of the type of men and their communities that populated the regiment's ranks in the years just before the war.

In the early 20th Century, Pforzheim, dubbed as the Golden City and the northern 'Gateway to the Black Forest,' was an idyllic, charming, and prosperous small city. Despite its small size, Pforzheim was a powerhouse of Germany's jewelry and watchmaking economy, and at one time, accounted for 80 percent of national jewelry and silverware exports.

Albert, the only child to Gustav and Karoline Rieth, was born in Pforzheim on December 12, 1891. The Rieth lineage can be traced in this region all the way back to 1530. Like many of his ancestors, Albert's father, Gustav, was a talented artist and metalsmith. A combination of tradition and local opportunity destined a young man like Albert for a career in Pforzheim's robust jewelry industry. As he came of age, Albert received formal training as a toolmaker from one of the city's excellent technical schools.

A young man growing up in Baden would have every reason to be optimistic about his future. At the time of Albert's birth, Pforzheim had a population of 30,000, a figure that would swell to almost 79,000 by the time of his Army enlistment in 1912. Western Europe was experiencing a tremendous industrial boom that was having a huge impact on the life of the average citizen. Those of Albert's generation experienced staggering technical advances bringing forth mass-produced automobiles, the world's first aircraft, telephones, and the common use of electricity. It was a time of great progress in international banking, communication and transportation – economically linking the major European powers to a common interest. John Keegan described this bright era:

"The economic outlook of the industrial nations was nothing but optimistic from the mid 1890's through 1914. New categories of manufacture – electrical goods, chemical dyes, and internal combustion engines – became available for purchase, while new sources of cheap raw materials were making them affordable for the common man. The rising population (43% in Germany) sharply enlarged the size of internal markets, and the growing immigration of Europeans to America created a world economy." [3]

Europe in 1913 was a continent at peace, and according to Scottish historian Gerard DeGroot, had war not occurred, it is likely historians today would analyze the overwhelming momentum of peace.[4]

With economic prosperity being what it may, the call of military duty for young men in Imperial Germany was never far off. Albert's journey as an apprentice toolmaker was interrupted in 1912 when, at age 20, he was called up for active army service.

Prior to 1914, Germany required the annual induction of 300,000 men to meet the needs of the standing army. At age 20, virtually all qualified German males were liable for some degree of military service, but with only about 30% being obligated to service in the reserves and another 20% conscripted into the active army. In comparison, France drafted between 50-60% of its military aged men. Conscription was categorized by the annual class year from which they were born, the *Jahrgang*. In Albert's case, his late 1891 birth date placed him in the class of 1892, with that year group entering the recruitment process in 1912. The author team of Frank Bucholz and Frank and Janet Robinson explained the induction process in their authoritative examination of the pre-war Imperial German Army titled, *The Great War Dawning; Germany and its Army at the Start of World War I:*

"Recruitment was a yearling cycle with the collection of lists of eligible men that culminated in a spring event called the *Musterung*, that classified candidates based on medical examinations and other criteria such as sole family providers and other exemptions. The candidates were ranked into groups of fit for service, fit for garrison duty, fit for labor employment and permanently unfit. Those men deemed fit were sent forward into a lottery system based on the number of vacancies to be filled. For the entire Empire, the 1912 Musterung reviewed 557,608 20 year olds from the 1912 Jahrgang, of whom 112,623 for selected for active or reserve service. An additional 732,000 from prior year groups and other categories were considered, with 127,000 of that number recruited. The total number of young German men inducted into active and reserve army rolls 1912 totaled 239,717." [5]

Great War Dawning explains the celebratory spirit that communities devoted to the annual musterings in the days prior to reporting for duty.

> "Those selected would march through the town beating drums and demanding money from folks to pay for a last drink. The local ladies would tie bright ribbons to the hats of the soldiers-to-be. The ritual lasted two or three days and was often funded by those not selected." [6]

Recruits reported to their assigned regiments in October, after the fall harvests. The new recruits were issued uniforms and equipment at the company level and began a period of intense basic training that introduced them to the harsh discipline of the German Army. The initial phases of new recruit school consisted of drill, hygiene, physical training and dry fire marksmanship. Later phases added weekly training exercises in the countryside where the weight of backpacks were increased to 60 lbs. The recruits were isolated during this period from any contact with civilians." [7]

In addition to the military skill training, recruits were indoctrinated on an overarching commitment to serve the Emperor and Germany and adhere to a strict obedience to superiors and their orders. The men were immersed in the traditions of their new regiments, binding them to a high degree of loyalty and sacred obligation to never dishonor their unit.

After a standard two year active duty enlistment for infantrymen (one year longer for cavalry and artillery), German males faced various levels of reserve responsibilities through the age of 45. [8] These rules changed in wartime, and men could be sent into combat before age 20 and were not automatically released until reaching 45. The strength of the overall active German Army at the start of the World War I was 870,000 men. The efficiency of the German mobilization system enabled the army to quickly expand to 3.5 million troops at the start of the war.

Throughout Europe, there were French, Austrian, and Russian equivalents of this system, rendering the potential to call up millions of citizen soldiers who possessed at least some degree of military experience. The trend of peaceful coexistence of the early 1900's aside, a glimpse of Europe's tumultuous history in the century preceding the Great War shows the demand for all rulers to possess a strong military reserve capability.

The single-most important military organization in the German Army was the regiment. Ranging in size between 2500 – 3500 men, regiments were usually affiliated with a specific town or regional area. At the start of the war, Imperial Germany counted 217 infantry regiments in its rolls. Regiments were rich in tradition, with the lineage of some of the oldest reaching back to the 17th Century. Individual regiments had different variations of colors in their dress uniforms and most boasted their own drinking songs and marches. The regional manning, and long-term association of reserve units tied to active regiments, ensured a strong social aspect of military service. Imperial German regimental beer steins, personalized for each soldier in the unit, illuminate the deep sense of tradition, pride and loyalty inculcated within the regimental infrastructure. The close personal ties provided within regiments established a strong sense of comradeship, inclusion and trust among the men.

Commissioning sources for the Imperial German Army in the early 1900's saw a clash of Prussian nobility ruling traditions and the need to create a well-qualified junior officer cadre able to meet mobilization requirements. In 1913, officers of royal bloodlines made up 80% of cavalry regiments, 48% of infantry regiments and 41% of artillery regiments officer corps. The more prestigious guards regiments had higher levels of noble-classed officers. A system of three yearlong cadet academies brought both noble and middle classes into pre-commissioning systems. In the ranks of lieutenant to captain, officers were poorly paid and expected to supplement their salaries from their well-to-do families. Those young officers without such patrons lived in virtual poverty. Still, in the militaristic society of Imperial Germany, the privileges associated in becoming a commissioned officer came with significant social status. This provided poorer officers with at least a decent chance to marry into wealthier families. Promotion in the pre-war army was slow, with the typical progression to first lieutenant eight years, 14 more years to captain, 25 to major and 30 to reach lieutenant colonel. Promotions from the rank of lieutenant to major were conducted within regiments, and centralized at General Staff levels for higher grades. Seniority and noble connections were important for advancements. Officers were held to high standards of conduct and were required to wear their uniforms at all times.[9]

IR 169's commanding officer at the start of the war was *Oberst* (Colonel) Spennemann. The regiment's second-in-command was graded for an *Oberstleutnat* (lieutenant colonel), whose responsibilities included backing up the commander and leading the regimental staff. The staff sections fulfilled such tasks as operational planning, communications, personnel administration, logistical and other tasks essential to supporting and coordinating the operations of the line units.

The regiment's three battalions [listed as 1st, 2nd, 3rd for the purposes of this book, but actually I, II and III in German numeration] were commanded by majors. Battalions were the nucleus of the regiment's core combat power. Each battalion consisted of four rifle companies, with 1st Battalion containing Companies 1-4, 2nd Battalion Companies 5-8, and 3rd Battalion with Companies 9-12. The lowest independent maneuver unit within an infantry regiment was at the rifle company level. Rifle companies were commanded by a *Hauptmann* (captain), and at full strength were manned by five officers and 250 infantrymen. Rifle companies were further divided into three platoons, led by a combination of *Oberleutnant* (lieutenant), *Leutnant* (2nd lieutenant) and *Feldwebel-Leutnant* (sergeant major-lieutenant). Resident within each platoon were four sections, with the smallest subunit being an eight man squad.

The German Army had developed a strong cadre of experienced noncommissioned officers (NCOs) who served at the regimental, battalion and company levels. German NCOs of the Imperial era were either re-enlistees who came up from the ranks or graduates of NCO training schools. These training schools took in volunteers from *Volkschulen* (German public school system) for a two year training program that graduated them in NCO ranks with four years of active service obligations.[10] Ranks of the NCOs included the E*tatmässige Feldwebel* (regimental sergeant-major), *Feldwebel* (company sergeant-major), *Vizefeldwebel* (staff sergeant), *Unteroffizier* (corporal) and *Gefrieiter* (lance corporal). The NCOs were responsible for maintaining the day-to-day operations and discipline of the regiment. While the officers may have commanded the regiment, it was the NCOs who truly ran things.

By 1913, the German Army had developed a doctrine that established a dedicated machine gun (MG) company for each infantry regiment. By September 1913, IR 169 had a machine gun company consisting of fifty-seven men, ten NCOs and a standard company level officer complement. While some variants of machine guns had been in existence since the 1860s, the large size and unreliability of the early versions led to their deployment more in the role of artillery, rather than a direct fire weapon. The fielding of the German Maxim 1908, 7.92 mm machine gun provided the Germans with an extremely effective weapon at the small unit level. Although weighing a hefty 58 pounds, not including the additional bulk of the carriage, water cooling system and ammunition, the gun was still mobile enough to be dragged into battle by a squad of gunners. With a rate of fire of 450 rounds per minute and effective range of 2000 yards, a distance that could be expanded further with specialized ammunition, this weapon had a profound impact on the WW I battlefield.

A German machine gun company of 1914 was armed with six Maxim guns. The company was divided into three platoons, each with two guns. Commanders were provided with the options to divide the machine gun platoons to each of the three battalions or concentrate the massed firepower of all six guns as a single company. The Germans were the only nation at the start of the war to integrate machine gun units into the regimental level. While machine gun doctrine, unit structure and weapon systems evolved throughout the war, this dedicated regimental resource provided the Germans with a distinct tactical advantage in its opening days.

German soldiers were issued a variety of full dress and field uniforms. IR 169's dress uniforms, worn in parades and on ceremonial occasions, consisted of visored caps with red pining, dark blue jackets, with a gold and red collar and brass buttons, and dark brown pants. The dress jacket had red shoulder straps with a yellow numeral 169. The standard-issue *pickelhaube* helmet was adorned with a brass plate, representing Baden's Griffin seal. Musicians adorned their parade helmets with a red plume added atop the spike.

The standard garrison uniform included a visor-less, *feldmutze* field cap that sported a red band, the type 1910 field gray, wool tunic, dark gray trousers and brown leather jackboots. The tunic included red shoulder epaulettes that had 169 embroidered in red. [Later in the war, troops were issued a wool band that would cover the number for security purposes.] Additional uniform accessories and trimmings varied based on the soldiers' ranks.

When worn in the field, the leather pickelhaube helmet was protected by a field-gray canvas covering with red 169 unit designation on the front [in 1914, green replaced the red numbering]. The classic spike on top of the pickelhaube was a throwback to the days when it was intended to thwart blows from enemy cavalry sabers. The traditional pickelhaube proved impractical for modern combat and provided little protection against weather, shrapnel or bullets. Soldiers initially adapted to the advent of trench warfare by unscrewing the spike to avoid telegraphing their helmets. Beginning in 1916, the pickelhaubes were replaced by the more practical *stahlhelme* steel helmet.

In full marching order, a German infantryman's field kit weighed well over 65 pounds. Much of his gear was packed in a large calfskin knapsack covered with a rolled blanket. Strapped on the back of the pack was a 1910-pattern mess kit. Soldiers wore a brown canvas haversack, containing a bag holding thread, needles, bandages and adhesive tape, and another with such items as matches, chocolate, and tobacco. A second bag contained 'iron ration,' a unit with two cans of meat, two of vegetables, two packages of hardtack crackers, one of ground coffee, and a flask of whisky which was only to be opened with the permission of an officer.[11] A canteen was strapped on this rig. A sturdy field belt, with a Baden belt buckle that depicted the imperial crown and proclaiming *Gott Mit Uns*, held an entrenching tool and two three-section leather ammunition pouches. Each pouch section contained three, five-round stripper clips, for a total of ninety bullets for ready access, with an additional one hundred and fifty rounds carried in the pack.

The infantryman's primary weapon was the 1898 model, 7.92mm Mauser rifle. The Gewehr 98, weighing 9.5 lbs, was a bolt action rifle that fired cartridges from a five round internal clip-loaded magazine. Quick to load and with an effective range of 500 meters, the Mauser was an accurate, powerful and reliable weapon that was the mainstay of the German Army well into the Second World War.

The authors of *The Great War Dawning* provide a vivid description of military life that reflected the IR 169 experience in its prewar garrison existence:

"When in garrison (*Kasernes*), each battalion was housed in its own barracks building, divided into squad rooms of 10-20 men each called *stubens*. Kasernes were enclosed by high brick walls and included an assortment of buildings that included barracks, headquarters, latrines, mess halls, armories, storage depots, tailor shops, barbershops, shoemakers and the like. A daily menu may consist of coffee and bread for breakfast, stew at lunch, and tea, coffee, bread and occasional soup at dinner. Fruits and desserts were seldom available and the troops were expected to supplement their meager rations with care packages from home. Privates were poorly compensated at a rate of 2.2 marks every ten days, and with a portion of that sum going to pay for their laundry and other services. During off duty time, the men could retire to their battalions' canteen, where beer could be purchased for five pfennig and a pipeful of tobacco for one pfennige.[12]

The morning routine was guided at the company level. A typical duty day began at 4:45 am when a member of the evening guard awakened the NCO of the day. The rest of barracks were woken shortly after, and the men were given one hour for personal and barracks hygiene and breakfast before being paraded for squad inspections. Ten minutes later there was a company formation led by the first sergeant. The company's lieutenants arrived at 6:00 am to inspect their platoons, and then report to the company commander. The company marched to the drill field where training was conducted until 11:15 am, and the men marched to the mess halls for lunch. Soldiers returned to the drill fields in the afternoon to continue training that may include physical fitness calisthenics. When afternoon training was completed, the men were released for dinner and, schedules permitting, evening free time.[13]

Albert Rieth was thrust into this, deep-rooted martial apparatus in mid-1912.

Following his basic training, Albert joined the 1st Badischen Leib Grenadier Regiment 109 at its Kaserne in Karlsruhe. From the mid 1700's on, Karlsruhe served as the Baden's capital city throughout the various evolutions of monarchy and parliamentary governments that followed. The Grand Herzog Palace sat at the city center, with outlining roads forming a pattern of spokes, leading to Karlsruhe's nickname as the 'fan city' *Fächerstadt*. In the early 1900's, Karlsruhe's population stood at just over 100,000.

Regiment 109 had a rich history that dated back to its formation as the *Infanterie-Regiment Erbprinz* in March 1803. Imposing the will of the Baden royalty, the regiment's battle record reflects the bloody and complex evolution of the various European kingdoms and formation of the Germanic states throughout the 1800's. In the 1813 War of Liberation, Regiment 109 fought first with France against Prussia and then switched sides to fight with the Prussians against the French. The regiment served alongside the Prussians against Denmark in 1848-49, but then fought *against* the Prussians in the three month Austro-Prussian War of 1866. Finally allied again with Prussia in the 1870-1871 Franco-Prussian War, the regiment fought the French at the Battle of Nuits.[14]

Regiment 109's standing was further elevated by its designation as the palace guard for the Regent of Baden. The Grand Duke himself was the ceremonial commander of the regiment, a tradition starting with Grand Duke Friedrich I, who ruled Baden from 1856-1907, and then continued by his successor, Grand Duke Friedrich II.

At some point in his induction cycle, Albert was selected to become a musician and was eventually trained as a bugler (*kornist*). Upon arrival in Karlsruhe, he was assigned to the 109th Regiment's 1st Battalion, 4th Company. Buglers had dual duties at the regimental band and company level. While in garrison, the regimental band would perform for parades and other ceremonial functions at the palace. In the field, and during routine fatigue duties, buglers were assigned down to the line company level, where they were directly detailed to the commander. Most mornings were spent on regular duties within the company, while afternoons were often dedicated to battalion and regimental band music practice. Through the early days of the First World War, a commander's most expedient means to communicate with his unit over the din of battle was via bugle calls. Another typical duty the bugler had was to serve as the commander's designated distance estimator, an important task when company fires were massed at long range targets. These responsibilities frequently placed the bugler at his commander's side. To further stand out among the ranks, German musicians wore a distinctive red striped band 'swallow nest' on the upper sleeve of their uniform jackets. As World War I progressed, there was little need for regimental bands in the trenches, and regiments converted their musicians to such roles as stretcher-bearers.

Back in garrison, service as a musician offered some advantages to a young conscript biding time until his discharge. At the very least, participating in routine band practice was a break from some of the tedious tasks of the afternoon training and inspection cycles that marked the life of the common foot soldier.

In early 1913, a realignment of Baden regiments resulted in Regiment 109's 1st Battalion being re-designated as the 3rd Battalion of Infantry Regiment 169. This addition finally provided IR 169 with a complete complement of three maneuver battalions. With this reassignment, the newly designated 3rd Battalion was transferred to the town of Villingen, 100 miles to the south of Karlsruhe on the eastern edge of the Black Forest. The Villingen posting separated the 3rd Battalion from the IR 169 regimental headquarters and the other two battalions headquartered in Lahr, 50 miles northeast. Soldiers of that era made frequent use of postcards that were created at the unit level and contained pictures of military life. One card from Albert Rieth's collection, dated January, 1914, depicts the newly re-designated 3rd Battalion marching into the streets of Villingen with the band leading the way. As in the case of IR 169's initial entry into Lahr in 1898, 3rd Battalion's arrival in Villingen was a major event, with thousands of residents lining the main street to welcome the newly arriving soldiers.

The collective unit training cycle of the German Army revolved around the two year active duty service obligation of the average enlisted man. During the late fall season, as new recruits went through their period of basic training, second year soldiers participated in a 15 week period of individual training and drills run by NCOs. Officers and senior officers used this time for advanced training such as staff rides, war games and other winter studies. From February – April, company level training was conducted focusing on live firing exercises and tactical drill at regimental training areas. Four weeks of battalion level training followed that included tactical maneuvers, long distance marches and live weapons firing. Summer training began in mid-May and lasted through July. This training focused on fixing deficiencies found in company and battalion level exercises. Soldiers from rural areas were allowed to go home during this period to help on their families' farms.[15]

At the end of July, regiments traveled by rail from garrison towns to their assigned corps level training areas. For IR 169 and other Baden regiments, this meant deployment to Troop Exercise Base (*lager*) in Heuberg. Located 100 miles southeast of Karlsruhe, near the large railroad station in Albstadt, the Stetten Lager was established in 1910 by the XIV Army Corps to serve as a base camp to support field training exercises. The German Army's XIV Corps' wartime function was to serve as the headquarters element commanding all of Baden's mobilized regiments. The Heuberg base facilities could comfortably house and support a force of over 10,000 troops and provide access to large weapons ranges and field maneuver spaces not available in smaller garrison towns. Albert Rieth's postcards from this era reveal scenes of soldiers relaxing during field training breaks, posing in a studio with a mock-up of an airplane and of the regimental band on a road march. Summer camp training began with company live fires on ranges followed by regimental and brigade exercises. In the third week of August, the brigade exercises pitted regiments, coupled with artillery and cavalry units, in mock battles.

Around August 20, the regiments would return to their kaserns for yet more tactical drills to prepare them for the large scale autumn maneuvers. IR 169's 1913 maneuvers took them to the southern Alsace region and locations where first saw combat a year later. These exercises featured brigade, division and then corps level maneuvers. With this final series of exercises concluded, regiments would return to their garrisons and those soldiers due for discharge returned home with one set of uniforms. The training cycle would repeat with the arrival of the next set of new recruits.

Great War Dawning's account of the infantry training cycle continues with the emphasis on rifle marksmanship.

"Initial rifle training focused on weapons handling, disassembly and theoretical lessons on bullet trajectory, range estimation, use of long range sights and firing positions. Reflective of following obsolete infantry doctrines, squads and platoons were trained to mass together to concentrate fires at longer ranges of 400 meters, where aimed fire was ineffective.

Marksmanship programs integrated a series of drills, local range firing and live firing exercises. The weapons training program included qualifications in laying, kneeling and standing positions. To meet basic second class ratings, soldiers had to score hits on six targets at the 150 – 200 meter range. First class ratings required firing to hit 200 – 400 meter targets. German infantrymen were trained to adjust rates of fire on the tactical situation. Slow fire (1.5 – 3 rounds per minute) was to engage distant or low visibility targets, high rates of (3-7 rounds per minute) to engage advancing marching columns and maximum rates of (7-12 rounds per minute) to prepare in pre-assault fires or sudden, close range combat.

To encourage marksmanship excellence, the army established a series of competitions to provide special awards on individual and unit levels." [16]

Despite the German Army's renowned efficiency, its tactical training and doctrine programs had severe deficiencies. Along with all the other armies of the day, and countless others since, the German military fell into the fatal trap of preparing for the last war. Anthony Farrar-Hockley, in *Death of an Army*, provides an apt description of the pre-war German military training and the consequences of drilling tactics that were quickly becoming obsolete.

"Above all else, a new recruit would spend the majority of his time suffering through drill after drill. In 1912, no army in the world had yet grasped the consequences of employing 19th Century tactics against the machine gun and rapid firing cannon. The school of military art dictated that infantry still be deployed in massed formations. While it was recognized that tight formations of hundreds of men were more vulnerable to concentrated fire, no one envisioned the slaughter that the first months of World War I would reap. Military tacticians of the day viewed the benefits of massing troops to include the discouraging of stragglers and deserters, and most importantly, the effect of shock action. At a time when the machine gun was just being integrated in line units, the concentrated fire of 200 rifles in a German company was viewed as much more effective than the scattered fire of 200 individuals. In sum, men massed to move and fire collectively as one was considered a controlled weapon of war in the hand of a skilled company commander." [17]

While the Germans may have advanced ahead of other forces in integrating machine guns for effective defensive use at the regimental level, they had yet to learn how to *attack into* enemy machine gun and modern artillery fire. While the German 1906 infantry field manual did take new technologies and tactics into some account, many officers still remained entrenched in traditions from 40 years past.

This description, taken from *Great War Dawning*, sums up the state of mind of the German high command in 1914:

"After 1914, an entire generation paid the price for this outdated picture of war. For those who think that the old 1870 way of attacking was outdated, we have to take a look at the order of XV Army Corps on 3 November 1914: "I direct therefore that the attacks are to be pressed home with bugle calls and with regimental bands playing. Regimental musicians who play during assaults will be awarded Iron Crosses" v. Deimling." [18]

The overwhelming objective of Germany's vast military capabilities and plans were designed to protect the Empire against the two biggest threats - France and Russia. Long before the events in Sarajevo that would trigger World War I, the German military leadership concluded that a conflict with France would also draw in Russia. In the early 1900's, the task of planning for a simultaneous war with France and Russia fell to German Chief of the General Staff, Count Alfred Von Schlieffen, the architect of the strategic plan which bears his name. In its most broad context, the Germans planned a rapid, knockout blow against the French, and would then turn to conquer Russia.

The Von Schlieffen Plan assumed it would take Russia at least six weeks to mobilize the forces needed to threaten Germany's East Prussian states [Eastern Imperial Germany included territory that is now the Czech Republic and Poland]. France, the more immediate danger, would need to be neutralized within 45 days. Forces freed by the defeat of France would then be quickly transported east to crush the Russians.

German military planners understood the pitfalls of attacking France directly from their common, southern Alsace-Lorraine border. One factor was that the French, deeply fearful of a repeat of Germany's successful 1871 invasion, had developed a network of powerful fortifications along their border with the Alsace-Lorraine. The Germans understood that a frontal attack against these defenses would be costly in terms of blood and time, spelling a fatal consequence to the all-important, six-week deadline. A second factor was the sheer size of the German forces, 1,500,000 troops, programmed to attack into France. This force was six times the size of the 1870 army and required much more maneuver space than was afforded in the Alsace-Lorraine. Only by going north and blasting through neutral Belgium would the Germans acquire enough room to support such a grand offensive.

German planning called for a Western Front force consisting of seven armies. An eighth army would be posted in the East to hold the Russians at bay for a month and a half. Five northernmost armies were to dash across Belgium, sweep down through the non-fortified French-Belgian border, and descend into the heartland of France. Heavily defended Paris would be avoided, with the French Army in the field becoming the primary target. Caught away from their fortified areas, the French forces would be subject to destruction by the German's superior combat strength and capacity for maneuver.

The two remaining West Front German armies were to be posted on the southernmost, left flank area that covered the Alsace-Lorraine territories. It was there that IR 169 and other Baden troops would be deployed. The deliberately weak German left wing on the Alsace-Lorraine front was designed to lure the French into a sack between the city of Metz and the Vosges mountain range. It was expected that the French, intent upon liberating their lost provinces, would launch their main attack there. So much the better for the Germans, for by tying up significant French forces in the south, the prospects of their invasion in the north would be enhanced.

The weak left strategy brought potential risks and advantages. Should things go wrong and the German defensive line break, the French could thrust deeply into Germany. Conversely, if the battle on the left went well, an aggressive German counter attack could put the main French Army in a decisive double envelopment, an ultimate military objective. Von Schlieffen, who died the year before the war began, was well aware that his masterful plan could be destroyed by the natural temptation to make the left more robust. So wary was Von Schlieffen of this threat, it is reputed that his dying words were; *"If it must come to a fight, only make the right wing strong."*

The Von Schlieffen Plan was an all-or-nothing strategy. Once launched, it was virtually impossible to dial back. Germany's survival depended on its success.

The French also developed elaborate military contingency plans, recognizing that Germany represented their primary menace. The consequences of the Franco-Prussian War had a seminal impact on French military strategists. An analysis of the 1871 debacle led to a conclusion that the defeat was due to a lack of offensive spirit. The French Army's most influential military mind, Colonel de Grandmaison, impregnated the French high command with the following dogma: "In the offensive, imprudence is the best of assurances....Simply attack, what the enemy intends to do is of no consequence. From the moment of action every soldier must ardently desire the assault by bayonet as the supreme means of imposing his will upon the enemy and gaining victory." [19]

This passion for 'élan vital' led the French Army to discount technological developments. Symbolic of this mindset was the French Army uniform of 1914, which essentially was the same uniform of the mid 1800's, a blue wool coat and kepi cap, and red trousers. Such impressive looking uniforms had merit in the mid-19th Century where black powder smoke obscured the battlefield and uniform colors distinguished friend from foe. As inspiring as images of heroic bayonet charges were, the French, like all the other contemporary armies, failed to account for the realities of 20th Century warfare – the machine gun, modern artillery, aviation, motor transport and communication technologies.

The French dogma for a bold offensive strategy was encapsulated in Plan 17. As the Germans predicted, the French intended first to reclaim the Alsace Lorraine, cross the Rhine in the vicinity of Mainz, and then march to Berlin. The French paid scant attention to German plans. Although they were aware of the possibility for a strong German attack across Belgium (on the French left flank), they discounted it as immaterial to their own intentions. In fact, some in the

French high command welcomed such a German move. By drawing enemy troops to the north, they would have fewer to resist their avenue of advance, which would create more opportunities to destroy the bulk of the German armies.

For all the machinations of German and French military planning and lingering resentment from a war that had ended 40 years earlier, few in the bucolic summer of 1914 would have predicted the outbreak of hostilities in Continental Europe. For the soldiers, the transition from peaceful garrison life into an actual war occurred with blinding speed. The powder keg to the crisis was the long simmering dispute between the Austria-Hungarian Monarchy and Serbia – a problem far beyond the awareness of IR 169 conscripts drilling in the Lahr and Villingen kasernes. The explosive spark was the June 28, 1914 assassination of Archduke Franz Ferdinand, the Austro-Hungarian heir apparent, in Sarajevo, Bosnia, at the hand of a South Slav nationalist. Austria-Hungary used the assassination as pretext to invade Serbia. Rejecting any realistic peace offerings, Austria-Hungary declared war on Serbia on July 29, with their artillery bombarding the Serbian capital of Belgrade.

The path to global war was further driven by an inexorable, cascading series of treaties. Russia, Serbia's staunchest ally, was committed to Serbia's defense and promptly declared war on Austria-Hungary. Germany, bound in treaty to Austria-Hungary, mobilized against Russia. France and Russia were locked in a mutual protection treaty, obligating France to mobilize against Germany and Austria-Hungary.

Germany's ultimatum to Russia, which demanded that the Tsar back off against its threat to Austria-Hungary, was the final act leading to war. When the ultimatum expired without reply, the Kaiser decreed a general mobilization.[20] Any deviation from the pre-existing scenarios and loss of the initiative was tantamount to certain defeat. There was no turning back the mighty German war machine that was now set in motion. The Kaiser declared war against France on August 2, 1914.

Germany's best hope for winning a quick victory against France was to pass through Belgium, a neutral nation. Kaiser Wilhelm II offered Belgium's King Albert significant financial compensation to allow the undisturbed passage of German troops. Albert rejected the offer and the Germans immediately invaded Belgium. Belgium's treaty with the United Kingdom drew England into the war against Germany.

While the diplomats failed to halt a rapidly evolving crisis, the soldiers of IR 169 went about their normal routine which focused on preparing for the annual autumn field exercises to the Stetten encampment. Albert Rieth, nearing the end of his enlistment, was no doubt counting down the short time until he could return home to Pforzheim for good.

Rieth's memoir begins with the opening day of the war:

August 2, 1914, Villingen
"One would hardly believe that it would come to a war. We were of the opinion that the thunderclouds would move away once more, and we told ourselves that no one would take the responsibility to call for a war involving the entire world."

Chapter 2
Opening Moves: The Battle of Mulhouse

August 2, 1914 began as a typical duty day in IR 169's Villingen garrison. All would be forever changed when, in the early afternoon hours, 3rd Battalion Commander, Major Lilienhoff-Zivowizti, received notice of the Kaiser's mobilization order. Rieth's account:

> Villingen, Germany, August, 2, 1914
> "It was the 2nd of August when we musicians moved out at noon as usual for practice. We had been practicing about one hour, when a man from battalion headquarters appeared. We were ordered to immediately make preparations to move out, as mobilization had occurred. Then we went to the depot to get our field gray uniforms. The depot was very busy as the uniforms and other equipment arrived on carts which we had to pull into the kaserne."

At IR 169 Regimental Headquarters in Lahr, similar orders put IR 169's 1st and 2nd Battalions into wartime motion. IR 169 had only five days to make ready before going deploying to the Alsace border. Reserve units and a small staff would remain at the Lahr and Villingen garrisons to train new recruits and execute other administrative functions.

The German Army had established elaborate plans to assemble its 2,000,000 man forces in the shortest possible time. Logisticians precisely calculated the number trains needed to move every corps, division and regiment and set tight timetables for movement schedules.[21] IR 169's entry to war was a cog in the machine orchestrated by Baden's XIV Corps. The task of assembling the widely dispersed Baden regiments in the first days of August fell to General von Huene, the XIV Corps commander. The XIV Corps staff frantically scrambled to collect Baden's two active duty divisions to meet the imminent threat of French invasion into the Alsace-Lorraine provinces. In 1914, XIV Corps, 44,000 troops strong, was comprised of the 28th Infantry Division, based in northern Baden, and the 29th Infantry Division, whose regiments (including IR 169) were garrisoned throughout southern Baden and across the Rhine in Alsace. The mobilization of reserve units followed shortly.

The 29th Division was commanded in 1914 by Lieutenant General Isbert. The division consisted of the following three infantry brigades, one artillery brigade, a cavalry regiment and a pioneer (engineering) battalion.
- 84th Infantry Brigade: IR 169 and IR 170
- 57th Infantry Brigade: IR 113 and IR 114
- 58th Infantry Brigade: IR 112 and IR 142
- 29th Field Artillery Brigade: FA Regiment 30 and FA Regiment 76
- 22nd "Prinz Karl" Cavalry Regiment
- 14th Pioneer Battalion

The 29th Infantry Division of 1914 was a uniquely large division, as it had three assigned brigades compared with most others that only had two. [By comparison, the XIV Corps' other division, the 28th, was more typical with two infantry brigades.] IR 169, along with sister regiment IR 170, fell under the control of the 84th Infantry Brigade, commanded by Generalmajor von Koschembahr.The 29th Division artillery firepower came from its 29th Artillery Brigade, which divided 72 field guns among its two regiments. Each artillery regiment had two battalions, divided into six batteries, each with six cannons. The 29th Infantry Division, adding in various field hospital, engineer, communication, and other logistics components, totaled approximately 17,000 troops.

At the XIV Corps level, other subordinates units included an aviation squadron, heavy artillery regiments, and other logistics and ordnance organizations.[22]

XIV Corps, along with XV Corps, the I Bavarian Corps, and the XIV Reserve Corps, made up the 7th Army, commanded by Colonel General Josias von Heeringen, who had previously served as the Prussian Minister of War. The 7th Army, 125,000 strong, was placed at the extreme left of the German western front. On August 9, 1914 the 7th Army was combined with the 6th Army and fell under the overall command of Bavarian Crown Prince Rupprecht. It was this army group, totaling 350,000 troops, which had the mission to hold as many French troops as possible across the entire Alsace-Lorraine front. In this role, 7th Army served as the anchor to the main push of the five northern-most German armies set to invade Belgium and France to crush the main French army.

To summarize Infantry Regiment 169's greater command structure, the regiment reported up to the 84th Brigade, then 29th Division, XIV Corps, and 6th Army (under 6/7th Army Group Command). This grouping would remain in place from August 1914 through early 1915.

The collection of Baden forces was a microcosm of the greater German Army build up occurring throughout the Empire. By mid-August 1914, the Germans were able to muster seven armies on the Western Front, with one army of 250,000 facing the Russians in the east.

While Baden troops were assembling along the southwestern border, the main German offensive was launched to the north. A mass of 34 infantry and five cavalry divisions were tasked to sweep over Belgium and northwestern France, pass to the west of Paris, and crush the French armies with their backs to their own frontier defenses. On August 4-5, a German force of six brigades attempted to rush the commanding ring of 12 fortresses surrounding Liege.[23]

Expecting only mild resistance, the initial German infantry assaults met with severe losses from the surprisingly stubborn defenders of the Belgian fortress complex. Onrushing German attackers were cut down in waves and in many places the German dead were stacked eight to ten men high. Monstrous 420-mm siege howitzers eventually blasted the shell-shocked Belgian defenders into submission. Although the route through Liege was finally cleared on August 16, 1914, it was an expensive victory for the Germans both in men, and most critically, time. To the southern end of the Western Front, events unfolded that soon embroiled IR 169 into one of the first large-scale actions of the War, the August 9 Battle of Mulhouse.

The fight at Mulhouse culminated from German and French maneuvering to control of the long contested Alsace-Lorraine provinces. The two provinces encompassed a 150-mile long region between the tip of Luxembourg, and south to Basel, Switzerland. Originally neither German nor French, Alsace had been snatched back and forth between the two until it was claimed by Louis XIV in 1648 and remained under French control for the next two centuries. The

German conquest of Alsace-Lorraine in the 1870-1871 Franco Prussian War left a deep scar within French pride. In the ensuing years, Imperial Germany administered the provinces with a heavy hand. By the time World War I broke, much of its populace was largely bitter and alienated against their German masters." [24]

For Berlin, control of these territories, populated by people who spoke Alemannic German dialects, was essential. Holding this territory provided the Germans with a deep buffer of ground on the east bank of the Rhine, control of the extensive fortifications of Metz and possession of significant iron resources.

The French Army, spurred on by both national pride and Plan 17, wasted little time to reclaim their lost territories. Under the command of General Joffre, the French had deployed a concentration of over 11 army corps along the western Lorraine frontier. To the south, poised to seize the Alsace, Joffre held an additional five corps and two cavalry divisions under General Dubail. Dubail attacked first. The French were confident the populous would support this liberation in a spontaneous revolt against their German oppressors.

The initial attack was led by General Bonnueau's VII Corps, a 70,000 soldier force that was based in the fortress city of Belfort, on the French/Alsace border. The objective was to cross over the Vosges Mountains, seize the cities of Mulhouse and Colmar, and prepare to establish a bridgehead over the Rhine. On August 6, VII Corps charged through the town of Altkirch where they easily brushed off a small German frontier force. Casualties resulting from this skirmish were less than 100 troops. After an unopposed 15-mile march, French troops entered Mulhouse on August 8. A prominent industrial city known for its textile manufacturing, Mulhouse sits six miles west of the Rhine, the actual historical German border, and about 10 miles north of Basel, Switzerland.

The French capture of Mulhouse was a significant milestone in the first week of the war. Tuchman described the scene in Mulhouse:

"The French cavalry in gleaming uniforms galloped through the streets. Almost dumbfounded at this sudden apparition, the majority of the residents stood first in transfixed silence, and then gradually broke into joy. A grand review of the French troops lasting two hours was held in the main square. Bands played 'the Marseilles,' and guns were draped with flowers of red, white, and blue. Chocolates, pastries, and pipes of tobacco were thrust on the soldiers. From all windows flags and handkerchiefs waved and even the roofs were covered with cheering masses." [25]

The French commanders were buoyed by this seemingly easy recapture of much of Alsace. On August 7, General-in-Chief of the French Armies, Joseph Joffre, declared a quick victory with this bold proclamation on Mulhouse's liberation:

"CHILDREN of ALSACE!
After forty-four years of sorrowful waiting, French soldiers once more tread the soil of your noble country. They are the pioneers in the great work of revenge. For them what emotions it calls forth, and what pride! To complete the work they have made the sacrifice of their lives. The French nation unanimously urges them on, and in the folds of their flag are inscribed the magic words, "Right and Liberty." Long live Alsace. Long live France."

As the French Army celebrated, the Germans readied for action. General von Heeringen, using air reconnaissance and intelligence gleamed from spies and retreating border troops, maintained a sound understanding of the French disposition. Recognizing that the French had employed only one army corps, the Germans assessed that the French advance was more of a local dash than a well-planned, greater offensive. The invading force would have to be quickly expelled before they could become entrenched on the banks of the Rhine.

The Germans were confident that a quick counterattack could at least disperse the French VII Corps and chase it back to Belfort. In a best case scenario, a collapse of the French left flank could even entrap their entire corps against the Swiss border. Late on the evening of August 7, the Supreme Army Command in Koblenz directed Heeringen to launch his XIV and XV Corps in the attack as soon as possible. XIV Corps was ordered to assembly points before Mulhouse, with the 29th Division moving to Neuneburg, a town on the German side of the Rhine, 10 miles northeast of Mulhouse. XV Corps was ordered to stage at the Alsace town of Colmar, 20 miles to the north of the growing French concentration around Mulhouse. [26]

IR 169 was set into motion on August 8, with orders to travel to the Neuneburg assembly area, 50 miles south of Lahr and 65 miles southwest of Villingen. A myriad of extensive deployment preparations consumed the regiment in the five days since receiving the initial mobilization order. Vast quantities of equipment, ammunition, and provisions had to be drawn, accounted for, cleaned, and readied for movement. 3rd Battalion's departure from Villingen, and transit across the Black Forest, began in the early morning hours of August 8.

The August 1914 train movements of WW I soldiers towards their first battles were well-documented events. Photographs and newsreels reveal enthusiastic crowds waving at trains packed full of eager German troops, with slogans such as *"Ausflug nach Paris"* (Excursion to Paris) chalked on the sides of the cars. Some soldiers described a sense of euphoria at the anticipated adventure of battle glory, a welcome release from the dull routine of the garrison.[27] Others of course, were more reflective when considering the prospect of bloodshed that lay ahead. Rieth's journal described the early morning train journey through the heart of the Black Forest:

"Finally the time to march out arrived, August 8, at 3:00 am. We marched to the train station where naturally the entire town was present to wish the young battalion the last farewell, after having been in this garrison for only one half year. We embarked with the song 'Must I Then Leave the Little Town.' The train started moving and the song finally diminished. One could only hear the vague hum of the wheels, and some told high-spirited jokes. But most thought about their loved ones, and some thought of the words "Who knows if we will ever see each other again!" Because no one could know what fate would present him? At dawn we were already in Offenburg, everywhere we were greeted enthusiastically by the population.

From Offenburg, the train went up the Rhine River to Mulheim [50 miles south], where we disembarked. From there we went to Vogisheim, where we moved into alert quarters. No sooner were we with our quartering hosts, the order came for me to report to the captain, and before long I had to give the 'charge' bugle call, as we were ordered to man the trenches across from the Rhine bridge. Now we marched back to

Mulheim, and then to Neuneburg. We heard the first cannon thunder from Fortress Istein, and it felt like maneuvers, but we learned differently the following day. It was our first mission to protect the bridge over the Rhine at Neuneburg and to man a trench on the other side forming a great arc. The night was perfectly quiet, except for the sounds of Fortress Istein grumbling madly all night, the mysterious rushing of the Rhine, and the firm footsteps of the soldiers continuously crossing the bridge to hold the loyal watch on the Rhine."

From Mulheim, the men marched on to occupy pre-established trenches across the river from Neuneburg, which guarded the far side of a Rhine bridge. Six miles to the south was Fortress Istein, a massive fortification that stood on high cliffs on the east bank of the Rhine, protecting the approach to the bridges and ranging miles beyond. Throughout the night, Istein's heavy artillery blasted at French forces deployed to the southwest. The explosions of these heavy guns reverberated among the German positions, giving the troops their first sounds of actual war. Fortress Istein's artillery continued to pound the French around Mulhouse during the next two days. Not all of the guns' victims were enemy troops. At one point in the battle, a German reserve unit came on the field without having had the opportunity to exchange their blue garrison uniforms for field gray. A German artillery observer mistook the unit for French infantry and directed Istein's guns upon the friendly troops, killing a number of them.[28]

Albert's journal makes reference to the iconic, patriotic song, *Watch on the Rhine*. As Tuchman records, "In the early days of the war, singing served as an important source of morale and inspiration for the German Army. When either marching or sitting by campfires, German troops would sing such staples as *Deutschland uber Alles*, *Die Wacht am Rhine*, and *Heil der im Siegeskranz*. They sang when they halted, when they billeted, when they caroused. Many who lived through the next thirty days of mounting combat, agony, and terror were to remember the sound of endless, repetitious masculine singing as the worst torment of the invasion." [29] On the night of August 8, 1914, while protecting an important Rhine bridge against a nearby enemy, no more poignant song spoke to the German soldier's sacred obligation to defend the Fatherland than did the *Watch on the Rhine*.

"For the Dear Fatherland to have peace,
Stands fast and true the watch,
The watch on the Rhine!"

Both the German and French armies spent August 8 readying their dispositions for the impending battle. Patrols were deployed to fix the enemy locations and regiments were moved into various defensive positions or attack staging points. The Germans made their upper Rhine fortifications ready for defense and constructed pontoon bridges at Neu-Breisach to the north of IR 169's position at the Neuneburg bridge and Fortress Istein to the south.

The French army, now alert to the coming German attack, put aside their celebrations and prepared a hasty defense across a 15-mile long line. The French line extended 9 miles out from Mulhouse and continued east atop the heights at the suburb village of Riedisheim. Control of the high ground at Riedisheim was particularly significant, as it covered the Rhine canals that served as a natural obstacle to any enemy attack. It was against this most heavily defended portion of the French line where IR 169 was directed to assault.

The Seventh Army intended to make a two-pronged attack on Mulhouse that begin in the early hours of August 9. The two divisions of XV Corps were to attack the French left on the outskirts of the city while XIV Corp's 28th and 29th Divisions would directly strike Mulhouse and the high ground on the French right. This was to be a direct, frontal attack, with both corps of the 7th Army moving abreast and assaulting in line from north to south.

The challenges facing the German troops were considerable. First, the 7th Army staff had the mammoth task of assembling 100,000 untested troops to execute a complex attack. The terrain favored the defending French, who held commanding high ground all along their lines. Furthermore, numerous brooks overgrown with brush, orchards, vineyards, canals and forest copses hampered the attacking Germans advance. Most of the German forces slated for the attack had to make a considerable march to reach the French positions. The severest obstacle proved to be the weather. August 9 was an extremely hot and humid day, debilitating many of these men before they even reached the battlefield.

The intended 7:00 am attack time proved over-optimistic, and few German units reached the French positions until early afternoon. The battle opened on the German right flank, spearheaded by XV Corps. The 39th Division first came under fire from French outposts in the vineyards northwest of Uffholz. Artillery was brought up and the German attack was fully underway by 1:00 pm. The XV Corps 30th Division, slowed by the difficult terrain and hot weather, did not get in the fight until 3:00 pm. Following a bitter street battle in the village of Seenheim, the 30th Division was eventually able to pierce the main French line at nightfall. By day's end, XV Corps had achieved modest gains on the German right flank. The heavy fighting and exhausting conditions left XV Corps spent. However, the French line was broken in several places, giving hope that if exploited, XIV Corps' direct attack on Mulhouse would lead to victory.

IR 169 began its advance in the predawn hours of August 9. Rieth described the difficult, ten mile march:

"When dawn came we awaited events to come, and as it became lighter we could slowly see more of our surroundings. The trench connected to the Rhine. There were strong wire fortifications before the trench, and then the ditch of the old Rhine, making a breakthrough by the enemy impossible. So we waited in vain for the enemy.

Finally, on Sunday, August 9, we vacated the trench at 6 am and moved in the direction of Mulhouse, where there were already small skirmishes between advanced guard posts. We marched along a seemingly endless straight road, and the sun burned down from the cloudless sky, making the march almost indescribably difficult if one considers the heavy load of equipment of an infantryman. In addition the new boots were burning and gave you the feeling of walking barefoot through a mowed cornfield.

The cannon thunder came nearer, and soon we could distinguish rifle fire as we marched along the street that led to the canal of Mulhouse. We then saw a picture of an endless column settled upon by a cloud of dust. There was not a bit of air and it seemed like we were suffocating. Some of the men were becoming quite pathetic, with their legs staggering as if they would collapse. Although each one pulled himself together, their faces looked feverish as if a heat stroke was imminent."

Rieth's account did not exaggerate the effects of the oppressive, muggy heat. The official German report of the battle estimated that ten percent of the German ranks that day fell to heat exhaustion.

Like their XV Corps counterparts, the XIV Corps movement also fell far behind schedule. By noontime, the exhausted XIV Corps was forced to rest, with the units on the right flank still not having moved beyond the woods east of Battenheim, still five miles north of the attack point. At 2:00 pm, XIV Corps Commander, General Von Huene, reported to 7th Army Headquarters that the sorry condition of his troops made it unlikely that they could attack Mulhouse that afternoon. He suggested delaying the main attack until the next morning.

General Heeringen proved unsympathetic and pressed XIV Corps to get into the battle as soon as possible, as any further delays would undermine the fledgling XV Corps attack to the west. Furthermore, newly arrived intelligence led the Germans to revise their understanding of the French dispositions. Reports from German aerial scouts indicated that there was a major French line being formed to the south, towards Altkirch. Other reports observed that additional French troops, under fire from the big German guns at Fortress Istein, were also retreating to the south. This led to the 7th Army's conclusion that the main French effort was now relocating several miles south of Mulhouse, and that the enemy forces defending in front of the city would be only a thin outpost line. In reality, this new estimate was flawed. The main French effort remained in strong defensive stance along the existing Mulhouse line, the target of the sputtering XIV Corps advance.

At 3:00 pm, General Von Huene re-examined the status of XIV Corps and his standing orders to take Mulhouse. The sounds of the furious XV Corps battle to the east punctuated the need to join the fight as quickly as possible. The impromptu midday rest had afforded his two division commanders time to re-establish better control of their units. Further movement for the day was now deemed possible. The newly arrived, albeit false, intelligence that the Germans were facing only a picket line before Mulhouse made the prospects of an immediate advance that much more enticing. At 3:15 pm, Von Huene resumed the attack upon the foremost positions of the French near Mulhouse.

The lack of a clear picture of the enemy situation continued to frustrate German commanders. Generalmajor Koschembahr, commanding the 84th Brigade, attempted a personal reconnaissance in his motor vehicle. The unarmored car was an inviting target and Koschembahr was killed as soon as it approached the French picket line.

IR 169 took advantage of the midday halt to seek relief from the heat among the tall pine trees of the Hardt Forest. With the XV Corps battle raging to the west, the men of IR 169 were able to get some hours of rest and even had the opportunity to eat from the field kitchens just brought up to the front. The confusion bedeviling the XIV Corps Headquarters spread down to the anxious troops, with contradictory rumors flying fast. One report would have "Mulhouse clear of the enemy," the next: "the Mulhouse front is still occupied by the French." Eventually, the 29th Division's final orders filtered down to the regiment at 4:15 pm, "Capture Hill 283." [30]

Hill 283 was a steep mass just to the east of downtown Mulhouse. The village of Riedisheim sat on the western portion of the hill with the village of Rixheim just to its east. The hill, and the two villages, were tactically important to the French, who defended the sector in strength. The German intelligence assessment that this position was held by only a weak picket line could not have been more wrong.

The area of Napoleoninsel, 2000 meters south of Hill 283, was in the path of IR 169's attack. This unique terrain feature was named for the small man-made island which was formed at the intersection of two Rhine based canals that flowed to Mulhouse. To the immediate south of the island, and along one side of the east-west canal, ran a railroad track with a steep embankment and train station. The open terrain directly to the south of the train station served as a pre-war military training area, which included a small airstrip and, ironically, two rifle ranges. The zone of attack also included a paper factory complex of several industrial buildings and warehouses. To reach Hill 283, the Germans would have to cross the canal and train embankment, and then assault across nearly one mile of open ground. The French entrenched on Hill 283 owned a commanding field of fire, with plenty of infantry, machine guns and artillery, poised to defend it.

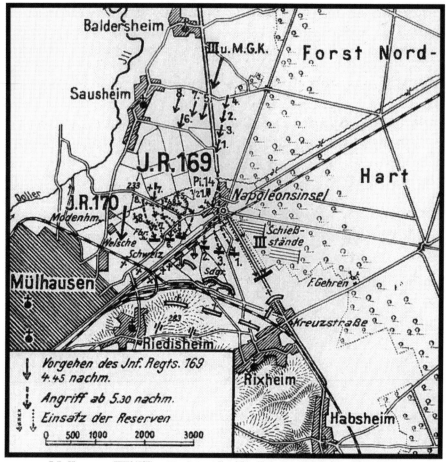

Mulhouse: IR169's attack on the Riedisheim-Rixheim Heights.
(BIWW)

On the order of Colonel Spennemann, the sore troops of Regiment 169 rose up from their rest, donned their equipment and formed a column on the main road leading towards Napoleoninsel.

A section of light infantry guard fanned out through the fields and farmland to screen the path ahead. The main body of the regiment marched in a long column along the dirt road. The dust rose in huge clouds, choking those in the rear companies. Just past Baldersheim, the regiment began to form a line of battle in preparation for the impending assault on a still unseen enemy. 1st Battalion (Companies 1-4) led the regiment as they continued to follow along the trace of the main road. The 2nd Battalion (Companies 5-8), moved off the road and deployed in the open fields to the right. 3rd Battalion (Companies 9-12), along with the regiment's machine gun company, followed in the center as the reserve force.

It was now 5:30 pm. On the regiment's left flank, 1st Battalion advanced towards the train station, its intermediate objective. The battalion used the cover of the small village north of Napoleoninsel to gain access across the canal and reached the train station and railway embankment without meeting resistance. 3rd Battalion followed across the canal as 1st Battalion deployed along the embankment in preparation for the attack up Hill 283, now one mile south.

From the heights of Riedisheim, the French coolly held their fire as they watched the gray columns made their way towards the Rhine canals, the train station, and the railroad embankment. The first shooting started when the 6th Company came under fire by a rock quarry near the railway embankment. The 8th Company deployed alongside, and both companies skillfully maneuvered against the French pickets in a sharp firefight. The French skirmish line withdrew, and 2nd Battalion secured a toehold on a street that ran from Napoleoninsel towards Mulhouse.

Rieth described the situation when the opening artillery salvos began to land:

> "Suddenly the order came to rest rifles near the train station of Napoleoninsel, one of the last stations before Mulhouse. We stacked the rifles and fell asleep by the side of the road because of the terrible exhaustion. All of a sudden a hissing and terrible burst, the first enemy artillery shell landed in the canal, causing a great fountain. But we could not admire this spectacle because soon a second, a third, and finally a downpour followed so that we quickly sought cover behind the railroad embankment. The enemy sent frightening greetings of flames over to us. We could not deploy, as only a few would have made it across the embankment, so we could do nothing but stay behind it."

With their picket line now clear, the French let loose a terrible fury of rifle, machine gun, and artillery fire across the entire IR 169 front. On the German right, the four companies of 2nd Battalion were fully engulfed in the firestorm. In the confusion, 2nd Battalion lost contact with Regiment 170, the regiment to the right of IR 169. This resulted in a gap in the German line, which the French exploited by pouring fire into 2nd Battalion's exposed right flank. The situation continued to deteriorate. The 5th and 6th Companies were able to fight their way across the embankment to their front, only to be trapped on the opposite bank. The 7th Company was now IR 169's right-most unit and was completely pinned down in an open field before they could reach the cover of the rail tracks. The 7th Company was left leaderless, when its commander, Captain Hensling, and his executive officer, Lieutenant Klotz, were killed. The 8th Company remained stalled at the rock quarry. Within moments, the entire 2nd Battalion was neutralized and no longer capable of supporting the main attack effort.

On IR 169's left, the eight companies of 1st and 3rd Battalions, along with the regimental machine gun company, were able to cross the canal and reached the rail embankment before the shooting started in earnest. In order to reach Hill 283, they would still have to cross over one mile of exposed fields under a terrific concentration of fire – all without the support of the beleaguered 2nd Battalion. The commanders of 1st Battalion's 1st, 2nd, 3rd and 4th Companies organized their men for the assault. While 3rd Battalion and the machine gun company remained behind to provide a measure of covering fire, the four companies of 1st Battalion jumped over the railway embankment and began to charge forward towards the entrenched French positions. The French guns ripped apart the German ranks from the moment they crossed over the train tracks. Almost immediately, all four companies had taken heavy losses and were pinned down a short distance from their starting point.

By 6:00 pm, seven out of twelve rifle companies were decimated and stalled. The right flank of 2nd Battalion was trapped with two companies on each side of the train tracks and under heavy fire from both the south and west. 1st Battalion was scattered in the open fields before Hill 283, taking whatever cover could be found in various ditches and buildings. While 3rd Battalion was holding firm behind the train embankment, French artillery had zeroed in, setting the roof of the station ablaze and flinging razor-sharp shrapnel into the ranks.

Despite suffering a grievous wound, 3rd Battalion Commander, Major Lilienhoff-Zivowizti, gave an inspiring speech that galvanized the battalion into action. [The stoic Lilienhoff-Zivowizti was made of hardy stuff. He survived his wound and eventually returned to duty. In March 1915, he was decorated for another act of valor.]

Now led by Captain Berthold, Companies 10, 11, 12, with two platoons of the 9th Company, prepared to assault on the left portion of the military training ground and rifle ranges. Perhaps it would be possible to gain a foothold at the bottom of the hill, and then roll up the French right flank. The machine gun company, along with a covering platoon from the 9th Company, was to take an over-watching position to provide suppressing fire in support of the main attack. With a hearty cheer, the 3rd Battalion leaped over the embankment - and into the same direct fire that was destroying the rest of the regiment.

Rieth described the attack:

"One man nearly penetrated the enemy position and was shot in the throat. Then the news came that our captain and battalion adjutant were killed because they had remained in a dangerous position too long, and thus died the hero's death after only being in battle for less than half an hour. The major wanted to advance with a company but it was impossible, he too soon came back with a bullet hole in his lower body. Our regimental adjutant [1st Lieutenant Eckardt] was hit on his horse while he was relaying an order, with a fragment of shrapnel caving in his skull.

3rd Battalion, to which I belonged, was ordered to retreat. We were just about to obey the order, when our major [Major Lilienhoff-Zivowizti] appeared with a dangerous wound in the abdomen. Holding his saber in his fist, and without a uniform jacket, he shouted to us: "Men before we retreat from these scoundrels even one half step, we should all wish to die!" This had a powerful effect, and with a "hurrah," we went over the embankment. One platoon of the company had to remain back to give cover for the four machine guns. These guns were located on the country road leading to Mulhouse. To the left was a big paper factory, behind a building of which we took position. The machine guns fired murderously, but since our fighting line had advanced already, we also had to go forward.

To follow the front lines, we crossed the yard when a terrible shelling came through the roof of the factory and exploded in the yard where we were. We had no choice but to leap across the yard. We made it just in time because a new steel rain began. I laid flat on the ground behind a big bale of paper stacked by one of the buildings. There I had the dubious pleasure to hear and see what artillery shells look like when they detonate at a distance of 3 - 4 meters away. I believed the earth was torn to pieces, and the shrapnel flew about my ears so I could neither hear nor see."

Finally, the 29th Division field artillery entered the battle, with the promise to provide some measure of covering fire. The initial volleys were ranged too short and shells exploded among the troops they were intending to support. Adjustments were eventually made, and finally, the rounds began to hit the intended targets. Rieth:

"To my horror, I realized that our own artillery was firing upon us, as the battery had just got into position in the dark, and without the target being exactly known. My situation became very uncomfortable and during a small firing pause, I was able to jump into the building. But as soon as I was in it, a shell entered through the loft. The building collapsed and I was buried under the debris, fortunately without injury. It was also the last shot fired upon our own position. A soldier had probably run back and told the battery that they were firing too short. It was a pleasure for me to hear how the shells now went high over my head, and I hoped that none would miss their targets."

A French soldier who viewed the battle from the heights at Riedisheim recorded this observation of the slaughter brought on by the deadly French '75mm field artillery pieces:

"...The enemy was greatly demoralized by the damage wrought by our field artillery, which was using melinite [high explosive] shells with terrible effect. From afar off we could clearly see whole sections of the enemy wiped out by our accurate fire. When a shell fell near a German platoon, it was annihilated. After a few seconds one saw two or three men get up and flee, the rest remained. It was a complete destruction. Our batteries of four guns do the work of four or six-gun batteries of the enemy. Our fire is quicker, and we can direct a hail of shells from a given spot in a very short space of time. Our gun-carriage does not move during fire. Only a very slight and a quickly executed adjustment is required before the next shell goes. The Germans find that their guns shift after each shot. In addition to the rapidity of our fire, our shells are extremely powerful. ... Our immediate success was due to our artillery. I saw the battlefield and the damage done was awful. Our shells compare with that of a gigantic blow of an axe. This is quite exact. The impression one has is that a giant had struck everywhere with some Titanic axe. Those directly hit are pulverized while others are killed by the shock of the explosion. Their convulsed faces are blackened with the powder of the enemy." [31]

The 3rd Battalion attack, now advancing with some of the machine guns, was able to make some progress and reached within several hundred meters of the enemy lines. The fighting continued past twilight. At 8:30 pm, one of the machine gun sections actually became the farthest leading element of the entire regimental attack, with their advance placing them directly on a roadside position to the front of Rixheim. Mercifully, as complete darkness descended, the firing began to slack off, and then finally ceased.

Those who survived were left dazed and exhausted. Many units were left leaderless, and dead and wounded were everywhere. Most critically, the threat of a French counterattack loomed large. At 2:00 am, General Isbert, the 29th Division commander, tried to stabilize the sector by bringing up Infantry Regiment 112. IR 112, relatively un-bloodied from the previous afternoon's fighting, was positioned at the edge of the Gehren Forest, the area immediately east of the 3rd Battalion's assault. The presence of IR 112 allowed the remainder of IR 169 to withdraw from the field in the early morning hours of August 10. IR 169 eventually reassembled in a field south of Baldersheim, where it first went into battle-line eight hours earlier. A number of the casualties were collected by the train station at Napoleoninsel.

Rieth described his night under the rubble of the paper factory building.

"Now I endeavored to dislodge myself from out of my unfortunate position. But as the night had completely come upon me, I did not know where to begin and all my efforts were in vain. So I remained still until the following morning. During dawn I crept away from the factory through a small aperture. But what a view presented itself there, I still think about it with a shudder! A few steps away from me lay a rider and his horse, both dead, and a musician's carriage totally shot to pieces. This was my road to reality after I had spent the whole night half unconscious under the debris. Soon I met a comrade from my company and went with him to the train station in Napoleoninsel. There lay our captain and the battalion adjutant; both had suffered to their end."

Elsewhere along the XIV Corps front that day, the German attack was met with brisk French resistance. On the corps' right flank, the 28th Division fought all afternoon and into the evening in an inconclusive attack. By 9:00 pm, the 28th Division was finally able to gain limited progress by taking control of the outskirt villages of Reichweiler and Burzweiler.

General Bonneau, despite being able to push off the worst of the German attacks, perceived that he was in a most precarious position. While the Germans never achieved a decisive breakthrough, they were able to fracture the French line at several locations, especially in the western-most attacks of XV Corps. The day's fighting also left many of the French units with considerable losses. To Bonneau's regret, reserves that would have otherwise been immediately available were deployed towards Altkirch, too far away to be of any use.

Just before midnight on August 9, General Bonneau concluded that he was significantly outnumbered. He expected a renewed attack the following morning and lacked the confidence that he could continue to hold. Above all else, Bonneau feared that a crack in his left flank would lead to his command's destruction. With no prospect for quick reinforcement, the French commander ordered an immediate retreat back across the Alsace – French border and a return to the protection of the Belfort fortresses. By dawn of August 10, the French had deserted Mulhouse and were well on their way to the 15-mile retreat back to France.

Within hours of discovering the French had retreated, the German 7th Army launched a pursuit. The enemy's head start was far too great however, and the French reached their Belfort sanctuary well ahead of the advancing Germans.

Rieth's journal on this battle concludes with this simple passage describing the situation on the morning of August 10. "There was no trace of the French, who had moved away swiftly. We pursued them across the border."

Throughout the day, wounded were collected and evacuated and the dead buried in hasty graves. For the next four days, IR 169 moved into quarters in villages around Mulhouse to recover from the battle and prepare for future operations.

Those Alsatians who rejoiced at their short-lived 'liberation' by the French were subject to harsh German retributions. Max Hastings, in *Catastrophe 1914*, provided these reflections of the Mulhouse battlefield by Warrant Officer Ernst Klopper, a peacetime artist from Pforzheim:

> "...Klopper's dead comrades were laid out in rows for burial, while the French village which they had died to capture was almost burnt out. Klopper was distressed by the clamorous appeals for food, water, rescue from horses, pigs and cattle trapped in their stalls and pens. "I do not like to record these wicked atrocities," he wrote in his diary, "I never saw anything sadder than a battlefield with so many victims dead and wounded. Despite our victory, I feel deeply depressed. It looks as though the ancient Huns had been here; everything is smashed to pieces, kitchens, trunks, cellars ransacked for food and drink. Even the manure heaps are burning." [32]

Total casualties from the Battle of Mulhouse were estimated at 4,000 French, and 3000 German losses. IR 169's toll on August 9 was severe. The regiment's field journal lists losses of 23 officers (8 killed) and 544 enlisted men. 7th Army was able to get about 30,000 troops into the battle. With IR 169 representing 10% of the total German infantry strength, they made up nearly 20% of all German casualties from the entire battle. The war was barely a week old.

For the French, the defeat at Mulhouse brought a national sense of humiliation. To finally liberate a large portion of the long-lusted for Alsace, only to lose it in a matter of days, was a disgrace.

The French Commander in Chief, General Joffre, was furious. He fired General Bonneau outright and blamed the French defeat on lack of aggressiveness and offensive spirit. The relief of Bonneau marked the first evidence of Joffre's ruthless intolerance towards failing subordinate commanders. Within the next three months, Joffre sacked 98 senior French officers whom he regarded as incompetent.[33]

Chapter 3
The Battle of Frontiers: Into the Lorraine

While the now-bloodied elements of the 7th Army regrouped after Mulhouse, major events in the eastern and western fronts shaped the start of IR 169's next campaign; the Battle of the Frontiers.

In the east, the Germans were surprised to learn the Tsar had mobilized much quicker than forecasted, with two Russian armies posed to threaten East Prussia. Although the Russians would be badly defeated in the late August 1914 Battle of Tannenberg, the speed of the Russian deployment, combined with Austrian-Hungarian setbacks, would siphon off important resources needed for a speedy and decisive victory over France.

On the Western Front, the Liege fortresses had finally fallen to the Germans on August 16. Germans were now starting to pour through Belgium and began their primary thrust into northwestern France. Scottish historian Gerad DeGroot described a million Germans tramping into France: "No longer was it regiments of men marching, but something uncanny, inhuman, a force of nature like a landslide, a tidal wave, or lava sweeping down a mountain." [34] The attack on Belgium drew the English into the war, and by the second week of August the British Expeditionary Force (BEF) had landed a force of four infantry and one-cavalry division on the Continent. By August 22, the BEF was in position in Mons, just south of the Belgian capital of Brussels.

The French remained slow to recognize the imminent threat to their northern homeland. Ten days into the war, they were still committed to their ill-fated Plan 17. "Whatever the circumstances," dictated Plan 17, "it is the Commander-in-Chief's intention to advance with all forces united to attack the German armies." Joffre's scheme of operations was to throw forward his five armies in two groups, 5th and 3rd on the left, 2nd and 1st on the right, and the 4th Army set slightly to the rear to cover the gap between the two masses. The leftmost force would attack through the Moselle Valley and Ardennes Forest, while the 1st and 2nd Army Group were to retake the Alsace-Lorraine, cross the Rhine, and invade southern Germany.[35]

The French blow to the south fell across the Lorraine. Situated northeast of the Alsace, much of the Lorraine is forested and mountainous. The Vosges Mountains rise to the east, giving way to the hilly Lorraine Plateau to the west, bordering Champagne-Ardenne.

On the German side of the Alsace-Lorraine front, Chief of Staff Moltke combined his two southern-most armies into the single 6th/7th Army Group. Crown Prince Rupprecht, who initially commanded the 6th Army, was placed in overall charge of the newly formed joint group, brimming with 350,000 troops. A common staff was created, with General Krafft Von Delmensingen designated as chief of staff.[36]

In addition to his military responsibilities, Crown Prince Rupprecht was the regent heir apparent to the State of Bavaria. The 45 year old Rupprecht proved to be a competent military commander who was well prepared and eager to bring battle to the French. Moltke's orders were for the 6th/7th Army Group to conduct a strategic defensive to tie down a large number of French forces – all in support of the grand German envelopment now gaining traction to the north.[37]

The resulting Battle of the Frontiers began on August 14, when the French southern-most forces, the 1st and 2nd Armies, crossed the western border of the Lorraine. Among other objectives, they focused on seizing the large German Army garrison at Sarrebourg. The French underestimated the size of the German 6th/7th Army Group; instead of six corps, Rupprecht commanded eight. The French also did not factor that the Germans might simply wait for their advance to overextend itself, at which time they would launch a powerful counterblow.[38]

Although assigned a defensive mission, Rupprecht initially wanted to attack deep to the west to seize bridgeheads across the Moselle and Meurthe rivers. A success there would enable his army to serve as the pivot point to the advancing 5th Army to his right, which could swing down for a war-ending blow against the exposed French armies. This scheme would require additional forces. In an order that drew IR 169 into motion, Rupprecht reached down and called on the 7th Army's XIV Corps to serve as his reinforcements. 7th Army's remaining forces, the XV and XIV (Reserve) Corps remained on the southern extreme of the German front, now serving to protect the 6th Army's left flank in its impending attack.

Fluid German estimates of the enemy strength forced Rupprecht to alter plans from offense, to defense and back to offense throughout the days of August 12-14. The change in the 6th/7th Army Group battle plans had little effect on XIV Corps' (and IR 169's) movement orders – Rupprecht still needed to shift multiple divisions north. XIV Corps departed Mulhouse on August 13-15, with instructions to assemble in the Sarrebourg area, 50 miles west of the Strasbourg.

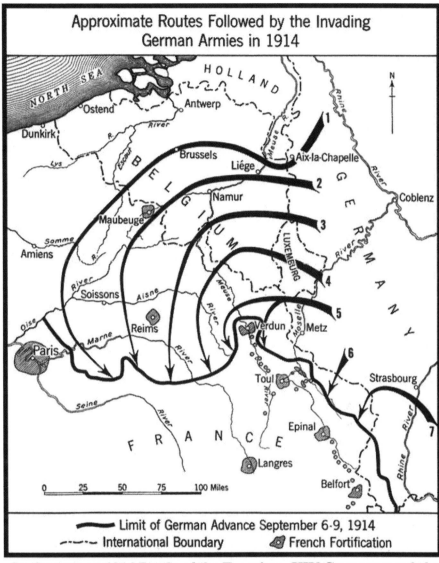

Approximate Routes Followed by the Invading German Armies in 1914

Limit of German Advance September 6-9, 1914
International Boundary
French Fortification

In the August 1914 Battle of the Frontiers, XIV Corps entered the fighting in the area between the 6th and 7th Army arrows. This map also reflects the greater Von Schlieffen Plan in motion, with the main effort of the German Army sweeping in from the north.

(AABE)

On August 16, the German commanders reassessed the number of French troops and correctly concluded that the enemy was considerably weaker than was earlier presumed. The reduction of French troops was, in part, due to several corps being funneled northward to meet the emerging German invasion. All considered, the Germans were braced to meet with the combined forces of the French 1st Army, commanded by General Dubail, and the 2nd Army, under General de Castelnau. Poised along the Alsace-Lorraine, the enemy line ran over 100 miles from the city of Nancy to the north down to Raon l'Etape to the south.

The French 1st and 2nd Armies' Lorraine offensive began in earnest on August 14, but quickly lost steam. Much to the frustration of the German commanders, the French armies were well abreast, which presented few vulnerable gaps that invited a German counterattack.

Rather than making a stand on a fixed position, Rupprecht proposed a plan where the German 6/7th Army Group would lure the French into a massive trap. Using terrain to their advantage, the Germans would contest the French in sporadic engagements. In doing so, the Germans hoped to draw the center of the French advance into a large kill sack. Then, by exploiting the weakened and exposed flank of the overextended line, they would launch a fierce counterattack where the enemy would be weakest. Rupprecht saw an opportunity to destroy the 1st and 2nd Armies and then envelop the remainder of the French field.

Rupprecht, waiting for the perfect moment to go on the offensive, was quickly losing patience. Finally, on August 18, Rupprecht received Field Marshal Von Moltke's reluctant approval to go on the attack with the full weight of both 6th and 7th Armies. With that decision, one of the war's greatest meeting engagements was launched.[39]

The French offensive reached a climax on August 20, with a massive left flank attack towards the hilltop village of Morhange. The French debacle before Morhange foretold the calamity that was about to descend upon their entire front. The Germans had established a virtually impregnable defense, with artillery, machine guns and infantrymen deeply stacked atop high ground and with miles of open terrain in front of them. Discounting recent intelligence that warned of the German strength, the French commanders ordered a grand assault. In Napoleonic tradition, 43,000 French soldiers, in gleaming blue and red uniforms, bravely marched towards the German defenses. The results were suicidal. Massed German fires ripped apart the French soldiers by the thousands. In a few hours, two French divisions were destroyed. As described in Hastings' *Catastrophe 1914*, a French officer wrote of the confusion: "a sublime chaos, infantrymen, brilliant motor cars of our brilliant staffs all meeting, crisscrossing, not knowing what to do or where to go." Across the entire front, the French assaults resulted in disaster, throwing back entire corps with heavy losses.[40] Into this greater morass came the full counterattack of the $6^{th}/7^{th}$ Army Group.

When IR 169 set out for the 6th Army sector on August 15, the intended destination was Sarrebourg, deep in the heartland of the Lorraine. However, as the trains approached the Vosges Mountains in the early morning hours of August 17, Sarrebourg was on the verge of falling under French control. In the first three days of the French offensive, most of the 2nd Army had advanced between 10 – 15 miles into the Lorraine. Its furthest penetration was Sarrebourg itself, which the French captured on August 17.

In its 40 previous years of German occupation, Sarrebourg held a sizeable German military garrison. Strategically situated, the town covered the midpoint of a railroad line that linked Strasbourg with the huge German garrison of Metz, further to the northwest. Sarrebourg also sat just west of a small passage through the Vosges that led to a natural exit of the Lorraine gateway to the Rhine Valley, a crucial objective for the French offensive. The Germans understood that the terrain around Sarrebourg did not favor a defense to the west, which was the natural direction of French advance. Rather than making a fight for the town on poor ground, the Germans elected to withdraw to the high terrain just to the east. They would then retake the garrison with the inertia of the pending offensive.[41]

Late on August 17, French cavalry took Sarrebourg with almost no resistance. Undetected by their foe, the Germans had stealthily deployed vast concentrations of infantry and artillery on the high ground to the east. The French 'victors' celebrating the capture of Sarrebourg soon found it a prize far more difficult to retain than to take.

IR 169 departed Mulhouse for Sarrebourg on August 15. Albert Rieth wrote of movement from the Alsace to the Lorraine:

"On August 15, we marched via Habsheim to Kembs. It was very evident how the fighting had ravaged the entire area, as there were shot up houses everywhere and torn telephone cables. From Kembs, we crossed the Rhine River to the Fortress Istein. Meanwhile, a strong rain commenced and we arrived wet to the skin at Efringen, the same town we had ended the maneuvers a year ago. We visited our host family where we stayed during the maneuvers and knew them well. They remembered us well but what a difference between the maneuvers and now, as the war situation had become serious.

The departure from Efringen occurred on August 16, and we did not know where the journey would lead. We rode via railroad through Strasbourg and Zabern, and then to the final station at Lutzelbourg. We arrived there on August 17, at 4 am."

IR 169's soggy, nine-mile march from the Mulhouse area to the Efringen railhead took back over the Rhine and into Germany. Arriving at the station, the men piled into tightly packed cattle cars, with 48 men, or 28 men and six horses, in each car. The XIV Corps men still fared better than other 7th Army units called later to battle in the Lorraine. Many of these troops would eventually be flung into battle after completing a 60 mile forced foot march.

The trains rolled away from Efringen and moved north, with the Rhine River to the immediate left. For the next 30 miles, the journey reversed much of the same route that brought IR 169 to Mulhouse nine long days earlier. Passing through Offenburg was a significant event for men of the 84th Brigade, as this was the garrison city for IR 170. The IR 170 troops were given a hero's welcome that featured a parade through the town, a comfortable bivouac and a special field religious service. Shortly after passing Offenburg, the trains crossed west over a Rhine railroad bridge and passed through the ancient cathedral city of Strasbourg. From there, the route moved northwest, and began to enter the foothills of the Vosges Mountain range and towards their destination of Lutzelbourg, one train stop east of Sarrebourg.

The final segment of the journey to the edge of the battlefront took them through the flat farmlands west of the city and into the canyons of the northern limits of the Vosges. Upon reaching the highlands, the train snaked its way along the Marne River Canal and through a series of tunnels that cut through the imposing mountainside. With Sarrebourg now in French hands, the closest destination to the German assembly point was Lutzelbourg, a three-street village on the edge of the canal and 10 miles southeast of Sarrebourg. The regiment arrived in Lutzelbourg at 4:00 on the morning of August 17. They were among the last troops of XIV Corps to join the 6th Army.

The men unloaded their equipment in the early morning darkness and marched three miles north to the village of Mittlebronn, where the regiment bivouacked for the next two days. IR 169 was now near the epicenter of the 6th/7th Army Group's impending strike.

Across the entire Alsace-Lorraine front, the sizes of the French and German armies were roughly equal, with the Germans having a slight overall numerical superiority. In the Lorraine gateway however, the critical region where the primary contest was to be decided, the Germans had assembled 19 infantry divisions against a force of 11 French infantry divisions. The Germans had succeeded in the all-important military principle of assembling mass at a critical place and time.

Throughout August 19, the Germans made their final preparations for their grand attack. Troops were supplied with ammunition and several days' rations, artillery was moved forward and unlimbered, reconnaissance patrols probed forward, and regiments either rested or marched to final assault positions. At 7:30 that evening, Crown Prince Rupprecht issued his attack orders: "Starting at 5:00 am on August 20, the four base corps of 6th Army are to conduct a surprise attack to south and west, across the French border and towards the Meurthe River."

XIV Corps positioned in the center of the grand German attack. Its task was to smash the French 8th Corps located along a five-mile line that ran on a southeast axis just below Sarrebourg. This zone included the village of Buehl to the north, continued south across the Marne Canal, and then through the villages of Niederviller, Bruderdorf, Hochwalsch [present day Plaine-de-Walsch], and Vallerysthal. In the coming fight, IR 169 would be sent into battle in the area between Vallerysthal and Hochwalsch. French forces opposing XIV Corps included the 1st Army's 15th Division.

Dubail, lacking accurate intelligence, sensed that the Germans were now close about him, and in greater numbers than in the opening days of the campaign. Despite this ominous premonition, Dubail estimated that a continued French attack, if rapid and determined, would probably suffice to chase the Germans out of their positions and open a road through the Vosges passageway and then to his Rhine River objective. The decision was settled. On the evening of August 19, Dubail ordered the 15th Division to undertake an eight-mile night march, and then mount a dawn attack on the Sarre River bridges beyond Sarrebourg. The French moved briskly into a 4:00 am attack. The first objective was carried at bayonet point as the French columns pressed nearly a mile up the Sarre valley. At that moment, an overwhelming barrage of German heavy artillery and small arms fire coming from both sides of the valley descended upon the leading French formations.[42] The battle of Sarrebourg had begun.

At 5:00 am, August 20, the Germans let loose with a ferocious artillery barrage all along the line. Much of this fire came from heavy caliber artillery. The French light field artillery that was so effective against infantry at close range was at a disadvantage when dueling with larger German howitzers – guns that lobbed shells at a higher angle. The French suffered the worst in this artillery contest.

The Lorraine counteroffensive began on another exceedingly hot day. The early morning attack of the German 6th/7th Army Group was aided by a hazy morning fog, which helped obscure their advance. Close on the heels of the heavy artillery barrage, German infantry quickly closed in on the battered French lines. Some of the French divisions crumbled and retreated, while others made determined defenses. Only to the far north, where the French 20th Corps held firm under the competent command of General Ferdinand Foch, were they able to hold fast. Casualties were heavy on both sides.

The XIV Corps' battle plans called for the 29th Division to attack the town of Buehl, which was on the far right of the corps sector. 28th Division, which would secure the center and left flank, had a wider sector that included the villages of Niederviller, Hochwalsch, and Vallerysthal. IR 169 was detached from 29th Division to serve as XIV Corps' reserve. In this role, IR 169 would be held back from the initial attack and be prepared for contingencies that included exploiting breakthroughs and responding to French counterattacks.

XIV Corps achieved initial success in the north and center portions of the attack. The 29th Division pushed past Buehl Road and cut off the French troops that were defending Sarrebourg. By late afternoon the French, having lost over 1000 casualties, retreated out of Sarrebourg to the strains of a regimental band playing *Marche Lorraine*.[43] To the left and center of the XIV Corps zone, the 28th Division ran into stiff resistance. Throughout the morning, the Germans absorbed heavy casualties while trying to breach the Marne canal and take the village of Niederviller. At noon, a more concealed approach through woodlands cloaked the next German attack. Bursting from the woods, the 28th Division quickly overran the French positions and were in possession of Niederviller by 1:00 pm.

Just to the south of Niederviller, the 28th Division's left wing had a much more difficult time in trying to dislodge the well-embedded French infantry at Hochwalsch. Hard fighting raged throughout the afternoon as German casualties stacked in the open fields before the town. The XIV Corps commander grew increasingly frustrated at this lack of progress, and demanded that the position "be taken at any price." By late afternoon, and XIV Corps still had yet to even launch an attack on Vallerysthal, their southernmost objective.

The limited successes in driving the French out of Buehl and Niederviller led German commanders to overestimate their gains and ignore the stubborn enemy resistance at Hochwalsch and Vallerysthal. With the misperception of a French collapse, the combined I Bavarian and XIV Corps' force was ordered to pursuit the enemy through a five mile zone beyond the initial breakthrough points.

The German troops fighting the battle understood all too clearly that the French had no intentions to give up the field without more of a fight. French infantry, well supported by artillery, launched a series of concentrated counterattacks against the 29th Division's gains. The fighting seesawed in the fields around Buehl and Niederviller for several hours. Finally at 6:00 pm, the nearly-exhausted troops of the 29th Division were able to take the village of Schneckenbusch, one mile west of Niederviller. This achievement was short-lived, for soon after, a massive French artillery barrage drove the battered Germans out of the town and back to Niederviller. The entire southern segment of the XIV Corps zone was now barely beyond its start point from the beginning of the day. By late afternoon, it was obvious that the effort to take Hochwalsch had stalled. With the 7th Army commander demanding the immediate capture of Hochwalsch, it was time to call in the XIV Corps reserve force – Infantry Regiment 169.

The day before the battle, IR 169 moved into battle position with a five mile hike from Mittlebronn to the tiny crossroad village of Hommarting-Post, a ramshackle collection of a half dozen farmhouses. The regiment spent the night in fields and used the village as a staging point for its corps reserve mission. On the morning of August 20, the land around Hommarting-Post shook from the firing of the XIV Corps artillery that brimmed the surrounding ridges.

Throughout the deafening day, IR 169 was repeatedly placed on and off immediate alert status. The final summons to the front came at 3:00 pm. These orders called for the regiment to bolster 28th Division's stalled attacks to take Hochwalsch, and then swing down to take control of Vallerysthal, just under a mile further to the south.

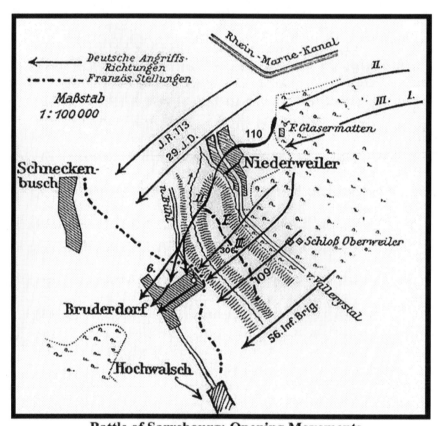

Battle of Sarrebourg; Opening Movements
In the August 20, 1914 Battle of Sarrebourg, XIV Corps' 28th Division attacked between Niederweiler and Vallerysthal. Late that afternoon, IR 169, as the Corps' reserves, went into action at Hochwalsch.
(BIWW)

Moving in columns to the front, the regiment trudged over dusty country roads, crossed the Marne Canal, and passed through the small villages of Arzviller and Guntzviller. One mile south of Guntzviller, they climbed a steep rise, and finally reached their staging area at a roadside intersection in the small hamlet of Renthal. At 6:00 pm, the three battalions moved off the road and deployed in battle formations. The French line was now less than one mile directly to the west.

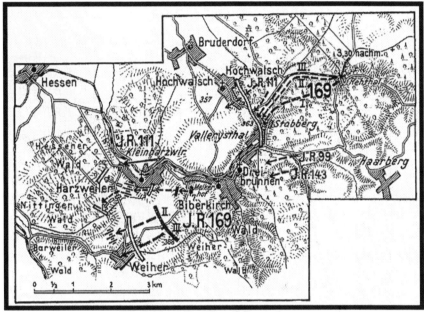

IR 169 at Battle of Sarrebourg
On August 20, IR 169 attacked Hochwalsch and Vallerysthal. The regiment captured two French batteries between Weiher and Harzweiler the following day.

(BIWW)

Rieth described the opening stages of IR 169's attack:

"On August 20 the order came for XIV Corps to attack. From Hommarting-Post, we marched in the direction of Vallerysthal. Then we had the report that the French occupied the town, and it was our task to take it over. We went steep up a hill and the French must have noticed us, as shrapnel began to fly high over our heads, but missing us. It was about 6 pm when we reached the top and took cover behind single houses. We could not remain here too long, because if the enemy artillery discovered us we would have been lost. There was a slight decline where the enemy had dug in. First the 1st, then 2nd, and finally the 3rd platoon (of which I was a member) were engaged, and with a "hurrah" we stormed down the hill."

The officers formed the regiment in a tight cluster with 1st Battalion to the south (left), 2nd Battalion in the center, and 3rd Battalion on the right. The individual rifle companies stacked their platoons in three lines. Shortly after forming into a line of battle, the regiment began to draw some French artillery fire. IR 169 commenced its attack.

With bugle calls blowing and a spirited cheer, IR 169 stormed downhill through exposed farmland and into a valley. The objective of the attack was to carry the French positions along the rise of the far valley ridge that stretched between Hochwalsch and Vallerysthal. Racing forward, the men stepped over the many dead and wounded left from the day's previous attacks.

Instead of making a stand, the French infantry abruptly left their main positions and retreated back to a second defensive line. The Germans occupied the first vacated ditch and prepared to continue the attack to the second line. Rieth described the French response:

"The French left their trench and retreated to a second one. They liked to construct trenches behind each other. We took the first enemy trench to rest up before taking the second trench, when the enemy artillery suddenly started to fire upon us. They knew the distance very well, and we laid flat into the trench but were nearly buried alive.

The shells and shrapnel so often burst in the trench that I thought the 3rd Battalion, Regiment 169 had ceased to fight. A piece of shrapnel took the drum out of the drummer's hands without injuring him. But meanwhile we had many dead and wounded. Next to me someone shouted, "Help, help me, I am wounded!" I wondered how one could best take him out of this witches' cauldron, because if we both exposed ourselves in full size we would have been easy targets for the French infantry. The wounded was the Recruit Schindler. My neighbor, Musketeer Schmidt told me that we should carry him out. We jumped out of the ditch. I took Schindler under the arms and

Schmidt grabbed his legs, although his thigh bone was completely shot off. Although the man was in terrible pain, we could not hesitate very long. We carried Schindler to the street and wanted to get to one of the houses behind which we had hidden before. As we got to the street, a shell hit the street about 2 meters in front of us. Schmidt fell down and dropped Schindler. I thought that Schmidt had fallen because of the explosion, but I soon saw that he was wounded. I got away with only a few lacerations in the face, which I did not initially notice in the excitement. First I took Schindler to a hay-shed, and then I helped the other. I noticed that Schindler had been wounded for the ninth time, mainly by the shell that also wounded Schmidt. A rather large piece of shrapnel had torn a big gaping hole in Schindler's chest, which I was not able to wrap up as my medical dressing kit was missing. I could wrap his foot with my remaining two rolls of bandage. Schmidt had a big wound in his thigh and his foot was completely severed from his ankles, so I could only tie it off to try to prevent his bleeding to death. So we sat behind the house in a terrible state as the shells continued to fly over our heads. It must have been terrible for the wounded, but I must admire them, as they said not a word.

Then we heard commands from the 2nd Battalion, 76th Artillery, which was now in position in front of us. They began to fire, and soon the French artillery became quiet. The medical corpsmen now had a lot of work to do, and I learned that the two wounded men had died. Our battalion spent the night in Vallerysthal." [Today, the names of Emil Schmidt and Alton Schindler are listed on a memorial that marks the mass grave of the German dead in the joint French-German military cemetery in Hochwalsch.]

The 3rd Battalion was lured into a torrent of artillery fire. Counter-battery fires from the 76th Artillery Regiment finally silenced the French guns, but further hopes of a breakthrough at Hochwalsch on August 20 was dashed.

With darkness descending, the left-most companies of IR 169 attacked into the small logging town of Vallerysthal, located one half mile from 3rd Battalion's stand near Hochwalsch. Vallerysthal was a

Y-shaped village wedged between high-ground outcroppings of the Vosges Mountains. The village's topography had important tactical considerations, with one road leading directly from Hochwalsch and a second to the southwest and deep into the Vosges itself. Control of this pass was essential, as it opened the exit point for other German forces battling up in the Vosges. Immediately adjacent to Vallerysthal is the adjoining village of Biberkirch.

The French took advantage of the village's sturdy stonewall factory buildings and homes to make a vigorous defense, and bitter, house-to-house fighting raged throughout the night. German units from both XIV and XIV Corps' regiments poured into the fight, contributing to the already chaotic nature of the nighttime melee. By dawn, the German officers had sufficiently regained control of the situation to collect their weary men for the mission ahead.

August 21 began with the French pulling out their remaining forces from Vallerysthal to defend the high ground by Weiher and Harzweiler, two miles to the west of the previous day's fighting. The French had organized a defense in depth, with advanced forces deployed along the expected German attack route. The terrain favored the defenders, as the Germans had to traverse villages, steep hillsides, and open farmland in order to reach their objective.

XIV Corps objectives for the day were to drive the enemy back across the French Border, ten miles to the west. IR 169 was ordered to a lead role in forthcoming attack, with its 1st Battalion being detached to serve as the 28th Division's reserve. This left Colonel Spennemann with only two battalions for the main attack. Combined with the severe losses from the previous day's fighting, IR 169 was going into battle with sharply depleted numbers.

Rieth described the advance towards Weiher and Harzweiler:

> "Our battalion spent the night in Vallerysthal. The next morning, the 9th Company was ordered to the front of the unit. No sooner had we progressed some steps, and then the shooting began again. On the left of the street was a rather steep hill, where the French had dug in. We lay down behind the houses and were thus out of reach of the enemy bullets. The bullets hit the walls of the houses in such a manner that we thought we were under fire from different directions. We had to search

each house painstakingly, but found nothing, so that the enemy could only be on the hill to the left of the street.

"Our next task was to take that hill, and we went through the back garden of the house to reach it. After we reached the hill the enemy had disappeared without a trace. We thought this was a trap and rested first. We then approached a little wood that we thought was occupied, but nothing was there except for an abandoned trench. We continued but then were showered by a hail of shrapnel making it impossible to proceed. The enemy had planned to lure us into the wood and then fire at us, in which they succeeded as we had fallen for this ruse.

The enemy artillery had fired into the entire wood, and we were wondering how to get out of it. Our major had died, so the captain of the 12th company took command of the battalion, and ordered that the battery should be stormed. We cautiously proceeded to the adjacent ridge of the wood, when our artillery started firing upon the enemy. The shells of our heavy artillery came with terrible noise. Some of the rounds fell too short, and landed only about 80 meters into the ground ahead of us. We thus had the opportunity to witness the effect of our shells, with a pine tree of half a meter being torn out just like a straw. We now had to retreat in order to get out of the range of our artillery, which was now firing intensively at the enemy."

A 6th Company patrol, commanded by Lieutenant Bertele, led 2nd Battalion's advance on Weiher. The patrol moved forward in two single columns on either side of a country road that crossed the rolling farmland. The scattered enemy resistance included an incident where a French soldier sprang from a ditch to be killed by 6th Company's Corporal Lohr. Midway to Weiher, 2nd Battalion began to receive an intensive artillery barrage. The opening rounds killed color bearer Corporal Buehrle as he stood by his battalion commander. The heavy fire halted the 2nd Battalion's advance forcing them to await the arrival of 3rd Battalion to come online to its left.

IR 169 was taking fire from two separate French batteries; one located at the northern outskirts of Weiher and the second, one mile north in the village of Harzweiler. French infantry was arrayed several hundred yards before each battery.

The toll on the German officer ranks was high. 3rd Battalion was now under the command of Major Hoffman, who only one week earlier had replaced Major Lilienhoff-Zivowizti, who was critically wounded in the Battle of Mulhouse. While organizing the final push towards the French lines, Major Hoffman was killed and replaced by the 12th Company commander, Captain Grasmacher. Grasmacher then ordered the 3rd Battalion to storm the battery. Moments later, Captain Grasmacher was decapitated by a shell.[44]

German artillery support finally came into action, and provided suppressive fire that allowed the advance of the infantry to continue.

In the midst of this artillery duel, a scratch force of various regimental elements was formed under the command of Major Teschner, the commander of the 2nd Battalion. This ad hoc task force consisted of the 2nd Battalions' 5th and 7th Companies, 3rd Battalion's 9th Company and the regimental machine gun company. Aided by the effective artillery support, Teschner was able to take advantage of the rolling terrain and skillfully maneuvered his force forward between the towns of Harzweiler and Weiher. The German artillery fire compelled the French infantry near Harzweiler to fall back into the woods to the west. Teschner led his force to a small depression just outside of the Harzweiler, where they lay undetected by the French.

The French battery that had been firing on the Germans from Harzweiler mounted up and displaced to a position to the south, towards Weiher. In the fog of battle, the French commander was obviously unaware that a German force had penetrated so far forward. The commander halted the battery in field a short distance out of town as the guns were unlimbered and readied for their next fire mission, all as three German infantry and one machine gun company lay waiting only yards away. On Major Teschner's command, the troops arose to pour concentrated rifle and machine gun fire into the unsuspecting artillerymen. Within moments, most of the French soldiers and horses were dead or wounded, with a few survivors managing to flee into the Harzweiler woods.[45]

The annihilation of the French battery outside of Harzweiler had a pivotal effect on the course of the battle, with the momentum swinging in favor of the Germans. The machine guns, which continued to be supported by the three infantry companies, advanced beyond the destroyed battery and took a strong position that overlapped the flank of the French infantrymen defending Weiher. These French troops quickly found themselves in an impossible spot. Already taking heavy artillery fire, the French infantry and the remaining battery were also facing a direct attack from IR 169's 6th, 8th, 10th, 11th and 12th Companies to the front, and from the machine guns and 9th, 5th and 7th Companies to their left flank.

Officer losses continued to stack up, with Lieutenant Bertele killed, and Lieutenants Roder, Winter and Unger seriously wounded. The accuracy and rate of fire of the German machine guns played a critical role in keeping the French pinned down. At a crucial point in the fighting, a machine gun support team arrived at the front with desperately needed ammunition. The timely resupply enabled to the Germans to continuing pressing the attack.

One of the French infantry units battling in the XIV Corps sector was the 86th Regiment of Infantry (RI). The 86th RI official history provides a glimpse from the French perspective of the fighting, which was characterized with "impetuous bayonet charges" and acts of great valor. At one point, Captain Degoutin, commanding the 6th Company, led his men through violent artillery and machine gun fire into the German lines. Degoutin fell dead, pierced with multiple bayonet wounds. Just prior to leading his men in a charge, recently commissioned Sub-Lieutenant Ely, calmly pulled off his white gloves and took position at the front of his platoon. He also fell dead. 86 RI left the battlefield losing over 1,000 men and 25 officers.[46]

The deciding point of the battle came when German battalions stormed towards Weiher, now only a few hundred yards away. Major Teschner ordered 9th Company to attack the French left flank. The French infantry line collapsed, with its survivors fleeing into the forest immediately behind the town. The artillery battery on the northern edge of Weiher was now trapped in a field, as a stream blocked access to the one road that headed away from the Germans. The remaining French artillerymen abandoned their guns and followed the path of their fleeing infantry comrades into the nearby woods.

The Germans swept over the French positions and to the edge of the forest and began to pursue the routed enemy through the Hessener and Nittinger forests. The French were still able to muster yet more artillery to the west and began to shell the Germans as they moved through the woods. The barrage lasted over an hour and finally halted the German advance of August 21.

As the fighting began to ebb on the evening of August 21, the German 7th Army command group realized they were on the verge of a major victory and directed an all-out pursuit. At 8:00 pm, IR 169 received orders to advance to the town of Niderhoff, several miles to the southwest. Further movement for the night proved impossible, as the troops had been in intensive combat for over 30 straight hours. The exhausted men of the 2nd and 3rd Battalions spent the night of August 21-22 bivouacking on the eastern edge of the Nittinger Forest. The close proximity of French troops denied the Germans the comfort of building fires to ward off the chilly night.[47]

Rieth's account of the Battle of Sarrebourg concludes with a simple summary: "When we attacked we found the enemy battery deserted, and we captured 32 guns and munitions carriers, as well as 100 prisoners. It was rather a victory as the enemy was pushed 20 kilometers past the border."

By battle's end, IR 169 had done its share to puncture a decisive hole in the French lines. The regiment was credited with capturing multiple artillery pieces, ammunition carriers and prisoners. A rough estimation of French casualties can be derived from examining the battlefield cemeteries that dot the countryside. Today, a cluster of four of these cemeteries from the XIV Corps sector of the 20-21 August 1914 battles list almost 4,000 French soldiers killed in action. Adding the wounded, missing and those taken prisoner, it can be conservatively estimated the French lost 20,000 men in this small pocket of the Lorraine Province.

This early stage of the Battle of the Frontiers gave evidence that the regiment was quickly learning to better adapt to modern warfare. Compared with their experience Mulhouse, battle of Sarrebourg showed the regiment was making better use of terrain as well as integrating machine gun and artillery support. IR 169's losses were steep. The two days of fighting resulted in losses of 19 officers (8 killed) and 807 enlisted men. The severity of the August 21 fighting hit the 2nd and 3rd Battalions especially hard, as a review of the regiment's losses for August 1914 shows the losses to 2nd and 3rd Battalions to be three time that of 1st Battalion.

Chapter 4

The Meurthe Campaign; Baccarat and the St Mihiel Salient

The German 6th/7th Army Group's August 20-21 counterattack into the Lorraine sent the French 1st and 2nd Armies reeling. By late afternoon on August 21, the 2nd Army was in full retreat to the Meurthe River, 20 miles to the west, while the 1st Army was stopped in its tracks in the Vosges Mountains. All French gains from the previous week were lost.

The Meurthe River, serving the tactical military functions of either an obstacle or sanctuary, dictated the direction of the next series of battles. Deep and fast moving, the Meurthe originated from the Vosges and flowed into the Moselle River beyond the city of Nancy. Quick German control of the river could trap an entire French army. Conversely, a failure to secure adequate bridgeheads would destroy Rupprecht's goal of sustaining the offensive into France. The race to the Meurthe drove the actions of IR 169 for the next three days.

With their left flank unhinged, the 1st Army was in danger of being cut off and destroyed. Crown Prince Rupprecht realized this opportunity and moved to cut off the westernmost routes of exit from the mountains. To accomplish this, the 6th/7th Army Group issued orders for the main German effort to attack to the west and secure a crossing of the Meurthe River. By August 23, the 1st Army commander, General de Castelnau, perceived the threat and organized a desperate retreat to reach the safety of the Meurthe's far bank. de Castelnau was dealing with more than just the heavy burdens of command; on August 21 he lost the first of his three sons to be killed in the war.[48]

Far to the south, and as a sideshow to the fighting in the Lorraine, the war revisited Mulhouse. Following a bloody contest on August 19, the French 1st Army reclaimed Mulhouse, and in the process captured 24 German cannon and over 1000 prisoners. Like their earlier capture of Mulhouse, this French victory was again short lived; a sloppily managed German counterattack again forced their retreat to Belfort on August 22. The French flag would not again rise over Mulhouse until the war's end.[49]

August 22, 1914 stands as a grim milestone in the tally of World War I losses. Although IR 169 was not directly involved in combat, this date marked the bloodiest day of the entire four-year war for the French army, as 27,000 French soldiers were *killed* on that day alone. In three days of fighting (August 20 – 22), the French suffered an astonishing toll of over 40,000 killed, with over one hundred thousand more wounded, missing or captured. The extreme casualties of August 1914 for all major combatants contributed to the long length of the war; this great cost in lives made a complete victory all the more imperative.

From August 22 – 23, XIV Corps' weary troops prodded on with gritty road marches in the race to the Meurthe. The intermediate objective for XIV Corps was the town of Badonviller, 14 miles to the southwest of the site of IR 169's August 21 fighting. Badonviller held strategic value as it contained a major roadway entrance into the Vosges Mountains. XIV Corps had only two primary roads available for the movement; one skirting the very edge of the Vosges foothills and the other, used by 29th Division, paralleled several miles to the west.

The 29th Division's August 22 march was a hot, dusty and slow ordeal. The Germans were hampered by an inadequate road network that led to the western approaches of the Vosges; there were simply too many troops for too few roads. The roads and fields were clogged by endless ranks of German infantry, cavalry and artillery batteries, as well as vast munitions and supply columns. Villages along IR 169's path included Laneuveville, Fraqueling, and Hattigny. These were all typically small Lorraine towns that dotted the open farmland and led towards the Hattigny Forest.

Distant French artillery fired on the German advance guard that approached the Hattigny Forest. Additional reconnaissance determined that the French XV Corps was in a defensive formation before them. This development forced the tactical deployment of German infantry and artillery units, which effectively ended the day's advance. By evening, the 29th Division had covered little more than six miles, but the short journey did leave IR 169 only a stone's throw from the border into France.

In the early hours of Sunday, August 23, 7th Army commander Von Heeringen reaffirmed his demands for XIV Corps to reach Badonviller, 10 miles distant, by the end of the day. There was expected enemy resistance along the French border at the Vezouze River.

At first light, a massed concentration of German artillery fired on the suspected French defenses along the Vezouze. At 9:00 am, the German infantry followed the barrage and advanced towards the river. The Germans were surprised to learn the French had pulled out overnight, leaving the path into France completely open. IR 169 marched into France at Taconville.

The entry upon French soil was a symbolic milestone throughout the German ranks. All indications suggested that the three-day old offensive was heading towards success. Rieth's account notes: "On the third Sunday we crossed the border, and our captain held an enthusiastic speech, stating that we would not return until the enemy was completely defeated, and we marched back into France singing patriotic songs."

Later that morning, German aerial reconnaissance observed long columns of French troops now crossing over the Meurthe River at various points to the southwest. It was imperative for XIV Corps to sustain the momentum and prevent more French troops from getting over the Meurthe. The 7th Army's objectives became more ambitious, with XIV Corps now tasked to have at least one brigade reach the Meurthe River at the town of Baccarat, 15 miles further southwest. Orders were personally issued by the German Supreme Army Commander, Von Moltke, who directed the efforts of all available men to march to the "utmost exhaustion" to accomplish this mission.

There would be no quick dash to Baccarat. Once again, clogged roads stymied the German juggernaut. Things got worse when the 1st Bavarian Corps strayed into the XIV Corps line of march, creating a hopeless traffic jam. More time was lost before XIV Corps troops were finally able to push through.

IR 169's 23 August movement carried them past the villages of Femonville, Harbouey, Nonhigny, Montreux, and Neuviller-les-Badonviller, a distance of 10 miles. Despite the Germans' all-out effort, the lead elements of XIV Corps were still five miles short of Baccarat at day's end. By nightfall, most of the XIV Corps units massed closely together and plopped down in a cramped three mile-long area between Saint Poole and Neuviller.

Up in the Vosges highlands, French *chasseurs-alpins*, specialized mountain infantry, made effective use of the difficult terrain to slow down and inflict losses upon the advancing Germans. Despite this valiant defense, the Germans were coming ever closer to cutting off the last of the escape routes out of the Vosges. To buy more time against the oncoming XIV Corps, the French 21st Corps used the shallow Verdurette River to form a defensive line. The Verdurette served as natural obstacle before Baccarat and Raon-L'Etape, the last of the key gateway escape routes still open to the endangered French 1st Army. The French needed to hold this ground until their forces were safely across the Meurthe.

XIV Corps' bivouac site the night of 23-24 August was a scant two miles south of the French Verdurette line. The French were posted in strength along the river, and the defensive line included the villages of Merviller, Vacqueville, and Pexonne. The Germans moved out in attack formation early on the morning of 24 August and were immediately engaged in a sharp contest against the French defenders. Rieth summarized the fighting along the Verdurette: "The first enemy contact was at Vacqueville, but they were thrown back with heavy losses."

The fight for Vacqueville was actually a bitter struggle that came to bayonet fighting. The French troops held on long enough to serve their purpose as a temporary blocking force. By mid-day, the French had retreated out of the Vosges and were over the Meurthe. The Germans had failed to realize their intended great prize - the destruction of the 1st Army.

After the French were cleared from Vacqueville, the 29th Division found that the remaining four mile trek to Baccarat to be a difficult, all day march. The terrain was heavily wooded and hilly, rising to a 1000-foot mountain peak at the summit of the Forest dom de Grammons. IR 169 did not reach the outskirts of Baccarat until nightfall. A small screen of infantry pickets and a cavalry squadron entered into the town while the remainder of 29th Division made a hasty bivouac on the suburbs. After three days of arduous marching, XIV Corps was finally on the verge of crossing the Meurthe.

In Koblenz, the German Supreme Command faced a momentous, war-changing decision. It had always been assumed that once Rupprecht's armies contained the initial French offensive and stabilized their front - goals that had now been achieved - they would halt, organize their defenses and free all available forces to reinforce the primary right wing effort.

A second option appeared that presented as a powerful temptation.

The Supreme Command dusted off an alternative known as "Case 3" for consideration. By applying Case 3, the left wing would advance west towards the Moselle River rather than stay in place. On August 24, the Supreme Command was filled with a strong degree of optimism, as their three right-most armies were on the verge of pouring deep into France. Should the $6^{th}/7^{th}$ Army Group achieve a decisive breakthrough in the south, the Germans could then force the French into a fatal double envelopment, and thus defeat France within their six-week time table. With France beaten, the Germans would be able to finish off the hard-pressed Russian Army, ending the war in a quick and spectacular German victory.

Case 3's steep cost was that it siphoned off forces available to the main German effort on the right. This violated the core precept of Von Schlieffen's dictum; "Keep the right strong!" Furthermore, the prospects of a successful German attack in the $6^{th}/7^{th}$ Army sector were questionable at best, as that region was considered France's strongest fortified zone. There, massive underground fortification networks defended such places as Verdun, Toul, Nancy, Epinal, and Belfort.

After significant debate, von Moltke issued the fateful order to "Pursue direction Epinal;" considered one of the seminal tactical decisions of World War I. This directive launched a major left wing offensive across the Moselle. It also meant committing the $6^{th}/7^{th}$ Army Group to a frontal attack upon the French fortress line instead of freeing up reinforcements for the right wing. In the days that followed, this decision locked Rupprecht's Army Group in a major struggle against the reconstituted French First and Second Armies, now backed by the heavy artillery of several massive bastion fortresses.

Elsewhere on August 24, the $6^{th}/7^{th}$ Army found a distinct stiffening of French resistance. Although the advance continued to make overall progress, signs were beginning to emerge that the French were recovering from their three day, free-fall retreat. [50]

In 1914, Baccarat was a small town that stood world-renowned for its spectacular crystal industry. One German soldier expansively recording his impressions in a letter home: "Baccarat, you delightful town, dear heaven, how your main street looked before that never-to-be forgotten day." On August 25, all that mattered about Baccarat was the control of a substantial stone bridge that gapped the Meurthe River.

The bridge divided Baccarat into east and west sections. On the east bank, a large estate, with an accompanying walled Castle Park was located 600 meters from the bridge. On the west bank, the large church of St. Remy occupied the southern corner of the bridge intersection. The church opened onto a wide village square, with the Hotel d'Ville on the north corner.

XIV Corps' August 25 plan was to first have the 84th Brigade of the 29th Division, including IR 169, cross over the Meurthe, take control of Baccarat and seize the high ground over the southwest bank. The 28th Division, along with 58th Brigade of the 29th Division, was to then move southeast to the Meurthe River towns of Bertrichamps and Thiaville. From there the corps would execute its primary objectives; take the towns of St. Barbe, six miles to the south, and St. Benoit, which lay another four miles south of St. Barbe.

The hasty French retreat left Baccarat, and more importantly, the bridge in the town's center, abandoned. The lack of an organized defense enabled the first German patrols to easily slip into Baccarat on the evening of August 24. One of the initial German units in the town was the 3rd Company of Regiment 113 (from the 29th Division's 57th Brigade), commanded by Lieutenant D.R. Banzhaf. Banzhaf entered Baccarat with orders to arrest the mayor and pastor, who were then to serve as hostages. [This was a common German practice in the early weeks of the war, where the leading officials of many occupied towns were held as hostages to safeguard the incoming German troops against the threat of civil resistance.] On his way into town, Lt. Banzhaf met a Baccarat police official by the name of Barbier, who volunteered to serve as the town's primary hostage representative. After the Germans accepted the offer, Barbier suggested that they move to the southeast part of the town to make additional coordination with other civic leaders. As the group moved out, Lt Banzhaf came across a German cavalry officer who advised that French troops were laying in ambush at their intended destination.[51] There is no record of what fate befell Barbier after the treachery was disclosed, but it was likely to have been harsh.

Later that evening, German vanguard units from the adjacent 1st Bavarian Corps, along with a squadron of the 29th Division's 22nd Dragoons, crossed over the Meurthe Bridge to the western side of Baccarat. The infantry troops from the 1st Bavarian Corps were to serve as the advance pickets, while the cavalry dismounted and rested in a park. IR 169 spent the night in the forest just to the east of the town.

In the early evening hours of August 24, French commanders realized that Baccarat had been left undefended. The 86th Regiment of Infantry (86th RI), which contested XIV Corps in the fields around Sarrebourg, was the nearest French unit. Commanded by the rather elderly Colonel Couturaud, the regiment was ordered to reverse its retreat, drive out the lead German patrols and establish a bridgehead on the eastern bank.

The 86th RI, which lost a third of its strength at Sarrebourg, had retreated across the Baccarat Bridge during the night of August 23, and then moved to the fields northwest of the town. On the afternoon of August 24, German artillery targeted the regiment's command post, killing the much-respected regimental second-in-command, Lt. Col Barral, Dr. Canel, the chief medical officer, and Captain Morel, one of the commander's aides. At 11:00 pm that evening, the regiment was ordered to seize the bridge in an early morning assault.

Inside of Baccarat, the advanced German infantry picket force shifted to a new location. The movement was poorly coordinated and the German cavalry squadron was left unaware it was now the front-most force. The cavalry troopers were caught completely off guard when the French attack landed at 4:30 am. In the ensuing panic, the cavalrymen lost most of their horses as they dashed over the bridge to warn the nearby Regiment 113 of the imminent assault. Albert Rieth's account described the action at Baccarat:

"We took bivouac overnight near Baccarat, where we arrived on August 25. Our scouts were stationed at Baccarat, and were provided cover by a squadron of dragoons. Then came the order for the scouts to retreat while being covered by the dragoons. But the infantry neglected to tell the dragoons of the retreat. So it came that the unwitting dragoons were attacked, and lost all of their horses, which were tied to the trees in a park. Our entire regiment was pulled in, but meanwhile about 200 Frenchmen had hidden themselves in church, and were prepared to ambush us as we marched through. But luckily we noticed this just in time when a French officer serving as an observer was noticed standing in the steeple. Our artillery fired on the steeple, which collapsed immediately. The church door opened. Apparently the French were uncomfortable in this house of God. Machine guns were now positioned approximately 400 meters away. The artillery shot into the church above and below the machine guns fired upon the Frenchmen trying to escape through the door. As we then passed, there were over one hundred dead and wounded before the church."

The details of the battle were considerably more chaotic but no less bloody. The French attack was led by the 86th RI's 3rd Battalion. After routing the small German cavalry detachment, the leading 12th Company extended its attack and raced over the bridge to the east side of Baccarat. 3rd Battalion's 11th and 12th Companies were to follow across the bridge and then fan out throughout the town and establish blocking positions. The 86th's 1st Battalion was ordered to establish a defensive position around the church and city hall square on the west bank of the bridge.

IR 113 troops quickly established a hasty defensive position on Baccarat castle's grounds. Other German units, including IR 169, joined the battle. A wild firefight raged in the streets. German infantry set up in buildings overlooking the bridge, plunging fire into the two French companies that were attempting to push over the river. French soldiers trapped on bridge were slaughtered, with the dead including Captain Shearer, one of their company commanders. A few made it to a parapet outcropping on the far side, where they returned fire at the Germans inside the buildings. The French attack pressed on, with some of the 1st Battalion men making it across the bridge to join their struggling 12th Company comrades pinned down by fire from the castle grounds.

The hundreds of German infantrymen swarming into the battle soon overwhelmed the few French troops still fighting on the east side of the river. While the combat swirled in front of the castle, additional German troops came in from behind the French. These newly arrived Germans set up machine guns with fields of interlocking fire over the entire bridge, blocking the only possible escape route for the beleaguered Frenchmen. Fighting was house-to-house, as the French valiantly tried to maintain their positions. With the hope of reinforcements fading, the French attempted to break off contact and raced back across the Meurthe. It was a disaster. Many of the troops were shot down before they even neared the bridge. About 30 French soldiers (including the wounded 1st Battalion commander and four other officers) managed to surrender. Those who made it onto the bridge were subject to the murderous German crossfire.

The French attempted another doomed assault across the bridge, this time with 1st Battalion leading. Just prior to the attack, guns from the German 50th Field Artillery Regiment opened up on the St. Remy Church, scoring direct hits on the steeple where French officers were observing the fighting. A French section leader from the 2nd Company, Lieutenant Aussedat, described the 1st Battalion charge. Aussedat, who was wounded and captured in this action, wrote this account in a letter to the widow of his company commander, Captain Souques:

"The intensity of the shooting redoubled in our movement toward the bridge. In the midst of the clamor, we could distinguish the maddening noise of the machine guns. At this time, the enemy artillery fires at church steeple next to us; the situation becomes untenable - we must act. From my position behind the bridge's parapet, I noticed Captain Souques calmly standing and giving orders despite the bullets whistling around him. The infernal machine gun fire did not seem to concern him. A bugle sounds "charge" on the colonel's order to attack. Immediately, 1st Company, led by the 1st Battalion and 1st Company commanders, moves forward at a run down the left side of the bridge. On Captain Souques order, 2nd Company follows on the right side of the bridge. I led my section from our sheltered position behind the parapet, and raced forward with the rest of 2nd Company.

This becomes the most terrible spectacle imaginable. From across the river, enemy fire comes at us from homes, street corners, and especially, the storied castle park gardens surrounded by large walls. From behind these walls, German machine guns rake the bridge with enfilading fire. The assaulting column fills the bridge, pushing forward with a great cry of 'In before we die!' Entire ranks of men are mown down by the enemy bullets. Piles of bodies block the path of those men courageously attempting to attack an invisible enemy. These men are also shot down and the attack is briefly halted. Officers and noncommissioned officers, through their example and encouragement, immediately restore the column's forward movement. All this happened in the space of thirty seconds.

The middle of the bridge, I see Captain Souques, with a sword in hand, and shouting 'Forward' with all his might, and leading his men over a clusters of corpses. Following his example, I increase my pace forward and into the hail of bullets. Unfortunately, the circumstances did not allow me to continue, as I fall wounded, dozens of meters away before the bridge exit. It was here that Captain Souques fell.

Captain Souques' leadership inspired the men forward, but their heroic efforts were unable to overcome the barrage of enemy bullets. They, like Captain Souques, are all fallen heroes, humbly and courageously fulfilling the most sacred of duties." [52]

The Germans later counted the bodies of 97 French soldiers killed on the bridge. One German noted that the firing was so intense that many of the dead were found with bullet holes in the soles of their boots. In the midst of the battle, some of the wounded were able to roll over sides of the bridge, only to drown in the river below.

The remaining companies of the 86th RI took up positions on the west bank of Baccarat. Colonel Couturaud had made a fatal error by positioning his machine guns too far in the rear, where they remained silent. The 86th RI was also devoid of any artillery support, which left the infantryman's individuals rifles - Lebel 1893's, which were inferior to the German Mauser - as the regiment's sole source of firepower. German cannon and machine guns fired with double-fold intensity, setting many of the west bank buildings ablaze. With other neighboring bridges across the Meurthe already in German hands, there was little value for the remaining 86th RI men to continue fighting. Cutting through the streets and alleyways, the remaining French troops pulled out of Baccarat and retreated west into the Forest of St Barbe and beyond. The 86th RI lost over 1,000 men in the 11 hour struggle. [Today, a memorial marker by the Baccarat City Hall lists the names of some 350 men from that regiment killed in the fighting.]

Adding to the pathos, a pig, with a French kepi pinned to its head, rooted through the bloody streets.

While XIV Corps' 29th Division was held up in the fighting at Baccarat, the 28th Division made good progress to the southeast, gaining uncontested Meurthe River bridge crossings at Bertrichamps and Thiaville. The Meurthe crossings behind them, XIV Corps next objective was to move five miles southwest to take the villages of St. Barbe and St. Benoit. XIV Corps planned for the 29th Division to take St. Barbe from the northeast, and the 28th Division to secure St. Benoit from the south, and through the ominous Forest of St. Barbe.

The ground before St. Barbe, a small farming village, formed the entranceway to a large swath of open ground to the west. The Germans needed to secure this area quickly in order to gain badly needed maneuver space to sustain the 6th/7th Army Group offensive. Other than a few, easily defended roads, the terrain between Baccarat and the two villages was a portion of the deeply wooded and hilly Forest of St. Barbe. The Germans did not have a clear appreciation of either the number or intentions of the enemy forces immediately before them, as the Forest of St. Barbe effectively cloaked a large number of French troops from German aerial observation.

The Germans were beginning to learn that the 25 mile-long French retreat was over. The French VIII and XIII Corps were the backbone of a strong new line that ran west to east, and squarely in the path of the junction of the German 6th and 7th Armies. The west end of the line began at Damas-aus-Bois, six miles west of the Moselle, and ran east for 12 miles to St. Barbe.

At midday on August 25, the 28th Division moved out of Bertrichamps into the fringes of the Forest of St. Barbe. The Germans had not gotten far into the forest when they collided with the lead elements of the French XIII Corps. The fighting in the woods that raged throughout the day. Eight miles further to the southeast, XV Corps was also facing trouble as it attempted to break through strong French positions in the rugged hills south of Raon-l'Etape. By late afternoon, the forest to the west of St. Barbe still remained in French hands.

After driving the last of the French forces out of Baccarat, the 29th Division's 57th and 84th Brigades moved out for St. Barbe. The direct route from Baccarat to St. Barbe was along a single road running south through a gap in the forest. Setting out on this approach, the lead 57th Brigade came under heavy artillery fire. German guns responded and a sharp artillery duel followed that knocked out a French battery, leaving shattered guns and abandoned caissons at the edge of the forest southwest of Deneuvre. This small accomplishment aside, the German commanders realized that if they intended to get to St. Barbe by nightfall they would need to take a different route. This mission would go to the 84th Brigade, consisting of IRs 169 and 170.

The 84th Brigade's route was to drive into the heart of the forest, and descend on St. Barbe from the east. Regiment 170, commanded by Colonel Tellenbach, led the advance. Departing Baccarat, the Germans crossed over a small open field, into thick brush, and up a steep 1000-foot hill. Once in the forest, IR 170 would have to advance through the woods for a two-mile journey directly south. IR 170 was to clear the woods of French forces, leaving IR 169 to follow in their path and then storm St. Barbe from the forest.

Elite French Alpine troops, specially trained for mountainous combat such as this, were waiting. The *chasseurs-alpins* made effective defensive use of the forest, placing sharpshooters behind rocks, thick tree trunks, and high up in the branches. German soldiers were shot down before they even had any idea of where the enemy was hiding. After a period of initial confusion, the Germans regrouped and fired furiously into the woods. The German troops were eventually able to maneuver through the forest and chase out the remaining French troops at the point of bayonets. IR 170 continued to advance into the dark forest.

Additional French forces, including the 56th Regiment of Infantry, were brought in to conduct a series of vicious counterattacks; the fighting was reminiscent of 19th Century warfare. Infantry still went into battle with their colors at the front. From deep in the forest ahead of them, the Germans first heard the enemy's distant bugle calls and drum rolls. Moments later, French troops, led by officers waving swords, came crashing through the woods and into the German ranks. Fighting was often hand-to-hand. At one point in the struggle, the flag of the 170th Regiment's 2nd Battalion was in danger of being captured. Lieutenant Meyer, commander of the 2nd Battalion's 7th Company, was able to maneuver his unit behind the French to break their attack and save the colors. French troops in this fight also included several hundred men from the battered 86th RI, who retreated into the forest after the slaughter in Baccarat. These men were divided in two groups, one fighting in the forest and the other forming part of the defense in St. Barbe. 86th RI's Commander, Colonel Couturaud, led the forest-based detachment before being wounded and captured. [The 86th RI took heavy losses in the late August fighting, from the time of Sarrebourg battles through the end of the month, the regiment lost 2,400 men and 53 officers.]

By late afternoon, the tide of the battle shifted towards the attackers. In the final phase of the fighting, elements of the 170th Regiment's 3rd Battalion rushed a battery posted at the southwestern edge of the forest, seizing three cannons. The Germans also captured 60 French prisoners, including the badly wounded commander of the 56th Regiment. Although it was a costly effort, IR 170 secured the high ground to the west of St. Barbe. A section of artillery from the 3rd Battalion, 76th Regiment was brought forward and set up on the site near where the French battery was overrun. The path for the attack by IR 169 was now open. Rieth described his journey over IR 170's battlefield:

"We now marched through Baccarat and had a short respite on a knoll. Soon the order came that the village before us was occupied by the enemy and had to be taken. It was almost dark when we reached the hill, from where we could see St. Barbe, located on the western side of a great plain. Our artillery had also positioned itself on the hill and so had access to the entire area. We now took a little rest as we had done a long march. In great intervals we spread out and slowly approached St. Barbe where it was very quiet, only far away the cannons thundered. One could see that a battle had raged here, as dead and wounded Frenchmen were lying everywhere, with some having been transported away."

It was now dusk. Poised on the high ground to the east of the town, IR 169 cautiously began its approach towards St. Barbe. 3rd Battalion, along with the battery from the 76th Artillery Regiment, was posted on a large hill overlooking the plain and village. From there, they could provide covering fire to support the 2nd Battalion, the regiment's primary maneuver element. It started as a well-coordinated movement, with the companies arrayed to provide covering fires to the lead-most elements. The 2nd Battalion advance was led by the 8th Company, followed in line by the 6th and 5th companies. With the 2nd Battalion's 7th Company in regimental reserve, a machine gun section from

Regiment 142 was attached and followed at the end of the column. The 2nd Battalion had swung well to the south, and approached the village from a southeastern direction. Traversing through a wood-line, the battalion crossed over the Belville Brook and made a final approach towards the town. 3rd Battalion, left a half-mile behind, moved forward as all units simultaneously descended on St. Barbe.

French troops were well hidden in buildings at the western end of the town, waiting for the Germans to wander deep into their trap. This tactic afforded the defenders the maximum shock effect in their first volleys as well as providing cover from the German artillery. Other French units were posted to the southwest of the town and were taking cover on the southbank of the Belville Brook. They also lay quiet as the lead elements of 2nd Battalion came into their fields of fire, awaiting just the right moment surprise the incoming Germans.

The French held their fire until the Germans were almost in the town. Rieth described the moment of contact:

"We got very close to the village without hearing a shot. Suddenly, we were received by a murderous fire, indicating a strong enemy presence in the place. We retreated and collected our resources, after which we stormed and took the village."

The 3rd Battalion fell back and returned heavy fire. French troops deployed along the south of Belville Brook came alive and fired into the 2nd Battalion, who were on the verge of entering the town. The three companies of the 2nd Battalion, supported by the IR 142 machine gunners, wheeled to the south and engaged the French defenders in a firefight across the brook. The 76th Artillery Regiment's guns fired away at French both along the brook and in the village. After regrouping, the 3rd Battalion again stormed into St. Barbe. Fighting house-to-house, the Germans were able to kill, capture, or chase out the last of the French troops. The gateway to the plains to Rambervillers was finally in German hands.

Albert Rieth's next entry speaks to the conclusion of the evening:

"It was determined that the villagers had shot upon us, and therefore all houses were burned. When the village was totally in flames it was a sad picture, as all the inhabitants had to leave. Mostly they were old men and women who had to leave their homes in the middle of the night. It hurt to see them go with only the necessities; everything else was burned in the flames. Since the wind came in the direction of the village, the bivouac was comfortably warm, which we appreciated."

IR 169's actions at St. Barbe reflected the harsh consequences of combat in populated areas. It is well documented that the German Army levied a heavy hand on the civilian populaces of France and Belgium in the early months of the 1914. The worst of the atrocities often occurred when German troops believed they were being fired on by French civilians, or *francs-tireurs*. As presented by Max Hastings in *Catastrophe 1914*, the German obsession with civilian guerrillas was conditioned by experiences dating back to the Franco-Prussian war. An account from a German soldier on August 19, 1914 reveals: "..to be shot at in the villages again and again. Several poor fellows have already lost their lives. Disgraceful! An honest bullet in honest battle – yes, then one has shed one's blood for the Fatherland. But to be shot from ambush, from the window of a house,,,no, that is not a nice soldierly death." [53]

German soldiers naturally resented exaggerated accusations of atrocities. Long after the war, Stefan Westmann, a veteran from IR 113 of the 29th Division recalled the early days of the war: "…Entering a small French village, the mayor came and asked our company commanders not to allow us to cut off the hands of the children. These were atrocity stories that they heard about the German Army. We laughed about it at first, but when we heard of other propaganda lies against our Army we became angry. …One of these rumors was that the Germans extracted the fat from fallen British and French soldiers to use for soap." [54] The facts remain however that a number of German deprivations, especially in the first months of the war, did occur. The Allies effectively used resulting propaganda to shape world opinion against the Germans.

As the fires raged in St. Barbe the night of August 25/26, Crown Prince Rupprecht's staff took stock of the situation. After enjoying a victorious five-day advance, the German fortunes were rapidly changing. The 7th Army and the southern portions of 6th Army had run into fierce French resistance everywhere on the southwest side of the Meurthe River. The French troops, already highly determined to defend their homeland, were suddenly much better organized. In areas where the Germans were making progress, it came as the result of hard fighting and steep casualties. The worst news came from the far right, where the northern corps of 6th Army were being pushed back by vigorous French counterattacks from Nancy. Rupprecht knew he needed to redouble his efforts to break the French lines and regain the initiative. The 6th/7th Army Group spent the next several days desperately probing the French lines in an attempt to find some vulnerable point for exploitation.

On August 26, XIV Corps and their I Bavarian Army Corps partners to their north, set their sights on seizing the town of Rambervillers. A town of 6,000 residents, Rambervillers lay six miles to the southwest of St. Barbe and served as an important road network hub. Possession of this large town was essential in moving forward to breach the Moselle River. To reach Rambervillers, the 29th Division would first have to fight through a concentrated French force in the village of Menil (just over a mile southeast of St. Barbe), as well as by taking a forested ridgeline that dominated the ground to the north and northeast of Rambervillers.

Rambervillers had a storied military legacy left over from the Franco-Prussian war. On October 9, 1870, 200 French National Guardsmen manning the fortifications around Rambervillers weathered a day long assault by 2000 Prussians. This feat of heroism won the town the Légion d'honneur medal, and had a street in Paris named after it. Efforts to take Rambervillers in 1914 presented the Germans an even greater challenge.

Updated intelligence reporting provided senior German commanders with bad news. They now understood that the entire French 13th Corps – at least 20,000 men strong - was located in and around Rambervillers. This contingent, consisting largely of fresh troops, actually outnumbered the German attackers. It was no longer a question of simply attacking; the Germans also now had to contend with the real threat of a major French counterattack.

Although the village of St. Barbe was in German hands, the forest to the south was still under French control. The 29th Division's 58th Brigade was ordered to clear this portion of the Forest of St. Barbe, the same area where they were defeated the day before. Again, the unsupported brigade battled in the forest, and again, was forced to retreat with heavy casualties. The 58th Brigade's losses in killed, wounded, and missing were so severe that its two regiments were no longer capable of further offensive action. On August 27th, the battered brigade was pulled out of line and sent back across to the north side of the Meurthe to be placed in distant reserve.

The uneven progress of the German advance past the Meurthe River had left a large gap between IR 169 and other friendly units to the east. On the morning of August 26, the regiment moved south, through the shattered Forest of St. Barbe, towards the neighboring village of St. Benoit. Rieth described this movement and the run-down condition of the now exhausted, filthy, wet and hungry men of the badly under-strength 3rd Battalion:

"The next morning we had a rather long march ahead of us, as we had to relieve our left flank, which was very vulnerable and manned only by our artillery. The march was exhausting as we went through swampy areas and through woods without passages. At 5 o'clock in the morning we had started and arrived at 6 o'clock in the evening, so we had come a pretty good distance. We immediately began to dig in, as we had to expect an attack by the enemy, who estimated us to be very weak here; and they were right. We were a rather dilapidated battalion. A field kitchen was still something that we had not seen for at least 15 days. There was no shortage of rain from early morning until the next noon. It poured so continuously that we had not a dry thread upon us. We were hungry and exhausted.

The road leading through the wood had to be blocked, for which the felling of 150 trees was necessary, all with dull saw blades. The trees came crashing down and we were sleeping standing up. Although we wanted to lie down, the fear of being attacked if this task was not completed kept us awake. The butcher slaughtered a calf, from which we cut pieces and roasted them over a single fire, which was hidden by four bed sheets so not to alert the enemy. The meat was unpalatable, sooty and burnt, but one had to have something in the stomach."

On August 27, the 6th/7th Army Group realized that their recent probes failed to identify any obvious vulnerability in the French lines.

The need to control the Rambervillers road network remained urgent, and IR 169 continued to be committed to this objective. Before the 29th Division could attack Rambervillers, they still needed to punch through the French line centered at the village of Menil. From August 27 – August 29, IR 170 battled the French for possession of the heights around Menil. IR 169 supported this effort from the right flank of the attacks. The house-to-house fight for Menil was particularly ferocious, with French wounded fighting from buildings used as field hospitals. The fighting surged back and forth, with each side at various points in the battle either attacking or defending. German officers killed at Menil included IR 170's commander, Colonel Tellenbach, and Captain Schmidt, the commander of the 9th Company. Just before the battle, Colonel Tellenbach was seriously injured in a fall from his horse and could barely move. He still insisted on being brought forward into the fight and subsequently was killed by a shrapnel burst.

Rieth described the events of August 27:

"By morning the trench was also completed, but only knee-deep, as the ground was so rocky that it was hard to dig. No sooner had we manned the trenches, the French artillery commenced firing. The first shells exploded very near, and later they hit the trenches, which we had to vacate in order not to sustain too many casualties. We had not seen any infantry, nor were we attacked. It developed into an artillery fight, and the shells went over our heads. Luckily everything ended and we lost not a man, at least in our company. It was clear that if that gang continued to shoot like that, we would not see our field kitchen again that day, and so it happened.

At 4 o'clock in the afternoon the order came to attack. We prepared ourselves and marched through the forest in front of us and came to a country lane. Here we stopped and our captain led the spearhead and I as trumpeter was with him. To the right of the street the forest climbed up a hill steeply. To the left of the street were also some woods, and then a meadow....." .

[This entry marks the final posting in Albert's journal, which he wrote in March 1915 from a military hospital in Schweinfurt. For years, the reason behind this abrupt ending remained a mystery. In researching this book, a listing was found in the official German World War One Casualty Rolls that recorded Hornist Albert Rieth as being wounded this day. Albert later returned to the ranks some months later and was again wounded in January 1915.]

The end of Rieth's memoirs also marks the far limit of the German offensive across the Meurthe. The Germans were never able to push beyond the little village of Menil, let alone seriously threaten the primary objective of Rambervillers. The most important priority for Rupprecht's 6th/7th Army Group's main effort was to take the city of Nancy, 30 miles north of IR 169's most advanced position. On the evening of August 29, XIV Corps pulled seven miles back across the Meurthe, and established their headquarters at Baccarat.

Rieth's description of 3rd Battalion being *a rather dilapidated battalion* on August 26, 1914 was an understatement. In the days between August 24 – August 29, IR 169 fought in four separate battles at Vacqueville, Baccarat, St. Barbe and Menil. Casualties recorded from this six-day period include 8 officers (4 being killed) and 810 enlisted men. Factoring in losses from the earlier fighting at Mulhouse and around Sarrebourg, IR 169 lost a total of 2211 men in the first month of the war. This represents a 63% attrition rate in the 20 days since the regiment first went into combat. It is likely that IR 169's effective strength at this point was well below 1200 men, less than a third of its authorized manpower. According to the "History of German Infantry Divisions" , a typical infantry line company in IR 169 was down to only 30 men present for duty by the end of the Meurthe Campaign.[55] The overall losses to the French and German armies in the first month of the war are staggering, with each side suffering over 300,000 killed, wounded or captured.[56]

While the German Army's 1914 mobilization infrastructure was impressive, a deeper examination of German logistics and command and control systems show critical shortcomings. The Germans were indeed able to quickly deploy a large force into combat but lacked the logistical infrastructure to sustain their early gains. Railheads grew too distant from forward deployed troops, motorized transportation was inadequate and the pre-war calculations for artillery ammunition was far too low. These problems, based in systematic failures long before the war began, became evident by the end of August.[57]

In late August, IR 169 was pulled out of line and sent to the Baccarat area for some much needed rest and replenishment.

Replacement troops, which included two officers and 556 enlisted men, reported to help fill the badly depleted ranks.

Rupprecht had one last hope for the 6th/7th Army Group's role in the definitive destruction of the French Army – the capture of Nancy and the mountainous region to the north, the Grand Couronne. The capital of the Lorraine, Nancy lay at a strategic point in the conflux of the Meurthe and Moselle rivers, and served as an entranceway to the fortified city of Toul. The battle-worn 6th Army was reinforced with troops from the German garrison of Metz. With these additional forces, the 6th Army had 350,000 men and 400 heavy artillery pieces in position for the September 1 attack.

The assault on the Grand Couronne began with barrages from a huge concentration of large caliber artillery. The French were well entrenched and prepared for the German attack. In just one location, the fields of St. Genevieve, 4,000 German dead lay before French defenses. The 11 day fight for Nancy cost the Germans approximately 100,000 casualties. By the end of the first week of September, it became clear to the Germans that future efforts to defeat the French 1st and 2nd Armies on the southwest side of the Meurthe were futile.

The German disaster at Nancy coincided with their more significant defeat at the Battle of the Marne. From September 5-9, this enormous struggle involved hundreds of thousands of combatants battling over a front that extended 250 miles. Four mighty German armies had advanced well into France, with some reaching within 30 miles of Paris and on the verge of encircling greater French armies posted along the banks of the Marne River. French commander Joffre took advantage of exposed German right flank and staged a violent counterattack. For the next four days, a great battle raged that consumed all the armies across the marshy Marne front. Ultimately, the growing gaps between its army groups would be the undoing of the German plans. By September 9, the German Supreme Command concluded further efforts along the Marne were futile. The German army retreated back along the Aisne River, a region where IR 169 would fight in 1917 and 1918.

The overall defeat of the German offensive in the Battle of the Marne had resulted in a general retreat of all German forces across the entire Western Front. On September 11-12, the Germans retreated back across the Meurthe, and gave up all the territory gained since

August 24. For the troops of XIV Corps, this meant retiring back to the area of the August 24 battle at Vacqueville, and taking up a line along the trace of the Verdurette River. Both sides started digging in, contributing to the continuous labyrinthine trench system that would eventually run from the Swiss border to the south all the way to the English Channel. For the most part, these positions would remain static for the next four years.

On September 10, IR 169 was completely pulled out of the front lines and sent 30 miles back to Dieuze, a town between Sarrebourg and Metz that served as 6th Army Headquarters. Here, IR 169 prepared for their role in the coming campaign that created the infamous St. Mihiel Salient.

In the wake of his disastrous attacks against Nancy's Grand Couronne ridgeline, Crown Prince Rupprecht's next move was an attempt against the fortified city of Verdun. To avoid a direct attack against the massive underground defenses in front of the city, the Germans launched a late September offensive intended to outflank Verdun from the south. A central component of this plan was to secure and then exploit a river crossing over the Meuse at a village called St. Mihiel. While the effort to surround Verdun failed, this small campaign did result in a 25 mile wide and 20 mile long bulge into the French lines, known as the St. Mihiel Salient. For throughout the remainder of the war, this small tract of ground played a significant role in shaping some of the most significant battles in the Western Front.

IR 169's refit in the village of Dieuze lasted less than one week. XIV Corps was transferred from 7th to 6th Army control, and by mid-September, was temporarily assigned to a large 6th Army task force known as "Army Detachment Strantz." Detachment Strantz consisted of the III Bavarian Corps, V Corps and XIV Corps.

Detachment Strantz's ambitious objective was to establish a bridgehead across the Meurthe at the village of St. Mihiel, followed by an attempt to cut off Verdun from the south. The detachment began to assemble its forces around the garrison city of Metz on September 15. IR 169 completed its 48 mile movement from Dieuze to the village of Pagny on September 18. Pagny, on the west bank of the Moselle River, several miles south of Metz, became XIV Corps' staging ground. Army Detachment Strantz occupied a 20 mile long front, with XIV Corps on the southern flank, III Corps in the center and V Corps on the right.

On the night of September 19, XIV Corps, supported by the 76th Field Artillery Regiment, moved six miles southwest to their jump-off position on the high ground above Regnieville. 29th Division's objective for September 20 was to break the French line located between the villages of Flirey and Limey, four miles south. The Germans were fortunate that morning to have a thick fog mask its movement out of the Regnieville Woods. IR 169's 1st Battalion led the way. As the mist began burning off at 10:30 am, 1st Battalion began drawing artillery fire from French artillery located one mile behind its infantry positions. The rolling terrain helped allow the Germans to minimize casualties, as the French skirmishers at Remenauville, midway to Limey, withdrew before the German advance. The 3rd Battalion, along with the IR 169's machine gun company, moved adjacent to 1st Battalion, and took up an overwatch position on the higher ground above Remenauville. Further to the left, IR 111, of the 28th Division also came on line as the Germans came within one mile of the French line at Limey.

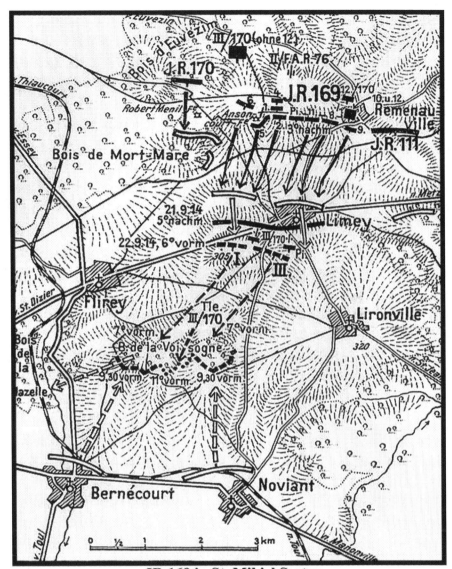

IR 169 in St. Mihiel Sector
From 19-20 September 1914, IR 169 led the 29th Division attack as part of the offensive that created the St. Mihiel Salient. A French counterattack blunted the German advance above Bernecourt and Noviant, marking the end of the regiment's maneuver phase of the war.
(BIWW)

IR 169's 1st Battalion continued to advance forward through the open field, with the Forest of Mort Mare to its right. The first determined French resistance came from infantry units posted at the eastern edge of the wood-line. While the 1st Battalion charged forward, the French were reinforced with additional forces from nearby Flirey. Eventually, the Germans were pushed back to the heights beyond Limey. Additional French troops arrived on the battlefield, and by 4:00 pm, French infantry, supported by an artillery fire, attacked the exposed 1st Battalion from two directions. Lacking effective cover, the Germans were forced back. The 1st Battalion was able to retreat in good order, thanks to the covering fire from 3rd Battalion and the MG Company, still posted at the Remenauville Heights. That night, Regiment 169 continued to hold its position as its men were ordered to dig in. Exhausted by the day's exertions and frustrated with the hardness of the soil, many of the Germans gave only a halfhearted effort to entrench themselves.

The early morning hours of September 21 again brought in heavy fog over the battlefield. As the fog lifted in mid-morning, the artillery batteries of the 2nd Battalion, 76th Artillery went into action. French artillery returned fire, and an all-out artillery contest was under way. Much of the French fire struck the 1st Battalion, which was now in reserve in the village of Remenauville. IR 169's commander, Colonel Spennemann was severely wounded and taken off the battlefield. The Major Teschner, the 2nd Battalion commander who had just returned to the field after recovering from wounds, replaced Spennemann.

The artillery battle continued until 2:30 pm., when IR 169 was again ordered to attack Limey and the heights to the west. After being heavily shelled in place for the better part of several hours, the German infantrymen were eager to move forward. The assault force was a combined group of IR 169 and IR 170 battalions. IR 169's 9th Company, along with the machine gun company, moved to a hill to the east where they could provide covering fire for the attack.

By 3:45 pm., the Germans closed into Limey where a street battle arose. The increasing pressure forced the French to slowly pull back. The assault force stormed forward, and by 5:00 pm, the village, along with a large number of French prisoners, was in German hands.

Once again, the failure of the 58th Brigade to keep up on the German right created another gap and exposed the right flank. The French quickly regrouped and launched a series of aggressive counterattacks against the assault force. Although the Germans were able to hold their ground and inflicted heavy losses against the attackers, they made no further progress for the remainder of the day. That evening, French forces retreated east, into the Forest de la Voisogne behind Flirey.

IR 169 spent an uncomfortable night in fields around Limey. Early the next morning, the regiment was ordered take Hill 305, just to the southwest of Limey. The regiment moved out by 6:00 am, and soon passed a recently abandoned French bivouac area. (Some of the Germans wrote of becoming aghast by the filthy conditions of the French campsite.) The Germans continued their advance, driving a few French patrols back before them as they entered the dark and thorny Forest de la Voisogne. The woods were so thick that the troops had to crash their way through the underbrush in single files. After much effort, Regiment 169 emerged from the southern edge of the forest and into a brilliant sunlight.

The Baden unit history described this moment in vivid terms, as it characterized a deeply symbolic and defining moment in the course of World War I - the end of maneuver warfare on the Western Front. Coming out of the forest, the Germans were presented with a huge panoramic view of open fields that led towards the city of Toul, 16 miles to the south. The sight was as dispiriting as it was dramatic, as French troops filled the horizon as far as the eye could see. In the distance, long blue and red clad French columns were snaking towards them on a number of roads. Midway, a number of battalions were pulling off the roads and into battle formations. Less than two miles away, before the twin villages of Berncourt and Noviant, were yet more French troops; furiously digging in the start of a new trench line.

The German commanders faced a conundrum. Orders were such that a retreat was not an option. Certainly, initiating an attack against this enormous host of oncoming French troops was a reckless move. Worse still, holding in place would give the French infantry digging in at Berncourt and Noviant a significant defensive advantage and allow more time for their reinforcements to come up. French artillery would soon have the Germans targeted in ground that left them completely exposed. The German junior officers and soldiers had enough combat experience at this point to realize the punishment that they were in for. Shovels and picks were pulled out and the digging began. At noon, a few French shells whistled over the forest. The next rounds grazed the tips of trees. The French were finding their range. In minutes, IR 169 was engulfed in a fearful barrage. The men in the front worked on their entrenchments with a renewed vigor, feverishly digging in a task that began with such initial reluctance. The barrage was even worse for several of the rifle companies that were being held in reserve in the woods as the forest was torn apart with bursting shells and flying splinters. The shelling continued until nightfall.[58]

By September 25, Army Detachment Strantz had pushed as far as it could and the German offensive had reached its limit. Trenches were dug deeper and IR 169 remained in line there through October 3, 1914. For the next four years, this area would mark the southern border of the St. Mihiel Salient. IR 169's casualties for this series of actions were 16 officers (with 8 killed) and 482 enlisted men.

The course of the war would take a particularly hard toll on a number of towns and villages fought over in this area; Fay, Regnieville, and Remenauville were completely blasted off the face of the earth. Even today these places are permanently listed on modern maps as *detruit* (destroyed). The ground taken by Army Detachment Strantz from September 20-22, 1914 came to play a large role as the war progressed. The bulge of the St. Mihiel gave the Germans their only permanent bridgehead across the Meuse River, the most important water obstacle on the Western Front. The French requirement to contain the salient would cause them endless trouble throughout the war.[59] The Battle of Verdun, one of World War I's most costly struggles, came partly as a result of the German Army's 1916 effort to expand it. The St. Mihiel Salient again came into to prominence at the very end of the war when the American Army reduced the position in September 1918.

Chapter 5

The Race for the Sea: The First Battle of Ypres

"Cuinchy bred rats. They came up from the canal, fed on the plentiful corpses, and multiplied exceedingly...." Robert Graves; *Goodbye to All That*[60]

By the middle of September, the entire southern and center portions of the Western Front had become deadlocked. All eyes now focused on control of a 60-mile wide narrow corridor in Belgian and French Flanders, nearly 250 miles north of Metz, as the sole hope for a breakthrough. In what history has dubbed 'The Race for the Sea,' this phase was a sequential quest for each side to turn the other's northernmost flanks before reaching the English Channel. The stagnation in the central front allowed both sides to free up extra forces to send northward to attempt to win control over this critical gap. IR 169, as part of 6th Army, joined in this race.

The German plan was to achieve a new drive through northern France. Possession of the Flanders region would provide the Germans an opportunity to outflank the French entrenched zone that stretched south from the Aisne River to Switzerland. The bulk of the German forces sent for the initial effort in early October were elements of Rupprecht's 6th Army Group, which now included XIV Corps. To the far north, the Germans dispatched a force of eight cavalry divisions (over 50,000 dragoons) to race towards coast. There, they established a tenuous hold on a large section of ground centered on the Belgium Flanders town of Ypres, an ancient walled city that would give the name to three of the most deadly campaigns of the Great War. This city became the epicenter of the 35-mile battlefield that stretched from Nieuport on the English Channel south to the canal of La Bassee. Keegan described the dreary landscape of Flanders as "a sodden plain of wide, unfenced fields, pasture and plough intermixed, overlying a water table that floods on excavation more than a few shovelfuls deep." Villages and farms were connected by scattered woodlands.[61]

Fighting in early October closed up 10 more miles of the southern and northern extremes of the gap. By October 8, German, French and British forces were concentrating in the Ypres front in great numbers. All armies were frantically seeking a gap to enable a breakthrough in the quickly shrinking, available ground. In reality, none of this ground was truly uncontested anymore; it was rather a degree of what terrain was more lightly controlled by either combatant. The British Expeditionary Force (BEF) made up the bulk of the allied forces. Consisting of five corps', the 160,000 BEF troops sent to France in August 1914 were virtually the entire pre-war strength of the British Army. Also included were the remnants of the Belgian Army, now only 60,000 strong, and the French 10th and 2nd Armies. Both German and Allied forces were on the offensive; it would be a thundering clash of two great armies.

During the first week of October 1914, IR 169 pulled out of the front lines in the St. Mihiel Salient, crossed back over the Moselle and returned to the Metz garrison. There was no time for recovery, despite their heavy losses from the fighting around Limey. Along with other 29th Division regiments, IR 169 departed Metz by rail on October 3, 1914 for the long, circuitous, 150-mile journey north to Flanders, where it disembarked at the station in Valenciennes. On October 5, the regiment hiked 20 miles west to the village of Douai. Days earlier, there had been heavy fighting at Douai when the Germans pushed the French 10th Army forces back towards the city of Lens, just to the west. At Douai, IR 169 made final preparations to go into combat, now only a few miles distant.

From 7 – 10 October, IR 169 engaged the French around Lens in a subset of the First Battle of Arras. Both sides had already started digging a rudimentary trench system by the time IR 169 reached the front. The costs of IR 169's troubles in Lens were 7 officers (1 killed) and 132 enlisted casualties.

On October 12, the Germans scored a significant victory by seizing the city of Lillie, 17 miles northeast of IR 169's position at Lens. The Allies responded by launching two British divisions to retake the city, which was one of the largest industrial centers of northern France. These events set into motion the Battle of La Bassee and the resulting campaign that consumed IR 169 from October 12, 1914 through March 1915.

IRs 169 and 113 pulled out of Lens on October 12 and marched 7 miles north to the La Bassee sector. The town of La Bassee, with a 1914 population of 6,000 residents, sat on the north bank of an extensive canal network that ran from the sea through northern France. The heaviest fighting would occur in a small area between La Bassee and three neighboring villages. Directly south of La Bassee, on the southern bank, was the town of Auchy. Two miles east was the village of Guinchy [often spelled in English accounts as *Cuinchy*] with its sister village of Givenchy located just to the north on the other side of the canal. The canal, with a large railroad embankment running along the southern bank, divided the entire sector. In the course of the campaign, the canal frequently split the efforts of attacking forces, favoring whichever side was defending.

The worst of the fighting would occur in a two-mile long-by-two mile wide area between Guinchy and Givenchy. One area that took on unique importance was a large brick foundry to the east of Guinchy. These brickyard grounds were covered with old kilns, smoke chimneys and 16 enormous piles of bricks. Rudyard Kipling, in his history of *The Irish Guards of the Great War* described this feature as "a collection of huge dull plum-coloured brick-stacks, mottled with black, which might have been originally thirty feet high." [62] The brickyard, which provided an untypically strong natural defensive cover for its defenders, came to be the most notorious feature of the coming battle. Between the brickyard and Auchy was a 'railroad triangle' that also offered defenders additional natural cover. In the five months to come, IR 169 took part in a mighty struggle that killed and maimed thousands; all in futile efforts to possess three shattered villages, a brickyard full of rubble and an inconsequential railroad junction. La Bassee marked the extreme southern border of the First Battle of Ypres.

In early October, the La Bassee area was occupied by German dragoon squadrons, which were soon pressed by French cavalry and infantry formations. To reclaim Lillie, the British II Corps was deployed to relieve French forces, sweep aside the presumably weak German cavalry and go forth to liberate Belgium. Starting October 11, the British came to learn XIV Corps had begun to reinforce the La Bassee villages with infantry and artillery units that included *Jaeger* (light infantry) battalions and IR 113. On October 12 the vanguard of the British troops entered Guinchy and Givenchy, but soon withdrew under heavy fire from well-placed German sharpshooters supported with artillery.

British regiments, largely comprised of men from Dorset and Bedford, moved in to replace the French. At the same time, IR 169 moved forward to relieve IR 113, which had been battered in the previous day's fighting. The following passage from *Baden in World*

War describes the activities of a small patrol from Regiment 169 that was settling into the front lines. This account informs us on the experience of moving into "no-man's-land" at the advent of trench warfare on the Western Front:[63]

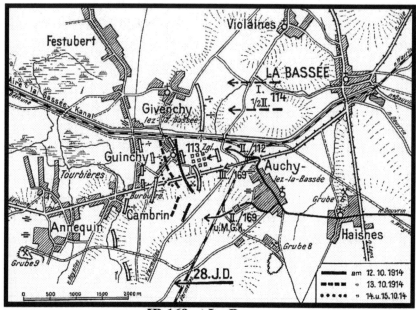

IR 169 at La Bassee

This map marks IR 169's 12-13 October 1914 entry in the southern Ypres front at La Bassee, where, through March 1915, IR 169 experienced some of its hardest fighting in the war. Much of combat occurred in the small area bounded by La Bassee and Auchy to the east, and Givenchy and Guinchy to the west. The notorious brickyards were just to the east of Guinchy.

(BIWW)

"On October 12, the 169th Regiment was ordered into action at Auchy. A patrol was ordered to establish contact with the front line and determine how things were going there. The mission fell upon the commander of the 4th Company, Lt D.R. Mayer. Accompanied by six troops of his choice, he left Auchy, following the railroad embankment. A soldier commanding a 113th Regiment position west of the harbor of Auchy told of heavy losses that his regiment had suffered on the previous day from fire from the opposite canal bank. As he spoke, he pointed to the earthworks around a small house on the north side of the canal. He said that was

~ 88 ~

where the British were supposed to be.

When the patrol looked down at the house from the high railroad embankment, they were able to confirm this remark. Broad flat English caps were visible above the earthworks. Lt. Mayer ordered, "Boys, before we head back, let's have a go at them. Take a good look at where they are so you can find them afterwards."

On the northern edge of Ziegelei, halfway between Auchy and Givenchy, the patrol again reached a small quay. Suddenly they heard a voice. In the railroad embankment a narrow passage about the height of a man was visible. Lt. Mayer crawled forward carefully, pistol in hand, and checked out the passage. But nothing there was to be seen. Again the voice was heard, and it seemed to be German. A few paces ahead the embankment was again traversed by the trench linking the harbor and the canal. Again the leader carefully slithered forward, checking out the shortcut. But there was nothing to be seen here, either on this side of the canal, and on the other side lay the small house and the English trenches, quiet as the dead.

The patrol made its way around the quay. There, just opposite the railroad cut, was the voice, this time very clear. It was a wounded member of the 113th Regiment. The patrol comforted their wounded comrade and promised to get him out of there as quickly as possible. In an instant more urgent demands would call, but a message about what had occurred, and the wounded soldier, was sent back immediately.

Again the patrol clambered up the high railroad embankment. They arrived just in time, because hardly had they gotten a glimpse of the area on the far side of the canal when the machine guns in the British trenches began to fire, directing their deadly rounds against other German troops that were attacking from the east. The patrol was ready to fire in an instant. At that point, a British soldier jumped from the trench to the house and sped westward - apparently he was a courier. A shot rang out, and the Englishmen in the khaki uniform collapsed without a sound. Soon other British troops, not realizing the danger on their flank, attempted to do the same thing, but again well aimed shots from German rifles laid their victims to the ground. Still more British troops followed them, but also suffered the same fate.

The patrol had its hands full. Even Lt. Mayer, armed only with a pistol, didn't want to just look on. A rifle lying down the railroad embankment was soon discovered. The increase in firepower may have been small, but it was certainly timely because the British had gradually recognized their danger and had begun firing from a hill on the far side of the canal. British artillery rounds impacted along the embankment, but fortunately, more in the direction of Auchy.

The gallant patrol stayed at its task untiringly and with its combined strength, it overcame all difficulties. Finally they were in position to take up the attack on the enemy's main trenches further to the east. It was from these trenches that the British machine guns spat death and destruction among the attacking German troops. The patrol had only this wish; help for the attacking German troops across the canal and vengeance for their wounded comrade down the embankment.

Soon the patrol, in heat of battle, crawled halfway up the embankment and started to pick off more British troops. Finally, a determined British soldier crawled forward and took aim at Lt. Mayer. He detected the danger just in time, and raised his rifle. Now it was man-to-man. The phrase, "just take it slow and easy; otherwise you'll miss," ran through Lt. Mayer's head. Slowly and just as assuredly as on the firing range, his trigger finger tightened, while the muzzle sought its target. Now front and rear sights were aligned on the target; the trigger finger tightened more, and a shot resounded. Stiffly and silently, the Tommy sank onto a pile of wood.

At length, the enemy guns fell silent, and north of the canal one could see the line of German infantry advancing toward Givenchy. The patrol had accomplished its mission."

The battle for La Bassee began in earnest on the morning of October 13. The German 84th Brigade, with forces from IR's 169, 112 and 114, stood ready to meet the British attack. At the beginning of the day, IR 114 was posted to the north and prepared to hold British forces advancing through Givenchy. The Germans to the south were positioned to defend against any attacks coming out of Guinchy. The 2nd Battalion of IR 112 occupied the brickyard and abutted against the railroad embankment and canal. Once again, German riflemen were posted in the piles of bricks behind Guinchy which provided clear fields of fire to the front, as well as to the opposite bank of the canal against any British troops able to occupy Givenchy. 3rd Battalion of IR 169 was next in line, covering the main road between Guinchy and La Bassee. IR 169's 2nd Battalion, along with the regimental machine gun company, was to their immediate left. Troops from the 28th Jaeger Division held the far left flank. Throughout the line, the Germans were supported by an artillery battery of 4-inch field howitzers posted at Auchy.

David Lomas, in *First Ypres, 1914* described the combat that typified IR 169's fighting from October 13-15. On the south side of the canal, the lead battalions of the British 1st Dorset Infantry Regiment emerged from the early morning mist. The Dorsets, accompanied by two 18-pdr field guns and a machine gun, advanced 2000 yards under heavy fire. They reached Guinchy and inflicted more than 80 German casualties. On the north side of the canal, a battalion of the 1st Bedford Infantry had established tenuous hold in Givenchy, but was being pounded by a fierce artillery and small-arms barrage. One platoon was wiped out by two howitzer shells in quick succession, and by noon, the battalion was virtually without officers. After fighting off two attacks, the Bedfords were overwhelmed by a third assault. Badly outnumbered, the British were forced out of the village, abandoning two guns of the 11th Battery, Royal Field Artillery. The Bedford's retreat isolated the Dorsets, who were still holding firm on the southbank of the canal at the edge of Guinchy. At mid-afternoon, the Dorsets, having lost their only machine gun, were in a desperate situation.

The next wave of German counterattacks was preceded by heavy artillery barrage and supported by fires from the IR 169's machine gun company. German troops from IR's 112, 169 and the Jaegers, attacked from all sides. The British fought furiously, with the 18-pdr fields guns described as firing "as fast as machine guns" until both gun crews were cut down. The Dorsets could hold on no longer and were also forced to retreat, leaving most of their wounded to be taken prisoner. In the day's fighting, the 1st Bedfords lost 117 men at

Givenchy and the 1st Dorsets lost 399." [64]

The British conducted another major attack on October 16. At a cost of over 1,000 casualties, they were able to finally take what was left of Givenchy, but failed to reach La Bassee. This attack marked the closest the Allies would ever get to La Bassee in the next four years of the war. From this point forward Germans lines stabilized at La Bassee and Auchy, with the brickyards between Auchy and Guinchy often serving as a no-man's-land. In this sector, the German and British lines would remain less than a mile apart.

Just to the north of La Bassee, the British suffered a major disaster on October 19, when an attack by the 2nd Battalion of the Royal Irish Regiment, seemingly at the verge of a breakthrough, captured the town of Le Pilly. This progress was short lived, as the Irish battalion first became isolated and then surrounded. Of the 900 Irishmen who went into the fight, only 300 survived to surrender to the Germans.

It was then the German's turn to attack. On October 20-21, the Germans launched a major offensive along their entire line from Arras to the sea. No gains, other than adding to the casualty rosters, were made before La Bassee. To the front of XIV Corps, the British regulars were reinforced and eventually replaced by the Lahore Division of the Indian Corps. These colonial troops had only recently arrived on the Continent. Although poorly acclimated and equipped to face the wet and increasingly cold weather, these troops fought courageously and the weight of their numbers had a telling effect. On October 24, a renewed German attack across the entire 6th Army front again failed to make progress. By October 29, both sides gave up prospects for success in the southern sectors, and moved much of their heavy artillery north towards the area directly around the city of Ypres. While this marked the end of 1914's major combat around La Bassee in the First Battle of Ypres, fighting would continue there for the remainder of the war. [65]

The BEF's 2nd Corps, which had done most of the fighting at La Bassee, suffered 14,000 casualties during October 1914. IR 169's losses were again severe. It is estimated that the regiment went into the La Bassee sector with less than 2,000 effectives. From the period between October 12 – 28, IR 169 lost 6 officers (1 killed) and 840 enlisted men.

Through early November, both sides attempted large scale assaults around Ypres, with neither side gaining a significant advantage. The last great German push came on November 10, when the entire German front attacked in an effort to halt the redistribution of Allied reserves. The casualties were extreme and the results were negligible. Between mid October – November 22, 1914, the recognized dates of the First Battle of Ypres, the Allies (French, British and Belgian forces) lost between 130,000 – 160,000 troops. The British, taking 80,000 casualties, finished November with a Regular Army force that stood at only 20% of the prewar strength. German losses for the entire battle were estimated at anywhere between 80,000 - 135,000.[66] IR 169's losses in the final stages of the battle, from October 29 – November 13 were 4 officers (2 killed) and 390 enlisted men.

IR 169's misery at La Bassee continued long after the main efforts of the combating armies moved north. Although major offensive action was put on hold, the threat of artillery fire and enemy assaults was ever-present. Along with the rest of the German Army in late 1914, IR 169 was introduced to the new realities of trench warfare. There was no blueprint for even imagining the intricate trench network systems that would evolve in the years to follow. Historian Sebastian Laudan researched the 29th Division's introduction to trench warfare through his study of IR 114's regimental history. The experiences of IR 114's trench digging efforts in 1914 paralleled to that of neighboring IR 169. Laudan described how Baden soldiers in the 29th Division first gained experience in constructing crude dug-out positions in the Battle of the Frontiers in August 1914. A dug-out was excavated in a few hours and consisted of a shallow hole just deep enough for two men to crouch in. Two benches were carved out of the hole, with the top covered by a door or other form of limber that was topped with a thin layer of soil. It provided the occupants no access point from which to shoot from no protection from indirect fire. Reflective of the prevailing, pre-war offensive doctrine, these positions were temporary in nature and were abandoned as the troops moved on to their next objective.

In comparison to those serving in other portions of the Western Front, German soldiers in the La Bassee canal sector of Flanders could hardly have been cursed with a more miserable proving ground for learning the craft of trench construction. The heavy rains and high water table in the Flanders region made it exceptionally difficult dig anything but shallow trenches. It was not uncommon for men to exist days on end in two feet of freezing, standing water.

In the earliest days at La Bassee, Baden troops found dug-outs to be wholly unsuitable for protective and defensive purposes. On October 20, Baden troops occupied a line of British constructed-works around Givenchy. This provided the Germans with the first understanding of how British troops, who by this time were slightly more experienced in static warfare, constructed field entrenchments. The British line was a series of square one-man foxholes separated by a small wall of earth. Dirt piled in front of the holes provided some measure of cover, although any rifleman fire out of them would have his head exposed to his direct front. Crude den-like segments, covered by canvas, were carved in the rear wall for protection against shrapnel and the elements. Flooding, a perpetual flooding, was mitigated by connecting individual holes into a core trench that further enabled construction of primitive drainage ditches.[67]

Laudan further presents the evolution of the German trench system in La Bassee in November 1914. As individual foxholes transitioned into trenches, soldiers excavated dirt bunks into trench walls that were just high enough to keep occupants above water. Shelters were provided by placing such material as doors and planks over the trenches. The narrow trench corridors, combined with muddy earth floors, made passage difficult. Defensive features were sorely lacking as there were no forms of protected breastworks to fire nor rolls of barbed wire entanglements to be issued. To provide at least some modicum of early warning, sap trenches were dug forward to provide cover for lookouts and thin barbed strands taken from cow meadows were strung when available. There was still no proper breastwork features or other forms of cover for effective defensive features. Despite the backbreaking and desperate efforts to construct these early trenches, they proved to be feeble defensive barriers when struck by a spirited French attack on 1 December. After four days of fighting, these forward German lines were pushed back several hundred meters towards Auchy.[68]

It was an awful, terrifying, filthy and freezing existence. Some units in the region recorded instances of men actually disappearing into and drowning in the muddy holes. As the war progressed, the German army eventually created *Schippen* battalions that leveraged manpower from men deemed unfit for combat duty, but still able to at least dig holes with a shovel. In the winter of 1914/15, these pioneer units had yet to be created and it was up to the infantrymen who would bear the fighting to build their own defensive works. While the grueling, unending tasks of trench construction at preoccupied the troops from the misery of their existence, they were left with in a constant state of fatigue.[69] As the weather turned bitter cold, losses, particularly from artillery, continued to mount. In the first two weeks of December, IR 169 lost 1 officer and 46 enlisted men.

During the La Bassee campaign, the 29th Division fought both Commonwealth and French forces. Stephan Westmann, a private with Baden's IR 113, a regiment often posted in the immediate proximity of IR 169, described instances of compassion and extreme violence:

"In front of our trenches near La Bassee was a brickworks. The enemy used to put their bricks together as high as houses and on top of these houses there were machine guns which prevented us from going near them. One day we got the order to attack these brickworks and to take them. The only possible means to take them was by a surprise attack in full daylight and we got orders to do so. We cut zigzag lines through our barbed wire entanglements and at noon we went over the top.

We ran approximately a hundred yards when we came under machine gunfire that was so terrific that the losses were so staggering that we got orders to lie down and to seek shelter. Nobody dared to lift his head because the very moment the machine gunners saw any movement they let fly.

And then the British artillery opened up. Corpses and the hats and the arms and the legs flew about and we were cut to pieces. All of a sudden the enemy fire ceased. Complete silence came over the battlefield and one of the chaps in my shell hole asked me, 'I wonder what they're up to?'

Another one answered, 'perhaps they are getting tea.' The third one says, 'Don't be a fool. Do you see what I see?' And we looked over the brim of our shell hole and there between the brick heaps, out there came a British soldier with a Red Cross flag which he waved and he was followed by stretcher bearers who came slowly towards us and collected our wounded.

We got up, still completely dumb from fear of death and helped them to bring our wounded into our trenches. One hour later a British Army doctor came out, again with a Red Cross flag and he arranged a truce for two hours to let us collect our dead ones. I never forgot this generosity of the British, which I must say took place shortly before Christmas, 1914.

Near La Bassee we lay in slit trenches with French trenches to our front. We really didn't know anymore what the first trench, the front trench was and what were the reverse trenches.

One day we got orders to storm a French position. We got in and my comrades fell right and left of me when I was confronted by a French corporal. He with his bayonet at the ready and I with my bayonet at the ready.

For a moment I felt the fear of death and in a fraction of a second I realized that he was after my life exactly as I was after his. I was quicker than he was. I thrust his rifle away and I ran my bayonet through his chest. He fell, put his hand on the place where I had hit him and then I thrust again. Blood came out of his mouth and he died.

I felt physically ill. I nearly vomited. My knees were shaking and I was quite frankly ashamed of myself. My comrades, I was a corporal there then, were absolutely undisturbed by what had happened. One of them boasted that he had killed a Poilu with the butt of his rifle, another one had strangled a French captain.

A third one had hit somebody over the head with his spade and they were ordinary men like me. One of them was a tram conductor, another one a commercial traveler, two were students, the rest were farm workers, ordinary people who never would have thought to do any harm to anyone.

How did it come about that they were so cruel? I remembered then that we were told that the good soldier kills without thinking of his adversary as a human being. The very moment he sees in him a fellow man, he is not a good soldier anymore. But I had in front of me the dead man, the dead French soldier and how would I liked him to have raised his hand.

I would have shaken his hand and we would have been the best of friends. Because he was nothing like me but a poor boy who had to fight, who had to go in with the most cruel weapons against a man who had nothing against him personally, who only wore the uniform of another nation, who spoke another language, but a man who had a father and mother and a family perhaps, and so I felt.

I woke up at night sometimes drenched in sweat because I saw the eyes of my fallen adversary, of the enemy, and I tried to convince myself what would have happened to me if I wouldn't have been quicker than he, what would have happened to me if I wouldn't have thrust my bayonet first into his belly.

What was it that we soldiers stabbed each other, strangled each other and went for each other like mad dogs? What was it that we, who had nothing against them personally, fought with them to the very end and death? We were civilized people after all. But I felt that the culture we boasted so much about is only a very thin lacquer which chipped off the very moment we come in contact with cruel things like real war. To fire at each other from a distance, to drop bombs is something impersonal.

But to see each other's white in the eyes and then to run with a bayonet against a man was against my conception and against my inner feeling.[70]

Beginning December 19, the German defenders around La Bassee faced an assault by some of the same British colonial troops they fought in October. This mini-offensive, consisting of six assault groups, was intended to relieve the pressure from French troops before Arras, 15 miles to the south. The bulk of the attack was conducted by troops from the Indian Corps, including the Garhwal Brigade and storied Gurkhas. While these men were fine fighting soldiers, they suffered terribly from weeks of continuous combat, shortage of food and lack of suitable winter clothing. British munition reserves were at a low point, with only 40 rounds allocated per gun. With weak artillery support, the Indian troops stepped off in a freezing rain from the direction of Givenchy. Some of the Indians troops were able to storm several German trenchlines before Festubert. The Germans quickly regrouped and blasted the Indian gains with grenades and artillery and detonated mines in nearby British trenches. By December 22, the Indian troops withdrew with UK losses tallied at 4,000 men, with many others suffering from severe frostbite and trench foot.[71]

The need to remove the many casualties remaining in no-man's-land at the end of the attack led, in part, to informal ceasefires that sprang up on Christmas day. In recent years, much lore, including books and movies, has been recorded about the famed Christmas Truce that occurred along the Ypres front lines in 1914. Indeed, there are well documented instances of scores of German, British and French units declaring informal truces and fraternizing in no-man's-land.[72] Those in the trenches at La Bassee, experienced anything but a silent night on Christmas Eve when the Germans launched futile attacks against British troops entrenched at Guinchy and Givenchy. These attacks contributed to IR 169 losing another 4 officers and 567 more men in the last two weeks of 1914.

A summary of IR 169's 1914 field records show the regiment suffered 3744 casualties from August 9 – December 24. To be sure, the regiment received a steady flow of new replacements as the war became more static. However, this loss ratio, when compared with IR 169's prewar, authorized strength, reflects an overall 1914 casualty rate of over 100%.

The German Army casualty rolls (*Deutshe Verlust Listen*) recorded that IR 169 suffered 12 losses between 19-21 January 1915. One those men was trumpeter Albert Rieth who suffered a serious wound to his left foot. Albert was evacuated through various field aid stations and eventually sent to *Hilfslazarett Sachs* (Military Hospital Sachs) in Schweinfurt, Germany.[73]

While few large-scale offenses were launched that winter, a number of nasty flare ups took place in the trenches around La Bassee. The most significant was a German demonstration directed along a three mile front to the La Bassee-Vermelles sector. The extremely muddy ground resulted in the British manning a relatively light defensive force, consisting only of a half battalion of Scots Guards and another half battalion of Coldstream Guards – both fabled English units.

The German assault began at 6:30 am, January 25, a date coinciding with customary military celebrations to honor the Kaiser's birthday. The Germans planned to bombard southern canal locks with the intent to flood the British trenches dug among the Guinchy brickyard. The attack was supported by the explosion of a series of mines under first line of British trenches.

The element of surprise was nearly lost when a German deserter snuck over the British lines just before the attack to warn of the impending assault. It mattered little, as the mines were detonated moments later and the German artillery barrage fired full-on. The mines obliterated a trench held by 4th Company, Coldstream Guards, which was centered between sister companies holding the embankment of the canal to their left, and the brickyard to right.

A British artillery officer, Frederick L. Coxen, described the furious exchange of fire that followed in his diary:

"When the bombardment started it was more horrific than any of the other ones I experienced. The sound of artillery fire was continuous, except when they fired their 17 inch guns... The whine of hundreds of shells going through the air, mixed with the explosion of both above and ground level shells, was deafening. All around me great mounds of earth were uplifted by bursting shells. We rapidly replied with gunfire of our own, which added greatly to the unbearable noise. The smoke from gunfire and bursting shells was so heavy, that at times we couldn't see our target... The heavy bombardment forced our infantry to retire. Since our battery position was the foremost battery behind their trenches, I knew if our infantry lost the small ridge in front of us, it would be the finish of us and our guns." [74]

While the barrage and mines failed to break the locks, they did severely damage the front line trenches. German infantry surged forward and closed in with bayonets, taking possession of several lead trenches and portions of the brickyard. Many of the British troops were pushed back across the brickyards and into the second line of trenches. Having regrouped, the British laid down terrific rifle and machine gun fire. The German assault force took heavy losses as it pressed into the British communication trenches along both sides of the canal.

By early afternoon, British and French reinforcements launched a forceful counterattack. The Allied forces maneuvered through the brickyard and over the muddy ground, but could not break the center of the German advance. The battle raged into the night. By the next morning, the British had cleared the Germans from the south side of the canal and recovered some of the brickyard grounds that had been lost the previous day. Over 50 Germans were taken prisoner, with hundreds more left lying dead among the piles of scattered bricks.

On the north side of the canal, German infantry were able to pass through the British front trenches and gain a foothold in the wreckage of Givenchy. House-to-house fighting, often at the point of bayonets, knives and fists, lasted over one hour. The Germans launched five separate attacks against the northern portions of Givenchy, all repulsed with heavy losses.

The fighting continued over ten days. On January 30, the British moved up fresh forces, to include the well-reinforced Irish Guards tasked to reclaim the brick stacks. Kipling recorded the following attack:

> "Five of the brick stacks were held by our people and the others by the enemy—the whole connected and interlocked by saps and communication-trenches new and old, without key or finality. Neither side could live in comfort at such close quarters until they had strengthened their lines either by local attacks, bombing raids or systematized artillery work.
>
> Early in the morning of the 1st February a post held by the Coldstream in a hollow near the embankment, just west of the Railway Triangle—a spot unholy beyond most, even in this sector—was bombed and rushed by the enemy through an old communication-trench."

The No. 4 Company of the Irish Guards rushed to support the Cold Stream men. All of the commissioned officers were soon killed or wounded with command devolving to a senior NCO, who refused orders to retire. At daybreak, the British infantry were supported by an intensive, ten minute heavy artillery barrage. Kipling wrote that the "spectacle was sickening, but the results were satisfactory. Then a second attack of some fifty Coldstream and thirty Irish Guards went forward, hung for a moment on the fringe of their own shrapnel—for barrages were new things—and swept up the trench." [75]

A precise ten minute artillery strike swept the German positions. With the Irish Guards on the left, the Coldstream Guards assaulted from the right. Citing of heroism that day was Private Duncan White of Sheffield, who had a particular expertise for throwing grenades.

Along with a small party of bomb throwers, White was able get within hand grenade range of the German positions. *Deeds that Thrill the Empire*, a 1919 collection of British Military acts of heroism, describes this action:

"The advancing Guardsmen, got within throwing distance and began to rain bombs on the Germans with astonishing rapidity and precision. High above the parapet flew the rocket like missiles, twisting and travelling uncertainly through the air, until finally the force equilibrium supplied by the streamers of ribbon attached to their long sticks asserted itself, and they plunged straight as a plumb line down into the trench, exploding with a noise like a gigantic Chinese cracker and scattering its occupants in dismay. So fast did White throw, and so deadly was his aim that the enemy, already badly shaken by our artillery preparation, were thrown into hopeless disorder; and the Guardsmen had no difficulty in rushing the trench, all the Germans in it being killed or made prisoners. A party of the Royal Engineers with sandbags and wire, to make the captured trench defensible, had followed the attacking infantry. Scarcely had they completed their task, when the German guns began to shell its new occupants very heavily; but our men held their ground, and subsequently succeeded in taking another German trench on the embankment of the canal and two machine guns." [76]

By day's end, the combined Coldstream and Irish Guards attack recovered their trenches lost five days earlier. At 2:00 am on the night of 5-6 February, British and French heavy howitzers bombarded the railway triangle area located between the brickyards and the outskirts of Auchy. The 30 minute bombardment was so intense that it could be heard 20 miles away. One house receiving a direct hit from a large caliber shell was blasted clean into the air. Shells exploding among the brick stacks, adding brick fragments into the spray of shrapnel. At 2:30, the fires lifted and three columns of British and French troops simultaneously attacked. The battered Germans offered little resistance and the position soon fell. The Germans tried to recover the lost ground the next day but were beaten back with severe losses by exceptionally accurate artillery fire. Later in the day, these same fires also destroyed a German heavy artillery battery.

IR 169's field journal recorded the regiment created a breach in the British lines 800 meters deep and 500 meters wide. The records further claimed the British Coldstream and Irish Guards suffered between 800-1000 men killed, 130 prisoners captured, as well as four machine guns, one heavy mortar, 800 rifles and a large quantity of ammunition and grenades seized. IR 169's casualties were 11 officers (5 killed) and 678 men.

Throughout the winter months, 29th Infantry Division regiments were rotated to various sectors in the XIV Corps area. In early December, IR 114 moved three miles south of La Bassee to occupy a position in front of the village of Loos. Sebastian Laudan, in his study of IR 114's education in trench construction, explains how the Badeners in the 29th Division advanced their craft during this period. In their first weeks at Loos, German trenches continued to be expanded in a piecemeal manner, where at best, were deep enough to enable some men to at least stand upright. These works failed to provide protection from the weather elements, let alone from heavy caliber artillery fire. Up until this time, the German troops simply did not have the construction material available to add the needed strength. Things began to improve when the Germans began to loot large amounts of timber from nearby coal mines. One of the first priorities were to construct deeper, reinforced dugout excavations that provided basic shelter and cover. This reduced the crowding of trenches and provided better free flow of passage. Creature comforts such as chamber ovens, furniture and bedding followed. A deliberate zig-zag design reduced the risk of shrapnel and bullets from traversing a long segment of trench line. Communication line trenches were constructed far to rear, which enabled troops to enter and exit the works without being exposed to direct enemy observation and fire.

The more primitive dugouts proved unable to withstand the heavier caliber artillery fires that were becoming more common to the battlefield. German pioneer troops designed a system that built layers of timber, buttressed by soil, over the dugout roofs. Shells would then explode on the top layers and cushioned the dugouts' actual roof.[77]

In early March 1915, IR 114 returned to the La Bassee sector to replace IR 170 in the vicinity of the Auchy brick stacks. This trench system was much weaker, given its close proximity to enemy lines. Still, the Germans redoubled their digging efforts, with a first priority to make the trenches deeper. The labor presented a daunting challenges, as the high water table by the nearby canal forced the digging to be incised at an angle, resulting in a funnel shape that exposed the top portion to incoming fire. The addition of additional fire loopholes and protected observation posts compromised the strength of core trench walls. The Badeners toiled hard to add thick layers of timber, rails and corrugated iron, topped by soil protect dugouts. Dugout sizes increased from two man to eight men bunkers and incorporated two exits, which added an emergency escape for partial collapses. Increased drainage drain systems were established and trench floors were covered by duck boards. Work began on establishing 2nd and 3rd line communication trenches.

Subterranean warfare brought the menace of tunneling operations. Throughout the war, combatant forces were constantly building tunnels to explode enormous mines under their foes' trenches, often as a prelude to an offensive action. Such was the case one morning, when at 8:30 a large mine exploded under IR 114's 10th Company, trapping 25 men. Although an expected enemy infantry attack failed to materialize, these now well-seasons veterans regiment quickly closed off the breached line, readied machine guns, organized reinforcements and prepared supporting artillery fires. The incident illuminated the need for more aggressive countermine tactics and forward deployed listening-post saps. When IR 114 departed this sector in on 20 March, they left a far stronger and comfortable trench system then the one they inherited only a few weeks earlier.[78]

A major organizational realignment of Baden troops in the Flanders front took place on 6 March, 1915. The 84th Brigade (including IRs 169 and 170) was transferred from the 29th Infantry Division to the newly formed 52nd Infantry Division. From this point until the end of the war, Regiment 169 would serve with the 52nd Division. The 52nd Division had only one infantry brigade (the 104th), which now included Baden Infantry Regiments 169, 170, and Magdeburg's IR 66. Additional divisional elements included the 4th Squadron, 16th Cavalry Regiment, Baden Field Artillery Regiments 103 and 104, the 52nd Heavy Artillery Battalion and Pioneer (engineering) companies 103 and 104.

On March 21, 1915, the 52nd Division finally pulled out of La Bassee after six months of a miserable existence. As fate would have it, IR 169 was only transferring from one part of compartment of hell to another. The regiment's next destination would eclipse even Ypres' stature for World War I horrors. IR 169 was headed to the Somme.

Chapter 6
The Battle of the Somme (Part I)
Britain's Bloodiest Day

In late March 1915, the 52nd Division traveled 30 miles south of La Bassee to what then was considered a quiet sector – the Somme. The assembly point for IR 169 was in the large town of Bapaume, 12 miles west of what would soon be the regiment's front line posting at Gommecourt. Gommecourt was marked as the extreme north of the eventual Somme battlefield front. In late spring 1915, French 2nd Army forces faced the Germans across the 6th Army front.

The tactics of trench warfare had evolved significantly in the six months since the IR 169 men first plowed their shovels into the soupy mud of Flanders. Historians John Keegan and SLA Marshall provide these overviews of the expanding German trenching system in early 1915:

> Keegan: "The entire German front was reinforced by secondary lines of trenches, two or three thousand yards to the rear, which were connected to the front by communication trenches. The trenches zigged and zagged at intervals in order to diffuse blasts, splinters or shrapnel, and to prevent attackers who entered a trench from commanding more than a short stretch with rifle fire. The German infantry burrowed as deeply as possible to construct shell-proof shelters, often heavily walled with timber or metal. In some instances, concrete machine gun posts appeared behind the trenches, interlocked in fields of fire with other bunkers to make enemy forays into the no-man's-land a deadly proposition. By the spring of 1915, barbed wire had become plentiful, and dense obstacle barriers, often 50 yards deep, sprang up between the combatants' lines. In a never-ending cycle, engineers strung the barbed wire by night and enemy artillery would blast it apart by day." [79]

> Marshall: "Distances between the opposing front lines varied from sector to sector. In some cases German and British/French trenches lay within talking distance. Elsewhere the lines were up to a mile apart. The pattern followed no sensible criterion.

The only common factor was the misery of the soldier. Where the lines were farthest separated, both sides pounded the hardest with large caliber artillery. Great gun duels would go on for hours, often starting from nothing more significant than a nose-thumbing from a soldier on outpost observed by a sharp eyed patrol in enemy country. First, the small weapons would get into play; shortly would follow the full barrage of heavy artillery. Where the opposing trenches were close-joined, they were mutually immune to the big guns, but they suffered all the more from grenades, mortars, machine guns, and from the ever-present threat of trench raids." [80]

Trench raids did little to alter the actual progress of either side's lines, but they did serve as a constant source of stress and terror for those either conducting or defending against them. Raiding parties, usually of company-sized strength, would sneak through the barbed wire fences and descend on unsuspecting defenders. Their mayhem accomplished, the raiders would slip into the darkness and escape back to their own lines before the defenders could organize a strong counterattack. In the years to come, IR 169's raiding tactics would evolve to the highest levels of storm trooper precision.

The introduction of chemical warfare added even greater lethality to trench existence. The first instance of chemical warfare occurred at Ypres on April 22, 1915 when the Germans unleashed a chlorine gas attack. Both armies soon developed more elaborate and lethal forms of chemical warfare that included phosgene and mustard gases that blistered the skin outside and inside the body. The unendurable pain could last for weeks and left thousands blinded. The imprecise delivery mechanisms, be they gas canisters or artillery shells, were dependent on the direction of the wind, often making these strikes nearly as dangerous for those initiating the attack. Early forms of protection were as primitive as urine or water soaked towels, with both sides adapting to more advanced forms of gas masks.[81] Employment of chemical weapons seldom made a decisive difference in battle outcomes, but certainly added more degrees of terror and misery.

The battlefield that defined the 1916 Somme Campaign was a 15-mile long line that connected a series of villages roughly centered near the town of Albert. The Somme River flowed through the region, bordering the southern portion of the battlefield. The Ancre, a tributary to the Somme, cut across the northern battleground sectors where IR 169 conducted its fighting.

The front lines were first established here in early October 1914, when Crown Prince Rupprecht's 6th Army forces clashed with units from the French 2nd Army. Heavy fighting raged through Albert, with the French eventually pushing the German back along a line two miles to the east. By October 7, both armies moved north as the Race to the Sea dominated the strategic direction of the Western Front's offensive actions. The general trace of this line would remain in place from October 1914 through the grand Allied offensive that began in July 1916.

The ground to the east of Albert enabled the Germans to possess the important high ground. The German trench lines integrated a succession of nine villages in a manner that blended the natural topography with some of the most fiendish defenses of the entire Western Front. Not only did the higher ground give the Germans an important tactical advantage, it also provided the drainage that made for superior trenches. The hard, dry, chalky soil was conducive for digging expansive trenches, deep dugouts and assorted strong points. Networks of machine gun bunkers covered all angles of approach across the bare fields and thick waves of barbed wire protected the first lines of trenches.

IR 169 spent its first weeks in the Somme in the vicinity of Bapaume, a major German logistical hub. The regiment rebuilt as new replacements were assimilated, equipment was replaced and training cycles established.

In spring of 1915, the vicinity of Bapaume was as pleasant enough of a posting, at least by Western Front standards. The lines had stabilized to the point where a large civilian populace remained within a near proximity to the front. Bapaume residents coexisted well with their German occupiers. Ralph Whitehead, in his history of the German XIV Reserve Corps, *The Other Side of the Wire, Volume 1,* records these observations of German soldiers during the time period that IR 169 was based near Bapaume.

"It is a terrific life in Bapaume. We slept splendidly in the last two nights. There are bedsprings and mattresses on the beds and for coverings we have carpets... The French are gourmets of goodness first and cook beautifully. The French women are naturally nice and also funny in trafficking with us. The church is beautiful and has a splendid organ. In front of and by the church there was an oratorio played from Handel and a symphony from Beethoven as well as something from the magic flute, simply wonderful... One could see French women in their extravagant clothes. Bapaume is in some ways a smaller version of Paris, although in other ways it is like a very large town although it only has 3000 inhabitants. Then a band played at the marketplace, with many soldiers and officers standing about. 15 kms behind the front! Is it possible? Many men did not know how beautiful they have it behind the front at all." [82]

Within a few weeks, the 52nd Division was deemed ready to return to the front and took up positions in the defenses around Gommecourt. IR 169 inherited a well-established and strong defensive system when they entered the lines in May 1915.

For most of 1915, the overall Somme sector was comparatively quiet. An exception to the calm occurred on June 7, 1915, when the French tried to reduce an exposed section of the German lines at the Toutvent Farm, three miles south of Gommecourt, and just to the west of the village of Serre. It was the 52nd Division's fortune that the most significant French attack at the Somme in all of 1915 struck squarely at its front.

IR 170 held the left flank of the 52nd Division's line and was at the center of the French attack. A successful breakthrough here would give the French a foothold on high ground that threatened the fortified village of Serre. From June 3-6, the French conducted a mighty artillery barrage which badly damaged IR 170's first line trenches. The shelling also telegraphed French intentions that allowed the Germans plenty of time to prepare for a counterattack against the inevitable infantry assault. On June 7, the French infantry surged forward out of the thick, early morning mist. Many of the defending Germans had a hard time clambering out of their damaged dugouts as the lead French infantrymen stormed into the trenches. German reinforcements from the 52nd Division's IR 169 and IR 66, as well as the 26th Reserve Division surged forward. The French were pushed back in close quarters fighting. In the week that followed, the French poured fresh regiments into the battle and made four more concerted attacks, all repulsed with heavy losses. The French finally gave up further offensive action by June 13, having fired over 150,000 artillery shells.

The French did make some small gains by retaining a section of German trenches but failed to take the key high ground surrounding Serre.[83] IR 169's casualties from this fight through late August 1915 were 5 officers and 200 enlisted men.

When compared to the scale of many of the other great battles that IR 169 participated in the war, this June 1915 French offensive was a relatively small affair. However, the near loss of Serre made the Germans appreciate the tactical value of the higher terrain and its role in protecting all-important Bapaume. A major investment was made in the next year to fortify Serre's defenses into a mighty stronghold.

Among notable occasions in August 1915, Friedrich II, the Baden Regent, visited his troops along the Somme Front. In the course of his stay, Friedrich officiated at the dedication of a monument for Baden dead in the quickly expanding cemetery in Bapaume. Also in early August came indications that the British were beginning to enter the sector across the central and northern Somme lines. By August 9, a sufficient number of British prisoners had been interrogated to confirm that the British replacement of French units across this sector of the front was complete. This was unwelcome news to the Germans, as the French had a reputation of adopting a less aggressive, "live-and-let live" approach to trench warfare. German corps and regimental notices were issued warning their troops of the daring and determined nature of British soldiers. They further cautioned how British troops were likely to feign surrender, only to turn on unsuspecting captors. Harsh orders were given to take "no notice of isolated enemy signals to surrender." [84]In time, a routine settled in with these foes as well. As recorded by Martin Middlebrook in *The First Day on the Somme*, Feldwebel Karl Stumf, of IR 169 wrote: "Before the bombardment started and while everything was peaceful, I could see through my periscope a young Englishman playing his trumpet every evening. We used to wait for this hour but suddenly there was nothing to be heard and we all hoped that nothing had happened to him." [85]

German commanders across the Somme were mindful to incorporate lessons learned from the evolving trench warfare into their doctrine. In particular, a review of the June 1915 French attacks at Serre provided several important teaching points. One area of concern was that some shelters had been dug too deeply, which prevented a quick response when the French infantry rushed forward. New orders came out that dugouts were not to be more than three meters deep (a calculation that would stop a direct hit from a 155 mm projectile). Dugouts were to be equipped with two entrances, and frequent drills conducted on getting the riflemen to the firing parapets as rapidly as possible. There was a realization that the best of trenches would still be badly damaged from a prolonged bombardment by heavy caliber artillery. This was a reminder of the importance of defense in depth and need for strong reserves available for counterattacks.

Detailed instructions were issued on the fine points of patrolling the no-man's-land. One set of instructions passed throughout 6th Army prescribed an in-depth standard operating procedure on the art of patrolling and conducting trench raids. Sparing no details, the document provided exact guidance on the fine points of general patrolling tactics, setting operational objectives, selecting the enemy break-in point, conducting mission rehearsals, intelligence collection, coordination with friendly units, weapons and equipment checklists, mission execution details, engineer support requirements, coordination for supporting machine gun, mortar and artillery fires, use of chemical weapons, coordination of counter-battery fires against enemy artillery and telephone communication. This SOP even detailed the type of awards that should be authorized and the standards required for earning the coveted Iron Cross.[86]

At the time of the July 1916 Battle of the Somme, IR 169 still had two machine gun companies, comprised of two platoons, each with two gun sections. The guns were manned by six-man squads, all qualified to serve as gunners and loaders to replace casualties. The men were trained to a high degree of proficiency, to include being able to quickly clear 36 different forms of jams or gun malfunctions.[87] German machine gun doctrine and tactical structures adapted to reflect the changes in warfare and advances in technology. Beginning mid-1916, German regiments were organized to have three machine gun companies each. Standing MG companies were augmented by independent machine gun troops. This included 'Musketen' sections; two-man crews who operated automatic rifles with a 25 round magazine. The 1917 deployment of the lighter Maxim Model 08/15 machine gun enabled each infantry company to have its own, dedicated machine gun.[88]

The German soldier of 1915-1916 had a decidedly different appearance than the first year of the war. German infantryman removed the spikes of their leather Pickelhaube helmets, which were then replaced altogether by the Stahlhelme steel helmets in 1916. Infantryman wore a more rugged and functional 1915 issue field tunic. This blouse did away with lavish pippins and was a simple, field-gray, single-breasted coat with a fly down the front that protected the buttons and large pockets that could hold extra ammunition. The only unit signatures were the regimental numbers on shoulder straps, which could be covered with gray slip-on tabs.[89] Beyond uniform changes, photos of this era depict lean, battle-hardened veterans that had become accustomed to skills required for survival in the trenches.

The late November rains of 1915 were unusually heavy. Freezing rain flooded the bottom of trenches and dugouts. Men wore soaked clothes and boots for weeks at a time, leading to many cases of crippling trench-foot. The walls of connecting trenches collapsed and became impassible. It was a full-time effort just to keep the front line trenches open and many units completely gave up on maintaining the secondary and communication trenches. The dramatic complexity of the 1916 trench systems, which tripled in yardage from the previous year, added to the burden. Plagues of lice and enormous rats added to the filthy conditions and contributed to diseases. Simply getting sufficient quantities of clean water to the front required great effort. To provide some measure of modest comfort, the Germans installed small stoves in some dugouts.

The logistical demands of supporting a field army of this size were enormous. Jack Sheldon, author of *The German Army in the Somme* describes some of this infrastructure: "Behind the lines, corps and divisional slaughterhouses, butchery departments, bakeries and mineral water bottling plants had sprung up everywhere. These were large scale operations. ...One of the Bavarian corps estimated that it slaughtered an average of 40 cattle and 50 to 90 pigs a day. Compared with civilian slaughterhouses, one corps was consuming more beef and pork a day than all but the largest cities in Bavaria." [90] Ordnance personnel had to transport and safely store vast tons of conventional and chemical munitions, to include hundreds of thousands of heavy artillery shells that could each weigh hundreds of pounds.

By late 1915, both Allied and German high commands had visions of taking the initiative in 1916 with large-scale offensives. Although both sides continued to underestimate the cost of attacking formidable trench systems, there was a growing realization that the prospects of achieving a master breakthrough was becoming more remote. Planners reasoned that if a limited objective could be taken, the attackers could then dig in and prompt their foes to absorb severe losses with futile counterattacks.

By late January 1916, the British and French set plans on a spring 1916 offensive against the Somme. The French were to commit the main effort of three armies (each with 16 divisions), supported by the British 4th Army. The Somme was selected less for any specific strategic or geographic purpose, rather because it simply bordered the French and British sectors.

The Germans focused their strike on the French fortified city of Verdun (130 miles southeast of the Somme). The Battle of Verdun, which ultimately committed 1.25 million French and 1.1 million German troops, began on February 21. For 10 months, both sides engaged in a pattern of costly attacks and counterattacks, with casualties mounting at a prohibited rate. By the end of March 1916, in just over a month of fighting, the French sustained 89,000 losses with the Germans losing 81,000. If left unchecked at this rate, the French would risk running out of manpower. The Verdun nightmare had a direct impact on French/British plans for the Somme. Two thirds of the French forces that had been identified for the Somme were now redirected towards Verdun. By late spring 1916, the French were desperate to get the British into the fight in the Somme, if for no other reason than to reduce the pressure at Verdun.

The reprogrammed Somme Offensive was slated to launch in late June 1916. The total Allied forces consisted of 20 British divisions from the 3rd and 4th Armies and 13 French divisions from the 6th Army.

IR 169 spent the winter of 1915-1916 in the trenches centered on Gommecourt. Even in the absence of major battles, routine service in the trenches took its toll. From 14 June 1915 – June 23, 1916, the regiment lost 17 Officers (4 killed) and 453 enlisted men.

The Germans, in anticipation to the Allied buildup, began to shuffle divisions across the Somme front. As part of this movement, IR 169 relocated from Gommecourt to Serre, four miles south, in mid-May 1916. Serre was a hamlet on the western end of a prominent plateau which extended two miles to the east of the village, and was on the northern side of the Ancre River, a tributary of the Somme. The village, with 25 structures, ran along a country road that led to Bapaume, 10 miles southeast. A mile and a half southwest of Serre, directly on the front lines, stood the German stronghold of Beaumont-Hamel. The capture of both Serre and Beaumont-Hamel were the primary northern sector objectives of the coming British offensive.

In the aftermath of the French June 1915 offensive, German efforts to fortify Serre made it one of the strongest bastions in the entire Somme line. Up until IR 169's spring 1916 reassignment, Serre was under control of the XIV Reserve Corps. Ralph Whitehead's *Other Side of the Wire* provides a detailed description of XIV Reserve Corps' construction of Serre defenses. The French 1915 offensive had pushed the front lines to the village's edge. IR's 180 and Reserve Infantry Regiment (RIR) 99 of the 26th Reserve Division were tasked to transform Serre's defenses in accordance to the latest German doctrinal advances. New, highly-skilled pioneer companies were assigned to divisions and dedicated labor companies, comprised of men not fit for combat but still capable of digging, augmented the construction.

Dugouts were substantially reinforced and provided with two exits. Many dugouts were interconnected or fitted with other means of escape in the event of partial collapse. An entire new front line was constructed by sapping individual positions that connected into a continuous trench. Company commanders operated from centrally located dugouts where daily orders were posted on bulletin boards. Ammunition storage portals were cut into trench walls and shellproof kitchens were constructed in rear sectors that were connected to the front. Trenches were named and marked with designations that soldiers were required to memorize.

The amount of materiel required for constructing a fortification the size of Serre's scope was staggering. Whitehead details the amount of supplies consumed by a single German regiment in this sector from the period April 1915-January 1916. A summarized portion of this long list includes nearly 10,000 beams, 1600 beds, 13,000 planks, 38,000 duckboards, 10,000 fascines, 13,5000 barbed wire balls, 3300 barbed wire coils, 3300 railroad rails, 28 complete sentry posts,

200,000 sandbags, 400 armored shields, 27,000 wooden posts, and 25,000 pounds of nails. Following an inspection, Second Army Commander General von Below was so impressed with Serre's defenses that he declared it a model position for other commanders to visit and replicate.[91]

When IR 169 took control of Serre, they inherited a fortified village that was surrounded by a four deep trench system. The thick barbed wire fields around Serre were arrayed in a manner to create false entrances that channeled attacking troops into machine gun covered killing fields. The far trench, known as the Serre trench, surrounded the village in a large, 1,400 yard semi-circle. Portions of this line were designated as Sectors 1-4 (S1-S4). Second and third trenches covered ground directly in front of the village, and the fourth "Munich Trench" ran on the left side of the Serre and then banked to cover the length of the rear. The village itself served as yet another defensive line. Most of the structures of the town were on the eastern side of the road, making them well-suited to serve as individual strong points. Some of the dugouts were 30 feet deep and with cellars used as barracks. Over time, as the buildings were reduced to rubble and the earthworks grew in height, the actual structures were no longer visible above the ground.

[Two significant primary sources, described in the Author's Notes, are introduced at this point in the narrative. The first is an account of the Battle of the Somme taken from IR 169's informal regimental history, the *Commemorative Publication for the 1st Regimental Day of the former 8th Baden Infantry Regiment 169 on 30th and 31st August 1924* (subsequently abbreviated in references as *Regimental History.*). A second comes from Otto Lais' brochure, *Experiences of Baden Soldiers at the Front, Volume 1: A Machine Gunner in the Iron Regiment (8th Baden Infantry Regiment No. 169).*]

The *Regimental History* provides glimpse of the daily routine prior to the coming battle:

> "The position looked something like this: The regiment's sector was usually occupied by two battalions, each of which had two companies in the first and second trenches; both remaining companies were billeted as reserves in the sector

of the Tuebingen trench and at the edge of the village, behind the sectors of their respective battalions. One battalion was withdrawn to the recuperation quarter in Achiel-le-Petit [four miles to the rear]. Relief and replacement usually took place on a 14 and 7-day schedule so that every battalion spent 14 days in the trenches and 7 days in recuperation. Of course their relief time did not consist of doing absolutely nothing. It included weapons maintenance, formations, instruction, hand grenade practice, and combat exercises. At night they usually dug trenches in the area to the rear.

From the middle of June onward the combat activity of the English increased daily. While light and middle caliber weapons had predominated up to this point, now heavy artillery and short-range mortar fire became noticeably unpleasant. More and more new battalions were ranging in their fire. Soon no one could have any doubt that the English were amassing an extraordinary supply of arms and ammunition for a major offensive." [92]

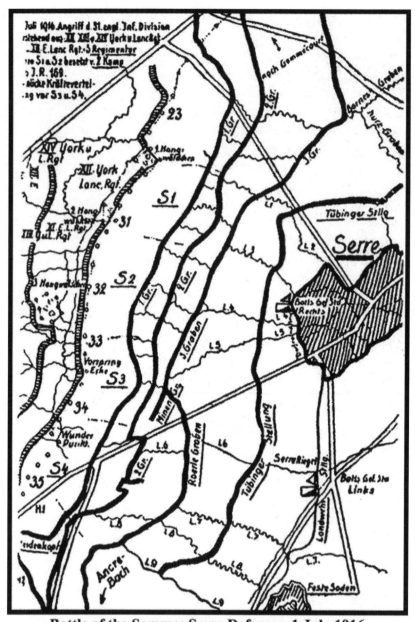

Battle of the Somme; Serre Defenses, 1 July 1916

A German mapping of Serre's defensive sector on July 1, 1916. Note intricate series of 'L' communication trenches, which were of great importance in the fighting in the later stages of the Somme Campaign.

(IR 169 History)

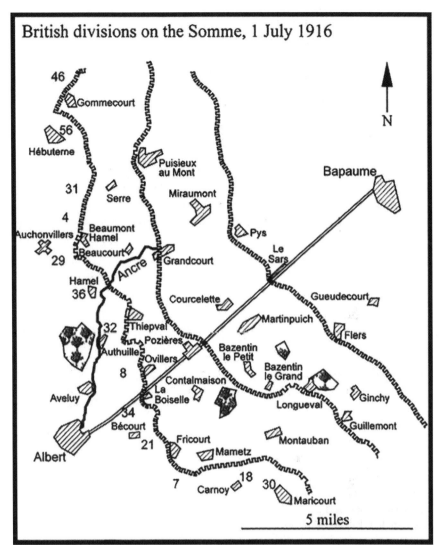

Battle of the Somme; British Attack, 1 July 1916
Courtesy of Andrew Jackson, this map, created for Accrington's Pals; the Full
Story, shows the three major German trench systems that stretched across the
Somme front, as well as the disposition of the British divisions that attacked on
July 1, 1916. IR 169 held Gommecourt from May 1915-1916, and Serre, May
1916 to December 1916.

(AP)

Otto Lais, aged 19, joined IR 169 ranks in the spring of 1916 and
was assigned, in the rank sergeant, as a machine gun squad leader in
the regiment's 2nd MG Company. Lais grew up in the small Baden

village of Wilferdingen, near Karlsruhe, where, before the war, he displayed early talents in the fields of music, art and horsemanship. Prior to his assignment with IR 169, Lais served in an engineering battalion that saw duty in the Aisne region of France in 1915. Lais began his account of IR 169's history in the Somme with this rendering of the defenses at Serre:

"There is an old Latin proverb: "Ora et labora!" In German it means "*Bete und arbeite*" [pray and work]. 'Curse and work' was our trench-motto in the positions in front of Bapaume in the Artois! This motto was a reference to the endless digging, to the drawing of wire entanglements, and to the never-ending construction of dugouts. One swore, one grumbled, one groaned at the nightly hauling of the rolls of barbed wire, the barricades, the wooden frames and all the other 'treasured' things in the life of an infantryman.

Particularly popular was the enjoyment we infantrymen had hauling the hundredweight mines. We have the feeling that nowhere on the whole Western Front is there as much digging and tunneling as here.

The divisional commander checks everything! In the opinion of us other ranks, His Excellency just has a digging-mania.

The second, the third, the ninth trench gets deeper and deeper dugouts. Thirty, forty and fifty steps go deep down. Hewed tree-trunks, beams and T-bars, sacks of angle irons and scaffolding clamps are hauled from the supply depots. The entrances to the shelters, the dugout recesses are strengthened and reinforced. Even some of the approach trenches, the L3, the L5 and the notorious and feared L6 get dugouts and depots are strengthened in rear areas. Our divisional commander, our beloved 'Little Excellency' (he is of small stature) often made daily inspections, coming in all weathers and worst of times! Usually unaccompanied, wearing a shabby windcheater, he went along the trenches, climbed down into the dugouts, clambered over the spoil, squeezed at night through the lanes of barbed wire, was here, was there, was everywhere. He had a particular liking for his machine gunners and it always gave us special pleasure when we were allowed to show and demonstrate our spick-and-span weapon to him. *Generalleutnant* [Major-General] von Borries never made a big deal of himself or of the performance of his division, just as his favorite Regiment 169 never made a fuss of itself and its successes.

So it was that on the gentle hill of Serre, to left and to right of the Bapaume - Puisieux - Serre - Mailly - Albert road, an ingeniously organized infantry fortress came into being.

Our grumbling falls silent, as the enemy calmly finds its range, as we realize that 'it starts' soon." [93]

From May through June, the British assembled the massive infantry and artillery concentrations needed for the attack. The planned date of the assault, referred to as "Z Date" was scheduled for the end of June. Come Z-Day, there would be 17 British divisions - well over 500,000 men available for the overall offensive - with 100,000 tagged for the initial assault. The six defending German divisions were outnumbered seven to one. To the south, five French divisions joined in the offensive.

A considerable percentage of the British troops sent forward were inexperienced in trench warfare. Britain's four regular army divisions had been decimated in Flanders and were filled with new recruits. The Territorial divisions [pre-war reserve units] were also hard hit in the previous year's fighting and were full of untested replacements. The so-called 'New Army' regiments, those formed entirely by new recruits after the start of the war, made up 60% of the British forces on the first day of the battle. These units, many formed from industrial areas, were nicknamed as Pals battalions, given the close connection to their hometowns. In the earliest days of the war, Lord Kitchener, the British Secretary of State for War, believed that it would help recruitment if friends and workmates from the same town were able to join up and fight together. A small number of the Pals regiments had experience in Flanders, Gallipoli and Egypt, but most were seeing trench war for the first time at the Somme.[94]

It was one of these New Army units, the Accrington Pals, which took part in the attack on IR 169 at Serre on July 1. A brief review of this unit represents a sample of the enemy that IR 169 opposed at the Somme. As described by Andrew Jackson, the author of the excellent history of the unit "*Accrington's Pals; The Full Story*," the battalion was formed in September 1914 by groups of friends from all walks of life in the northwestern British town of Accrington. The battalion reflected the enlistment fever of the first month of the war, with 1,100 volunteers filling the ranks within ten days of the unit's establishment. While informally dubbed the 'Accrington Pals,' the official designation of the unit was 11th Battalion, East Lancashire Regiment. In December 1915, the 11th Battalion, as part of the 31st Division, deployed to Egypt to counter a Turkish threat against the Suez Canal. The danger soon receded and, in the last week of February 1916, the 31st Division was ordered to France, to take part in the joint British-French attack on the Somme.[95] The battalion landed in Marseilles, France in early March, and was integrated into the Somme front by the first week of April. Like the thousands of other British troops assembling for the major offensive, the Pals first set to work at adapting to the cadence of war in the trenches.[96]

The attack would be preceded by one of largest artillery barrages in the history of warfare. In the first weeks of June, the British brought guns of every caliber available into line. In the end, they were able to mass 1,000 field guns, 180 heavy guns, and 245 heavy howitzers. Throughout the 15-mile front, a gun, howitzer, or mortar stood at 17-yard intervals.[97] The general British scheme was to use an enormous, five-day bombardment to pulverize the German front line trenches and blow apart the barbed wire fields that protected them. With this array of firepower, the British hoped the bombardment would result in a relatively simple advance through no-man's-land where their infantry could then mop up any survivors in the shattered trenches. The British then intended to repeat the process with the second, then third trench lines. The new batteries would move up at night into prepared positions. Once the guns were moved in, fires would be registered on assigned targets. The British gunners would then await the command to initiate the bombardment.

The order came at 7:00 am on June 24. The crash of artillery could be heard all the way to England. For the British infantry, who had long been suffering from German artillery, the fireworks display was spectacular.Middlebrook wrote that the cannon fire so suppressed the German trenches that British soldiers could actually walk in areas above the ground that would have otherwise resulted in instant death. One Tommy described the effect of fire on the German defenses: "The enemy's trenches look very pretty sometimes in the sunlight, our shells bursting over them in yellow, black or white puffs." The nighttime scenes were especially dramatic, "It was a real sight to see for miles to left and right, all the guns flash as they fired, and with the Very Lights (flares), machine gun, it was something to remember." Most impressive was the firing of heavy 15-in howitzers, which were manned by the Royal Marine Artillery. These behemoths fired huge shells, each of which could be "watched in flight for some time, until it dipped at the top of its trajectory. A few seconds later a distant 'boom' would tell of its arrival in the German lines." For five days, the British artillery followed a consistent pattern. Each morning, every gun on the entire line fired a concentrated 80 minute barrage. For the remainder of the day, continuous, but more regularly paced firing continued. At night, half the guns would rest, but machine guns picked up the slack, with the intent of cutting off the front lines from any source of support from the rear.[98] The British fired 1,500,000 artillery rounds in the seven-day bombardment phase of the battle.

The sheer scope of the fires provided great confidence to British soldiers of all ranks. It understandable why the prevailing thought was that certainly no organized resistance could possibly withstand that degree of punishment. The *Regimental History* told of the impact of the fires in the IR 169 trenches:

"On 24 June a hurricane-like barrage began with one blow. Massed artillery batteries and mortars, which had previously ranged in individually, began a devastating coordinated attack. In the course of the war we had experienced a number of artillery attacks and had become generally accustomed to them. But what now took place was unknown, terrifying, and frightful. This raging fire simply did not stop. Sometimes increasing, sometimes letting up, but continuously by day and night hundreds and thousands of rounds rained down on our trenches. By day and by night maddening explosions roared, shrapnel screamed and the earth trembled. Here, the expression *Trommelfeuer* (drum fire) was introduced for the first time. This continuous fire soon rendered our defensive positions into rubble. No speck of earth was left untouched. Every square meter of earth was rooted up; every centimeter lay in the trajectory of millions of shell fragments and pieces of shrapnel. The trenches were torn apart. Beams, planks, and barriers blocked the ones that still existed. Soon there was no more communication with one of the positions. Although circumstances allowed for some return fire, they were simply not protected against direct hits from this caliber of weapon.

Tremendous demands were placed on the brave men of our 169th Regiment. It was simply impossible to imagine this maddening bombardment and sounds or the continuous explosions from light and middle caliber weapons up to 30 centimeters. Thousands upon thousands of shells and shrapnel fell day and night upon the entire position. And throughout this storm of steel our pickets stood unmoved, despite their meager protection. Their faces, hollow, tense, and with deep wrinkles, stayed turned toward the enemy. Hardly a tremor when a hand-sized piece of shrapnel whistled past, hardly any movement when a shell impacted a few meters away. Everyone knew it was a miracle if he could remain unwounded until he could turn his post over to his relief.

Everyone had to figure on getting hit. And despite all, nowhere was there any dereliction of duty! With firm step, clinging to his rifle, wearing his gas mask, hand grenades at the ready, the relief advanced to the picket position through the expected chaos. From time to time, a nervous blinking of the eyes was the only acknowledgement of the situation. Under these conditions, there was no time to relax, no rest. Crammed tightly together in damp, stale air, everyone laid down where he could and waited. Waited for what? Well, for the attack! There was no fear. To the contrary, it would be relief if the English would finally come. But they took their time. First they wanted to wear down the damned Germans pretty well. Their barrage continued without interruption. They had even brought up naval artillery rounds and were using these 30 centimeter shells to make the German position level with the earth.

What could survive such a bombardment? It was an exception if a particularly deep bunker remained undamaged, if only a stair shaft was blown in. But what if the second exit was also filled with rubble? Then they remained in place, and before rescuers could arrive, carbon monoxide brought on death through asphyxiation. At night the destroyed positions had to be repaired; the pickets had to be reinforced; defensive barriers had to be restored. Every last man was needed. The only approach from Puisieux [2 miles behind the German defenses] to Serre was under heavy fire, particularly at night. It was impossible to bring anything forward. There was no longer drinking water and no regular supply of food. They lived off of preserves and zwieback. They boiled thick, dirty mud from shell craters into something that resembled evil-smelling coffee."

Otto Lais provided this description of the bombardment:

"On 24th June, hell broke in upon us. There was an unimaginable fury of an uninterrupted week-long drumfire by all calibers into the infantry trenches and artillery emplacements.

Over more than a 50 km breadth, the gentle hills of the Somme and of the Ancre River sink behind the brown curtain of millions of shell-bursts. Those of us whose dugouts had not been crushed, crouched below on the alert, took breaths, whether of smoke, dust or shell-bursts, gasping and with difficulty, believed by the third day that the unrelenting booming, rolling, cracking and bursting, on top of the shaking and trembling of the earth, would drive us mad. On the sixth and seventh days the fury seemed to increase, the dugout entrances were mostly blocked leaving, where it was going "well", space to crawl through; the nerves of the occupiers were dulled, a suppressed rage lay in the tortured minds and souls of the defenders, one thought dominating all: when will they finally come?" [99]

Breaks in the nighttime bombardment allowed each side to resume limited patrols and trench raids. It was now more important than ever to determine what the enemy was up to. During these lulls, a third of the German soldiers would emerge from the dugouts and occupy what remained of the firing positions. Others would scramble to make repairs to the trenches and barbed wire fences, and then scramble back underground when the inevitable firing soon resumed. With trench conditions never sanitary even in the best of circumstances, the unceasing shelling made it truly unbearable. In addition to the horrors described in the IR 169 field journal, there were other deprivations. The dead could not be removed and they were left to rot for days on end. Trench latrines were inaccessible, requiring the men to use buckets for relief. It is little wonder that the Germans were praying for the ground assault to begin.

Four days into the bombardment, British scouting parties returned to their lines with bad news. The artillery was failing to cause the damage needed to rip apart the German barbed wire fences. Heavy rains were also turning the ground to muck, a factor that would further impede the British advance. The attack, originally planned for June 29, would be pushed back two days. The delay to Z-hour, the actual time of the assault, added to the British difficulties of massing 100,000 men to make the attack. The bombardment resumed, with 7:30 am, July 1 tagged as Zero Hour of Zero Day.

BEF Commander-in-Chief Douglas Haig designated the large German supply depot at Bapaume as a primary target of the offensive. The Serre defenses blocked an important road that linked the northern sector to Bapaume; making it an essential objective for the attack. The British 31st Infantry Division was assigned the mission to secure Serre and the surrounding areas. Once this objective was captured, additional British forces were to come through and then swing northward, into the German rear areas. The specific task of seizing the fortified village of Serre, fell to the 31st Division's 94th Brigade, consisting of the 12th York & Lancasters (Sheffield City Battalion), the 13th and 14th York & Lancasters (1st and 2nd Barnsley Pals), and the 11th Battalion, East Lancashire Regiment (11/East Lancashire) -- the Accrington Pals. The three battalions of the 94th Brigade would be among the 129 English battalions going over the top of the 15 mile long line in the July 1 attack. Most battalions went into battle with about 25 officers and 700 men.[100]

The Accrington Pals final journey to the front represents the experience of the other British forces executing the attack on the Serre fortress.[101] Throughout late April – mid June 1916, the Accrington Pals had been rotating their four line companies (designated W,X,Y and Z) in and out of the front line trenches. German shellfire accounted for 14 killed and 24 wounded during this period, with illness incapacitating a number of others. On 24 June, the day the artillery barrage started, the Pals were pulled back to the 31st Division reserves at the Warnimont Woods, seven miles behind the front lines. The Pals spent the final week before the attack rehearsing assault tactics and readying equipment.

In the early evening of June 30, the Pals departed Warnimont Woods for the six-mile hike to the assault trenches. The men were laden with their rifles, bayonets, ammunition pouches with 170 rounds of ammunition, water bottles, groundsheets, haversacks (with mess tin and two days of iron rations), toilet gear, field dressings, spare socks, two gas masks and goggles.[102] The troops were also issued four empty sandbags and two Mills bombs [Mills bombs were British hand grenades; developed in 1915, these were the first modern fragmentation grenades ever used on the battlefield]. Half the men carried shovels and a quarter toted pickaxes. The average soldier carried no less than 65 pounds; many others were loaded down with well over 80 pounds of gear.

As the columns approached the front, they were directed into the communication trenches. The great volume of men advancing through the muddy trench floors made for an excruciatingly slow march. After two hours, the battalion advanced only 1000 yards. In frustration, the Pals commander, Lt Col Rickman, ordered the men to advance outside the trenches. Incoming German artillery fire soon forced them back in. Finally, near 3:00 am, the men piled into the badly damaged, front-line trenches to await the orders to attack. They had four and half miserable hours ahead of them, with many spending those final hour hours up to their knees and waists in mud and water.[103]

The Germans knew that the main attack was imminent. While a number of German batteries were knocked out in the week-long barrage, many more remained intact, and held their fire to the point of inflicting maximum damage to the massing infantry attackers. At 4:00 am, Germans artillery began to rain down on the jam-packed British trenches. A more ominous signal of German readiness came at 7:00 am, 30 minutes before Z-Hour, when German machine gun fire ripped into the sandbags over the heads of the waiting Tommy assault forces. On the morning of the assault, the British planned for the concentrated morning barrage to be shortened from 80 to 65 minutes. The intent was to allow the lead infantry waves to go over while the Germans were still expecting 15 minutes more of a heavy barrage.[104] The last few minutes of that barrage were particularly intense, with the British mixing in smoke shells among the high explosives. In supporting the attack against Serre, the British 94th Light Trench Mortar Battery fired a final hurricane mortar barrage of 1,150 rounds in the span of 10 minutes. The IR 169 *Regimental History* depicted the final days and moments of the great barrage from inside the German trenches:

"And the drumfire still continued. On the night of 29-30 June enemy patrols were observed that were apparently sent to determine the condition of the barbed wire before our positions. A few times shortly before dawn enemy fire had intensified considerably, apparently a coordinated probe. Nerves were gradually threatening to break. The tension increased by not knowing when the English were going to attack, how long this hell would last. This uncertainty was more demoralizing than the certainty of an eventual attack. Notably, during the night from 30 June to 1 July, the artillery gave us a little more peace. But when our companies noticed activity in the enemy trenches, the riddle was solved. Now the time had come."

The British infantry attack was entirely dependent on the effectiveness of the artillery support. From the senior commanders on down through the ranks, there was a presumption that the German defenses must have been shattered. On average, the British and German trenches stood about 500 yards apart. The basic scheme of attack was for the infantry, under the cover of the barrage, to advance to within 100 yards of the German trenches, and then assault in as soon as the fires lifted.[105] At that point, it should be a simple matter to mop up any enemy survivors, and then move on to the next objective.

Andrew Jackson detailed the 94th Brigade's assault plan for Serre, describing how the attack was designed in a series of four waves. The first two waves, under the cover of the bombardment, were to enter no-man's land at Zero minus 10 minutes and advance as close to the German lines as to close to the German wire as their artillery fires allowed. At 7:30 am, Zero Hour, the division artillery fires would shift off the German front line and creep forward 100 yards every 2 minutes until it reached the fourth German line on which it was to continue firing for 20 minutes. By this time, the first two waves of infantry were expected to have crossed three lines of enemy trenches and be ready to lunge into Serre Village. Follow-on platoons would clear the second, third and communications trenches. At Zero plus 5 minutes (7:35 am), the third and fourth waves would advance into the now-cleared German second and third trenches, and be in position to assault into the final 'Munich' Trench. At "Zero plus 40 minutes" (8:10 am), the 31st Divisional artillery would rake Serre Village. As these fires lifted, the third and fourth waves, led by strong grenade parties, would assault into the village. Specific platoons were tasked to clear 17 separately designated structures. By 9:10 am, the barrage would lift and the British would finish clearing the village and trenches and then prepare a defensive flank facing north-east and north." [106]

Across the 94th Brigade front, the attack would be led by the Accrington Pals on the right and the Sheffield City Battalion on the left. The 1st and 2nd Barnsley Pals were to support the two leading battalions. Each battalion front was about 400 yards wide. This attack was the British Army's first attempt at executing a rolling barrage, where the infantry would advance just behind the slowly creeping artillery fire. In time, the British would become adept in this form of fire and maneuver. However, on July 1, 1916, the execution of this complex tactic would prove completely unworkable. Another failure was the intended smoke screen intended to blanket the British troops moving over no-man's land. What little smoke was produced only covered a fraction of the assault area, and even then, only served the Germans to better silhouette their targets.

At Serre, the IR 169 front line was held by 1st Battalion on the right (Sectors 1-2) and 2nd Battalion on the left (Sectors 3-4). Each sector was defended by one rifle company in the front trench with a second company deployed in trench immediately behind. Machine guns were deployed among the first three sets of trenches, with the guns from the 1st MG Company in Sectors 1-2 and the 2nd MG Company covered Sectors 3-4. 3rd Battalion served as the regimental reserve in the Tubinger Stellung. IR 169's ranks were also augmented by sections of external pioneer sections who were trapped in Serre during the days of the bombardment. [107]

Many of the Germans later recalled that they were ready, and even eager, for the ground assault to begin. An extract of a war diary from a member of IR 169's 6th Company tells:

> "If the English thought they could wear us out after the unprecedented fire of the past few days they were badly

mistaken… The most ardent wish that we all cherished was that they would finally come. Everyone was aware of their duty. The look-outs were standing when the shrapnel flew like hailstones. The actions of our company commander, Hauptmann Haufer, acted as a shining example to us all. Almost constantly, day and night, he was in the trench and looked out. Who could have hidden their cowardice? Now everyone knows that the hour of retaliation will soon come. Cartridges and hand grenade reserves are made ready; everything is ready….” [108]

In the moment before the attack, an eerie, rare instant of silence descended across the battlefield as British gunners adjusted the quadrants on the next program of targets. The silence lasted only seconds as the barrage resumed. Whistles blew, orders were given and the Brits went over the top. The first challenge was simply for the overloaded infantryman to struggle out of their trenches and cross through gaps in their own barbed wire entanglements. The German reaction was instantaneous. Artillery, machine gun and rifle fire erupted across the front. Many of the first of British troops fell back dead into their trenches. The highly disciplined and courageous British infantryman did their best to form into lines and advance in the orderly fashion. The British troops were stunned, as they surely believed only a few Germans could have possibly survived such an intense bombardment.

The Germans were also bewildered at the sight of waves of British infantry stoically walking towards them in a path to certain destruction. Musketier Karl Blenk, IR 169 recalled:

“When the English started advancing we were very worried; they looked as they must overrun our trenches. We were very surprised to see them walking, we had never seen that before. I could see them everywhere, there were hundreds. The officers were in the front. I noticed one of them walking calmly, carrying a walking stick. When we started firing, we just had to load and reload. They went down by the hundreds. You didn't have to aim, we just fired into them. If they ran, they would have overwhelmed us.” [109]

As soon as the British had cleared their own barbed wire entanglements, they became perfect targets for the German machine guns. "Whole waves were swept over by fire. The dead lay in long rows where they had fallen, the wounded lay with them, pretending to be dead, or took cover wherever they could." [110] IR 169's *Regimental History* recorded how "Our companies had hardly assumed the highest state of readiness when the running fire resumed with monstrous vehemence. Then a black-grey cloud of smoke came slowly and heavily sweeping over the ground toward our trenches. Very suddenly, fire was redirected against the rear trenches." While many of the attackers first and second waves were mowed down, others reached the trenches, as hot rifles were discarded for grenades.

Lais: "After a terrible night, after the inferno of dawn 'they're coming'. - Finally! - relief - that the enemy turns to the attack. The sun shines brightly. It is the 1st July 1916. In the splendor of this summer's day the English columns advance to the attack. They have the certainty, that their week-long drumfire, precisely calculated to the square meter, has destroyed every atom of life in our position.

The enemy's artillery fire suddenly transfers to our rear positions, onto the grounds of Serre village, onto the approach roads and the villages beyond. 250 to 400 meters away from our destroyed trenches they advance to the attack! They advance in columns, in thick, packed lines of attack, behind which are drawn up support troops, ready to turn the English breakthrough on the wing of the attack front into a devastating defeat of our center. The English infantry have their rifles at their necks, hanging from their shoulders, ready for the stroll to Bapaume, to Cambrai, to the Rhine!

The idea that there could still be life or any resistance in us (after this week) seems absurd to them!

But now our men crawl out of half-crushed dugouts, now men squeeze through shot-through tunnels, through buried dugout entrances, through broken, shattered timber frames, now they rise up between the dead and dying and call and cry out: 'get out! get out! it's the attack!'

'They're coming!' The sentries, who had to remain outside throughout the drumfire, rise out of the shell-holes. Dust and dirt lay a centimeter-thick on their faces and uniforms. Their cry of warning rings piercingly in the narrow gaps that form the dugout entrance. 'Get out...get out...they're coming!' Now men rush to the surface and throw themselves into shell holes and craters; now they fling themselves in readiness at the crater's rim; now they rush forward under cover from the former second and third lines and place themselves in the first line of defense.

Hand-grenades are being hauled by the box from shell-hole to shell-hole. There's a choking in every throat, a pressure which is released in a wild yell, in the battle-cry 'They're coming, they're coming!' Finally the battle! The nightmare of this week-long drumfire is about to end, finally we can free ourselves of this week-long inner torment, no longer must we crouch in a flattened dugout like a mouse in a trap.

No longer do we feel the dull impact of the shelter-breaker exploding downwards (an impact like a hammer-blow on the helmeted skull).

No longer must we calm, hold down, tie down those men whom almost lose their minds through this pounding, booming and splintering, through difficulty in breathing and through the jerking and swaying of the dugout walls, and whom with trembling limbs want to get up away from this hole and this mousetrap, up into the open air, into a landscape of raging flames and iron - a landscape of insanity and death.

We call for a barrage!! Red flares climb high then fade away as they fall to the ground. Barrage fires leave masses of green and red marks in the sky!

Dear God! The German barrage fire! Behind us the guns lie destroyed in their emplacements, their wheels upwards, their barrels in the dirt. An enormous crater left by the impact of the English heavy shells yawns at the site of the gun emplacements. Most of the crews are dead, lying buried in tunnels and bunkers. On the wagon-tracks that led to the gun batteries lie shot-up ammunition caissons, shattered gun-limbers, spilled cartridges and shells, dead drivers, and the carcasses of horses torn apart by direct- and near-hits. Our barrage is pitifully weak; there is no artillery in reserve. The summer of 1916 was a time of the great artillery shortage. So it was that on 1st July 1916 almost everything depended on us - the infantry![111]

Shots flew, whipped and cracked wildly into the enemy ranks, above us it hissed, whizzed and roared like a storm, like a hurricane; the path of the English shells which fell on what little artillery was left, on the support troops, on the rear-areas. Amidst all the roar, the clatter, the rumble and the bursts, the lashing out and wild firing of the riflemen, the firm, regular beat of our machine guns is solid and calm; -tack-tack-tack-tack....this one slower, the other faster in rhythm! It is precision work! - a terrible melody to the enemy, it gives a greater degree of security and inner calm to our own friends in the infantry and to the other ranks." [112]

The British 94th Brigade surged forward into the fire. C Company, Sheffield City Battalion, which served as the left flank of the 94th Brigade formation, had a particularly hopeless task. The barbed wire fields to their front remained intact and were defended by a slew of machine guns. In the first moments of the fight, the C Company Commander was killed by a shell burst and the entire left half of the company was wiped out before reaching the German wire. A few troops were able to crawl along a shallow "Russian Sap" ditch and make it near the German trench, only to be isolated and then hit. To their right, in 94th Brigade center, A Company fared little better, with most of their troops, to include their company commander, cut down by machine gun fire while trying to seek an opening at the wire's edge.

Only on the brigade right, to the front of the Accrington Pals, were there any gaps in the German entanglements. Leading X Company of the Pals, Captain Tough received his first wound even before the attack kicked off. He was hit again in no-man's-land and then killed by a machine gun bullet as he neared the German trench. Any semblance of an orderly attack had fallen apart, and only those now dashing forward, or taking cover in shell holes, were able to survive. Incredibly, some men from the first two waves were able to reach the first German trench. Lt Gay, one of the few British officers still unhurt, led his platoon into the trench and was shot through his neck. His orderly, trying to dress his wound, was also shot down. More British troops, remnants from the first two waves led by W Company's already wounded Captain Livesey, were able to leap into the trench and close in upon the defenders.

The third and fourth waves, designated to assault deep into the Serre Village, lost 50% of their strength, to include both commanding officers, before they could even enter no-man's-land. Those who were able to continue forward joined others from the first waves who were now in a desperate struggle for control of the first German trench.

German officer ranks, like their British counterparts, also paid a toll for leading from the front. Oberleutnant Emil Schweikert, commanding officer of the 6th Company, was wounded in the head with a shrapnel fragment during the final bombardment. Bleeding heavily, he stood by his command post for much of the fighting until finally agreeing to be evacuated. Five other IR 169 officers, Lieutenants Beck, Hoff, Jenisch, Neck and Imle, were killed.[113]

Lais' narrative continued:

"The machine gunners, who in quieter times were much mocked and envied (for being excused from hauling ammunition!) - are popular now! One belt after another is raced through! 250 Shots - 1000 shots - 3000 shots.

'Bring up the spare gun-barrels' shouts the gun commander. The gun barrels changed - carry on shooting! - 5000 shots - the gun-barrel has to be changed again. The barrel is scorching hot, the coolant's boiling - the gunners' hands are nearly scorched, scalded.

'Carry on shooting' urges the gun commander 'or be shot yourself!'

The coolant in the gun jacket boils; vaporized by the furious shooting. In the heat of battle, the steam hose comes away from the opening of the water can into which the steam was meant to re-condense. A tall jet of steam sprays upwards, a fine target for the enemy. It's lucky for us that the sun's shining in their eyes and that it's behind us. Had the enemy used close-in covering fire in 1916 as became customary for both sides in 1917 and 1918, the situation would have been highly critical for us.

The enemy's getting closer; we keep up our continuous fire! The steam dies away, again the barrel needs changing! The coolant's nearly all vaporized. 'Where's there water?'" shouts the gun-layer. There's soda water (iron rations from the dugout) down below. 'There's none there, Corporal!' The iron rations were all used up in the week-long bombardment.

Still the English attack; even though they already lie shot down in their hundreds in front of our lines, fresh waves continue to pour over from their jumping-off positions. We have to shoot! A gunner grabs the water can, jumps down into the shell-hole and relieves himself. A second then also pisses into the water can - it's quickly filled!

The English are already in hand-grenade range; grenades fly to and fro. The barrel's been changed and the gun jacket filled - load! Hand-grenades and rifle-grenades explode violently in front of the gun – the loading begins to tangle! You recite loudly, slowly and clearly saying to yourself: 'forward - feed - back!'....tack-tack-tack-tack....a furious sustained fire once more strikes the "khakis" in front of us! Tall columns of steam rise from almost all the machine guns. The steam hoses of most guns are torn off or shot away.

The skin of the gunners, of the gun commanders, hangs in shreds from their fingers, their hands are scalded! The left thumbs reduced to a swollen, shapeless piece of meat from continually pressing the safety catch. The hands grip the lightweight, thin gun handles as if locked in a seizure.

Eighteen thousand shots!

The platoon's other machine gun jams. Gunner Schwa. is shot in the head and falls over the belt that he feeds in. The belts displaced, taking the cartridges at an angle into the feeder where they become stuck! Another gunner takes over! The dead man is laid to one side.

The loader takes out the feeder, removes the cartridges and reloads. Shooting, nothing but shooting, barrel changing, hauling ammunition and laying out the dead and wounded in the bottom of the trench, such is the harsh and furious pace of the morning of 1st July 1916.

The harsh, clear report of the machine guns is heard on every division front. England's youth, their best regiments, bled to death in front of Serre. Our machine gun, right by the Serre-Mailly road, commanded by the brave Unteroffizier Koch from

Pforzheim, shoots through the last belt! It's driven twenty thousand shots into the English!" [114]

The frantic rate of fire from the German machine guns drew heavy enemy attention and created numerous gun malfunctions. A machine gun operated by Unteroffizier Adelbrecht in the front line of Sector 1 laid down an especially devastating base of fire that forced oncoming British waves to the left. As Adelbrecht was clearing a gun jam he was hit in the head and instantly killed. Another shot hit a hand grenade carried by Gunner Heinrich Pfahler, causing it to explode, killing Pfahler and wounding four other members of the section. On receiving word of the dire state of this gun, 1st MG Company Commander Oberleutnant Faller ordered Unteroffizier Johann Wilhelm to lead a gun from the reserve trench forward to replace the fallen Adelbrecht's squad. Soon after putting his gun into operation, Wilhelm was also shot in the head and killed. British troops had advanced within grenade range of this gun, and rained Mills bombs among the surviving crew members, who continued to sustain fire.

In the Sector 2 front line, a machine gun commanded by Unteroffizier Fritz Kaiser came under heavy enemy fire that killed two crew members, mortally wounded another and slightly wounded a fourth. Remaining gunners continued to fire the weapon until its firing pin broke. No sooner had it been replaced when the water jacket was hit with shrapnel, rendering it inoperable. The gun was pulled back to the reserve trench where repairs were quickly made. Platoon commander Leutnant Bayer led the surviving gunners back to the first trench where it resumed firing. [115]

The melee in the first German trench was desperate for both sides. For a few moments it looked as if the British may have been able to fracture the German lines. A group of especially intrepid British soldiers surged over the German second and third trenches and into Serre Village itself. At 8:16 am, a British signal unit observed a signal flag briefly wave inside Serre, only to disappear and never be seen again. [116] [The British never learned the specific details of what happened to this group that made it so far into the IR 169 lines, but their ultimate fate was certain. The following year, after the British eventually controlled the area, the graves of a dozen York and

Lancaster men were found in the ruined houses and gardens of Serre.][117]

At 8:00 am, IR 169 Regimental headquarters received reports that their 2nd Sector was penetrated. The regiment's 2nd Company was immediately ordered to counterattack in platoon waves from the third trench.[118] Inside the German first trench, the surviving Pals were battling for their lives. Captain Livesey continued to fight like the devil and made an especially valiant stand. He had been hit in the arm when going over the parapet, shot in the chest in no-man's-land and hit again in the head going through the German wire. Livesey cleared and then held a portion of the trench until he was killed when a rifle grenade smashed into his face.

The fire had become so concentrated that it was impossible for follow-on British troops to reach the few defenders still holding on in the German trench. Even so, the British still attempted to push reinforcements into the melee. After 8:00 am, B Company of the Barnsley Pals made another attempt to cross over no-man's-land. The company commander, Major Guest, actually made it near the German first trench, only to be hit and never seen again. Most of the remaining men in the company were also soon shot down. By 9:15 am, the German counterattack had gained full control over positions that had previously been threatened. No other British soldiers would get close to threatening any of the Serre positions that day. Lais described the final phases of the battle:

"After the initial confusion and panic caused by our unexpected resistance, after the horrific loss of life in their closely-packed attack formations, the English re-form. For two hours and more, wave upon wave breaks against us. With incredible tenacity, they run towards our trenches. In an exemplary show of courage and self-sacrifice, they climb from the safety of their jumping-off position only to be felled, barely having reached our shot-up barbed wire.

Twenty, thirty meters in front of our guns, the brave ones fall, the first and the last attack waves together.

Those following behind take cover behind their dead, groaning and moaning comrades. Many hang, mortally wounded, whimpering in the remains of the barbed wire and upon the hidden iron stakes of the barbed wire barricade. The survivors occupy the slight slope around and behind the remains of the barbed wire and shoot at us like things possessed, without much to aim at. They make cover for themselves from the bodies of their dead comrades and many of us fall in the fire. We shoot into the wire shreds, into the belt of barbed wire that winds to the earth. The hail of bullets breaks up at the wire and strikes downwards as an unpredictable crossfire into the protective slope. Soon the enemy fire dies out here as well.

Fresh waves appear over there, half-emerge from cover then sink again behind the parapets. Officers jump onto the thrown-up earth and try to encourage their men by their example. Flat-helmets emerge in numbers once more only to disappear again immediately. The hail of bullets from our infantry and machine guns sprays over their defenses.

Meanwhile the English support troops fared badly. Closely packed, caught between their jumping-off positions and advanced units of all kinds, they were unable to move forwards, backwards or sideways once the catastrophe began. Machine guns mounted on sleds, elevated from the front line, with sights set at 500 to 700 meters, shot accurate bursts of fire into the English support troops. The deliberate fire of the few German guns had a devastating effect on their ranks. Still shooting somewhere in the sector are two *Minenwerfers* [trench mortars] and a makeshift mortar put together by sappers, a so-called Albrecht-mortar [a wooden tube wrapped-around with thick coils of wire or steel bands.] With a low rate of fire but with all the more terrible effect, this sent its shaky "jam-bucket", filled with a highly explosive charge, iron and thick glass, swaying through the air in the direction of Hebuterne [two miles northwest of Serre]. Wherever such a monster exploded 3 to 4 meters above the ground, the result was terrible to see.

The English officers no longer lead their men out of their trenches. The sight of the field of attack takes the breath away from the attacker.

The attack is dead." [119]

Although IR 169 lines ultimately held throughout the attack, the English made gains directly to the north and south of the regiment's stronghold at Serre. Of particular concern was the threat of British control of the nearby *Heidenkopf*, a quadrilateral fortress 1000 yards southwest of Serre. German commanders had long acknowledged that the Heidenkopf was located on indefensible terrain. In the event of a major attack, the Germans had essential written-off the position and planned to use it as an enormous booby trap against advancing British troops. German engineers waited until the lead British elements reached the walls and blew up the position with a massive demolition charge. The detonation was slightly premature, as a defending German machine gun squad did not get the word to pull out in time and was destroyed along with the fortification. The four large craters left in the aftermath of the explosion were occupied by the oncoming waves of British infantry. Although the original fortifications were no longer intact, a fixed British possession of the craters remained problematic. A German counterattack, supported by an IR 169 platoon commanded by Lt. Hoppe, cleared out position later in the day.[120]

Lais described the situation:

"At the adjacent regiment on our left, situated in front of Beaumont, the enemy succeeds in breaking through to the third line. Our left flank is threatened. If the enemy occupies the Heidenkopf, it looks bad for us in the valley.

The 169th Regiment, whose battle-sector included the north- and northeastern sides of the Heidenkopf, sends help to the *Landwehrsmen* of Reserve IR 121. The slight, dashing Lt. Hoppe from Magdeburg throws the English out from the breach with a single infantry platoon from the 3rd Battalion in dazzling close combat. The English reserves that try to penetrate the gap are caught in the flanking fire of one of our machine guns - the Death Reaper! Here too the English soldiers fall to the ground in rows." [121]

By day's end, the British only made slight gains in their southern sectors. Further to the south, the five French divisions engaged in the offensive made somewhat greater progress. July 1, 1916 marked the bloodiest day in the entire history of the British Army. The British committed 13 divisions, a force of 100,000 men into the Somme attack. 57,000 were listed as casualties, with almost 20,000 of those being killed. IR 169 bore the brunt of the 31st Division attack. By early afternoon, this division lost 3,600 men. The lethality of the combat is reflected in the statistic that only nine men of the 31st Division's losses were listed as prisoners.[122] The Accrington Pals went into battle with about 700 men, with 584 reported as killed, wounded or missing. Almost every officer (including three of the four company commanders) in the attack was either killed or wounded. IR 169's losses from June 24 – July 1 totaled 591 casualties.[123] Most of these casualties came from the fighting of July 1, where IR 169 reported 141 killed, including five officers, and 219 wounded. In the day's fighting, the regiment expended over 70,000 rounds of small arms ammunition and 1000 hand grenades.[124]

Lais on the battle's aftermath:

"Our losses are very heavy. The enemy's losses are inconceivable. In front of our division's sector, the English lie in rows by company and by battalion, mowed-down, swept-away. The no-man's-land is one great scene of misery. The battle falls silent; it seems to have frozen through so much misery and misfortune. Medical orderlies hurry into the battlefield, an English medical team appears from somewhere with many stretchers and unfolded Red Cross flags, a rare and shattering sight in trench warfare.

Where to start!? Whimpering confronts them in almost every square meter. Our own medical orderlies, those who can be spared, join forces on the battlefield and place the enemy just as carefully into the hands of his people.

Evening is drawing in. In front of the sector of the 52nd Infantry Division, the enemy's attack is defeated. Some kilometers further left, at Ovillers-Contalmaison, at la Boiselle, the enemy succeeds in breaking through the less-well consolidated position to a depth of one to two kilometers. The French succeed in breaking through at Peronne to a depth of 3 to 4 kilometers. Local successes, which they were able to extend to some two to four kilometers in a six-month long struggle - this loss of material, this sacrifice of life for that!

The English-French dream of a bright and cheerful war of movement, a march to the Rhine, is over by the evening of 1st July. What happened on the part of the allied military command over the course of the next six months of the Battle of the Somme is the cruelest and the most incompetent bungling ever indulged in by an army command.

The bases of Serre, Gommecourt, Beaumont-Hamel, which dominated the open-country towards Bapaume, remain in our hands. The 8th Baden Infantry Regiment 169 has the fame to be one of the few regiments which did not allow the English to gain a foothold in their sector on 1st July 1916." [125]

The IR 169 *Regimental History* recorded the German treatment of wounded British soldiers:

"There was notable praise from the enemy side. On 24 July 1916 the *Morning Post* wrote, at a time of strong anti-German feeling, the following: "The German troops opposite the London regiments were the 52nd and a Guard-Reserve Division. All officers confirmed that during the battle the enemy acted as Europeans in their comportment. The enemy permitted our medical corpsmen to come onto the open battlefield to evacuate the wounded back to our positions, even those lying close to the German front line, without any harassment. And it was not rare to encounter such experiences in these engagements, where we confronted German troops with excellent discipline. The troops of a nation that had been waging war with barbaric intensity for almost two years even showed themselves capable of occasional acts of compassion."

[Given the tactical situation, Andrew Jackson questions the extent that medical assistance could be afforded to the combatants on July 1. In 1972, as a young man, Andrew toured the Serre battlefield with Accrington Pals veteran, Harry Bloor. Bloor described being wounded in front of the German wire during the July 1 attack. For 38 hours after being hit, he survived by lying in a shell hole. He eventually crawled back into the British front line trench, to find it filled with other wounded Pals. It wasn't until the night of July 3-4 when he was able to make it to an aid station for treatment.[126]] Middlebrook also painted a grim description of the fate of the British casualties trapped in no-man's land. He documents how the practice of the British placing upturned rifles at the site of their wounded resulted in drawing deliberate German fire. Outside Serre, a British soldier in the Barnsley Pals observed one British corpse, "propped up against the German wire in a sitting position" being used for German target practice throughout the day, with shooting continuing until the head was completely shot off.[127] While there certainly were acts of compassion, the intensity of battle made for an awful existence for those left wounded.

Chapter 7
The Battle of the Somme (Part II)
Serre Besieged

In the aftermath of the Allies' disastrous July 1 attacks, the Somme Campaign devolved into a five-month campaign of attrition. Through July, the British and French continued localized attacks that resulted in more heavy losses. The Germans in the northern sectors, to include IR 169's position at Serre, held firm. To the south, the Allies did somewhat better, and eventually pushed Germans lines back three miles. By late August, the lines once again stabilized. These limited gains provided the Allies with little tactical benefit and came at the cost of 180,000 casualties to both sides. The British and French continued to apply heavy pressure through sustained artillery fires and occasional offensive action. On September 15, 1916, one of these attacks struck at the village of Flers, 10 miles southeast of Serre. The British use of Mark I tanks in this action was the first ever battlefield deployment of a tank.

At a strategic level, German resources were stretched thin. The ongoing Battle of Verdun continued to consume men and material at a terrific rate. Since February, Verdun had cost the Germans more than 200,000 men and millions of artillery shells. By summer 1916, the Germans were absorbing more infantry losses and weapons and ammunition expenditures than could be replaced.[128] The Germans defending along the Somme saw few reinforcements.

All through the autumn, Serre, and the surrounded strong-points north of the Ancre River, were among the few German positions that remained unmoved since the British offensive began on July 1. This stubborn hold-out became the source of increasing British attention and artillery fire.

IR 169's *Regimental History* recorded this period:

"After the failure of their hopes, the French and English concentrated on the area between Ancre and the Somme. From our position, from the heights above Serre, we followed with fearful eyes the attackers' advances. Often when in the night the entire sky, all the way to the south, was colored by a sea of flames, when sharp explosions rent the darkness, when massive tremors in the earth gave us no rest, we stared with dark thoughts at the cruel but beautiful theatre of war. Little by little, meter by meter, but inexorably, the front south of the Ancre was being pushed back; the distance between the new positions on our flank up to Serre was getting shorter and shorter. Soon our artillery was involved in the battle; there was brief flanking fire from the south that covered our emplacements. The enemy infantry again became active, digging 4-5 meter deep mines approaching our position in order to blow up our trenches at a time designed to pave the way for their own storm troops to advance."

Lais on the weeks following the July 1 attack:

"The English prepared the next major attacks on the Serre heights more thoroughly due to the failure of their artillery barrages, as well as the collapse of the spirit of élan from their original attack in front of the Serre defenses. July passed. The many unburied Englishmen in no-man's-land rotted. At night both the enemy and we buried the mortal remains, (you can hardly call them bodies), all those who were lying within reach. It was only into the second half of August when the sweet, heavy, nearly unbearable smell of decay finally disappeared.

Our position is bearable. Small probes, forceful explorations, artillery duels; those are the daily occurrences of the months of August and September.

Rockets, like the sound of a giant organ, are launched from a division to our left, less than three kilometers south from us. Every day, the unceasing drumfire fills the brown, black curtain of earth with smoke, fire, and whistling steel; descending over the heights as well as the slopes. To our south, forces on both sides, regiment by regiment, division by division, are burning themselves up, and are being swallowed and consumed by the wavering flame.

We of the 52nd Division receive new reinforcements. Our entire Division manning is down to one-third of its original total strength. Units in the trenches were being manned at only one-fourth of authorized levels. Companies are now being filled and otherwise refurbished. The class of '97 comes to the front, to which our volunteers of 1914 all belong. They are tough, still well-fed, 19 year old boys who, in a few weeks, will be steeled to men.

We remain in our positions at the Serre. The shot up trenches are being reconstructed; the leveled communications trenches are newly dug out. Everything is being made a bit flatter and more open. But they still are not as nice, tight, and protective as they were before the beginning of the late June barrages. There were beautiful September days where we lay half naked in the ditches, getting sunburned; or we would sit on the trench steps and catch lice.

I was cleaning the machine gun at the entrance to the bunker. In our ears droned the distant rumbling and rolling raging battle of Thiepval (two mountaintops - five miles - left of us), and of Ovillers (two miles further south), of the vast St. Pierre Forest. Thiraatsch! Boom, Boom!

Attack by Fire!

We are lying on the bottom of the ditch, mud sticks to our mouths, sand sits in our eyes, ears, and nose. We hit head-first into the bunker. This damn Tommy does not even stick to his shooting schedule. Since it had been quieter here with us, the 'Beefs' transmit only at very special times. This evening shelling, five o'clock aperitifs, are not welcome here. Heavy shells fly over, mostly towards Puisseux.

As a special surprise, the British like to fire all calibers of artillery into Serre Village. There you quit laughing. In these moments, the cooks are especially worse off, because the kitchen trenches are in Serre. It's always especially bad in these trenches." [129]

On August 6, Colonel von Westernhagen took command of IR 169. Other leaders rotated in, to include the assignment of one particularly harsh disciplinarian who briefly led Lais' machine gun company in September 1916:

"Our situation at Serre had not exactly turned into a life insurance policy, but compared with the hot, major battle days of June and July, the decreased activities of the Tommies make it seem like paradise. The entrances to the bunkers, which had been mostly badly shot-up, are being repaired and improved. New bunkers are being set up as well. We accept the nickname of 'trench rats' (*Schanzenfimmel*) without complaint, as we now know the value of a good bunker in drumfire.

Unfortunately, we suffer with the temporary assignment of a new machine gun company commander, a real martinet, who doesn't understand the basics of trench warfare. When enemy shelling fills the trenches with dirt and splinters, this Unterfuehrer immediately orders the floors swept in order to preserve the cleanliness of his highly shined boots. Up until now, we had served under only one, fabulous company commander, whose leadership had prompted our motto 'Our chief is a hell of a guy!' But now we were to suffer four weeks of bad luck. This replacement is an active service lieutenant, a not very youthful, but rather pompous-looking gentleman. He rarely came to see the guns, but he always found something to criticize. It seems he found special pleasure to harass the platoon and section commanders by demanding the excessive rotation of new passwords. When artillery fires started up again at the end of September to early October, the daily 20 minute run to get the new passwords became a race with the Grim Reaper. When our real lieutenant returned, this nonsense stopped, and Mr. Sadist reported sick and withdrew to the rear." [130]

From July – October 1916, the Allies concentrated all offensive actions on the Somme's center and southern fronts. Beginning late September, their attack focus turned northward. The results of the gradual German retreat in the south led to IR 169 serving in a northern salient that eventually jutted out six miles north of the Ancre River. This holdout sector of German strongholds was a five mile stretch of ground that ran from Serre in the north, down to Beaumont Hamel, Beaucourt Hamel and St. Pierre Divion to the south. In mid-October, the British began to make plans to reduce this troublesome salient in a decision that was partly political and partly tactical. A success there might somewhat redeem the failure of the July 1 attacks as well as allow them to gain high ground needed for the long-sought effort to take Bapaume.

The IR 169 *Regimental History* recorded the increasing British artillery and aviation attacks upon Serre:

"In September, the artillery fires resumed in earnest. If the enemy had relied on the extent of his week-long artillery barrage before the July offensive, now he was learning from his most recent experience. Aided by aerial observation, trenches and bunkers were systematically targeted until the enemy could conclude he had accomplished his purpose. Anyone on location would believe this. In addition, the enemy was now using a new artillery round with a delayed action fuse that would explode only after penetrating several meters into the ground. The effect of the tremendous concussion was devastating. Every bunker was crushed with no hope of rescue. Woe to the occupants buried in the rubble! If they weren't killed outright by the explosion, they faced death by asphyxiation from the gas of the explosion or from lack of oxygen. Every rescue party was subjected to enemy artillery, with fire directed from aerial observation. For the same reason it was impossible for the regiment to receive any relief. For week upon week, month upon month they had to remain in their positions with no break. Relief was possible only between the first and second lines, and with that came hard, laborious work in rebuilding damaged trenches and bunkers, constantly under terrible artillery and mortar fire. When weather conditions permitted, the English released clouds of gas and smoke against us, with the goal of reducing our forces and eroding our alertness. The effects of hard, never-ending physical work on the emplacement and of continuous lack of sleep gradually became noticeable. Constant exhaustion; care-worn faces. Constantly the question of how long we were going to have to hold out. Haven't we earned some relief? We continued to suffer losses. Half of the companies consisted of newly arrived replacements that did their best but lacked the combat experience of the 'old boys'. They lacked the composure and inner balance that the battle-tested hero possesses."

Lais vividly portrayed the effect of a particularly deadly British projectile (which he describes as a mine) delivered by a 2 inch, 'Toffee Apple' Medium Mortar.

"They throw many medium and heavy shells at us; you can hear these beasts come in. You can be lying in the first trench, enjoying the sun half-naked, when there comes a distant alarm, followed by many deaths. Some of the shells can be seen wailing in the air, like thick black tadpoles, which, moving their tails, sail towards us wavering to and fro.

While lying in a forward position with my machine gun, I receive a visit from engineers who belong to a signals interception unit. We can smell the fuse of these mines that pass-over beyond us. One then lands in a sentry post. Two sentries were blown into the air; one is killed with a broken neck while the other was flung high into the air and dropped into the second line of trenches. He landed in the latrine, but alive. For him, the results of this aerial excursion are three days shock, eight days of the shakes and four weeks leave.

Now comes the opposite: how the latrine took an aerial trip. 'Attention, mine' shouted the machine gunner as we take cover. A large mine with a tail sailed majestically very close over us. We lie in the trench and press our body against the wall as the mine will impact on the other side. These mines have sensitive explosive warheads and produce a terrible shrapnel effect. The ground shakes, the dirt of the trench falls and we hear a subdued detonation.

And then what? These monsters usually make an earth-shattering sound. Something is coming over us, something from above falls on us. It is wet. It splashes onto our back. We shake ourselves with terror, jump up. Oh hell, how it smells. The large mine skidded into the newly-furnished, frequently-visited latrine in our trenches and only exploded once it had dug itself very deep into the cesspool.

In this war, the grotesque and tragic are very close.

I have prepared a big bucket with water and creosote to clean myself of this terrible shower when an intense mine attack hits the first trench. I stand on the second to last step and wait for the barrage to stop. Suddenly the entry to the bunker turns dark.

Three engineers from the depot jump in and sit down on the steps at the bunker entrance. I call for them to come further down, since mines often explode in the trench. They don't listen to me, but just sit there. One of them stands up, at the same second as a heavy mine hits the back-wall trench directly in front of the bunker. The entire charge blasts into us. I'm being pushed against the door of the bunker. The bucket in my hand is completely riddled and above my head, pieces of the door frame turn into splinters. The bodies of the three engineers, which covered my body, are cut up by thousands of small sharp splinters. They were killed instantly. The tunnel is filled with smoke and dust. In the evening, a group of infantrymen take the dead to Serre in canvas bags.

Machine gunners may leave their position only individually or two at a time, but only for a short time. On the same night, we go back to the third trench-line again. Be careful, we tell the machine gunners of the 1st Machine gun Company who replaced us; trouble is brewing." [131]

By 1916, the use of aircraft by both armies for reconnaissance and attack purposes had become commonplace. Wireless capabilities allowed planes to adjust artillery fire rapidly on targets far beyond the visibility of ground observers. In an instant, an enemy plane could swoop down and strafe an unsuspecting trench-line with machine gun fire. For the German soldier in the trenches glancing upward, there was a three-to-one probability that any aircraft flying overhead was that of the enemy. In the Somme in early July, the Allies' airpower (201 French and 185 British machines) significantly outnumbered that of the Germans (129 planes). Anti-aircraft defense technologies and tactics were continuing to evolve, with the sighting apparatus needed for accurate deflection shooting yet to be fielded. [132] Gunners of the day adapted as best they could, and in the following passage, Lais described the art of firing the machine gun against aircraft in 1916:

"Regimental headquarters issues orders that drainage holes, covered by grates, be dug in all the trenches. Bunker entrances are to be reinforced with sandbags. Our position looks downright feudal. I wish we had not done all of this. Even the English couldn't have liked it better for their aerial photography which they took from a low altitude. The Beeves must have had a good time when they developed the film plates; they could perfectly well see the grates and improved positions we had made, including the newly painted bunkers and fighting positions.

In the second half of the month of September, the English planes appeared again, in formations of two or four; sometimes a whole dozen. They would fly down, turn to us, and then fly up again at a sharp angle. Their observations are used to assist the English commanders' planning in a major battle which will happen shortly.

In the middle of October 1916, while IR 169 had been under heavy, continuous destructive fire, my machine gun was assigned for a few days to another position with the neighboring regiment to our north. Infantry Regiment 66 from Magdeburg was being transferred from our division and sent away. IR 111, which in the future will belong to our division, and the 52nd Jaeger Division are still engaged elsewhere. A newly formed regiment (numerically numbered in the 400s), is being assigned to the lines vacated by IR 66 that stand between us and IR 170 in Gommecourt. This new regiment is composed nearly exclusively from the same year/class Jahrgang which are now entering the trenches for the first time. Only a limited number of their officers and NCO's are familiar with battle, and most of those were wounded in the first days of the beginning of the war. Having been recently called back to active service, they have no clue about the survival tricks of trench warfare. The confidence of the division leaders in the battle value of these troops is minimal. Therefore a very wise decision of our division commander was made: groups of two machine guns, not as part of a platoon but independently as an assault group from the left (IR 169) and right (IR 170) regiments were sent to the new regiment.

While incoming enemy artillery in our new position is light, IR 169, hardly 300 meters south of its new battle station, lies under very heavy bombardment. The English know that if they can capture the Serre heights, they can take our new section without any effort. Our ability to attack the English line from our position is impossible; this must be why the English did not waste any ammunition on us.

Directly behind our bunker we discover a completely untouched antiaircraft position for the placement of four machine guns. A massive, hardwood beam stands rammed into the ground vertically. A cylindrical hole which has been lined with fascines is about two meters deep. On the upper end is an auxiliary platform for positioning of the machine guns. This auxiliary platform sits on hard rubber in order to neutralize the recoil. We were very happy with our new discovery and immediately installed our MGs on to the position. We then stacked a row of ammunition boxes around us, loaded the guns and waited.

The English planes arrived. At a maximum 200 meter altitude, they circle above the smoke and clouds of the Serre positions and direct artillery fire. Two of the planes circle close above us and turn. We stand in the emplacement with our guns and wait for a good firing opportunity. So often we have fired at aircraft and never shot one down, but we certainly chased many away. So we do have experience shooting at planes. We do not shoot at planes that pass us to the flanks, parallel to the gun barrel. The chance of success at this is zero. The expert marksman understands that he should wait until the target is so many plane-lengths ahead, flying at an angle that is towards the direction of the gun.

We don't put much trust in the new airplane sight/crosshairs for the MG, which look so nice in the toolbox, but bends in our pants pocket. Like the old German proverb, 'What the peasant doesn't know, he doesn't eat.' All these theories were created with the best of intentions, but once the planes are hit (in a non-critical area), the crews only have to glue on a panel to repair the wing again.

We'd rather just shoot according to the bead sight, even though the platform shakes so much, and the novice loses the sight picture. We don't let any new gun crew member shoot. Anyone who wants to be promoted from munitions carrier to touch the MG must first have significant combat experience.

Every time, before and after the airplane turns, we send a series of 50 shots against the fuselage of the two airplanes. Our

MG is the oldest gun of the company and it's called *Schneddelich* (an old, original piece). The boxed parts of this unique gun had been worn away; but they run better like this. The spring on the left of the MG, which absorbs the recoil and brings the bolt forward again, can be set at the strongest tension. Every normal gun with this level of tension would jam after the tenth shot. Our Schneddelich ate belts of 250 bullets with a monkey-like speed and sent the bullets with the extremely high rate of fire of a French machine gun. The belt is delicately fed into the MG.

Shooting a MG is a sensitive matter, a skill that cannot easily be accomplished by any carnival shooter. That's why the loader who feeds the belt deserves the highest praise. Without his cold-blooded concentration, which can see only the belt and not the opponent in front of him, the actual gunner would be lost. The incorrect feeding of the belt is the first step to jamming.

The two English pilots begin feeling annoyed by our shooting. They glide down to about 200 meters and attack us. Their bursts of fire impact irregularly around our emplacement. One of them shoots; the other turns. By now we already have wasted quite a lot of ammunition, and fire just in ten-shot bursts. It becomes uncomfortable for us when one of them shoots at us from the left, and the other from the right, while we are just busy feeding in a new belt and loading.

Unexpectedly quickly, one of the English pilots drops down to 50 meters, and fires a 3-4 second burst directly into our platform. It hits the fascines above, by a fingers width above our heads. We go down to our knees and press ourselves against the opposite wall, and raise ourselves in the next second while I lift the boxes and the shooter raises the belt.

Having felt that he went too low, the Englishman gives full throttle and rises steeply and nearly overturns. He moves directly into our line of fire, and with his steep angle of ascent, he cannot evade our burst. Had he been able to turn, he could have escaped, but his very steep ascent was for us the perfect target, which became smaller, but also remained fixed.

Now we have him! Our guns stand at a very bad angle. I hang with my hands at the grips of the box. My upper body back, my stomach against the vibrating oak beam; my knees nearly on the floor, I pull the trigger with both thumbs. Loading the belt into the gun from this position is a difficult matter. The corporal in charge of us performs a masterpiece of juggling to feed the belt directly into the gun. Our trustworthy Schneddelich grabs the belt with no problem, and with fantastic speed, pulls it through. The English plane does not escape our gun. The bead of the sight is constantly on the lower fuselage of the Englishman. At an oblique angle, our burst goes into the plane's fuselage. After I shot nearly 200 rounds, the Englishman tips over onto his right wing towards the village of Hebuterne and then crashes in a dive between the English trenches.

Somewhere, an alert artillery observer in our section calls in what is happening, and three seconds after the plane touches the ground, nose in the dirt and tail in the air, a German battery fires a round ahead, then below, then a direct hit. The plane is a smoking pile of rubble. The reward is equally divided between the MG Company and the field artillery battery. The other English plane quickly heads away. Five minutes later, an English artillery attack against our anti-aircraft stand begins. The next day, when we again fired at planes, we were attacked so violently that we hardly got 20 bullets out of the barrel. We received so much heavy fire that we had to stop. On the third day, our beautiful MG position vanished and a huge crater took its place.

It now starts to get bad in our sector, too. The inexperienced young regiment is not up to the difficulty and starts to fail. The English assault troops have immediately recognized that the new German regiment is not up to the situation, and take groups of prisoners every day from within their bunkers. Every night we have to kick the Tommies out. We MG gunners and our assault troops of IR 169 don't get a minute of rest. The nervousness of the 400'ers has gone to the extent that when faced with an English attack, they were ordered to the rear trenches to allow us IR 169 troops, who knew what we were doing, to repel the advance. One night I fired an entire belt against Englishmen who came close to our barbed wire obstacles. So when my MG hammered so hard into the quiet evening, they thought again that the Englishmen must be attacking from their trenches. These rookies were completely taken aback when we restrained them and laughed at them. After a few days, they were replaced by battle-proven troops. They reformed behind the lines, filling one-third of each company with veteran soldiers. Lo and behold, with the next major battle this regiment proved itself superbly." [133]

The Allies continued to hammer away at the southern shoulders of the German lines. In late September, a bloody push by three Australian divisions (at a cost of 7,000 casualties) took a German stronghold at the Mouquet Farm, four miles south of Serre and located along the strategically important heights of Thieval Ridge.[134] The Germans could not allow a breakthrough and pulled in units from northern positions as reinforcements. In early October, a company from IR 169, supported by Lais' machine gun squad, took part in this effort. Lais described the perilous venture:

"Through the October mud, we carried our guns and ammunition to leveled trenches that were a few hundred meters to the left of our regimental sector. The company commander told us, 'Well you've had quite a bit of pressure over there. Tonight you will replace the first line.' We think, 'Well, pressure! Everything is relative. In hell, the waiting room to hell is paradise.' We will be ordered to go south, past the sectors of two divisions, to the infamous Mouquet Farm. The division's Uhlans [long since dismounted cavalry troopers], which are by now able infantrymen, stand ready to replace us.

We have to go to the place where, since the first of July, constant, day-after-day and night-after-night fighting burns the marrow out of your bones. We are ordered to move to a fragment of a large farm, a murderous hole where at any hour of the day or night, the closest distance to the enemy trenches is only 12-30 meters; where the soldiers throw hand grenades at each other, where large blue flies decorate the reinforced basements and bunkers, where the moaning of the heavily wounded lie in rows to await for transport along the death road. Where fighting troops are pressed together like herons, with their hands on the grenades that stand in the entrance of the bunkers.

We only had to climb down from Serre into the valley of the Ancre, in the direction of Miraumont, to climb to the other side of the valley, and we would be at our destination. However, the road had a sinister name. It was called the 'Death Road.'

The valley of Miraumont, which we would see again in a very bad reprise during the withdrawal of 1918, has the most beautiful clouds in the sky (detonating shrapnel). This lovely, so green valley of Ancre, in whose swampy ground, black brown cypresses and pines stand, which grow from the ground and are then swept away by the wind that comes from heavy caliber artillery. It is a valley whose depressing memories last an entire lifetime.

After a few days of being bled and burned down to the marrow, the company and the MG squad came from the heights, marched back through this valley, and rested a few days at Achiet Leptit or Achiet LeGrand [two adjoining villages west of Serre]. Within the Serre positions, the battalions rotated their companies between the front and the rest areas. Three companies were forward, while one rested at Achiet. The MG company was always forward, and rotated only one gun crew out for rest at any time.

It's a peculiar rest quarter, these two villages of Achiet. Seven or ten miles from the front, they are under continuous English long distance fire. Constantly, people run from the open fields into bunkers. There is always a brown curtain of dust over everything, the rumble of thunder, and the sound of the powerful melody of the battle of the Somme and of the Ancre.

The 'rest' was a nightmare, since you have to go through the valley either tomorrow or the day after tomorrow again. And then, when you are at the area of greatest danger, you lay down with your nose in the mud, pulling yourself up again while clumps of earth fall on your head and body. You then run through shelling while beams shatter, stone breaks and walls collapse. You run through trenches on the heights of Serre, resting for the first time at the kitchen bunkers, while still having the worst to come. All of your senses become sharp and awake, as if you are an animal. Then you hear the orders; "Cover! Forward!" [135]

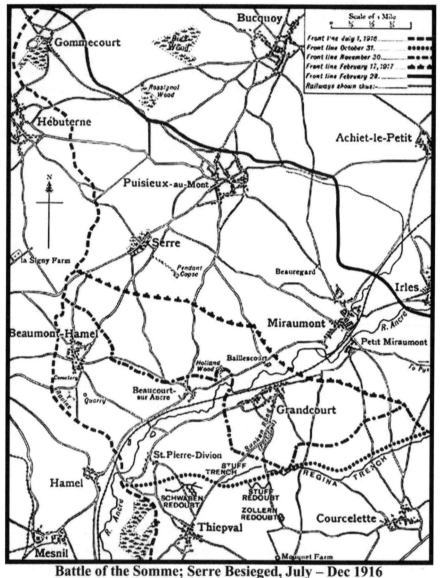

Battle of the Somme; Serre Besieged, July – Dec 1916
Serre, a stubborn German holdout, became increasingly isolated in the later stages of the Somme Offensive.

(PD)

In the ranks of any infantry squad, few skills were more highly valued than that of the scrounger. Despite the worst deprivations, these soldiers possessed an inherent aptitude to obtain all manner of food, supplies and creature comforts outside the bounds of the official supply system. Here, Lais describes one of these men, referred to only as Rifleman "B" from Berlin:

"Rifleman B. was one of our few northern Germans; he was a Berliner. Accordingly with his origins, he was always running his mouth off. 1.94m tall, broad-shouldered, he had military bearing - when he wanted to! But most of the time he didn't want to, and was then unbelievably worthless. He was almost ten years older than us nineteen and twenty year olds and possessed the wisdom of the world of a big city man, and the 'sans gene' that only a Berliner has.

At home he had a wife and four children, to whom he punctually sent his pay, except for 30 cents, which he kept for himself. When he needed to keep himself amused (which mostly depended on his stomach), he scavenged here and there, but not usually from us, but with the even-poorer infantry companies. He sought out the staff bunkers, the depots in and around Serre, he combed through the constantly under-fire Puisieux, and God only knows where else he got to. He most frequently requested to be sent to fetch rations, so that he could get to the engineer depot. 'Just wait a bit, B., until it's dark and the shooting lets up.' 'I'll get there (in his Berliner dialect), Sergeant', and he's gone.

Often he doesn't come for two or four hours. I get nervous. I just shouldn't have let him go alone. At nine in the evening he comes with a big grin plastered to his face and dragging: Three big cans of Leberwurst, a can of ham (still in fat), zwieback, butter, and seltzer water. In the next few days he's "loaded up" out of a basket of sizable dimensions. Caraway is there as well, which is a very much desired article. One can drink it for themselves, or trade it for candles, sweets, or other things. No one can figure out where he steals the things. He 'finds' everything in empty, abandoned shelters and depots and tells the most credible fairy tales about his finds.

You just can't keep B in one place; if you order him to stay, he is entirely useless. He has to stray, to wander about, and find sweet things. He is quite comradely, and shares with everyone. B possesses a fine sense of incoming shells; he can smell the shot being fired on the other side and is already lying down, nose in the mud taking cover, before the shell arrives.

We are lying at the street Serre to Wailly oriented towards the hill of the Heidenkopf. The bunker is deep, and has 5 to 6 meters of earth cover. It is a few meters from the fighting position for the heavy MG, so-called shatterproof (a type of bunker with 1 1/2 to 2 meter earth cover, in the interior strongly reinforced and strengthened with beams and iron rails). An eminently deep and wide firing slit looks out on an ideal field of fire. The MG fighting position is approximately 30 meters in front of our own first trench, in a kind of sap. The sap is a deep groove with very flat walls. The sap can hardly be recognized, out of the many rumpled grooves and ridges of the hillsides of the Heidenkopf. The personnel bunkers and shatterproof bunker have stood up under the eight days of drumfire due to their nested position within the hillside in front of the first trench-line.

Alarm one October evening! On the first trench-line, left of the street Serre-Mailly, is a pounding drumfire. At the same time with the arrival of the bombardment, a strong English battalion advances against the sector - a powerful reconnaissance!

There's not a shot near us. The silhouettes of the English assault troops, who are advancing hard against our half-right, are recognizable in the evening twilight. We have an outstanding fire opportunity. At a distance of 50 meters we hold a clear, enfilading angle against the hastening shadows, firing from the MG carriage within the firing position. The infantry of the second and third trenchlines provide a constant fire, and in seconds as the darkness falls, flares are fired and make the terrain as light as day. The English attempt has failed. In the no-man's-land, someone screams long and loud the entire night. The night is restless. Nervous popping off comes from both sides. Towards 4 o'clock in the morning the wounded man is now quiet, perhaps they have picked him up, perhaps he has died.

In the morning, things are very restless; we aren't in the bunker but in constant readiness in the combat positions. Around noon the bombardments are around us and damned near to us; it looks like they'll hit; an airplane flies above us - boys, if only they haven't spotted us. Around one in the afternoon it starts. In the entire sector there's the constant drumming of artillery fire. We crouch, ready to fire, in the fighting position - highest readiness! Suddenly, darkness, mud, pain, stifling, dust and four versions of explosion, just a hair's distance from our viewing slit. The firing slit is blocked - they have us!

To the left and right everything is crashing in. The shatterproof shelter is hanging crooked to the left - backwards and smashed - stifling and bending the wood - the shatterproof shelter is also hanging crooked to the right, crooked to the front, and is suddenly pushed back. Its square basic form has become a rhomboid, pointed in various directions, according to wherever the impacts are. Up and out of the hole; over to the secure bunker; unload MG and take the belt out; dismount the MG and take it off the carriage; let the carriage and munitions stay, just get the MG and the crew out in one piece!

We have more than enough munitions in another bunker, ten meters distant. Our seven man crew and one NCO must get there. Over this small short distance, this ten meter long trench groove, lies death and rot, lies a hair's distance from the range of the enemy's trench mortar shells, which land one after another. Rack-rack-rack-rack, a short three second pause while the ugly black puffs of smoke still are there; rack-rack-rack. The pillars of suffocating earth indicate where the impact fuse shells strike at the bunker and at the fighting positions. With a sensitive ear, we can even pick out the firing of the enemy artillery. In these short three seconds, in which they over there slam open the cannon breech and haul out the cartridge shell; load and return the breech, we must run over to the bunker.

First the MG. Be careful! In a fraction of a second, after the pausing of the battery fire, up and out of the hole and in long strides to the bunker entrance, always two at a time, and last Rifleman B and I.

'Be careful!' Shots fired over there; detonations, puffs of smoke, OK, now we go over. In the same moment comes a whistling barrage of a new battery which has just joined the bombardment. 'Take cover!' I shout and throw my body against the flat wall of the sap, rack-rack-rack. B makes one stride towards the shatterproof bunker backwards, and is a half second too late in taking cover, calls out, falls backward into the entrance, collapses and crouches on the floor, his head falls forward and he moans, deeply and heavily. With one stride I am next to him and pull him further in; what is happening, where was he hit? He doesn't answer, he just moans. Blood is soaking through his upper thigh. Stand up, I help him to orient himself; 'hold on to the cover beams.' His belt away, unbuckle; unbutton his tunic, he silently moans and holds with both arms fast above. His trousers pulled down; I see something worse than a shot to the leg - a shot to the belly.

An explosive has torn away the lower part of his belly, his intestines are visible and pressing out. B. sees that, and loses his nerves over this terrible change to his body. He moans and screams, 'let's go above', and then falls into my arms, shaking. 1.94 tall, 180 pounds heavy, how should I even control him? Outside its railing away just like before, the shells impacting and smashing above the sap. No one from the bunker can come over. In my desperation I yell at him: 'Man, pull yourself together! Think of your children and hold tight above!' He struggles up with his hands with his nails in the protective beams, takes his shirt and tunic corner between his teeth until I have bound it all up with his gas mask strap. I rip open his and my own bandage packet with flying fingers, slap them into a big wad, and press it against the large wound and wind as much gauze around it as I have. His strength is failing.

Ready! I bed him down on two 1.8m frame beams, which we have positioned over the munitions boxes as a bench. Outside it's still raging; the rifle stand outside is destroyed; in the position further back where we both are lying, it's so crooked that the corners and seams are so out of joint that it's a wonder that it hasn't fallen apart. If we hadn't reinforced the struts at the corners with scaffolding joints, the structure would have already collapsed on us.

One single heavy shell lands on top of our shatterproof bunker. Right afterwards comes another; they seem to really want to pack it in over there. Suddenly on the left wall, which was previously at an angle from us at a distance, is suddenly pushed over right on top of us. The beams break, earth trickles on to us - for two full hours this purgatory continues.

Two hours long Rifleman B., with his fatal wound, lies on two hard wooden frames, under his head a roll of empty belts. He lays his broad heavy worker's hands around the hands of his NCO's and looks at him with feverish, distant eyes: 'Sergeant, don't leave me alone.'

'Just don't leave me alone.' He can't feel the ranting and shaking anymore. 'B, I'm being straight with you, I will stay with you, you won't die. Even some stomach wounds have been healed - you'll get to the military hospital and all will end well.'

He isn't moaning any more, he is speaking as if in a fever, irrelevant and crazy things. He is slowly fading into another consciousness; his face is becoming hard, heavy, as if carved out of wood, like a sculpture of a farmer. His eyes are a great dumb question, as if questioning the way ahead.

I am becoming anxious about him; he now appears like the typical image of a serious stomach wound, which will with 99 percent certainty bring death.

The bombardment is now on the entrance to the aid station, at Communications Trench 6. After 3 o'clock the fire breaks off; it is quiet in our sector. But now it speeds up. Rifleman B is laid into tent halves buttoned together, which are fastened to two poles. Four men have to carefully carry him. Two medics of the infantry company around us, two riflemen from my MG crew carry the heavily wounded comrade to the battalion doctor.

We dig our MG carriage out of the rubble and recover the ammunition. The fighting position has become useless. We are all restless. If only they hurry up with B. If they weren't shot up on the way, they must be at the aid station already. Three explosions over there; low above the L6 Communications Trench are three shrapnel rounds; then nothing more. The afternoon becomes entirely peaceful, like it hasn't been for days. None of the people come back. Towards 6 o'clock, I hang my gas mask around my neck and head towards the battalion doctor, along the L6 trench. My platoon leader, who has arrived at our location in the meantime, takes over the MG.

Half of the way towards the aid station they are all lying there, all five are dead. They were surprised by the shrapnel attack, which hit them as they were carrying Rifleman B along the trench.

The four carriers, left and right on the slanted walls of the trench at which they tried to take cover, are riddled through with shrapnel holes. Inside the tent covers, B is dead; the released fuse of a shrapnel shell made a ruin of his forehead. Death was sudden and without suffering for all five. Three shrapnel rounds land above the L6 Trench, it is an unusually quiet afternoon. During the night, infantry of the third trench carry the dead to the casualty collection position in the engineer depot behind Serre." [136]

The British intent to reduce the north Ancre salient came with a renewed appreciation of the German's strength. The hope belief for a successful autumn offensive here was based on the premise that 20 weeks of hard trench warfare, combined with an enormous artillery barrage, would wear down the German defenders to the point of collapse.[137] Heavy October rainfall delayed the attacks, as the British needed at least some measure of dry ground to sustain such a large-scale offensive. Although the rain continued and the mud became deeper, the British eventually committed to a November 13 attack date. By early November, the British assembled a force of 12 divisions to take this five mile length of trench lines. The average width across no-man's-land was now less than 250 yards.

One of the British units brought forward for the coming offensive was the reconstructed 31st Division, which had virtually been destroyed in the July 1 attack at Serre. Included in the 31st Division was the 11/East Lancashire Accrington Pals, who went back into the Serre Front in late October. It was an emotional journey for the survivors of the July 1 assault, one of whom recorded "...A lump came to many throats and unspeakable thoughts flashed through men's minds at the sight of the old camp which only a few months before had heard the joyous ring of Lancashire voices." [138]

The British began increasing the intensity of the bombardment of the Ancre positions. The advance of British forces to the south enabled them to place multiple artillery batteries in a semi-circular pattern to the front and left-rear of the German lines. The Germans in Serre were now slammed by heavy guns to their front, south and southeast. Lais wrote of the effects of the severe October and early November bombardment of the Serre trenches:

"By the end of September, we were constantly in a high state of alarm. As it happened, we would not be relieved for a three week period. It became very bad from end of October until 18 November, 1916, when we were unceasingly engaged in the most intense and difficult of battles. From the end of September through the beginning of October, we noticed the attacks were about to start. Things were getting serious. The Englishmen were sighting in their rifles. Low-flying planes, protected by higher flying battle squadrons, circled from early morning until very late over our trenches. The brown curtain of smoke and fire has again taken possession of the valleys and heights of Serre.

But what is happening? Are our own artillery fires landing too short? We are now receiving incoming fire from the rear, directly into our shelter entrances.

Oh no, my boys, those are the Beefs, who bit-by-bit at Thiepval, Contalmaison, Ligny-Thillon and Sailly, have taken terrain and now can molest the defensive point Serre with long range guns firing from our half-left and rear. At night you can see it clearly, how they are already around us in a widely-bent semicircle - a nice view! A half-circle blaze of fire at night around us!

With a precise and sadistic pedantry and mathematical exactness; shelter by shelter, trench by trench, are in turn taken under fire. While the heavy fire lands throughout our positions, every shelter which was recognizable as such by the English aerial photos is worked over individually by the heaviest calibers. Shells from 15 to 38 centimeter arrive, heavy naval artillery; detonations of horrible strength that blast craters in which you could set a house down in. These dull blows of the heaviest bunker-smashers don't just create craters, but they throw up entire hills. With a direct hit, these shells will bury into and crush a bunker. Near misses cause the entire gallery of the bunker to shake for seconds, which makes the beams and joints rattle. All this landing onto one single, poor bunker with two to three entrances and five to seven meters cover out of built-up earth.

Finally it's had it! The naked, split beams and framing wood jut out of the rubble of the shot up bunker entrances - fifteen dead. The fire then moves further to the next shelter, where the airplanes are circling.

That's what it's like day-after-day, week-after-week. When will it be our turn?

The top of the bunker rolls and bumps as it sounds like an organ playing on and on with the frantic drumfire. The casualties of the regiment since the beginning of the battle are enormous. Will we never be relieved from this hell? The communications trenches don't look like trenches anymore, but like baking dishes; the position trenches are buried, the parapets and breastworks have been leveled. It starts to rain.

Sacks are hung next to the shelter entrances, smeared with wet clay. Destroyed and shot up entrances are left in this condition. Anyone who can be seen moving from above while the enemy aircraft are active is brutally chewed-out. If the Beefs get even an inkling that something is still alive in the bunker, then it's over for us.

Tracks are eventually covered and the airplanes are successfully fooled; we have learned a lot in a week. The ration carriers and the couriers run for their life at every turn; no one walks anywhere, everyone runs or trots, or creeps over rubble; no one wants to go alone on these tasks.

For us machine gun squad and platoon leaders, the path back to the company commander in the fourth line of trenches is a race with death. With whirring and gurgling whistling sound, the fragments of shrapnel travel a hand's length behind our heels into the earth - a horrible noise - this ffff-grrrr. Entire enemy batteries set off fused shells, aiming for the individual man, whom they discover while he tries to crawl or dives headfirst over the rubble. Some lie dead in their own blood, some remain helpless and lay wounded, until others arrive after running through the ruined trenches.

Exhausted, with trembling body and head pressed to the earth, one can figure out, even in the heaviest fire, which battery is firing from where and to where. With the instinct of an animal and schooled ear of an experienced frontline soldier, one knows exactly when he should begin to run again. Go - further! Until one can determine the time between the droning of the shots fired and the fraction of a second before the impact; then take cover with your nose in the mud.

It gets bad when they have ranged us and then mix in time-fused shells with impact-fused shells. Cover doesn't help much in the trenches when timed fuses are used. The only thing that helps is running like crazy and being lucky.

It's particularly awful in the first trench-line, which in and of itself is surprisingly the least destroyed of all the trenches. But it is now the constant target from a downpour of shells from these unpredictable *Stielminen* trench mortars, of both light and heavy calibers.

One night there is a rotation. The machine guns from the first trenches are sent to the third, and those of the third trench-line are sent to the first. We have the choice of occupying an established shelter in the third trench-line with 16 steps and two entrances, or a newly started shelter with 36 steps but only one entrance. A direct hit from an 18cm shell would knock our 16 step shelter pretty much to pieces, but if everything wasn't completely destroyed, we could at least escape through the second entrance. We go for the 16 step shelter and warn an infantry group by the new bunker that it is still under construction (which they certainly must know) and that there is still plenty of space with us. In the next evening, the 36-step shelter receives a direct hit and collapses. Through the night, we try to dig the infantry troop out. All nine are dead - suffocated.

Our 16 step shelter is known in the sector as the 'swinging boat.' During our presence, the swinging boat gets some stiffening through thick beams, tree trunks and T-girders which, despite the shooting, we get in the night from engineer depots. Terrain-wise, the swinging boat is a bit high, and so it occasionally shakes a bit due to the heavy impacts all around. For anyone especially nervous or fearful, being inside the swinging boat would not be the right place to be! The insides finally consisted of screwed and clamped supports, through which one had to push into place. Without the supports, it would have collapsed. We stood sometimes with white lips pressed together, hand clamped around our weapons, at the strongest points, when this 'box' would begin to sway so that it would throw us against posts and beams. The deepest shelters to our left and right, in front of and behind the swinging boat, were knocked around.

The swinging boat even survived the Battle of the Somme - in the middle of October! Dong, dong came the sound. Gas, gas - alarm! From the enemy trenches, they are blowing across a cloud of green-yellow chlorine gas which slowly, and without great effect, draws over us. There are some casualties in the kitchen in the rear, where the people didn't hear the gas alarm and didn't have their gas masks ready.

Inside our position it is getting harder and harder to stand it. We had to carry so many of the dead to the engineer depots because the baggage trains couldn't keep up with the number being killed. During one bombardment on a wet, misty October day, a disconcerted infantryman hastily comes to our bunker. 'Come quickly - our bunker has collapsed.' He himself had been on sentry duty in the moment of the catastrophe. In the third trench-line a double bunker was hit, with both entrances being left hopelessly buried. There's no way to work through the masses of earth jumbled together with bent wooden frames and beams. The only thing that helps is a new angled shaft, with a frame size of .8 meters by 1.2 meters. Entire infantry groups take off to get wood frames - and the engineers bring them along! The position where the rescue work takes place lies under constant artillery fire. At a crazy pace the construction of the angled shaft goes on. Engineers work first with mining frames, and we work afterward to replace the mining frames with a bigger profile frame. Arms are racing, earth is flying and sandbags are filled and distributed - a real human excavator! The medical bunker is repositioned, oxygen apparatuses are brought. Attention, airplanes! - take cover. (That was just what we needed...) Our work tempo is furious; every ten minutes the crews are replaced. Everyone gives it all they've got. In 12 hours we've done it - bring the oxygen apparatus - careful, the last breakthrough. Fast, get belts to haul the people out. Seventeen are dead, five are still alive, but they were almost gone. Most of them suffocated, a few sitting at the crushed entrance.

Among the rescuers, one was killed and four were badly wounded from shellfire while getting the frames." [139]

Chapter 8
The Battle of the Somme, (Part III)
The Last Stand

Beginning November 5 1916, the British launched a seven-day artillery bombardment north of the Ancre that was twice the strength of the one that preceded the July 1 attack. The progression of the bombardment was designed to create tactical surprise, with heavy artillery firing on the German front lines thirty minutes before dawn each morning, combined with an intense, hour-long barrage by field artillery. This tactic intended to lull the Germans into a routine and slow their reactions when the actual attack opened. Lais:

> "We come now to November. The firing on the position intensifies in the early hours and in the evening to a wild drumfire. There is not even a question of rotation. By day and night, we stand at the highest levels of readiness. They don't come, they don't attack, they only fire an unimaginable number of shells from ahead, from the left and the half-right at our positions.
>
> In the first days of November my machine gun is placed in reserve in the notorious and feared communications trench Number Six, the 'L6.' Our bunker lies between the third and fourth trenches, has two entrances with the respectable depth of 52 steps. The bunker also serves as an engineer station and hand grenade depot. L6 is the most hated trench in the sector. It leads from the left of Serre to the hillside of the Heidenkopf ruins. The word trench is, applied to this one, a rhetorical exaggeration in a most euphemistic sense. This pile of rubble, splinters, and uneven surface called the '*Backmulde*,' (baking trough) as it isn't even a trench anymore. The L6 previously was reinforced with shoulder embrasures and partially completed breastworks. It was intended to defend against an eventual breakthrough by the Englishmen from Beaumont or Grandcourt, and serve as a cordoning-off trench for the southern flank of the Serre position, with a field of fire towards Miraumont-Grandcourt.
>
> The 12th of November 1916. Frost is coming. The position is under fire every day. In the morning at 3:00 – 4:00 am, a

regular drumfire beats upon the entire position. Between 7:00 – 8:00 am it suddenly breaks off - a pause in fire - one can even rise above cover - a quiet agreement with the opponent - wounded can be carried back.

10:00 am, everything starts up again. Woe unto him, who after 10:00 am lets themselves be seen above cover. Heavy, interdiction fire continues until late in the night in our sector; creating a barrier to paths and village trails to the rear.

You must go through Puisieux at a run. The narrow pass from Puisieux up to the heights of Serre is a murderous gully. To the left and right of the narrow pass stands German artillery; field pieces up to 38 cm and 150 mm howitzers. These guns cannot be avoided as they pound on and on.

The carcasses of horses and shot up vehicles of all kind litter the approach paths. Here and there are dead infantrymen, artillerymen and transport drivers, who will be brought to the cemeteries around Bapaume in the early morning.

Every morning, around 3 or 4 am, increasing fire becomes concentrated on the infantry positions. Divisional and regimental orders come down: 'It is certainly to be reckoned with that in the next few days we can expect a major offensive. The daily drumfire at exact times is an attempt to wear us down and lull us out of our state of constant preparedness.'

It's raining, it's freezing, and thick, thick November fog builds up. Every day brings losses, ration carriers, signalmen run for their lives every night. The dishes are usually half-empty due to their haste. The first week of November passes by in constant readiness. The second week is already almost half over. When will the opponent attack?'[140]

The IR 169 *Regimental History* described the build up to the attack:

"Since the beginning of November the artillery fire on our entire sector had increased daily. Our position was destroyed to the extent that even our couriers could no longer recognize the trenches. On 9 November, a captured English sergeant reported that an attack was imminent. On 10 and 11 November constant artillery fire began, and on the morning of 13 November, under cover of thick fog, the English attacked anew with very strong force. They desired to seize the heights because they then could easily roll up the entire front north of the Ancre. Precise British attack orders directed those occupying individual positions in the shot-up village Serre: *'Confirm immediately when hidden objectives are reached. After this bombardment, what resistance is still possible? It is altogether certain that the first German trenches are either empty or full of the dead. After the softening-up by artillery, serious resistance is improbable.'* So figured the English leadership. However, at the first signs that an attack might be coming, our companies were at the ready."[141]

The gas attack portion of the artillery plan was designed to inflict maximum casualties. On November 12, the final stages of the artillery fires included a midday gas bombardment to wear down the German defender's respirators, followed by an evening phosgene attack intended to kill.[142] In the minutes just before the attack, an intense machine gun barrage was directed on German machine gun positions. At Zero Hour, a creeping barrage was scheduled to advance forward at 100 yards every five minutes, followed by an hour-long concentration of fire on the enemy rear trenches.[143]

The British units tasked to attack Serre included the 3rd Division's 76th Brigade (two battalions forward and two in reserve) on the far north (left), and all four battalions of the 8th Brigade on the right. The 76th Brigade carried 36 machine guns. The 92nd Brigade (31st Division) supported the southern flank of the 76th Brigade's main effort. [The 92nd Brigade was the same 31st Division unit that attacked Serre on July 1.] The primary 92nd Brigade battalions employed in this attack were the 12th and 13th/East Yorkshire. At midnight, a detachment of the 92nd Brigade, consisting of snipers and Lewis machine gunners, moved out to establish over-watch positions to support the early morning assault.[144] While the Accrington Pals were not involved in the main attack, the battalion did provide two platoons to carry supplies to the 92nd Brigade.

If anything, the challenges facing the British assault force before Serre were even worse than back in July, with a sea of deep mud topped with more densely concentrated barbed wire entanglements."[145]

The main attack kicked off at 5:45 am into a thick fog. Immediately upon entering no-man's-land, many of the Tommies were quickly mired in waist-deep mud. The mud so slowed the advance that the creeping artillery barrage shifted well before the troops neared the German trenches. A handful of British tanks supported the attack, but they all either broke down or were stuck in the mud, rendering them useless. While the fog helped cloak the advance, it also added to the confusion among the British ranks. The shattered, cratered landscape was devoid of landmarks. Many British units became disoriented and lost in the maze of wire, shell craters and trenches.

Lais on the opening of the attack:

"The morning of 13 November breaks - thick, dense fog. Around 4 am the daily drumfire begins - are we fooling ourselves or does it seem heavier than usual? We step out of the bunker entrance and try to orient ourselves. The fire is now only in and around the Serre village, and more to the rear. One can't even see five steps away. Everything is covered with a thick, milk-like fog. The fog seems to swallow up sounds. Ahead, in the first trenches one can hear individual machine gun rat-a-tat tat, and individual rifle shots. Then it is still again. But what is happening now; a new enterprise? After 9:00 am the fog lightens, one can see 10 or 20 steps. In any case, an unpleasant situation, we are, as before, in a certain state of tension and unrest.

The air is smoking and hissing; detonations are far away and can be perceived as a dull rolling; everything is far off in the hinterlands. We anxiously listen in the fog - nothing is happening!

One of the engineers with whom we share the bunker, is gripped by a cramp in his bowels. He runs back about twenty steps in the direction of the valley and sits down in a crater with unbuttoned tunic. All around us it is hissing and whizzing and howling on and on. Hastening back with wide strides, the engineer appears out of the fog and shows a small stripe of blood that runs on the back of his hand - apparently a shot from an infantryman. 'Sergeant, down below there are Englishmen!''Man, who are you kidding, that was just a wild shot, did you see any Englishmen? No. Did you hear a shot, close-up? No.' He insists, there are Englishmen in the valley. I am standing with the engineers in their bunker and call to my crack shot, Mall (from Sollingen) to come over." [146]

Once alerted, the Germans raced to get machine guns in position and riflemen to the firing steps. In many ways, it was a repeat of the July 1 attack. On the far left, a few of the 76th Brigade platoons were able to penetrate the German wire, but received no support when follow-on troops were blasted apart in no-man's-land. Officers attempted to rally men taking cover in shell holes, but it was no use; by 6:30 am the attack faltered.

The British had better results on their right. Under the cover of the fog, a group of British infantry pounced into the lead enemy trenches before the Germans could react. Waves of British troops poured through this breach and made it deep into the Serre inner defenses. A wild trench brawl ensued.

The IR 169 *Regimental History*:

"As soon as the running artillery fire began targeting the rear area, all of our troops poured out of their bunkers. They were not a minute too soon. Already long rows of forms were emerging from the thick fog. There was terrible defensive fire. Both sides exchanged rifle, machine gun and hand grenade salvos. The waves came to a standstill; they banded together and continued the advance. But it was in vain and the attack withered away. Heroic deeds were performed. Our courageous 169ers defended their positions standing and without bothering to seek cover. Gun crews lifted machine guns from out of the trenches, set them up on rims of shell craters, and without the slightest protection, they served their guns as smoothly as if they were at the firing range."

The *Regimental History*, and an article titled "Atmospherics from the Battle of Serre" included this account, credited to Vice-Sergeant-Major Spengler-Hugsweiser, who was awarded the Iron Cross First Class in the action:

"The early morning was pregnant with anticipation. Weird nightmares had terrified us during the night. The fog lurks like a lingering breath; in huge, grey shreds it veils our eyes, which, like daggers, try to see through this milk-colored wall. We are a four man machine gun crew, five meters behind our first trench.

Since daybreak we have experienced hammering running fire from enemy artillery. Suddenly it stops as if it had been cut by a giant knife. Our hearts beat as though they must burst. We know that now they must be coming. But we appear quite calm: one man whistles softly through his teeth; another draws fitfully on his unlit cigarette. I go down into the bunker to make coffee for my brave lads; otherwise they would fall over from exhaustion. The brown mixture was just beginning to boil and my nose twitched in anticipation when someone shrilly screamed my name. With a final glance I see that the coffee is boiling over.

And then I am standing at the machine gun and rush amidst the ghost-like forms that suddenly crop up on all sides. They disappear in the mist, reappear in front of us, to the right and left, and now even behind us! They have overrun the first trenches. But my machine gun does not sweep well in all directions. The forms rushing forward come to a halt and then fall back. But soon they rush forward again, trying to bayonet us. The devil! Right at this instance the action of my machine gun jammed! Already we see the triumphant blaze, the glaring gleam in the bloodshot eyes of the khaki-clad forms rushing upon us. Should we, must we surrender? A real soldier doesn't consider this very long. What do we have our hand grenades for? It is laughable, this inner tranquility that I have! And the joy in seeing how the English tumble down! My people laugh loudly over each one. How these rascals shame themselves, I see them doing it, we with only four men and they with so many. But now the bullets are impacting around us as thick as hail.

I wonder whether I would die straightaway if I were hit. My mind is working feverishly. Countless images appear and disappear. My entire life flashes past as a man presses hand grenades into the palm of my left hand. I draw back and throw, right, left, and straight ahead. Boom! Boom! Boom! Won't they ever run off from us? Or do they just want to wait until we don't have any more grenades? No, suddenly the entire specter disappears into the same mist from which it had emerged. Deep exhaustion sinks over me; I can't even feel my limbs. Sleep, only sleep! These torments since July, and now it's November!

Then - a new danger. The enemy artillery begins to fire with a vengeance. Explosion after explosion, blast after blast. Faster and faster, raging ever more. Now we have to get out and fall back. We jump up, run, fall down, and for a few seconds take cover in newly made shell craters. I touch a piece of shrapnel and burn my fingers. Shrapnel whistles by our ears; my breath is short. No word is spoken. The wide open eyes of my people, a particular movement of the mouth speak clearly. And the race between death and life begins anew. Our breath whistles between clenched teeth. Finally we are safely out of the impact zone and are safe! A genuine miracle. Thank God!"

Lais:

"Mall is an outstanding guy, a mason by trade, he is one of the best and bravest soldiers and will soon be promoted to NCO. 'You come with me,' I call to him; we want to take a look and see what's up. We are both completely convinced that the engineer's wound was a coincidence and that his observation is a complete fantasy. Where would the English come from; we don't hear any rifle fire? We grab for our gas masks and prepare to leave. I will never forget how I turn back to the engineer, with the gas mask canister swinging on its strap around me, and say 'For your Englishmen, this gas mask will be enough.'

Some kind of good omen inspires Mall and I to take a couple of hand grenades that are in the bunker entrance; two in our belt, two in our hands, and we head out to the L6 in the direction of the trenches, at the intersection of the fourth trench - 20 paces within sight. After a few meters something uncertain, something in the air, forces us to be careful. We don't see anything, we don't hear anything other than the deep rolling and spitting of the cannon tubes, and the dull impacts in the rear area.

This fog is vile. We unscrew the security pins of our stick-hand grenades. After 30 meters our way leads around a shot-up breastwork. With one step we are behind the breastwork, Mall pulls me down by my belt, and we both call at the same time 'Take cover.' Simultaneously, our hand grenades fly, in the direction half-right. In the same second the English hand grenades crash around us - twenty steps ahead of us to the right, to the rear of the three first trenches. English flat helmets appear over the edges of the parapet. We miss with our hand grenades, but anyway there is so much cover in the trench, that in a few strides we are back at our gun. Everyone up and out - alarm - to the sandbags - load, pull back the bolt; tack-tack-tack... it whips above the dug-out in front of the gun.

The Englishmen don't dare push ahead, they duck into the dug-out and throw hand grenades. (They later told us, after being taken prisoner, that they had lost every sense of direction because of the thick fog.) Some of us throw hand grenades, three others serve the gun. We throw the sandbag onto cover, one here, one there, and then lay up the gun. 'Man, lower your head!' Raise the head of the gun, draw a bead and pull it through! First fire in the air, then let the gun sink - let loose burst above the dugout. The sharp angle of fire forces the Englishmen to take deep cover. 'Go up and throw hand grenades over.' Fire until the belt is empty - load a new belt!

The same thing is repeated - shoot up the belt! Get a new load of hand grenades! What's up, aren't our hand grenades working anymore? We unscrew the stick and find they haven't even been fused. 'Give me a fuse - put it in!'

Our otherwise, so obedient engineers have been messing around, dawdling. In their carelessness, they have only loaded fuses in one case of the hand grenades that have been placed in the area between the third and fourth trench lines. It was a nightmare, when none of them went off.

In a split-second, we have now armed the hand grenades - attention! The nose of the gun lifts high, sights around as a new belt is inserted. Let it sink. The burst showers the edges of the trenches towards the valley 20 meters away. Six at a time, riflemen and engineers, draw the lanyard of the hand grenades... twenty-one...twenty-two...up onto the firing step and throw - we aren't new at this and throw them in the air, because the Englishmen have too much cover for rifle fire. In the meantime, Mall along the L6 trench, bends around the trench intersection to the fourth trench, and is suddenly standing as a sharp silhouette. A few meters from the next occupied trench, he throws two hand grenades, one after another, in the middle and then jumps down back into his own trench. Boom, Boom. Cries. And they come; hands held high, all injured, two seriously wounded and still lying in the trench. It was a strong assault troop. Kohler, our youngest, has to bandage them. He then sends them down below into the bunker. All around us, other groups of them are still crouching in shell holes. Soldier by soldier, we round them up, the best English assault troops; Royal Scots, who had lost all their orientation in the fog and are quite confused.

They don't surrender all at once; they defend themselves bravely; their fight is lost, meaningless; and they get in each other's way. The machine gun, firing in the closest proximity, completely demoralizes them. They are completely taken over by us, a handful of people (18 machine gun crewmen and 6 engineers), although they are more than ten times our number.[147]

In the meantime the valley wind blows the fog away. We now have a line of sight from 100 to 150 meters and shoot a precisely accurate fire at the individual lines. From the Heidenkopf, from the battalion trenches, the enemy infantry advances and becomes surrounded; they are captured to the last man.

The Englishmen are running loose upon all sides. In addition to us, German grenadiers and the machine gunners at the Heidenkopf are starting to fire. The confusion begins to reign among the Englishmen, who are helplessly caught in pockets. Some try to make their way through and are caught in a crossfire among three machine guns, not ten meters away. In groups of platoons and companies, they lie trapped in shell craters in the ground among the trenches.

But what has happened? In the night between 12 and 13 November the Englishmen brought a great deal of infantry together, and attacked at first light. Some were repulsed at the first trench-line, when they encountered machine guns or alert infantry. Many of the other English attack columns marched forward, unhindered and unseen, in thick fog through our lines. They came left and right of the Mailly-Serre street, they came over the Heidenkopf, the Lion's Back, by way of Beaumont, Grandcourt, Beaucourt, through the valley of the river Ancre and landed in our rear, in Serre, between our positions. They lost their bearings and often, in heavy fog, made their way in circles. If hand grenades were thrown at them, they took cover and returned fire.

Entire English platoons and companies marched according to compass direction, and appeared in front of German artillery positions, where they were received with carbines and hand grenades; disappeared into the fog again and penetrated rather deep into our rear areas. We were later told that a complete English company in march-order suddenly appeared out of the fog in the middle of German troops at Achiet Le Grande [five miles from the front]. Alert German companies to the left and right of the village street saw them appear like a mirage, and then disarmed them without a fight.

The focal point of the enemy attack lay between us, sideways from our flank, and behind us, in our rear. The first and second trenches (as far as one could still speak of trenches) were in our possession, and the enemy partially possessed the third trench-line. In the terrain left and right of the Communications Trench 6, in the Ligny low ground southwest of Serre, English assault troops were trapped, and did not know where to go next.

The positions at the outer edge of the Serre Village (which had completely disappeared under all the earthworks), were partially occupied by us, and partially by the Englishmen; who sat at the southern edge of the village. In the interior parts of the village, where our kitchens and supply depots were located, the cooks traded their kitchen implements for hand grenades. The administrative clerks and engineer NCO's blocked the southern entrance to Serre with improvised rolls of explosives and satchel charges connected by a long lanyard *"geballte Ladungen."* This mixture of German, Englishman, Englishman, German on top of one another went on as far as the regimental sector between Serre and Puisieux and up to the artillery positions. The English leadership must have been in a desperate position. They couldn't see anything from over there, there wasn't more than 150 meters' visibility during the day. The English attack columns were swallowed up by the fog. After initial reports of success, they heard nothing more and received no more couriers. We had retaken the first and second trench-lines, and did not allow any more to pass through or to go back. Those of us in Communications Trench 6, and the occupiers of the Heidepot (also known as the Lion's Back) blocked every attempted English breakout. Around midday the English artillery went completely quiet. They had no clue as to the location of their infantry, and didn't know if further barrage would shoot up their own troops." [148]

German NCO's led frantic, localized, small-unit counterattacks. Lais told how British prisoners were collected in the bunkers:

"Our bunker is full of wounded and unwounded Englishmen. Whoever hasn't been caught by us, or shot down, falls into the hands of other German troops who are mopping up. These captured English assault troops are first class material, all the same age as us, 19, 20, 21 years old, but better nourished. Royal Scots - none of them behave pitifully. Their faces are quite unsettled due to their own misadventure. The more heavily wounded, some with two or three machine gun bullet wounds in the thighs or shoulder, don't complain a bit. A very young boy, whose arm has been torn to pieces by a hand grenade and is dangling from the shoulder and swinging back and forth when he moves, moans, but very softly so that one can hardly hear him." [149]

By 1:00 pm, Lais' squad, with assistance from members of the battalion staff and troops from the Heidenkopf, were able to clear the British invaders from the southern portions of the Serre stronghold; the low ground between the Heidenkopf, the L6 and Battalion Staff

Trench. Still, a large number of scattered British troops had established positions in the northern portions, to include the area between the L6 to L5 Communication Trenches and the third and fourth trench-lines. Many of the British troops displayed great tenacity and heroism in the face of overwhelming odds.

Lais on the clearing process:

"To the northwest of our bunker, many English individual soldiers have settled in. In groups of two, three and four at a time, they bravely defend themselves and answer every call to surrender with wild shooting. A Lewis machine gun is there too and it makes things very uncomfortable. We bring our own machine gun into position at the higher trench intersection of L6 and the fourth trench-line. With two belts (500 rounds) we defeat the Lewis gunner. He survives, with five clean shots through his shoulder, hand, and upper thigh. He was still shooting, as his comrade later tells us, even with the shot through the upper thigh. These Englishmen are tough!

We work over the positions right of the L6, exactly as we cleaned out the positions left. Burst of machine gun fire above the sandbags; aimed fire at individual positions. Our position is unfavorable, as the level elevation of the ground results in the MG overshooting the target and forcing our own infantry beyond the third trench line to seek cover.

A courier comes running from there by taking a detour through the second trench-line along to the L6. 'Cease fire immediately;' the infantry from the third trench will assault the occupied positions and we would endanger the advance of our own people by continuing to fire.

"Man, get your head down." Tommies in the position, now unmolested by our MG fire, are no longer forced to keep their heads down." [150]

Lais' friend, Corporal Mall, went into action:

"Mall has taken the war into his own hands. He doesn't at all like how we can't fire due to the coming assault from the third trench. He tucks two hand grenades into his belt, hangs two sandbag sacks full of more grenades around his neck, grabs an engineer's Model 98 rifle, stuffs a few cartridge cases in his pockets, and heads out along the L6 in the direction of the third trench-line. Because the L6 in this sector position is almost level with the ground, Mall creeps on his belly to reach a position within hand grenade range of the enemy. With three or four hand grenades, he opens up a one-man attack on their positions. The grenades barely reach the positions, but their fragments strike the heads of his targets. Fast as lightning, Mall jumps from his cover and takes aim into the enemy's positions with his rifle. He draws a bead, pulls back, and shoots – and then with one stride is back under cover again - all in two seconds. Bullets fly all around him, a finger's breath away.

Mall is possessed by unbelievable cold-bloodedness and shooting accuracy. He creeps a few steps further and repeats the cruel game from another position. Again, someone falls. The Englishmen fire wildly at Mall. The man is so bold, that when he shoots the third shot, he sets his rifle down and raises it again, while standing completely in the open.

When the third Englishman falls onto his face with a bullet wound in the head, the fourth man, and only survivor gives up and comes out, with his hands up, his face ashen grey. He runs over to us at the same time our infantry advances with hand grenades and bayonets.

Detonations - dense smoke, puffing out here and there, in half an hour everything is ready, the Englishmen are dead, wounded, and captured.

Close by, out of a fold in the ground, someone comes hobbling to us, whose calf of his right leg is half taken away by one of our hand grenades. He has tightly bandaged his serious wound. He is a big, handsome chap with the typical English face, and he is entirely unsettled. Mall calls to him, and signals where he should go. It's difficult for the two of them to make themselves understood, because despite his best efforts, the Englishman can hardly understand that unique 'Badish' dialect which is spoken between Durlach and Pforzheim. He hobbles along and hops on one leg with a combination of sheer anger and pain from his wound, confusion about being taken prisoner, and in shock from the hand grenades that were thrown at him just a few minutes ago. He moves like a chicken back and forth. (A tender reader will think 'what a raw compassion for a poor wounded soldier.' The wound wasn't bad enough to touch the heart of our 'front soldier souls' - and besides, the poor lad really did look humorous!).

My good Mall, who didn't have the slightest intention of doing anything harmful to the wounded soldier, loses his patience and curses at the poor Tommy with an unsurpassable vocal effort and gestures frightfully with a stick grenade in the air around him.

The scared Englishman only sees the hand grenade and doesn't see that the pin is still screwed in, so that it is not armed, and in the worst case could only be used as a cudgel. He seems to believe that his last hour has come. With a great leap and the courage of desperation, he jumps on his good leg into Communications Trench 6, and then sees our grinning faces and notices in the tone of our shouts that we did not mean anything by it, and we didn't intend to put the fear of God into him.

Quickly his face changes, he beams and presses our hands (Mall and I are embarrassed and say 'Yeah, that's fine, enough already'), he stammers the few pieces of German that he knows 'gut Kamerad, gut Kamerad,' then he slips on the seat of his pants, protecting himself with his hands and good leg, all the way down the 52 steps of the bunker entrance, and as we from above observe this descent, with one voice all break out in hearty laughter." [151]

By late afternoon, most of the Serre strongpoint was cleared of the British combatants. Tommies trapped in no-man's-land were allowed to surrender and enter the German lines. The German bunkers soon swelled with prisoners, with those still able to walk sent back to the rear. Still as Lais described below, a few die-hard British soldiers continued to fight:

"In the third trench-line, sector to the right, sits an English infantry platoon down below in one of the large shelters with three exits. They aren't surrendering, and answer every call to surrender with wild shooting. Our infantry squads stand above next to the entrances, throw hand grenades in. They must be about to suffocate from the smoke. Still, they shoot at anyone who yells at them. The shelter is sealed off, and we will wait for the next day.

When our last demand to surrender is answered by shooting again, engineers come and demolish the shelter with charges. A shame for the brave lads, but one couldn't allow this 'thorn in our side.'[152]

As in the case of the July 1 battle, would-be British reinforcements were slaughtered or pinned down in no-man's-land; whatever foothold the British may have gained inside the Serre trenches could not be supported. By 5:25 pm, the British realized further efforts were hopeless and ordered a retreat. The fighting continued until 9:30 pm.[153] Lais described the disposition of the many POWs that filled the German trenches:

"In the late evening the English leadership understands that their prepared attack has led to a terrible defeat. A wild artillery fire descends on our sector. Over there, they must really be annoyed. With increasing strength, the fire continues for all of November 14. It is now impossible to bring back a single additional prisoner, never mind the heavily wounded. In the night from 13th to the 14th of November we concern ourselves with the wounded prisoners. Some of them are quite apathetic and have a fever.

The sick Englishmen are packed underneath our blankets and tucked into corners of the bunkers. It is the Englishman with the smashed and hanging right arm that we are most worried about. He's completely exhausted, both physically and mentally. His wound means nothing to him, so he hasn't even bothered to have it bound up properly. The arm has been tucked underneath his shoulder and bound by a leather strap. I cut the strap through, hopefully not too late, and apply pressure to stop the wound from bleeding again. With the help of the medical NCO, I have it bandaged properly. The arm will have to be taken off, and the boy with the dirty wound will be lucky to get through it. So, each of our wounded Tommies are indeed conscientiously taken care of.

In the lower corridor of our bunker, between the wire posts and the niches; the unwounded Englishmen crouch, stand or lean against the wall. The situation takes a comical turn, when one after another of the captives has to answer the call of nature. We can't let any of them go out up above. So, we develop a cycle; from time to time an Englishman, accompanied by one of our good-willed infantrymen or engineers, carries up his waste in a steel helmet.

From the English assault packs, which plentifully lie about, we get the most beautiful foodstuffs. English corned beef, preserved fish, white bread, and marmalade, chocolate; everything is distributed fairly. We only act greedy when it comes to white bread, which is such a rare pleasure for us. The captives get some of our kipper (smoked herring), which tastes very good to them. We are not particularly impressed by the preserved fish. It is supposed to be a delicacy (tuna fish), but our uncomplicated and unspoiled infantry stomachs can only barely remember salted cod, which is a horror and causes a shudder that goes through us. Early on the 15th of November a barrage starts up again. Heavy artillery fire lands all around. We are constantly lying with our nose in the mud. The Englishmen have learned in the Battle on the Somme. There is only a light shooting directed at the Heidenkopf, and still a strong barrage of fire heavily on us.

Despite the black fountains of earth that strikes frightfully near us, we hammer away at figures now silhouetted against the hillside towards the heights of the Heidenkopf. Not just us, from everywhere the machine guns are hammering, twittering, and whipping away. The infantry rifles knock against the hillside and dome of the hill. The attack is breaking up

In the meantime, a section of engineers guard the shelter exits, watching the Englishmen who were taken prisoner on 13 November. They see a glimmer of hope in their eyes. When we come down again and quietly clean our rifles, they look at us cagily.

In the late afternoon of the 15th, the firing at the position lets up, although heavy fires still impact upon the access trenches, particularly around L6. In groups of 10-30 men, prisoners are evacuated through the L6 from the first, second and third trench-lines. They are hot from running, from constantly throwing themselves down, and have a harried look. It's bad for prisoners; it really gets you, to be brought back under constant fire from one's own artillery. We push them along, including the wounded. 'Go - run - trot - whwww! - rack! - take cover!' Behind Serre there is a prisoner transport. Hurrying along, with faces twisted by fear, they run by our reestablished and newly engaged batteries, and cringe at their firing." [154]

The British November 13th attacks had significantly better success to the immediate south of Serre, leaving the Serre defenses as the northernmost shoulder of the entire Somme line. The British attention to the southern portion of the Serre defenses increased. A new German unit, IR 23, took up position in IR 169's left flank. Veteran IR 169 companies were called in to shore up the spine of these inexperienced troops and stabilize Serre's southernmost defenses. The British threatened Serre with another infantry attack in the early morning of November 17, but their attack formations were destroyed by German artillery. Lais:

> "In the night of the 17th the fire increases into an early morning barrage - a spectacle of hell. Our own artillery lands with devastating impact upon the English assault positions. It's a salvation, that since the replacement of the highest Army leadership in August 1916 we now have our own strong artillery. 15cm howitzers fire from the positions around Puisieux, around Bucquoy, from the artillery hollow of Beaucourt, from Erlenbusch at the intersection of Signy hollow - Beaucourt hollow; the heavy mortars at the railway embankment of Miraumont, all fire. Finally it roars and screams and rolls in unheard of strength at the Englishmen. The English attack which began early on the 17th has been halted, our artillery smashes everything to pieces. They can't even get a single attack wave together. The dust and earth raised by the bombardment blocks our vision through the curtain of smoke of the countless explosions." [155]

Since the July 1 attacks, Lais' gun crew had come through countless lose calls without suffering many casualties. Their run of good fortune ended in the final hours of the Somme Campaign:

"Around 4:00 am it is hammering away again at the Heidenkopf. Alarm, everyone out of the bunkers! Bring your rifle into position and load. The position is covered by clouds of smoke and fumes. One can't see into it at all. Our artillery shoots constantly. Mall and I rush to an escarpment and take turns observing through a telescope the Heidenkopf. Everything is covered by the curtain of fire. Suddenly it is blasted open and takes our breath away as the barrage presses us down against the ground of the crater. Slowly clumps of frozen earth clatter back to the ground and hit our backs, strike against our steel helmets.

A direct hit lands between us. Three men are dead. The gun is lying crosswise somewhere. The cooling jacket is ripped open from front to rear. The barrel and tracks are bowed, and the box sides are pressed in and the sight is ripped off. We recover our dead - the English attack isn't further developed. Around 6:00 am the engineers have two casualties - there's an impact on the left entrance that crushes two sentry posts. Ten minutes after that a courier from battalion arrives; as he attempts to take cover in our shelter at the last second he is riddled through with shrapnel, as if he is cut up by a thousand knives and falls dead in pieces.

An hour after that we drag the six dead, these poor bundles of humanity riddled through, with broken and smashed limbs, in tent halves to the engineer depot, to the kitchen shelter, where the wagon stops. After the recent battle of 13 November, in which my crew had no casualties, a heavy hand has taken us. The evening is quiet. Artillery on both sides are still. A general sense of relief settles over the combat sector, the calm before the storm! Then a solitary heavy shell rolls and whooshes deep into the rear area, and thunder breaks upon Achiet, on Ablainzevelle, on Grevillers, on Bapaume; our long tubes smash back on to St. Amand, Spuaftre behind Hebuterne, Bertrancourt, Mailly and so on, and bring death and destruction down on both sides of the nightly columns of artillery and the trains.

We report to the company commander, Lt Karl Winter, on our casualties and are praised by him that we had comported ourselves impeccably. He is an officer whom we love and honor; he is a very sharp, very serious and entirely just superior." [156]

On November 18, after seven consecutive months of holding Serre, IR 169 was finally programmed to turn over the position to relief troops. The relieving troops began arriving the night of November 16-17. There was immediate work to be done, as the L9 communication trench still remained in British hands and needed to be retaken. Two storm troop companies from the newly arriving unit were designated for the attack. When these companies failed to arrive on schedule, IR169 troops, eager to leave, finished the job themselves by storming the L9 after a short hand grenade battle. The balance of the relief battalions arrived at dawn, allowing most of the IR 169 troops to pull out. IR 169's regimental staff, along with a small reserve force, remained behind to ensure the new unit was securely in place.

The sporadic artillery fire turned into an intensive, drum-fire barrage. From the south, rows of distant figures could be seen moving in the heavy fog, but in the confusion of the ongoing transfer activity, it was uncertain who were the friendlies or enemies. At 150 meters, it was finally understood these were British troops, the vanguard of a major enemy ground attack. The attackers stormed deeply into the German lines. The assault was so swift that the lead companies were able to penetrate the Serre Village stronghold and capture one of newly arrived battalion staffs.

The relieving force battalions, manned largely by untested recruits, appeared helpless to stop the British attack. The entire Serre defensive sector was now at great risk of falling. IR 169's withdrawal was reversed and the regiment returned to counterattack. [157]

Lais on the unexpected return to Serre:

"At the same time we were informed that the regiment will be relieved after midnight and in the early hours of 18 November. We can hardly grasp this fortune. We'll be relieved? We will finally get out of this murderous hellhole of Serre! We go back to our bunker and take the ruined gun on our shoulders, put on our assault packs, take the munitions that can be carried and take off to our company commander. We are to go back with him and his company staff.

The night is uniquely quiet; we have wondrous thoughts; perhaps the Englishmen, humiliated through their disasters, have given up their thoughts of the Somme battle, and will stop - wishful thinking! It can hardly be believed, the whole night through there is no shooting.

Around midnight, the first infantry relief comes, and they appreciate the need for a quiet operation. No shovels, no drinking cups, no hand grenades clatter, no word is spoken; quickly and carefully at the same time they enter the positions. If only shooting doesn't start! It's an old, proven western regiment of men, who with just a look at the terrain already know that it's nasty and horrible. The machine gun relief, by platoon and guns, arrives at 2:00 am. Munitions and reserve barrels are exchanged and signed for; the individual company couriers pull out with the relief troops. Tie everything down and make it fast, so nothing will rattle. It is getting foggy.

Orders in a whispered voice, and now there is nothing left to do but to depart the combat positions. Everything works perfectly.

These new troops who have already been dragged through the hell of Verdun and Peronne know what to expect. When the company commander of the replacing machine gun company still hasn't arrived by 5 am, Lt. Winter orders us out: 'Off with you, children, and beat it, it won't stay quiet here for long.'

We want to take the ruin of our gun with us, but Lt. Winter orders we leave it in the bunker. 'That's junk' he says; he himself will submit a report on the missing gun. (In 1916, a report still had to be filled out for every single missing machine gun of the type 08/14, and describe how it was lost.)

We shouldn't see our brave Lt. Winter again. In the thick fog, ten to twenty steps visibility, we head out, direction Serre, Puisieux and then Achiet.

We don't get far. Just as we reached the supply depot of the former field railway stop, explosions go off into a half-crushed bunker! With all calibers they're pounding away on the heights of Serre. This is a real fix. In the middle of the relief - our poor infantry companies and crews, who are now on the way to the rear, have to go back again. Infantry troops and companies, who were involved in the relief and were supposed to assemble by Puisieux, are halted by fire and seek shelter in the bunker around us in the Serre cordon. One comes running: "The Englishmen have gotten through!"

Damn, that we have no more machine gun. Out of the hole, over to the southwest hill of Serre! Infantry, engineers, relieved artillery observers and so on all behind Serre, surprised by fire and who sought cover, are running, racing through the impacting shell strikes, through splinters of stone flying all around, through smoke and dust clouds, past the whistling shell splinters, and back into Serre." [158]

British infantry, under the cover of a thick fog, infiltrated Serre's southern defenses and took possession of a battalion command bunker. Now devoid of their ruined machine gun, Lais' men returned to Serre and joined the counterattack armed with pistols, grenades, spades and axes.

"Mall has a big pioneer axe. In a grisly close combat, the Englishmen are wiped out and flee in the direction of the Heidenkopf. Fleeing is the only expression for their retreat to the Heidenkopf. The Englishmen could not stand up to this counterattack, carried out by us in cold blood, without orders, originated by us alone." [159]

The retreating British tried to evacuate the German prisoners they had taken during their brief hold in Serre. The attacking Germans killed a number of the British guards and rescued most of the prisoners. The well-respected Lt Winter was killed in the final efforts to regain control of the last of the Serre defenses. German losses in the counterattack were heavy.

Lais and his squad finally exited Serre and, upon reaching Achiet, learned of another complication. With Lt. Winter now dead, there was no proof of his order to leave the ruined gun behind. Lais and Mall had to return to Serre once again to try to retrieve the machine gun:

"Mall and I look at each other without saying a word, stick our caps in our pockets, put our steel helmets back on, and join up with an artillery munitions convoy traveling from Achiet le Petit to the narrow pass in Puisieux. There, we run for our life down the street through Serre again. The gun is still there in the bunker of our fallen company commander, in the same corner in which we had placed it. After midnight we reached Achiet again and brought proof, that our gun really had been destroyed. The armorer examines the weapon; aside from a few bolts and rods it's entirely unusable. The weapon is thrown onto the junk heap.

A MG squad commander who had lost his weapon through his own fault or through dishonor would be brought in front of a court martial. A heavy machine gun was as holy a thing with us as if it was the regimental flag."

Lt. Otto Winter, the younger brother our fallen company commander, temporarily took command of the machine gun company. [Otto Winter was killed in early 1917.]" [160]

One of the great honors a German military unit could receive was recognition from the senior command in the form of special orders or through mention in dispatches. The following two documents, taken from the *Regimental History*, cited the 52nd Division and IR 169 for its service in the Somme:

On 18 November, 1916, the Army senior command issued the following order to commend the service of the 52nd Infantry Division:

"After heavy fighting the courageous 52nd Infantry Division left the positions that they have watchfully guarded since they were created. Here, between Gommecourt and Serre, the young division earned its first laurels. During the accompanying months of calm during the stationary war, officers and men produced results through their creativity and ingenuity. Model emplacements arose, and in them men were transformed into heroes who, in the heated fighting during the battle of the Somme, neither wavered nor weakened. Loyal to the death, the brave troops held their emplacements and the Division remained in full possession of their old position.

With pride the Division can leave the battlefield it so victoriously held and with pride it can look back on its deeds of arms.

I ask that my warmest thanks be conveyed to all members. As a token of my inestimable recognition, I award to the Division in appreciation for its outstanding service five Iron Crosses First Class, and 200 Iron Crosses Second Class."

The Supreme Commander
Signed: Von Below"

In one additional honor was the regiment being mentioned in official dispatches:

Western Theatre of the War (November 1916 Dispatch)
Front of Crown Prince Rupprecht of Bavaria

"The battle north of the Somme continues. The constant, ongoing combat won a place in the major events of the war on 14 November.

Hoping to exploit their initial success, the English attacked once again with strong weapons north of the Ancre and several times between Le Sars and Guendecourt. Although they were able to capture the village Beaucourt, at all other points along the broad attack's front, the force of their attack collapsed with many losses before our positions. Units that particularly distinguished themselves in defending against the enemy attack include the Magdeburger Infantry Regiment 65, the Baden Infantry Regiment 169, and the regiments of the 4th Guards Infantry Division." [161]

Serre was the only German position held throughout the three-day battle for the Ancre. At an enormous cost in men, the Germans were pushed out of St. Pierre Divion, Beaucourt and Beaumont-Hamel. With the coming of winter, General Haig, the British commander, recognized the folly of continuing further attacks. The 1916 British offensive of the Somme was officially declared over. [162]

From the period of November 11-24, the British 5th Army, which did most of the attacking at the Ancre, took 23,274 casualties.[163] In front of Serre, the British 3rd Division reported losing 2,400.[164] The German toll for the Ancre fighting were also high. Between 1-18 November, the British 5th Army reported total German losses of over

45,000 men, with 7,183 of these being prisoners. From July 20 - November 18, IR 169 lost 11 officers (4 killed) and 907 enlisted men.

The Battle of the Somme, which spanned July 1 – November 18, 1916, stands today as one the bloodiest battles in modern history. In the course of these five months, the Allies committed 99 divisions (51 British and 48 French) against 50 German divisions. Records show the Allies suffered 623,907 casualties (419,653 British and 204,253 French), with 146,431 of these being killed. German figures are more difficult to ascertain, but it is estimated their losses stood at over 465,000 men, with 164,000 being killed.[165] IR 169 contributed a large proportion of its ranks to this roll. From May 1915 – November 1916, IR 169 served in the trenches of the Somme for 18 consecutive months. IR 169's total losses in the Somme were 84 officers (18 killed) and 2,474 men.

Jack Sheldon, closes his book *The German Army on the Somme* with this passage from a poem written by a German veteran of the battle:

> "Homeland, dear beloved homeland, whenever you see a fighter who was there at the Somme, bow low to the ground, because you simply do not know what he did for you." [166]

Chapter 9
"This Terrible Bench"
Serre, December 1916 and Altkirch, Early 1917

On November 19, 1916, IR 169 finally pulled out of Serre. After spending 18 months in the trenches of the Somme, and virtually 28 months of continuous combat, this would be IR 169's first opportunity for a real refit and rest. The regiment traveled by way of Ervillers, 15 miles east of Serre, where they had a short but emotional reunion with the British prisoners they captured in Serre on November 13. Continuing on, the regiment halted in a rest area outside the city of Cambrai, 18 miles east of Bapaume. [In November of 1917, Cambrai would join the annals of the great World War I battles, when a British, tank-led offensive temporarily pushed German lines back a distance of several miles. In late November 1916 however, Cambrai remained a quiet, rear area.]

On November 21, Major von der Becke-Kluechssner was named as the IR 169 commander. During this period, the regiment's depleted personnel table was back-filled by reserve troops. The regiment conducted individual, unit and physical fitness training and took part in a 52nd Division review before Crown Prince Rupprecht.

One month later the regiment returned back to Serre to reinforce the 14th Bavarian Infantry Division. This brief campaign was known, quite appropriately, as the 'Mud Offensive.'[167] Lais:

> "At last we are relieved from the five months' battle on the Somme. Our seriously depleted companies assemble behind Achiet le Grand by Ervillers. On the way, the vehicles of the machine gun company rattle over the rough cobblestones of Gommiecourt. We stop at a collection point for lightly wounded. The drivers water the horses and the riflemen get hot coffee from the field kitchen. We sit on the wagons, on the towing shaft, on the low wall around the church, drink, eat, smoke, and are liberated, relaxed, and far away from the blaze, from the droning and shelling noises on the heights. We face in the direction of Cambrai - the rear area!
>
> At the open window of the aid station, two men are standing and waving their arms like crazy. Man, those are the Englishmen! One of them has a bandage on his arm, the other

supports himself with a stick. Hello, hello, they call with English accent. 'Hallo'! All kinds of troops are bivouacked here; everyone is astounded at these foolish Tommies. 'Hallo - our comrade machine gunners' - they try it in French.

Finally I figure it out. Those are the wounded Tommies who we interred in the L6 Trench. I quickly call my machine gun crew together, and we go over to the window. The Tommies are thrilled to run into us here. A lively discussion arises. English, German, French are all mixed up on both sides in order to make one understood. One of them is the Englishman who had lost half his calf. The entire company, the entire aid station and half of Gommiecourt look around and curiously take part in this reunion of former opponents. One trades the most improbable souvenirs, from a pence to a *zehner* [ten pfennig piece], from a pocket knife to a sewing kit, from the beautiful Royal Scots cockade to uniform buttons - one wouldn't have dared to do this at the front. People are writing their home addresses and promising to write after the war. The canteen at the church has cigarettes and chocolate - the Tommies get their tunics stuffed full. This encounter, far from the shooting, is somewhat touching. 'Fall in!' The company marches on. The Tommy with the half calf takes my hand with both hands and presses it to his throat. As long as they can see us, they wave from the window.

We arrive at the rest quarters in the villages and settlements around Cambrai. All kinds of rumors are running through the company. We are supposed to be sent to Russia or even Serbia. There is just one hope above all - just away from the Western Front, away from the Somme battle, to see something else and to be able to participate in a war of mobility. The middle of December comes. The companies are filled up; we perform field exercises, practice at firing ranges, and in measure, recuperate.

Among our assumptions and desires, in all the rumors and gossip that fill the air, suddenly an order strikes like a bolt of lightning: 'The Regiment will again occupy the battle sector Serre over Christmas.'[168]

This was the German Army's third winter in the Somme. Just as in the experiences of 1914 and 1915, the heavy rains turned the chalky soil into large fields of impregnable mud. Trenches and bunkers became impossible to maintain and the simple act of walking with heavy equipment was an ordeal. Lais told of his machine gun section's struggle to reoccupy the Serre position:

"It's raining cats and dogs and all roads are soft. The combat baggage and the MG vehicles remain at the rear and we are brought forward in cargo trucks. The guns are removed from their wagons; we have auxiliary carriages with us. It's impossible to use a sandbag as firing support for the gun in this weather. Everything is mud. We run and make haste again through Puisieux, which is under heavy fire, and arrive before midnight, damp with the exertions, steaming and trembling from sweat, cold, and the damp. The night is pitch black, rain is lashing us in the face, streams run off our steel helmets. Not a soul is there to lead us to the positions; apparently they have all taken off during a pause in the fire. Our orders are: MG position, third trench-line. It's pouring, and to our luck, the English artillery fires only occasionally. We know the position like our vest pockets, and orient ourselves on the location of the kitchen bunker, and have a clear picture in our inner eye; we take off into the darkness.

My loyal Corporal Pfefferle (who in 1918 will also become one of my reliable platoon leaders), alternates with me in carrying the heavy gun, which is stored on the auxiliary carriage.

The crew drags the heavy double munitions cases. Every soldier carries two cases, almost 90 pounds, as well as an assault pack. Bent over, silent, freezing from the cold, we put one foot in front of the other. We have a tough path; soaked through clay, mud, and sludge. Not a trace of a trench, everything has fallen apart in the constant rain, all around gigantic craters filled to the top with water. Pitch black night! We sink in up to our joints. The tough clay of the Artois holds our feet fast. Every individual step is a battle with the tough clay. Our legs and our feet become broad, unformed clumps of earth. Some are already going barefoot. The clay sucks off their boots. I myself have wound puttees around my boots and even inside the boots between the sole and mud. After half an hour I am walking with my heel in the tube of the boot, since the tough clay is pulling so strongly. After futile attempts to get my foot completely in the boot, I try to unwind the puttees, but can't find the beginning or the end, so I pull out my knife and cut through it. I pull off the boots, tie them together, and throw them over my shoulder. Almost all of us are barefoot.

'Attention, wire!' We sink in up to our knees, up to our bellies, and help each other get out. One falls into the darkness of a gigantic crater, and is saved in the last moment from drowning - two munitions cases and his assault pack are gone; we are deadly tired.

Rain pours down; we can't see anything. The English appear to have sniffed out the relief and fire nervously. Fortunately, flares can't climb high in this cloudburst of rain. It's out of the question to take cover, we need seconds to pull our legs out of the mud. Fortunately the shells bury themselves deep into the mash of clay and rainwater, which minimizes the effects of the shrapnel. And for that, fountains of mud splashed down upon us.

The usual, covered path from Serre to our combat positions takes 25 minutes. We have been lost for two hours in the pitch black gloom and have lost all orientation. We call to groups, who wander around just as lost and call out to us. Suddenly the Englishmen start up a wild machine gun fire. Flares are fired, but don't get far in the streaming rain. Lost groups of our infantry and machine gun crews pass through our lines and go further -- anything like wire entanglements are long since gone. They land in front of the English positions and call out 'Hello!... Which company?' As an answer they get hand grenades thrown at them. 'Back, go back!'

After 2:00 am we step from the mud onto a chalk outcropping. Our sense of direction has succeeded. We are at the Heidenkopf, in the forward left sector, all the way forward. But our assigned fighting bunker is in the extreme right sector, in the former third trench-line. Nothing to be done, we have to go back to Serre. Pfefferle, the strongest and toughest among us, starts sliding and sinks in up to his knees, and loses his balance due to the heavy gun, and stumbles. It is a strange, improbable fall. The viscous clay holds tight to his feet, so he slowly topples forward, arms outstretched with the gun, so it won't get dirty.

Quietly stumbling forward we proceed with the compass back to the village area of Serre. We rest for a quarter hour, sitting on wire spools that are lying around and nod off a bit.Further! Now, back again to the third trench-line, 20 minutes distance at most. We head out and have the sensation that our direction is just a bit off. We don't want to go back - infantry sentinels, which we bump up against in the dark, have no idea, or are just too tired to react to our questions.

It's 5:00 am, and since midnight we have been wandering through the sector, and we've been on our feet since 9:00 am the previous morning. In the certain instinct, that we can't go further straight ahead, we stop at a chalk overhang. We don't even care that it's oriented towards the enemy. We don't have shelter there, but at least we're out of the mud and slime. Freezing cold; we lay the gun and the sack with the replacement parts, over our knees, throw some munitions boxes together and wait for dawn. Between 7-8:00 am the sky lightens. Now we have to be ready, before our opponent has visibility to our location.

Pfefferle, in order to orient himself, goes a few steps back and comes back beaming; it can hardly be believed; we sat two hours in the cold night, ten steps away from our bunker. The overhang was the last remnant of a former line of the third trench-line; the bunker, our fighting position, is the 'much loved' Swinging Boat. No one of the troop which is to be relieved is to be seen; they must have taken off at midnight. Ten minutes later our company commander arrives, who was smart enough to wait out the night in Serre after he and his courier got lost. We share the bunker with him. The bunker is under water. There's no rest, two men have to stand guard, we have to screw on the sights for the gun, prepare the box covers, the locking mechanism, oil the charging mechanism - the gun is ready for action.[169]

Everyone else bails water, starting with the company commander, down to the MG commander and the lowest MG private. In two hours of hard work we have the water bailed out. The pickets are relieved; two others go out, from the same group of people who have this horrible night and exhausting work behind them - infantry existence, trench swine, as the infantry ironically call themselves! We warm up the tea with schnapps which we brought with us in canteens; that does a body good! The troops relax in their wet clothes on benches in the shelter.

In the meantime the company commander and MG platoon commander relieve the pickets so they can get something hot to drink also. Just a few meters from us, close to the bunker entrance, is a gigantic shell crater full of water, almost a small pond.

Towards 6:00 pm, the 'evening prayers' come from the other side. A barrage from just behind the battle area hits the side of the crater towards our bunker, so that the contents of the crater pour into our bunker. A flood of water shoots in, and we are standing up to our bellies in water. We bail away the whole night; sentry duty, bailing, and digging. During the night we direct the rest of the crater water towards the falling ground off to the right. Caked with mud, soaking wet, steaming from sweat, we are finally finished with the work towards morning, and go down into the bunker where we drink cups of schnapps and caraway, and then throw ourselves down on the benches. 'Relieve the sentries' comes the command from above.

Inside the bunker, the air is dreadful. We warm ourselves at a peculiar oven. In a corner of the bunker we found a whole depot's worth of big cans of rifle grease; lots of bottles, and two-liter cans of machine gun oil, a magnificent find. We pour the oil into a flat bowl, throw a handful of cleaning wads onto it, and light it. One of the soldiers always performs 'oven duty;' he has to keep it filled with oil, or throw on small chunks of gun lubricant. It smokes, it gives off soot, it stinks; our wet uniforms, which hang on posts, and despite having shelter halves hung around them, stay wet and have to dry off while on our bodies. But at least it's warm down below.

Outside it pours rain, day-after-day.

Our bunker is once again flooded; we bail endlessly. Every shell, which comes screaming in, whether with a high-pitched

'Huiiii!' or a heavy rolling sound, buries itself in the ground, throwing up a geyser of mud. The machine gun, which has to be ready for action above, constantly has to be cleaned of slime. In this hole of water and slime, we celebrate a dreary Christmas Eve." [170]

Despite the implausibility of any type of offensive action through the deep mud, a British commander orders a futile attack. Lais:

"Outside something is up again; we fire light flares; is it an operation? Tack-tack-tack-tack we fire; aiming at the wire obstacles of the English and on to Sector 7. We have hardly fired a minute, when the English battery positions around us throw mud and slime into our faces. Angry, we fire yellow light flares into the air, a signal for our counter battery fire. Promptly our artillery responds. Our Christmas Eve is spoiled (below we have a harmonica and a 15 cm tall fake "Christmas Tree"). We are on constant readiness.

On the day of the Christmas celebration, a barrage fire begins at 2:00 pm. 'Call in the sentries - Gun below into the bunker.' Individual sentries are placed out into the hell for observation - are relieved every 10 minutes. At 4:00 am the sentry is blown into atoms by a direct hit. An NCO and company commander are lying outside in the mud and are observing with their field glasses. 4:30 pm! It's getting hard to see – damn, and it's half dark! The experienced gunner, Corporal Pfefferle, throws himself next to us – "Alarm, out!" Half-right before us, out of Hebuterne, they are attacking, no lines, just thin rows of riflemen. Load the MG, charge the bolt. Some loose cartridges on the base of the bolt block the return by the spring. Haul it out! Man, just get your fingers out of there! A piece of clay in the inner receiver and we have a new blockage. Load...tack-tack-tack-tack... Damn!

I have thick clumps of clay deep on my nose and mouth, over the gun sight. It's even worse for the gunner, Corporal Pfefferle. He is bleeding from his nose and mouth; a thick clump of clay smashed the heavy gun into his face. A shell impacts and creates a new blockage! The gun is hopelessly filthy. Two men take the gun away, and everyone else stands ready with hand grenades. But we didn't need to get that far!

The Englishmen, after going down into the hollow between Serre and Hebuterne, first sink in up to their knees, and then up to their bellies; the sticky clay is holding them fast. They have ended up in the worst possible marsh and mud hole. Painfully they have to work their way out. Their rifles, which they have laid down to push against them to get out, are lumps of clay. No attack more to speak of, just the obvious thought: How do I get out of this sauce? Our rifles are ready to fire, but we don't fire any more. It is too unpleasant, to shoot at this miserable and lost opponent. The infantry all around us feel the same way. And besides, the rifles of our infantry are so dirty that they can only fight for close combat with the stocks.

A comic from the infantry takes a small white piece of tin, and fixes it to his rifle, and waves the Englishmen off. Just exactly like that well-known signal from our firing ranges - you missed!

For the most part without their rifles (which are sunk in the mud), the Englishmen disappear in the direction of the English trenches. Not one shot is taken at this miserable retreat.

It gets dark. The last English attack has been choked in mud and slime.

It is a small demonstration of a less pleasant aspect for the English of the greatest of all battles, the Battle of the Somme, on the Ancre.

The land, torn by millions and millions more of shells, earth plowed over, catacombs of human victims, unimaginable waste of material, waste of hundreds of regiments on both sides, every step of earth drowned and fertilized in blood of the bloom of three nations, and everything ossified/congealed, choked on mud, flooded in the cruel morass of this last December day of the year 1916.

It's still raining; hour-after-hour we sit at our smoking and sooty oil flame, drying and warming us. The opposing fire stops and goes to sleep." [171]

The regiment's Christmas-time occupation of the Serre defenses was mercifully brief. On New Year's eve, IR 169 was finally allowed to pull out of Serre for good and transported by train to a rest area in Bouchain, another 20 miles northeast past Cambrai. Lais:

"Three days before New Year's it finally started to freeze. In the night from the 30th to the 31st December we were relieved. It became a bit warmer, with a strong fog, but the ground was still somewhat frozen. We assembled ourselves by platoon left and right of the street Serre - Puissieux. In a half hour we were there.

2:00 am! We are the first to arrive, and wait and sit down on the tree trunks which were collected and piled around the pioneer depot. The position is deathly quiet, there's no shooting at all. We nap a bit while crouched over. Around 3:00 am the other platoons arrive, by and by. The night becomes clearer, the fog lifts, and it is freezing again. Our platoon leader wants to sit down next to me, so he takes a sharp look at the tree trunks in the darkness, and grabs my arm. 'Men, for God's sake stand up and look at that.'

We weren't sitting on tree trunks; we sat on fallen comrades whose bodies had been piled up and laid in rows. The dead are smeared with mud and clay and had frozen stiff onto one another during the last two days. This is the body collection point; with dead comrades of our own regiment from the hard November fighting; dead comrades of successive regiments; probably dead Englishmen there as well. They are all equal, no more recognizable with centimeters of clay covering them, practically already 'dust to dust.' The image seemed like winter timber clearing in a beech forest. The wagons, which were to have brought the fallen to the rear to the soldiers' cemetery, are lying smashed in Puisieux, shot up and ruined on the street and on the narrow pass to Serre.

Regiments come, regiments go. Forgotten - unknown soldiers. We machine gunners, who have already set much death and distress in front of our guns, we rise above this terrible bench of rest and tentatively step out along the path carved out between the craters, which once, and on the maps of the General Staff, is called Puisieux-Serre-Mailly.

This image, a memento for us, we suppress out of our consciousness. It is not good, when an infantryman begins to think, as we are still young and our nerves aren't used up yet. In the early morning of the New Year's Eve 1916, we arrive by way of Bucquoy, where we are picked up by transport trucks and taken to St. Leger.

There, they have lit a big fire of chopped wood on the cement floor of a large warehouse. Smoke escapes through the holes in the roof. We push our way to the fire and dry out our wet clothes and gear, which has frozen on to our bodies. Our front sides are baking and our backs are freezing - turn around! Now our backs are backing and our other sides are shivering.Gradually we are almost even dry. But man! How we look! Even for St. Leger, which is used to everything, we are quite a spectacle. Our uniforms, practically impregnated with yellow clay, don't even look a trace of field gray anymore.

After this fast drying process we appear in a light ochre yellow, through which one can see an occasional glimpse of gray green. Our faces are covered with a thick, greasy, black gray soot, which can hardly be scrubbed off. (The effect of our genius rifle grease oven.) With our black faces, our clay covered uniforms and our filthy dark olive green steel helmets we look like English black colonials! The medical company takes good care of us. There's lots of hot, sweet coffee and we can eat as much as we want.

In the dry cold of New Year's morning, just finished roasting ourselves in the warming hall, we travel with the field railway, into the open lower Loren, in the direction Cambrai towards Bouchain, a French little town in the country. In a bit more than an hour's rail travel when we arrive at the place.

Our good first sergeant, who has been instructed by the company bicyclist (messenger) about our condition, in his role as the "mother of the company" - in the best meaning of the word - has taken care of everything. Washing, soap, replacement trousers and drill uniforms are all ready. The drivers help out. In the quarters are buckets and pails with warm and hot water. Our appearance is a sensation for Bouchain. Our rear area troops are astounded to see us. The civil population knocks their hands together over their heads at our appearance. Whether it's 'quel malheux la guerre - oh ces pauvres garcons,' and even though they are fanatic French patriots, they helpfully take our frozen boys. They loan us wood slippers, warm underclothes and such things, so that we can get out of our trench gear as quickly as possible. Madame Fleurn from Estaminet in the Rue d'aigle, sends douze cafes au vert, 12 hot, steaming, pleasant-smelling glasses with raven-black, sugar sweet coffee next door to our quarters.

In the afternoon of New Year's Day 1916 we are wearing the most unbelievable getup, for example two pairs of underwear, civilian vest, wood slippers and caps of 'monsieur', and stand at the canal of Bouchain and busily swill our gear and our clothes around in the canal, until the mud of the Battle of the Somme darkens the dark winter water of the canal and turns it the color of clay.

On the threshold of the year 1916 we learn that the regiment's baggage was picked up at Fourage for a longer rail transport. The company breathes a sigh of relief and we are relaxed.

Around midnight there is a whistling and roaring, and the air explodes. We empty out the clip of our pistols and the infantry fire one clip after another in the air, which lights up red, yellow, green and white one after another. All the flares available on the front line are fired up. Hand grenades are exploding all around the canal. Somewhere a machine gun is firing against the embankment of the canal.

We are crazy with joy, with happiness, that our transport away is assured. Adieu Serre, adieu Heidenkopf, goodbye to the Battle of the Somme, to this craziness of a materiel war of attrition in the morass - may we never see you again!

This would not be the last of the Somme for IR 169. To foreshadow events that would occur in the summer of 1918, Lais hints: "Twenty months later the ground of the battlefield of Somme and Ancre drank the blood of our regiments again." [172] Serre remained in German hands through February 20, 1917 when it was abandoned in a prelude to the German reconsolidation to the newly established Hindenburg Line. In the Somme sector where IR 169 was engaged the lines shifted east, between Bapaume and Cambrai.

After departing the Somme battlefield, IR 169 returned to their comfortable Bouchain quarters and resumed their recovery from January 1 – 12, 1917. The next assignment returned IR 169 to familiar grounds closer to their Baden home; the Alsace, and the very southern portion of the Western Front.

On January 13, the 52nd Division boarded trains for a 300 mile trip that took them past Trier and Strasbourg and to the southern outskirts of Mulhouse, the site of their August 1914 baptism of fire. The regiment detrained at the village of Landser, just beyond the Rixheim battlefield of 1914, for a 13-mile hike to the front lines at the town of Altkirch, only 12 miles from the junction of the French/German/Swiss border. The front lines here had remained, more or less, in the same location since September 1914. Altkirch's origin dated back to a 13th Century fortress. The center of this picturesque town was dominated by the 19th Century Church of Notre-Dame de l'Assomption, which sits atop a steep hill mass. The French border was eight miles west. The French Army evacuated the civil population in early 1915 before the lines stabilized to its current configuration, leaving Altkirch under German possession.

IR 169's march brought them into Altkirch after nightfall. Lais wrote of how the men were left wheezing at the exhaustingly steep climb up the winding town roads to the church plaza. In the darkness, it appeared that the town seemed remarkably intact despite its close proximity to the front. This point was further confirmed when an illumination round revealed front trenchlines that stood only 1200 meters distant. After becoming numb to the urban destruction that typified other forward areas, the men were left amazed at the absence of damage. This new posting further boded well when the troops were assigned billets inside the town, with the 2nd MG Company spending their first night in a school house.

IR 169's new area of responsibility was a three-mile sector of line centered in Altkirch, with the left flank anchored at the village of Carspach and the northern sector at Aspach. French lines were dug in 600 meters to the west. The regiment was replacing a German reserve unit. Some of the 2nd Battalion men received an orientation from an older Landstrum soldier as they took over trenches west of Carspach. The 169 men marveled at the comfortable qualities of the trench and its spacious bunkers. The boarded trench floor were swept clean on a daily basis. Bunkers were covered with 1.5 meters of earth and machine gun bunkers and artillery observation posts were made of concrete. The Lanstrumer warned the 169 troops 'not to provoke the French,' as his unit had not experienced any casualties for months. Indeed, conditions were such that German regimental bands entertained the soldiers in Sunday morning concerts from the Altkirch church plaza. The IR 169 troops needed little further encouragement to sustain the peace, for after the hell of the Somme they were more than content to preserve the sense of tranquility.

Lais described this situation as 'trench paradise' and how the men felt like they were on top of the world. Unseasonably warm weather suggested that an early spring might arrive. The regiment continued to rebuild and the ranks swelled with new recruits – Baden men who came from IR 169's garrison induction and training pipelines in Lahr and Villingen. The occasional shots that rang between the French and German trenchlines usually meant that a rabbit or bird was targeted for a frying pan. Rather than run for cover, many of the troop nosed their heads over the parapets to see what prey had been scored. In one of the early days in the trenches, Lais wrote how a bored German corporal noticed a hawk flying overhead and took a lucky shot, plummeting the bird into no-man's-land. Cheers erupted from the French trenches as they applauded the German's marksmanship. Later that night, a patrol of Germans ventured out of the trenches and came back to roast the bird without further incident. Lais summarized, "The idea of shooting another human being came from neither side."

The peace before Altkirch was not to last. Strategic miscalculations at by both German and French high commands set into motion events that disrupted the laisse-fare mindset of field commanders in the southern Alsace. In early 1917, German intelligence picked up on rumors that the Swiss would be joining the Allies in declaring war against Germany. If true, a Swiss invasion against the thin German defenses along the southwestern border would pose an existential threat. As a precaution, the Germans began to mass troops by Fortress Istein, above Mulhouse. The French became aware of this buildup, which they mistook as a sign of a coming German offensive. The resulting increase of French activity led the Germans to believe a French offensive was forming to attack Mulhouse. Altkirch, just as it did in August 1914, stood in the middle of a French avenue of advance. All of spelled an end to the period of 'trench paradise.'

The first sign of trouble came not long after IR 169's arrival in Altkirch. One evening, a great deal of noise from came from the French trenches. The sound of marching troops, rattling of equipment and truck engines made it clear that the placid French reservists were being replaced with new units. A German artillery battery located at the Monastery of St Morand, fired a salvo of harassing rounds towards the French lines. Artillery fire echoed through valley as the French replied with a barrage three-times the power of the German shelling.

The artillery contest continued the following days. The Altkirch plaza, recently the site of concerts, was now under a steady rain of exploding shrapnel. At Carspach, troubling signs were visible with the observation a new French sap trench being constructed. Soon, the sap trench extended 300 meters into the no-man's-land, half the distance between the two lines. A German reconnaissance patrol, led by Master Sergeant Spies, took up position in a reedy marsh beyond the German trenches. Spies, whose future wartime exploits are told by Lais in coming pages, was the regiment's preeminent small-unit combat leader. Lais, as well as the rest of the regiment, held Spies in deep regard. Lais recorded these memories:

> "Spies, our most successful patrol leader, was a physically small, amiable and very modest man. In civil life, he was a baker, and came to the unit as a reservist replacement. He quickly rose through the ranks to NCO, warrant officer and eventually Leutnant, and was highly respected by his men. He was awarded with the Baden Gold Order for Gallantry, a highly prized medal that came with a lifetime annuity. There were hardly more than 20 awarded of these in the entire war." [173]

Spies and his men lay undetected in the reeds for two days, carefully watching the French pioneers at work and formulating plans for a trench raid to gather some intelligence.

The attack was set for late on the following evening. White clouds covered the moon, making for a dark night. Spies guided a raiding party into a position close to the sap trench. Earlier that day, Lais laid his squad's machine gun into a position perfectly situated to fire into the trench. The firing of the machine gun would initiate the attack, timed to begin at a predetermined hour. Lais anxiously glimpsed at the luminous dial of his watch, waiting for the exact moment to pull the trigger. He recalled the evening being dead-still, except for the faint noise of the French pioneers digging inside the targeted trench. Finally, Lais' watch marked zero hour, and his machine gun thundered as a full belt was fired into the sap. The ceasing of the machine gun burst was the signal for the raiding party's attack. In seconds, Spies' squad leaped into the sap trench and set into the stunned defenders. Moments later, Lais heard the labored breathing of the raiders returning back to the German trench with a collection of French prisoners.

Some of the prisoners were demoralized but otherwise intact, others were grievously wounded and close to death. Spies hurried the unwounded prisoners back to regimental headquarters for immediate interrogation while the wounded were treated by German medics. Lais, who saw more than his share of death in the course of the war, was moved by the passing of one particular French soldier:

"We carefully placed the injured French pioneer from our arms and onto the firing platform. The medic examined his body for wounds. He pulled some debris from one of the wounds and looked up at me, saying "hopeless." The signs of death were clear in the face of this French soldier. He pleaded at me with his large, fearful eyes. I took his hand as he moaned. The life goes from him as his eyes gaze in death. "Out" says the medic in a matter of fact voice, as he closes the eyelids shut. A young soldier who recently arrived from our home garrison watches this pensively, it is the first time he has seen a soldier die. …The moon comes from behind the clouds. The rest of the French dead are laid out on a path towards the rear. The gentle light of the stars flow over the fine, still French faces. Later, after midnight, the dead sappers are taken back to the St. Morand Monastery where its cemetery's winter earth receives them."

The interrogations revealed the prisoners were from a regular French pioneer unit attached to a colonial division, made up of men from north and central Africa. The rest of the night remained eerily quiet, prompting Corporal Pfefferle to remark at what all were fearing, "Strap your helmets on tight boys, it will be a sour morning."

By mid-morning, there was still no evidence of French retaliation. A high state of tension remained, knowing that some sort of enemy response was inevitable. The men continued about their usual routine. The field kitchen supporting the Carspach trenches were located in the cellar of the municipal hall in the center of the village. Nearing 11:00 am, food carriers set out from the village towards the trenches to bring forward pots containing the mid-day meal. Just then an enormous explosion came from beneath the German trenches, destroying an artillery observation post and a large section of a communication trench. The French had tunneled below the German lines and detonated a massive mine.

An instant later, multiple French batteries from the front and both flanks opened furious bombardment. French guns had registered the exact ranges of the German trenches. Some of food carriers were caught in the open fields between Carspach and the communication trenches and caught the worst of the initial fire. One young German recruit, who was under fire for the first time, returned screaming and tumbling down the kitchen stairs with a bloodied arm. The veteran mess sergeant, Popp, quickly soothed him with a comforting 'come hear Sonny,' as he bandaged the wounds. Another food carrier suffered a worse fate when his body was pulverized by a direct hit from a large caliber shell.

The shelling fully revealed the deficiencies of the Carspach trenches. The earthworks were set in a hollow depression, providing the enemy perfect observation into the rear sectors. The entrance/exit points of the communication trenches led to open ground before the village, making it impossible to transit without being exposed to fire. The Carspach position also created a forward bulge in the German lines, making it vulnerable to fire from three sides.

German heavy howitzers and mortars returned a vigorous fire. Some of the mortars targeted a wooded trench-line by the village of Dammerkircher [modern day Ballersdorf]. The effectiveness of this shooting was evident by the sight of colonial troops in olive green and light blue uniforms fleeing from the trenches.

The Germans expected to receive a ground assault at any moment. French helmets were observed scurrying about the front enemy trench. A German NCO directed his men in a group-fire exercise. As if in a marksmanship training course, he called for adjustments of 10 and 20 clicks to the Mauser sights to walk-in rifle fire against the distant targets.

The ground attack never came and the heavy shelling eventually slowed. The trench-life grew in a routine more typical of the Western Front. In Tagsdorf, a logistics base two miles east of Altkirch, Friedrich II came out to review the 52nd Division. Those having to defend the Carspach trenches were angry that the high command dismissed its fatal topographical weaknesses. A repositioning of only a short distance back would have made for a far superior defense. Lais speculated that it was perhaps more of a matter of pride of holding fast than addressing a tactical reality. The veterans were bitter at the senior decision-making that led to bloodshed at Altkirch, as it was more palatable to bear combat losses when there was a worthy objective at stake. Lais summarized the losses of the regiment's two-month stay at Altkirch:

> "The bill, a result of error and confusion, is paid by the infantry on both sides in these 'quiet' trenches. The losses of IR 169 was two officers killed, including one of our very best [Lais referred to Lt. Otto Winter, the brother of Lt. Karl Winter, who was killed in the final November fighting at the Somme], and 88 men, including 21 dead. These are small losses compared to a major battle, but too much for adventure caused by needless hysteria." [174]

On April 2, 1917, IR 169 was replaced by Infantry Regiment 470, part of the 240th Infantry Division. IR 470 was a new unit that was made up of primarily of Baden men; its entry into the Altkirch trenches was its introduction to combat. The 52nd Division pulled back 25 miles and crossed over the Rhine, where it was quartered in the vicinity of Fortress Istein. While there, the division joined the reserve of the Supreme Command in the Army, Department B. This three-week period marked the only time in the entire war that IR 169 was stationed on German soil. IR 169 took in new recruits and reorganized. Otto Lais' descriptions of his specific rank and title throughout all of 1917 is vague. As best can be deduced, Lais most likely served in the rank of sergeant as a platoon leader in IR 169's 2nd Machine Gun Company.

Elsewhere in early 1917, momentous events were churning that shaped the future direction of the war. To the east, the Russians had suffered as many as seven million casualties and were continuing to lose men at a rate of 200,000 per month. In March, a revolution and the establishment of the Provisional Government forced the Tsar to abdicate. Although Russia remained at war through November 1917, its days as a combatant power fighting against Germany were few.

Counterbalancing Russia's demise, the United States declared war on Germany on April 6, 1917. While it would take another year before American troops would enter the war in significant numbers, the shifting balance of powers added yet another nation that Germany would have to fight.

Severe food shortages left much of the German civilian populace and the soldiers the trenches suffering from malnutrition. Known as *Kohlrübenwinter* (turnip winter) of 1916–17, a rainy autumn caused a blight had reduced the harvest to about half of the previous year. As a last ditch measure, turnips – traditionally used as animal feed – were distributed in cities and towns. Two pounds of turnips per week were allocated for each civilian. The turnips were prepared in every conceivable variation. However, there was a total lack of other important nutrients, especially oils and fats.[175] Lais' 1917 account makes many references to the 'Starvation Year of 1917,' a time when IR 169 soldiers were often left hungry.

Karl Merkler was one IR 169 soldier who laconically recalled the lack of food during this period. Merkler, who came from the village of Mörsch [present day Rhinstetten, a suburb of Karlsruhe] went through IR 169's recruit induction cycle in late 1916. Long after the war he recalled how NCO's emphasized that they would mold the new recruits into men of steel. "*Zu Stahl Muss Ihr Werden.*" After a few weeks of such meager rations, he cynically joked they instead must have meant "*So Schmal Muss Ihr Werden;*" (how slender you will become).[176]

On the Western Front, the German push at Verdun and corresponding British offensive at the Somme had petered out. Verdun's losses resulted in over 300,000 deaths for each side. All the Germans had to show for this investment of blood was an advance of just five miles along a 20-mile front.

In March, the German Army made a strategic readjustment back to a largely pre-established *Siegfriedstellung* defensive system [known to the Allies as the "Hindenburg Line"]. The Hindenburg Line linked a system of fortified areas that stretched from the North Sea to the area around Verdun in mid-France. At its core was a 100 mile-long segment that ran from the vicinity of Arras to southeast of Soissons, and just north of Reims. While this consolidation resulted in a loss of ground (6-30 miles in various places), it put the Germans on better defensive terrain, straightened out a number of vulnerable salients and freed up 10 infantry divisions and 50 batteries of heavy artillery.

The establishment of the Hindenburg Line also marked a distinct shift in German defensive tactics. Throughout the first two years of the war, German doctrine called for a hard defense of front-line, fortified positions, backed by reserves poised to counterattack any breakthroughs. [IR 169's resolute defense of Serre is an example of this tactic.] One of the consequences of such a rigid defense was that it ultimately made the defending troops in the first series of trenches more vulnerable to heavy artillery barrages. The design of the Hindenburg Line afforded the German defenders more protection and provided a greater capability for defense in depth. The most forward positions would be a two-mile series of steel-reinforced, concrete bunkers intended to slow, disrupt and grind down attacking waves. Behind this sector was a quarter mile 'Battle Zone' backed by an intensive network of integrated machine gun and artillery fire. A triple layer of defense ranged back over 8,000 yards. Extensive use of barbed wire and mines added to the overall strength.

Beginning in 1916, German trench construction was guided by the manual *Stellungsbau*. Dr. Stephen Bull, author of *Trench: A History of Trench Warfare on the Western Front*, described the doctrine as a series of main positions:

"…each of the positions would consist of at least three lines, and between the lines of each position, every spot was to be prepared for defense, with many strong points, holding points and posts. Strong points were such features as defended villages and woods, while holding points were smaller features such as shell holes, ruins and small trenches. Strong points were to be linked by fire trenches with blockhouses built of wood. Artillery observation posts were placed in crucial forward areas and when possible, defensive lines were on the reverse slopes of hills. …Machine gun positions and dugouts formed the framework of all infantry fighting lines. One hundred meters or less was considered a sufficient frontal field of fire. Machine guns were to be concealed in emplacements; they must enfilade the obstacles. ...The few guns used in the front line must endeavor to increase their power by mobility." [177]

Chapter 10
The 1917 Aisne Campaign: Juvincourt and the Winterberg

In early 1917, recently appointed French Commander in Chief, General Robert-Georges Nivelle, proposed a new offensive strategy to break the front-wide stalemate. Nivelle, while commanding French forces in the last three months of the Verdun campaign, was recognized for his successful implementation of a series of short assaults supported by creeping barrages. With the support of the French and English governments, Nivelle set his sights on a segment of the German line in the heart of France's Champagne region along the Aisne River. One of the primary target sectors was the Chemin des Dames, a 20 mile road below the ridgeline along the Aisne River that connected Laon to Soissons. The southeastern anchor of the French trench-line was the cathedral city of Reims, which had been converted into a fortress bastion in the years before the war. The French assessed that the German positions northwest of Reims was less developed than the rest of the Hindenburg Line and more vulnerable to Nivelle's brand of offense.[178] The resulting Aisne campaign consumed IR 169 for seven months of 1917.

Nivelle's Aisne's offensive began along a 25-mile front on April 16, with the Chemin des Dames as the focal point of the attack. On April 2 began a two-week long artillery bombardment, where over 5,000 guns hammered the German positions with millions of shells. The April 16 ground attack, consisting of seven corps from the French 5th and 6th Armies, was supported by over 100 tanks – the first significant use of tanks by French forces. Most of the German defenders were able to weather the barrage by taking shelter in the substantial underground stone quarries that ran throughout the region. The creeping barrage intended by Nivelle failed to materialize, allowing concentrated German machine gun and artillery fire to rip apart waves of French troops and tanks. The French suffered 40,000 casualties on the first day alone. The French tanks fared badly, with German artillery fire knocking out scores before they could depart their own lines.

The only glimmer of hope for the French was on their right flank, where their troops were able to penetrate the Chemin des Dames road at the village of Juvincourt, 15 miles north of Reims. The German high command responded to the threat by surging strategic reserve forces, including the 52nd Division, to the Juvincourt area.

Jack Sheldon, in *The German Army in the Spring Offensives, 1917,* presents the following account from Oberst Leupold, Bavarian Reserve Infantry Regiment 12 of the French infantry and tank attack on Juvincourt on April 16:

> "The column continued to advance despite being under the heavy fire from the machine guns and quick-firing 37 mm guns. Some tanks were halted; the remainder ended up several hundred meters in rear of the command post, where most were knocked out by two still intact light field guns from a range of a few hundred meters. A mere few escaped to the rear. It was a wonderful sight when there was a direct hit: huge clouds of smoke with the flash of exploding ammunition. This, together with burning fuel heated the tanks red hot... There were destroyed tanks everywhere, thirty two of them in front of our divisional sector." [179]

The 52nd Division, garrisoned at Fortress Istein, was alerted for deployment to the Champagne on April 17 with orders to join the 7th Army's Sissonne Group. On April 20, the division loaded on trains in Efringen [the station from which IR 169 departed Mulhouse in August 1914] and traveled 250 miles north and unloaded at the village of Fourmies, 50 miles north of Reims. IR 169 conducted a fast road march to join the Sissone Group, which was surging five divisions to support the beleaguered German defenses around the Juvincourt area. The regiment's 35 mile hike passed through villages of Ertreaupont and Notre Dame de Liesse, and went into bivouac in a wet forest south of Sissonne. The troops bedded down on the soggy earth as fire from a nearby line of heavy artillery batteries blasted away. The 52nd Division was now positioned to enter the easternmost portion of the Chemin des Dames line.

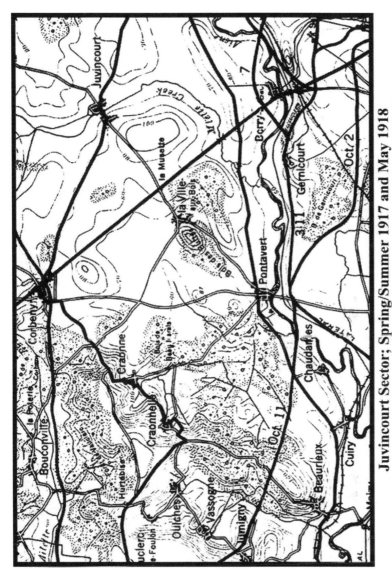

Juvincourt Sector; Spring/Summer 1917 and May 1918

This small segment of terrain was great significance to IR 169 in the 1917 and 1918 Aisne Campaigns. In 1917, IR 169 manned trenches before Juvincourt from 22 April – 17 June. From 21 July – 6 August it fought upon the Winterberg (high ground NW of Craonne) and occupied the Hurtebise Spur (south of Bouconville) 7 August – 15 September. (AABE)

The Juvincourt sector was engulfed in heavy combat during the six days between the initial attack and the 52nd Division's April 22 arrival on the battlefield. While the right flank of the French 5th Army attack penetrated the German second position south of Juvincourt, the rest of the French attack were disastrous. The French had underestimated the strength of the German defenses, which in many places were four lines deep and often out of the range of French artillery. Many of the French division suffered such extreme losses they were incapable of resuming the attack. German counterattacks, at a high cost of casualties, reversed many of the French gains.[180]

The ground situation had largely stabilized by the time IR 169 went into the front lines, with both sides having suspended offensive operations. The previous week's battle destroyed many of the pre-existing trenches, causing new lines to be repositioned. There was much digging to be accomplished as Lais described how "bayonets were sheathed and spades were drawn." The stacking of multiple German reinforcements in a tight space created a target rich environment for French artillery. The task of transporting provisions and new troops into IR 169's new front line positions was extremely treacherous. In the 52nd Division area of responsibility, IRs 170 and 111 at least had protected lines of communication into their positions. IR 169 was not as fortunate, as the positioning of IR 88, a regiment from a neighboring division, restricted covered support access to the front.

This situation led to a tragic circumstances in the regiment's first day in the Juvincourt trenches. That evening, field kitchen wagons attempted to transport food that had been prepared in rear areas. Segments of more secure routes were blocked by both gas contaminated areas and IR 88 defenses. This path diverted the wagon teams to elevated ground that exposed them to enemy observation. It was a wild ride as the drivers cursed and lashed at their horses in an effort to complete the journey as quickly as possible.

The wagons finally arrived at the collection point as food carriers came out of the trenches to draw the pots of hot chow. Coinciding with the arrival of the kitchen wagons, a group of new replacements reported to the front. Unteroffizer Lais was on hand to collect some of the new replacements designated for the 2nd MG Company. Lais, already nervous of being anywhere near an exposed road at the front, approached the replacements and warned "We always travel away from roads." No sooner had he spoke when multiple flashes came from the French lines. Seconds later came the howling of incoming shells. The first barrage scored a direct hit on the field kitchen wagon just as the food carriers were collecting their pots. Torn bodies lay everywhere as horses writhed in death agony, still tethered to wagon fragments. Dr Tebbe, the 1st Battalion surgeon, was in the vicinity of the attack and led efforts to treat the wounded. Moments, later, second barrage struck, severely injuring Tebbe and taking out others trying to assist those initially wounded.

When the shelling finally ceased, 30 men lay dead and a greater number wounded. IR 169's regimental command post used a field phone to call for support from a medical company posted in the nearby village Amifontaine. Wagons from a forested depot collected the casualties and returned them to the rear along a railroad embankment passageway. Lais accompanied the wounded and returned back to trenches at 5:00 am the following morning. A freeze had set in and the early morning hours were bitterly cold. Lais recalled: "After washing our filthy and blood-stained hands in the pots in this cold April night, we filled our bellies with flour paste and noodle soup; this was the infantry substance in starvation year of 1917!" [181]

The new trench system IR 169 inherited was in a dismal state. The crude trenches were so narrow that it was impossible for more than a few men to find places to sit at any one time. Dugouts had yet to be reinforced with timber frameworks, leaving them vulnerable to withstand the impact of even medium caliber shells. French artillery fire, especially in the first days of IR 169's deployment, remained heavy. As the position was under constant observation, any movement was certain to draw fire.

As the troops got their bearings, they noted several major terrain features that would eventually become prominent landmarks in IR 169's future combat history. The first location was the forested hill mass 1.5 miles to the south, known to the Germans as the La Ville aus Bois [and to the Allies as Boise des Buttes]. Three miles to the west, stood the beginning of the Californie Plateau, a steep, long and flat ridgeline that sat directly above the village of Craonne. In the months to come, the Germans nicknamed these heights as the *Winterberg*, a small piece of ground that witnessed some of the most brutal fighting of the war.

One notable feature of IR 169's new trench line was that it nearly intersected the center-point of the ill-fated April 16 French tank assault against Juvincourt. Lais, along with 2nd MG Commander Morgenhaler and his platoon leader, Leutnant Wenzler, discovered this 'tank graveyard' during their second day in the Juvincourt position. The trio had to venture across open ground in order to coordinate defensive plans with the neighboring IR 88. The journey was a frantic dash, with the MG leaders coming under fire as soon as they left the trenches. Midway, the men made a head-first leap into a shell crater to await a break in the fire. When the barrage slowed, they realized they were in the midst of 18 destroyed French tanks. Also strewn about the battlefield were shattered German artillery pieces of every caliber. French artillery had been keeping up a steady fire on the abandoned tanks and guns, making it impossible for the Germans to retrieve material of any possible value. Lais and his superiors completed their mission and returned back to their lines, but remained curious about the field of ruined tanks.

Soldiers are inquisitive creatures, and the lure of exploring the ruined French tanks at a later time proved impossible to resist. The French had created a pattern of halting artillery fires between the hours of 2:00 to 4:00 am. One rainy night, when visibility was particularly poor, Lais and a group of comrades set out to examine the tank graveyard at 3:00 am. Lais described his exploration of the shattered hulk of a French Schneider tank.

> At 3:00 am we dared to set out in a stormy night, with rain-scourged faces to examine the tank ruins. Eerily, the shredded outlines of a tanks appeared in the darkness, with storm winds mournfully blowing through their gaping holes. We crawled into the belly of one of these giants whose doors had been torn off. Once inside, the cover allowed us to shine a flashlight. A ghostly image was offered to us. There, in the crew compartment interior, were the twisted remains of the crew, with limbs resembling charred branches of a burned tree. We soon had enough of this tour. We hardly departed this tank graveyard when another artillery bombardment begins." [182]

On April 30, a heavy French bombardment lasted from 5:00-7:00 am. 18 French observation balloons flew overhead, leading to concerns that a French ground attack was imminent. German artillery responded with a strong counter-fire. The earth shook as a massive explosion came from the French lines. The German shells had scored a direct hit on a French ammunition depot. Innumerable secondary explosions and plumes of dark smoke filled the air, blanketing some of the balloons. Although no infantry attack followed, the artillery duel lasted throughout the day, damaging the German earthworks and killing scores of infantrymen. Lais wrote how that night "sad loads of the dead" awaited the pack wagons that would transport them to the rear.

The Germans observed a new sap trench under construction on the very edge of the French obstacle field opposite 1st Battalion's sector. The level of effort being applied suggested the enemy could be constructing a tunnel or perhaps digging a staging point for a hasty attack. This troubling development prompted the Germans to plan a trench raid in order to capture prisoners for intelligence. Leutnant Fritz Rombach, one of 1st Battalion's company commanders, was designated as the patrol leader. Rombach, a teacher by profession, was regarded as one of IR 169's best storm troop leaders. Lais described how Rombach's reputation as a personal daredevil was balanced by his great care to not expose his men to undue risk. Rombach was a meticulous planner who oversaw the smallest details in his many ventures into no-man's-land.

IR 169's senior commanders entrusted Rombach with full latitude to plan and execute the raid against the new French sap. To keep the operation as simple as possible, Rombach was adamant to only use the resources organic to his own company, and declined the support of heavy artillery and mortars. The raiding party would consist of a squad-sized group a volunteers, a single light machine gun from the 1st MG Company and three *Granatenwerfers*. [The Granatenwerfer 16 was a grenade launcher which bridged the gap between hand-thrown grenades and the light minenwerfers. Throwing a small grenade with a 400g high explosive charge to a maximum range of about 300 meters, the Gr.W.16 with a practiced crew could maintain a rate of fire of 4-5 rounds per minute. The Gr.W.16s proved to be effective trench weapons for the Germans. They had a high rate of fire, practical range and delivered a powerful detonation punch.][183]

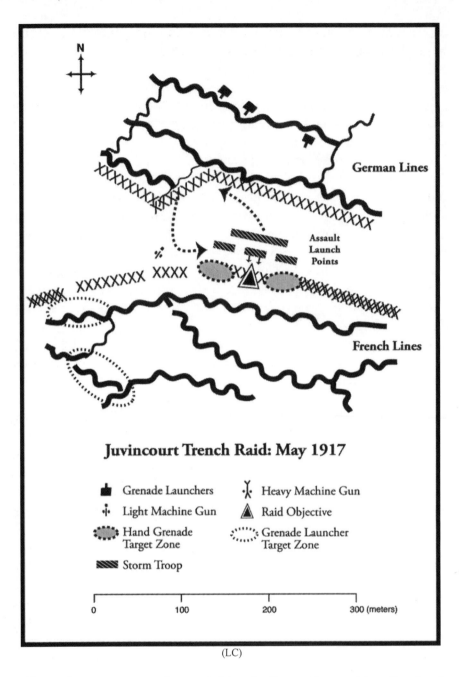

Juvincourt Trench Raid: May 1917

German Lines

Assault
Launch
Points

French Lines

■ Grenade Launchers   ⟋ Heavy Machine Gun

⫶ Light Machine Gun   ▲ Raid Objective

⬬ Hand Grenade   ⬭ Grenade Launcher
  Target Zone   Target Zone

▨ Storm Troop

0   100   200   300 (meters)

For three consecutive nights before the raid, Rombach, accompanied by one man, crawled through no-man's-land to conduct a personal reconnaissance of the French digging. He carefully recorded their activities, habits and time schedules. On the fourth night he was ready to execute the mission. The storm troop was made up of 17 hand selected men, including Medical Orderly Jung and one light machine gun crew. The infantrymen were armed only with pistols and as many hand grenades as could be carried. The three granatenwerfers were positioned in the second trench-line of IR 169 trench section *Abschnitt* 04. The explosion of the patrol's first hand grenade would be the signal for the grenade launches to open fire.

Rombach divided the patrol in five groups. He personally led the assault team of three men, with the objective of snatching a French prisoner. Two hand grenade teams, of three men each, were to align on the flanks of the attack area to disrupt the enemy response. A third team of the remaining seven men were positioned behind the assault element. They were to throw the first volley of grenades into the trench. The machine gun was placed to the west of the patrol and just outside the German trenches.

In the early morning hours, the storm troop crawled out of a forward deployed sap trench and carefully cleared a pathway through the German obstacle field. The raiding party silently crept through the no-man's-land and took up their assigned positions near the objective. The assault team snipped the outer strands of the barbed wire that protected the target. The storm troop waited in complete silence for 30 minutes. Just as Leutnant Rombach was about to give the attack command, he detected a large mass of French troops, with rifles, picks and shovels strapped on their backs, enter the trenches before him. He estimated there were now about 100 enemy troops now before him, too many for his small raiding force to take on. The Germans waited another endless hour.

Rombach finally detected that the majority of the French troops were moving off to right. After waiting several more minutes, Rombach blew a whistle to signal to attack. An instant later, a wave of hand grenades were tossed as Rombach fired a flare pistol that illuminated the scene of panic and destruction inside the trench. The assault team, led by Rombach and Unteroffizer Ruhmann, slipped through the cut wire and leapt into the trench. The French in the second trench were quick to react and a furious grenade battle erupted, with the German squad throwing 150 hand grenades. Ruhmann, fighting with great fury, was hit in the leg and evacuated by Orderly Jung. The assault team grabbed a stunned French sapper and the entire raiding party raced back to their lines. To cover the retreat, the machine gun fired 500 rounds while the three grenade launchers laid a barrage of 80 grenades on the patrol's endangered right flank.

Rombach's troop, along with their prisoner, made it safely back to German lines. The only casualty was the lightly injured wounded Ruhmann. Unteroffizer Ruhmann received an Iron Cross First Class and Medic Orderly Jung an Iron Cross Second Class. While any tactical benefits derived from the raid were short-lived, the action was recognized as 52nd Division exemplar on how to conduct a successful raid. Resulting teaching points included the importance of detailed planning, violence of action, designating soldiers to evacuate prisoners and use of concentrated indirect fire to protect the raider's flanks.[184]

On May 5, the men in the trenches of Juvincourt observed an enormous bombardment on the cusp of the Winterberg. Lais recalled how the entire crest of the ridgeline was seemingly wrapped in fire, with so much blood was to be spilled on and around it.[185] What the IR 169 men witnessed that day was the climax of a 72 hour sustained French assault on the Winterberg. This steep high ground above the destroyed village of Craonne was tactically significant, as it marked the far eastern beginning of the Chemin des Dames ridgeline. A French breakthrough at this point would split the German lines between the Aisne Valley heights and the eastern plains before Juvincourt.

Sheldon provides a vivid description of the horrors facing the German defenders of the Winterberg in this attack;

> "The expression 'a living hell' is a much overused cliché, but it is hard to think of any other way of describing the situation in the Winterberg Tunnel." The entrance to a tunnel that was used to house forward-deployed reserves and ammunition stocks caught fire and exploded. The opening, as well as ventilation shafts, were blocked and the enclosure filled with poisonous fumes. Two complete companies of Reserve IR 111 were trapped, with almost all of those not immediately killed in the explosion died of suffocation, dehydration or suicide. When engineers finally dug into the tunnel six days later, only three men, all close to death, were left alive." [186]

By the end of May 5, French troops, at an enormous cost of men, finally reached the summit of the Winterberg. Desperate German counterattacks in the next two days pushed the French back. The sum of this fighting resulted in a stalemate of French troops holding the southern slope and Germans the northern side. The artillery of both combatants ruled the flat plateau that, for a time at least, became the no-man's land.

While the French officially ended major offensive operations on May 9, intensive combat continued along the eastern portion of the Chemin des Dames sector. On May 21, artillery and infantry small-arms fire drove back a German counterattack on Winterberg, with 350 men lost as prisoners. The Germans again tried to take the heights on the night of June 2-3, when two German divisions made five attacks on the east, west and central parts of the Winterberg and the west end of the Vauclerc Plateau, just to the west. German infantry, stacked in waves and supported by flame-thrower detachments, gained some ground but were eventually pushed back by French counterattacks. This pattern of combat, with neither army able to retain decisive control over the Winterberg's summit, continued through the summer.[187]

As the artillery fires by Juvincourt subsided, IR 169 set about constructing a full battle zone defensive system as prescribed in the *Stellungsbau* doctrine. At the company and battalion levels, the centerpiece of this effort was to establish networks of reinforced machine gun nests that could enfilade all obstacles. Lais detailed how the regiment inserted machine gun positions that dominated every transition of terrain, every hollow and slope.

The troops went to extreme lengths to camouflage the machine gun bunkers, aware that the looming La Ville aus Bois Berg, with an elevation of 108 meters, provided the enemy with constant observation deep into their lines. Netting supported placement of vegetation over newly constructed bunkers, and care was taken to not to create visible trails to the resupply paths leading to Juvincourt. To preserve the image of fresh early morning dew on the grass, a series of removable planks were connected to permit foot transit during hours of darkness.

Strict orders were given for gunners to not fire their machine guns at aircraft or other fleeting targets. This mandate was so heavily reinforced that it became the basis of a sarcastic joke, with the sergeant asking a private what he would if coming under attack. The response; "Sir, I would make a report!" [188]

Although incoming artillery strikes had become infrequent, the effects of gas shelling across the front made for an uncomfortable existence, especially for those posted in lower hollows and gullies. The amount of time spent wearing gas masks was reflected in the regiment's high consumption rate of gas masks inserts. In mid June, the troops were pleased to learn that they would soon be replaced by a new unit. The displacement occurred on the night of 17 June, as IR 169 silently left the trenches in an eight mile hike to forested reserve camp. Lais remarked on how lush the magnificent forest was, respite with large quantities of small strawberries. The next day the regiment continued on to its next reserve destination, the village of Lappion.

The eight week posting in the Juvincourt trenches cost IR 169 ten officers (three killed) and 201 enlisted men.[189] History largely remembers the opening of the 1917 Aisne Campaign less for any of the few yards gained or lost, but rather as the catalyst for the infamous French mutiny of 1917. On May 27, up to 30,000 French soldiers along the Chemin des Dames abandoned their positions. In many cases, this was less of a mutiny than a refusal of French soldiers to submit themselves to pointless attacks they knew were suicidal.

The grievances of the common French soldier in this offensive were well founded, as their Army lost 130,000 men between 16 and 23 April alone. In the end, Nivelle was sacked and replaced by Petain, who quickly restored order and sought to improve the miserable conditions suffered by the French troops.[190]

The Lappion base camp was by a poor farming village, 12 miles behind the front lines. As well as resting and refitting, the regiment established a program of individual training, field exercises and area familiarization. On June 23, the regiment was reviewed by the Supreme Commander of the 7th Army, General Max von Boehn.

In the summer of 1917, Germany's logistical apparatus was stretched to near breaking point, making this period of refitting remembered for the abysmal quality of the food. The variety and quantity of food was severely lacking, and weeks would pass without the provision of meat. In typical rear area settings, established commissary and canteen dining facilities provided primary feeding services. In Lappion, there was simply not enough food available to keep the men from remaining hungry. In Lais' platoon, one of the soldiers, a man named Schmalhans, was tasked be an informal cook and oversee the augmenting of food provisions. The men scraped by as best they could, with illicit late night forays conducted to take livestock and crops from local farms.

In mid July, there was a dramatic increase in the quality of rations, including the serving of ox meat, high quality bread, artificial honey and cherry cakes, fresh fruit from Belgium and caraway beverages. As Lais explained, 'When the soldier only has something to eat, drink and smoke, then he is made.' While all enjoyed the improvement in their diet, the veterans knew it meant one thing – a pending return to the front.

Sure enough, orders soon came for IR 169 to be prepared to march, but with no specific location designated. Speculation was rife. Soon it was leaked out that the regiment was destined the Winterberg. The news could not be worse, as the Winterberg, above all possible locations along the Aisne front, was certain to be a bloody grist mill. At one point, 'latrine rumors' speculated that the regiment would only be deployed to the Winterberg for only three days, and then rotated. Veterans scoffed, remembering that the their six months of intensive combat in Serre kept the men in the trenches for weeks, rather than days at a time. At 2:00 am on the night of departure, it became certain, IR 169 was deploying to the Winterberg.[191]

Lais' memoirs of his 1917 service with IR 169 is titled *"Die Schlacht im Kreidekalt; 1917."* (*The Battle in the Limestone Chalk*). The book's title was inspired by the unique clay-based qualities of the soil in this region, a defining feature in the terrible fight for the Winterberg in the spring and summer of 1917. The sustained impact of heavy-caliber artillery fire battle so deforested the Californie Plateau that it took on the appearance of a snowy white Alpine mountain, given origin to the German moniker of 'Winterberg.' Just to the north of the destroyed village of Craonne, the Winterberg stood at 200 meters of steep elevation and a 1.5 miles in length. Its defining feature was a broad plateau, which in some places a third of mile in width.

Lais was one IR 169 veteran who could contrast the transition of the serene Californie Plateau [so named for long ago imported American trees] into the hellish Winterberg. Lais, when assigned to the 12th Pioneer Battalion, briefly served in this region in early 1915. He recalled:

"When I saw the Berg for the first time, I could not suspect what would become such terror two years later. The densely wooded peak was now bald and the luxuriously forested slopes were left with only a few, wretched broom-like trunks. Where the Berg sits it looms over the Aisne River. Light reflected off this rumbled mountain of chalk-clay, revealing the carcass of a savage, bloodletting drunk on the Western Front." [192]

Nearly a year later, German General Von Unruh wrote the following description of the Winterberg, then under French possession, from a personal reconnaissance he conducted on the eve of the German's May 27, 1918 Aisne Offensive:

"At first sight the heights of the Chemin des Dames at Winterberg seemed to be dead. There were no signs of life. I saw only the white chalk crest of the Winterberg, so dazzling in the sunshine that it looked as if covered with snow – a fact which had given the name to the hill on and around which so much blood had flowed in the war. It seemed to tower over the whole district with its steep slopes, close pitted with a hundred thousand shell holes, and barred by formidable wire entanglements, looked to be impregnable." [193]

Fighting on the cursed Californie Plateau was as horrifying for the French soldiers as it was the Germans. One of the war's enduring folk songs, *La Chanson de Craonne*, spoke to the despair of the common French soldier – sentiments that sparked the rebellion of 1917.

> *Farewell to life, farewell to love,*
> *Farewell to all women*
> *It's all over, it's forever*
> *For this infamous war*
> *It's at Craonne on the plateau*
> *That we must kick the bucket*
> *Because we're all condemned*
> *We're the sacrificed*

In mid-July 1917, the French were able to wrest control of the northern edge of the plateau. Starting July 19, the German 21 and 42 cm mortars pounded the French positions, followed by a 22 July ground assault by the 5th Guards and 5th Reserve Divisions. The German attackers absorbed heavy losses as they stormed over the French positions and pushed on to the southern portion of hilltop. There, scattered remnants of French units desperately fought and slowed the oncoming German tide. French commanders, disregarding the fate of their own courageous defenders, launched a massive artillery strike across the general battle line. The fires, which blew apart both friends and foes alike, succeeded in stopping the German attack. The plateau again became the no-man's-land. It was at this point when IR 169, temporarily detached to the 5th Reserve Division, entered the Winterberg fray.

IR 169 arrived in the vicinity of the Winterberg on July 21. For the next several days, Lais' machine gun platoon was detailed to guard a section of artillery that included two batteries of 21 cm mortars and one battery of 42 cm mortars located between the village of St. Thomas and the Ailette Creek, two miles northeast of the Winterberg peak. The 42 cm battery was segregated by barbed wire, with access tightly limited to assigned battery personnel.

Further to the rear, the Germans put into action one of their super-heavy 'Big Bertha' howitzers, gigantic cannon that could propel a 1,800 lb, 16.5 inch caliber shell a range of nearly eight miles. The German Army only fielded a dozen of these guns in the entire war. Its investment in this fight signaled the imperative placed on holding the Winterberg. The firing of the Big Bertha left a powerful impression on those veterans who experienced its mighty blast. Lais described how the cannon's roar came with a thunderous muffle that swayed large tree trunks and trembled their branches. The resulting detonations rattled the earth, and as Lais declared, announced that "Lucifer had come to the Berg!" [194] In his immediate vicinity, Lais observed the 21 and 42 cm mortar batteries fire in support of the 5th Guards and Reserve Division's attack. Elsewhere, German 15 cm howitzers joined the action as the crest of the Winterberg was again consumed in blaze of smoke and dust.

The IR 169 line battalions were ordered forward to regain control of the plateau. The regiment proudly marched through the Ailette Valley singing martial songs, causing Adjutant Muller to remark what an excellent impression was being made to on-looking, senior Prussian commanders. Nearing the northern slope, the regiment had to cross over a series of planked bridges that covered the marshland over the Ailette creek. It was nightfall when the companies deployed in a battle line and labored up the steep slopes to the summit to take positions across the center of the plateau.

The plateau had been turned into a sea of giant shell craters. There were no fixed trenchlines, so the men did their best to scrape and connect individual fighting positions among the shell holes. The French launched their own counterattacks as a desperate struggle fell over the entire plateau, where squads and platoons fought from crater to the next. Hand grenades were the weapon of choice and were thrown in copious quantities.After the first day of fighting, the Germans exhausted their entire grenade stocks, leaving them to toss captured French grenades, which lay about in the hundreds. The infantryman preciously conserved their rifle ammunition and resorted to hand-to-hand combat fought with spades, shovels, knives, bayonets and rifle-butts.

The Ailette marshland behind the Berg became a logistical Achilles Heel. French artillery precisely targeted the primitive plank bridges over the swamp, strewing the mire with splintered boards and shattered bodies of dead supply carriers. On the hilltop, food, ammunition, and most importantly water, fell to critical levels. Men were practically dying of thirst as their tongues stuck to the roof of dry mouths. One item that was not in short supply were the many dead of both armies that had fallen in weeks of unrelenting combat. The constant fighting prevented the burials or evacuation of the bodies, leaving them to decay and ferment in the burning July sun. The omnipresent, toxic odor was truly unbearable. Smoking was forbidden, as the consequence of lighting a cigarette invited a barrage of grenades. Men resorted to placing tobacco ripped from cigarette rations into their parched mouths for a moment's relief from the taste and smell of rotting corpses.

Communication with the front began to fail. Dispatch carriers were killed in the shelling and field phone lines were ripped apart and could not be repaired. A signal light connection from atop the Berg to the relay station to the west was briefly established. No sooner had the first message been transmitted when a direct artillery hit took out the far station. Carrier pigeons were deployed, but none managed to land in designated locations. German commanders, both on the hill and in rear areas, lost all sense of situational awareness on the locations of both friendly and enemy forces.

The fighting in these squalid conditions sustained over three days without relief. On the fourth night, it appeared that commanders on both sides gave up hope on sorting out who was fighting where. French and German heavy artillery joined forces in frustration and randomly fired with all their collective might onto the plateau, with the consequence of killing their own men be damned.[195]

Lais' MG section remained with the artillery through the fourth day of the Winterberg battle. While this guard duty in no way compared with ordeal faced by their comrades atop the plateau, the conditions were still hazardous. The heavy German mortar batteries drew the attention of French railway cannon, which pounded the area with high explosive and gas shelling. Gas residue affixed on surrounding undergrowth, requiring the men to frequently don gas masks. The non-stop firing of the German mortars began to compromise their tubes, resulting in the bursting of a 21 cm mortar that wiped out its crew.

That evening Lais' section received orders to displace from the mortars and join the fighting on the Winterberg. The regular night-time artillery fire had slacked off somewhat, making it possible to send reinforcements and supplies up to crest. The platoon set off after midnight as it followed an infantry company that advanced ahead of them. Lais, rather dramatically, recalled this movement as "a gruesome passage up to this mountain of horror."

Before ascending the steep slope, the men had to first get through the Ailette swamp. Scattered incoming artillery began to resume, with shells exploding in the marshland. The MG platoon, burdened with the heavy machine guns, carriages, ammunition and other accessories, gathered at the edge the marsh and waited for a gap in the firing to race across a dike. An interval seemed to emerge, and the Germans set off at a run. The dash was especially difficult for the men having to lug the carriage mounts. Midway across the marsh the platoon heard incoming shells and leaped face first into the mud. After the near-miss detonations, Lais looked around and saw the still-warm bodies of dead infantrymen from the column ahead, mixed among the rotting corpses of supply bearers from the previous weeks' shelling. The section picked themselves up and hurried as best they could through the marsh. One of the privates, a giant of a man who was carrying a gun carriage, collapsed, gasping "I can do no more." An NCO came up behind and helped him drag the piece until they finally reached dry soil at the base of the Berg.

The platoon continued up the start of the slope when Lais called a halt to account for personnel. It was determined that two men were killed by a direct hit. Also lost were a gun carriage and three, 250-round cases of ammunition. Now close to the front, the remainder of the hike needed to be conducted in silence. NCO's inspected the men to make sure all equipment was re-secured as not to rattle. The climb up to the top of the plateau remained grueling, with the men left breathless and exhausted when they finally reached the summit at 3:00 am.

With daybreak, Lais and his men witness how awful the preceding four days of combat had been. The stress of days of extreme battle showed on the faces of the survivors, many who carried shell-shocked, vacant expressions. Their faces were masked with the white dust of the clay soil, cheeks were hollowed from lack of food and dehydration and exhaustion marked by heavy bags under their eyes. The moon-like landscape was different from other battlefields. There were no barbed wire entanglements nor fixed trenches, just a network of loosely connected shell craters.

A limited resupply line up to the summit had been restored. Every other night, carrier squads brought up essentials such as food, water, schnapps and rifle and machine gun ammunition. There was no need to carry up more hand grenades, as there were still plenty of captured French ones about, weapons that the men preferred to their own, German-issued grenades. It was impossible to bring up the heavy construction materiel need to build reinforced dugouts. At best, some of the squads were able to salvage scraps of sheet metal from earlier defensive works to cover new positions with. This would at least provide some measure of protection from splinters and shrapnel from lighter caliber artillery shells.

The heat was insufferable. There was no shade from the direct July sunlight and the humidity was unusually high. Supply bearers arrived on the mountain soaked with sweat. One of the more bizarre supplies that were brought up were tins of butter. The heat liquefied the butter, turning it into a sticky, inedible mess that absorbed the taste of death.

One reason the 'rotgut quality' schnapps was deemed an essential item was that its consumption helped numb the horrible stench of the dead. With the fighting now on its fifth day, the accumulation of so many bodies in such a small space had become a major problem. Lais provided gruesome descriptions of how the decomposing corpses bloated to the point of bursting, revealing inner organs that oozed from bellies. The dead could neither be carted off of the plateau nor buried, as there was little remaining ground not already filled by hastily dug graves.

The repositioning of lines required one Lais' MG teams to move into a shell crater filled with enemy dead from the previous night's fighting. These bodies were those of Senegalese troops, men from the French II Colonial Corps. The Germans held a deep loathing of these African troops, whom they considered barbaric in respecting the fundamental laws of warfare. The MG crews simply tossed out the bodies of the Senegalese dead out of the crater to build a crude rampart. The German's disdain of this enemy was such that the dead's 'soul of brutality left them unaffected in this act.'

Events of the fifth night of IR 169's presence on the Winterberg provided an example of the German's hatred of the colonials. The absence of barbed wire and established trenchlines created a fluid battlespace, especially during the hours of nighttime. As some point in the early morning hours, a burst of horrible, animal-like screams came from the front, followed by sudden silence. Sometime later, Lais observed two badly wounded Germans, whose blood-soaked uniforms were shredded to tatters, being carried off to an aid station located midway down the rear slope of the Winterberg. The casualties could be heard moaning, '*der Schwarzen, der Schwarzen.*'

Soon word filtered back to the front what had happened. A resupply squad became lost while trying find a forward position and wandered close to enemy lines. A patrol of Senegalese soldiers, apparently drunk, set upon and captured the German team. They first ravaged the food and drank the schnapps rations. With that finished, they then began to murder the German prisoners with bladed weapons. Two of the badly wounded Germans managed to escape to tell of the atrocity. The German were enraged and looked to revenge. In the next several days, the Germans had occasion to take approximately 50 Senegalese troops as prisoners. Twenty of this number were summarily executed upon capture. As Lais wrote: "Hatred was large on the Berg."

On the sixth day of the battle, the intensity of the combat seemed to diminish. It appeared that the French began to accept their efforts to capture the Winterberg had failed and that further offensive action was fruitless. Presence on the Berg still remained a highly lethal existence. The French were able to establish a position on an elevated saddle on the eastern portion that afforded them an excellent, enfiladed field of fire into a section of the German lines. So many men fell victims to the French snipers that the Germans nicknamed the targeted area as a 'head shot paradise.' Lais contrasted the reality of death on this battlefield with that of fanciful, glorious depictions of death in German newspapers. Those men killed here instantly dropped into a 'pig's tomb.' Lais also recalled the macabre sense of trench humor that developed among the cynical combat veterans, and how some laughed at the image of death on those comrades killed by headshots. These bodies tended to retain the facial expressions on the instant of the bullet's impact, rather than be contorted from the pain of a mortal wound.

The Germans sought payback to this sniping. Among one of the many recently captured French weapons was a carbine that impressed the Germans with its compact size, quick reloading capabilities and accuracy – a perfect trench-fighting weapon. Armed with this carbine, a German marksmen crawled forward to position himself in a crater near the enemy line. He didn't have to wait long for a target. A Senegalese soldier, seeking to defecate, emerged at the lip of an opposing crater, his backside exposed the German's sights. Lais described this man as being incomprehensible stupid or bold, and how he 'floated away to his Islamic paradise' in this circumstance.[196]

It became clear on July 28, IR 169's seventh day on the Winterberg, that the French abandoned efforts to take the plateau. Enemy fire all but ceased, and French troops returned back to the southern edge of the plateau, leaving the Germans unmolested on the northern edge.

IR 169's regimental history quantified the fighting by recording how the regiment repelled four distinct French attacks, captured 22 prisoners (to include those from Senegal) and took possession of five enemy machine guns. The casualties, of course, were atrocious. Reported regimental losses were 14 officers (2 killed) and 870 men. As was typical, the regimental log fails to detail the mortality rate of the enlisted men. Lais explained that the death rate at the Winterberg was considerably higher than other battles, given the difficulty in evacuating the wounded during the five days of unremitting close infantry combat and artillery bombardment. Lais also speculated that the French losses must have been inconceivable. His assessment was in-part based on the comparison of prisoners taken by both sides, with the 52nd Division losing 18 men as prisoners while capturing 160 French POWs.

Lais, speaking on behalf of the veterans who had fought through Flanders, Verdun and the Somme, contrasted those battles with six days of combat on the Winterberg. Considering the appalling amount of blood was spilled for such a small piece of ground, one could 'award all the horrors' of these great battlefields of the war upon the Winterberg.[197]

With fighting on the plateau suspended, regular resupply schedules were resumed and proper trench lines and bunkers were constructed. Lais recalled how he could comfortably sun himself outside of a crater, with his steel helmet off and his gas mask firmly secured in its case.

The dead were finally removed off the summit. The Germans did their best to provide dignified burials for the dead of both armies in mass graves dug behind the Winterberg. The rapidly decomposing corpses, almost all unidentified, were sorted based on scraps of uniform. Strands of barbed wire were used to bind French helmets to mark the enemy burial trenches.

German soldiers, now able to explore their surroundings, witnessed more of the horrible aftermath of the battle. A hospital tunnel had been dug midway up the northern slope of the Berg, and the ground below its entry point littered with amputated limbs. Lais' travels took him to notorious tunnel were the two companies of Reserve IR 111, Baden men, were trapped and perished in the terrible explosion of May 5. "The sight of the now-exposed tunnel entrance is shocking. Many of the dead lay with rifles in arms and helmets on their heads, others were stripped of uniforms, and some had silently suffocated further inside the tunnel."

IR 169's departure from the Winterberg finally came on August 6, when it was relieved by the 12th Reserve Infantry Regiment at midnight. German artillery, in an effort to mask the relief in place, fired at regular intervals. As Lais' men returned across the foot bridges over the Ailette marshland, they actually made something of an effort to find the machine gun carriage that was lost in the mad dash back in July. Such was the German Army's insistence to account for all equipment, even when missing in the direst of combat circumstances. The regiment reassembled in the forest lager camp by St. Erme, four miles northeast of the Winterberg. The camp also served as a base station for an observation balloon. The men were treated to fresh fruit, to include the locally grown, sour apples the French used to make cider.[198]

The displacement provided only the shortest of respites as the regiment was immediately sent back to the lines. A crisis was brewing five miles to the southwest, by the destroyed village of Bouconville. The origin of this emergency was traced back to a May French assault in the vicinity of the Hurtebise Farm. The farm was set on the Chemin des Dames road, two miles west of IR 169's former perch on the Winterberg. In one of the few French breakthroughs across the Chemin des Dames, the French attack left a narrow finger-shaped spur, a mile deep and a half mile wide, into the German lines. The limit of the penetration pushed almost mile southwest of the Bouconville. Renewed German and French activity in mid-September resulted in a surge in reinforcements that called for IR 169 to replace IR 3.

IR 169's with fighting positions taken up around the arch of the bulge and on through the eastern portion past the ruins of the Abbey de Vauclair, a Cistercian abbey founded in 1134. The regiment's base of operations was established in around Bouconville. While in a rear area, Lais wrote of bedding down in the rubble of the Bove Chateau, the site of grand estates dating back to the early 1700s.

The position was essentially the western edge of the high ground that included the Winterberg. The terrain around the battle line was dominated by a crisscross of marshes, steep escarpments, ravines and snarls of tangled underbrush. Once again, the Ailette swampland posed an obstacle to resupply operations and bred insects that tormented the men. The only paved road leading back to rear areas passed by the abbey, which was rendered unusable as it fell under direct enemy observation and constant artillery fire. Resupply was dependent on the use of mules and donkeys, loaded with side-packs, and guided along footpaths up to the trenchlines. These approaches were also targeted by artillery, and the carcasses of many of these animals were strewn along the pathways. Lais credited these brave transportation troops and their animals as the real heroes of this deployment. Despite these efforts, there was never enough food at the front and the men stood their posts suffering from perpetual hunger.

While an enemy ground assault before Bouconville never materialized during the regiment's six week assignment, losses totaled 8 officers and 205 enlisted men.[199]

Chapter 11
The Battle of Pinon

On September 15, IR 169 was relieved in the front lines by IR 66 and redeployed to a reserve camp at La Selve, a 15 mile road march northeast of Bouconville. The regiment had been in sustained combat for much of the past five months and suffered over 1,300 casualties since April. A proper rest and refit was badly needed. La Selve served as a French garrison before the war and its facilities could accommodate the entire 52nd Division.

One notable occurrence from this period was a 52nd Division athletic competition held on October 2. IR 169 conducted its own competition four days earlier to select the best athletes for the big divisional event. Divisional contest winners included IR 111 men who took the 100 meter race, 100 meter hurdles, 400 meter race and stone toss. IR 111's Sergeant Backer won the hand grenade competition by landing a dummy grenade within 3 meters of a 52 meter target. [Lais' memoir expressed his irritation on having to rely on IR 111's official history for this data, as clearly felt IR 169's performance was under recorded.[200]] Other events included a machine gun carry obstacle course, marksmanship contests and a singing competition that was won by IR 169. Lais took pride in noting that the athletic achievements were quite impressive when considering the deplorable nutrition and battlefield conditions the men had long been subject to. At least one German necessity that wasn't lacking that day was beer. The evening closed with officers and enlisted men joining to consume copious amounts of beer in the garrison's large, wood-planked dining hall.[201]

Elsewhere on the Aisne Front, the final act of the great French 1917 offensive was taking shape. The French were determined to gain full control of the Chemin des Dames Ridge before the onset of winter. Having little to show for the costly battles on the eastern portion of ridgeline, they now looked to the west.

The final French push, set for mid-October attack date, is known as the Battle of La Malmaison, named for the large German fortification in the central sector of the 10 mile long attack zone. The French intent was to break out of the western-most lines and secure the Oise and Aisne Canal. Deeper objectives included capture of the Chemin des

Dames. The pre-offensive front line began two miles west of Pinon and sloping southeast to the village of Bray, and to the western portion of the Chemin des Dames.

The French assembled 14 divisions for the offensive. Six divisions were assigned for the assault, two designated to cover the flanks and six more for follow-on missions. The vast artillery concentration brought to bear 812 field guns, 862 heavy guns, 105 super-heavy guns and 66 trench mortar batteries. This artillery firepower totaled 1,790 guns, distributed with an average of 180 guns for each kilometer of the front. The French owned the airspace, doubling the German 168 aircraft with 300 of their own.

German intelligence identified the French preparations for the attack and pushed reinforcements to the western sector. When the attack came, the Germans were still only able to muster three and half divisions in the trenches backed by another two in the immediate reserve. The 52nd was one of the divisions designated for the reserve mission. German artillery strength was less than a third of the French, totaling only 580 guns, with 225 being of heavy and super-heavy calibers.[202]

The 52nd Division was alerted for deployment on October 11, at 2:00 pm. The following day, the division uploaded on trains for destined to Laon, 15 miles west. The division then marched on to its designated reserve assembly area in a forest lager between the villages of Premontre and Suzy, 10 miles further west. It was a rainy day and the French had begun the shell Laon and the surrounding areas with long range, heavy caliber artillery. This area was heavily populated with refugees and inhabitants who clogged the road and slowed the march. There were a number of civilian casualties from the shelling. Lais wrote that it was a dreadful feeling to see old men and young women killed by the shellfire. "Even though we were accustomed to death, this image made us ill."

The men were grateful for the rain as they headed into the forest, as the downpour diluted the lingering effects of poison gas. It was an unpleasant march, with the increasing rate of shelling forcing the men to often scamper for cover. These shells appeared to have a higher explosive quality and were assumed to be of American manufacture. The animals also were victims of the circumstances. Several horses were killed in the shelling and most were in poor health from illness, poor diets and the effects of gassing.

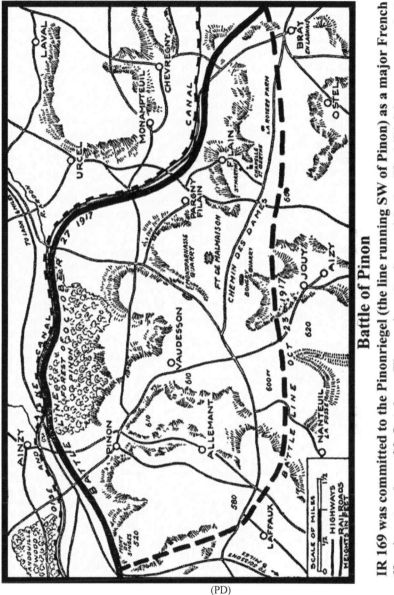

Battle of Pinon

IR 169 was committed to the Pinonriegel (the line running SW of Pinon) as a major French offensive struck on 23 October. The regiment, along with the 52nd Division, was crushed while defending a line extending from Pinon and its forest to the east, in an effort to allow German forces to escape across the Aisne Canal.

(PD)

The lager site was a disappointment. Tucked in the woods, the camp had little protective cover to support this large concentration of troops. Although tents were provided, there was no straw ground covering, forcing the men to sleep directly in the mud. The intermittent shelling caused the men to frequently scurry out of the tents to seek shelter behind embankments. The terrible quality of food did little to improve morale. Officers, NCOs and messengers were sent forward at the beginning of each day to reconnoiter the front around the village of Pinon. They returned long after dark, exhausted.

The imminent battleground that IR 169's leaders scouted was referred to the Germans by the Pinonriegel. The village of Pinon stood in the northwest corner. At the western extreme, the front ran in an arch-shaped line beginning the village of Vauxaillon and continuing 10 miles southeast to the start of the Chemin des Dames ridge by Braye-en-Lonnois. The 52nd Division prepared to stand as the reserve force for the southwestern portion of the Pinonriegel, under the command of Group Crépy. At the eastern center of the line was anchored by the German-held Fort Le-Malmaison. The original pre-war fort was constructed by the French Army in the 1870's and was deemed obsolete by 1913. Outdated as it may be, the fort served the German occupiers well, as its subterranean galleries could garrison an infantry brigade its hardened machine gun bunkers controlled a large swath of ground across the front.

The most significant terrain feature was the Canal de l'Oise à l'Aisne (Oise-Aisne Canal) that channeled the Ailette River. The canal ran north of Pinon, continued four miles east, and then towards the Chemin des Dames further to the southeast. There were only a few bridges that spanned the canal and the Pinonriegel. The positioning of the front lines only four miles south of the canal violated fundamental tenants of the German's 1917 strategy to defend in depth. The Germans placed much of their artillery on the southern bank, making them vulnerable in the event of an enemy breakthrough. In such a crisis, the canal would greatly restrict the flow of supplies and risk entrapping retreating defenders. It proved the Pinonriegel's fatal flaw when the French blow struck.

On October 15, the 2nd Battalion men were eager to leave their miserable forested lager for an advanced reserve deployment position nearer the front. Although the shelling would be heavier, there was hope they would stand a better chance of protection from more conventional defensive works. 2nd Battalion's new position was behind a railroad embankment by the Oise-Aisne canal, in a line between the villages of Anizy in the west, and Challevos to the east. Just over the stone bridge at Anizy was Pinon village, with the front beginning two miles further to the west of the village. A unique geographic feature of Pinon, and one of prominence in the coming battle, was a series of large, natural cave systems.

The forward reserve troops attempted to establish a typical front area routine. Efforts to improve the defenses along the canal's railway embankment were in vain, as the high water table precluded any form of serious digging. The intermittent shelling remained irritating, but nothing that veteran German soldiers hadn't experienced before. Troops involved in unit movements and supply operations remained wary of incoming shells, but continued with their tasks.

All changed on the morning of October 17 when the great French barrage opened. The minor shelling of the previous days were actually ranging fires in preparation for the big strike. IR 169 had the misfortune of being in the target area of some of the most epic artillery bombardments of the war, and this was among the worst of them. The onset of the drumfire condemned many of the Germans who were not near cover. The canal bridge between Anizy and Pinon immediately became tangle of smashed artillery limbers, pack wagons and dead and injured soldiers and horses.

The German counter-battery artillery response was at first feeble, then almost nonexistent. The French deluged the Ailette Valley with gas shells. German artillery batteries were so heavily targeted with gas that their gunners could not remove their masks eat or drink. Many of the batteries south of the canal were silenced when they could not be resupplied with shells. The German's inability to return artillery fire not only allowed the French guns to fire with impunity, but was also devastating for the morale of the German infantry.

IR 169 weathered the first two days of the bombardment hugging the northern slope of the railway embankment. German doctrine called for reserve forces, such as the 52nd Division, to remain in position behind the pre-attack impact zone. The intent was to ensure the reserve forces would then be intact when called upon for counterattack orders. This core precept was ignored when, on October 19-October 20, Group Crépy ordered IR 169's 1st and 2nd Battalions to forward positions to reinforce IR 79, of the 14th Infantry Division, in the trenches southwest of Pinion. The movement exposed the two battalions to into the midst of this terrible barrage.

When the orders were received, a momentary reduction of shelling made it possible to at least contemplate the movement. Heavy fire or not, it remained a perilous undertaking. The main stone bridge between Anizy and Pinon was badly damaged by bombing and still being struck by well-placed artillery fire. Pioneer troops labored to build crude plank bridges to support crossings elsewhere. French aircraft flew overhead and were certain to detect any obvious activity.

2nd Battalion started across the foot bridges during a brief break in the firing. The movement was especially difficult for the overloaded machine gun teams who were soon exhausted as they climbed the high ground past the canal. French planes bombed and strafed the exposed troops and the drumfire tempo artillery fire resumed.[203]

With the journey to the front now impossible, Lais watched infantry formations ahead of him disappear into an opening in the Pinon heights. Lais led his men into what was an enormous cavern system, so large it was already contained battalion-sized elements. For the rest of his life, on the anniversary of October 19, Lais would pause to remember his 1917 stay in the Pinon cave, as this was the circumstance of his 20th birthday.

Lais despaired when he realized that the cave only had one entrance and exit point. The veteran German soldiers had plenty of experience in subterranean warfare and knew they this circumstance violated the core rule of ensuring multiple exits. Lais had only recently witnessed the horrors of Reserve IR 111's death trap in the tunnel at the Winterberg and feared the same consequences here.

The Pinon caverns had a centuries-long history of providing refuge to residents of the Laon region in times of revolution and invasion. The French army knew they would be occupied by German troops and targeted the caves for bombardment by super-heavy siege artillery. This included several batteries of 15-inch and 16-inch guns which fired non-explosive shells with armor-piercing points that could penetrate roofs of the tunnels. The accuracy French gunnery was such that one aircraft was able to the direct the fire of one 15-inch cannon to land five consecutive shells in the same hole.[204]

In the first night in the cave, Lais' men huddled together in an alcove as the ceiling shook from the impact of large-caliber shells.

Sleeping men awoke to put on their helmets as small rocks and pieces of clay began to rain on their heads. The intensity of the shelling increased as the ear splitting overpressure blew out candles and loosened ever larger chunks of rocks to fall into the masses. At daybreak there was a short respite in the artillery bombardment. An outpost was established at the cave entrance. The sentries reported a flight of 18 French planes flying around the cave. 15 of the aircraft flew at high speeds, with three others slowly looping around to observe their prey. The artillery attack resumed as great geysers of earth flew up as a walking barrage was directed towards the cave's opening. The lookouts were prepared for such a contingency and had oiled the floor of the entrance to make their reentry faster. At the very last moment, they slid into the cave with a spray of shrapnel and rock splinters ricocheting on the entrance walls. The worst fears of the Germans holed up in the cave were realized – they were trapped.

The bombardment during the second day in the cave was much worse. French gunners were arming the large caliber shells delayed action fuses that enabled the projectiles to burrow deep into the cave's exterior before exploding. For hours on end, the concussions came so fast that it felt as if the men's helmets were being battered by jackhammers. The thick chalk dust was choking and turned the men's faces and teeth into white masks of clay. Waves of overpressure frequently extinguished the lights and plunged the cave in darkness. Many of the German troops were young replacements who only recently joined their units in the Sissonne lagers. This terrifying bombardment was their first exposure to shell fire, leaving some to shout and cry in a panic that began to spread to the veterans. Lais wrote how the prevailing, claustrophobic urge made it seem preferable to run out of the exit and be blown apart by the shell fire rather than be crushed or suffocated to death inside the cave.

It was at some point in the afternoon when the disaster struck. A mighty crash was followed by a dull thud. All lights went out and the chamber was filled with a thick dust cloud of lime that filled the men's lungs. The sounds of moaning and whimpering were joined by cries of 'pioneers here!' and 'bring lights!' When lanterns were relit, the flickering scope of the calamity became apparent. A 20 meter section of cave roof fell upon a platoon of infantry, crushing two squads under tons of rock. The surviving squad sat stunned but unscathed on the other side of the cave. After realizing the fate of their comrades, these men began to scream in panic. Veterans came over and tightly held the survivors in an effort to sooth them back into control.

Lais observed how the horrors of the cave illuminated the limits that the human soul could bear. He remarked some of the strongest men, 'bulls of soldiers' were driven mad by claustrophobia. In comparison, he described the example of one gentle, weak-appearing young men who previously was written-off by his NCO's as a poor soldier. When conditions inside the cave were at its worst, this meek boy became of pillar of strength as calmed an outbreak of panic swirling around him. Lais concluded: "It is the power of a soldier's soul that is most decisive, and not the strength of his biceps that enables him to throw a hand grenade five meters further than the others."

The artillery fires finally slackened at dusk. Squads, platoons and companies were counted off as the cave was evacuated in a two hour process. It was later estimated that 60 German soldiers remained entombed in catacombs of the Pinon cave. Lais likened his experience to that of Dante's Inferno.[205]

The dazed survivors emerged from the cave to find a scene of great chaos. Group Crépy had now ordered the 52nd Division to commit six of its nine maneuver battalions to take positions immediately behind the 13th and 14th Divisions defending the Pinonriegel. This decision, well before the French ground offensive had yet to launch, left the entire army group with a reserve force of only three battalions. Any counterattack capability was lost. Worse still, the individual 52nd battalions moving to the front would be subordinated to 13th and 14th Divisions and be divorced from their own regimental structures. Lais' MG platoon's ordeal in the Pinon cavern was for naught, as they, along with a scattered collection of other 52nd Division companies, were pulled back north of the canal.

Heavy rains on October 21-22 grounded French aircraft, bringing some relief from the accuracy of the enemy artillery pounding. The continuing artillery fires still restricted the overtaxed German supply routes. Food supplies were scarce and soggy bread was primary source of sustenance. Musketeer Hans Schadt, the leader of the IR 169's 8th Company's supply troop, proved a hero when his four-hour scrounging foray led to a discovery of a shattered baggage wagon. On his return to the company, the resulting booty of a bag of meat cans and wet bread was gratefully devoured. Field telephone wires were constantly cut by shell fire and communication between command posts and front line units were tenuous.

The French ground offensive began in the early hours of October 23. IR 169's 2nd Battalion command post, located near the village of Vaudesson and two miles northwest of Fort Malmaison, received first word of the attack at 3:00 am. A terse telephone report came from the front that enemy tanks were advancing upon them. The line then went dead. The pre-attack artillery barrage, described by Lais as 'an unimaginable vortex of fire,' began at 4:00 am. A rolling barrage across the front signaled the assault had begun.[206]

The first wave of the French offensive was led by six divisions attacking across a 7.5 mile front. The attack included 63 Schneieder and St-Chamond tanks, only 21 of which were mechanically sound enough to get through the mud and into the battle zone. The six day long bombardment churned the German front line trenches into crater fields. French infantry closely followed behind the creeping barrage that fired 16 shells per minute and advanced in 50 meter bounds. The weather favored the attackers, with a heavy fog and rain that obscured the assault waves as they closed in and stormed the Germans lines.

The German defenders stood little chance to slow the attack, let alone repel it. Artillery support remained ineffectual and the few strong points that remained were surrounded and attacked from the rear by tanks. Fort de la Malmaison, blasted into ruins, was easily overrun and its garrison was killed or captured. The 13th and 14th Divisions were shattered and front completely collapsed. Germans losses included seven regiments and large quantities of artillery. With the front line trenches conquered by 8:00 am, the French commanders halted for several hours to regroup and prepare to resume the attack. They had an enormous opportunity before them, for a rapid dash to the canal could entrap all Germans remaining to the south of the Ailette.

The Germans now paid the consequences for having deployed their main battle line only a few miles in front of a large water obstacle. The immediate priority was to organize enough resistance to slow the French offensive. At best, even a modest delay of the enemy would allow the Germans to evacuate as many men and guns as possible across the few remaining canal crossing points. A permanent defensive line could then be established north of the Ailette.

The Group Crépy command and staff element was in such disarray it was no longer functional. The 52nd Division commander took over this role and assumed operational control for the remaining Pinonriegel sector. The division leadership had an enormously difficult task to cobble together enough battered and disparate units to confront the French avalanche. Much of the task fell to 52nd Division staff officer Captain Preu, who commanded the three remaining reserve battalions. Using his adjutant and an ordnance officer as messengers, he hastily pulled together the division's widely dispersed battalions and other local units to establish a thin defensive line. The six 52nd Division battalion's that had been committed forward had already suffered heavy casualties. Whatever 13th and 14th Division remnants that could be found were used as 'stuffing' to fill the gaps between existing units. This position ran two miles north of the former front lines and stretched just south of Pinon and through the Pinon Forest to the east. Failure to hold this line risked destruction of the division and capture of most of the remaining troops and material still south of the Ailette canal.[207]

The thick fog continued well into the morning and masked the renewed French advance. One of the first 52nd units to encounter the surging French were IR 169's 3rd Battalion, which fended off the initial French attack in a wild fight before being pushed back to the heights overlooking the Pinon Forest.

IR 111's 2nd Battalion, commanded by Captain Seth, faced dire circumstances with the attack from French forces that included African colonial troops from Regiments of Infantry 109 and 149. Lieutenants Merker and Meldung were sent to scout the woods before the battalion and found themselves surrounded by the enemy vanguard. A section of tanks blocked a return to their unit. Their mad dash enabled them to escape back to regimental headquarters, sparing them the fate of what befell upon their battalion. Waves of French colonial infantry, supported by tanks came out of the fog from both the left and right flanks as heavy artillery barrage hit the battalion. Seth sent back breathless couriers to the regimental command post with pleas for reinforcement, but there was little help available to provide. In a rare display of fire support, German artillery did briefly slow some of the armor at the edge of the fog, and even scored a direct hit on a tank. It was too little and too late. The French tanks rolled forward and the infantry closed in with grenades. Captain Seth was severely wounded by tank fire as a violent, but brief close quarters melee ensued. The French numbers overwhelmed the defenders and the 2nd Battalion was overrun.

During the battle, a number of the German wounded had been moved into and around the 2nd Battalion command post bunker. The first squads of the French colonials arrived and began to club and kick those wounded German prisoners found outside the bunker. Others opened fire through the bunker slots into the wounded sheltered inside. An infuriated, captured German medical officer, wearing a red cross arm band, sprang forward to try to stop the shooting. When he refused the colonials demands to first treat the French wounded, he was severely beaten with rifle butts. Other colonials began to toss hand grenades into the bunker as screams of agony came from within. A French medical orderly finally put a stop to massacre. Lais' memoirs record him as remaining forever embittered by the instances of atrocities inflicted by colonial troops upon German prisoners. He cast the responsibility for their behavior on their white French officers.[208]

IR 170's 1st Battalion also made a determined stand but was slowly pushed back. Only 40 men remaining in ranks by the time the battalion eventually withdrew across the canal.

IR 169's battalions were equally hard pressed. Its 3rd Battalion, commanded by Captain Engel, defended in front of Pinon Village. In the 12th Company, the renowned storm troop leader, Sergeant Spies, took advantage of a fleeting tactical opportunity when he observed that a French detachment had become separated in unfavorable terrain. He led a small patrol in a counterattack and returned with 14 enemy prisoners and a captured machine gun.

The 3rd Battalion struggled to maintain connection to its neighboring left flank unit, which was separated by a gully. French infantry, supported by tanks, were pushing through the low ground and threatened to break the tenuous link. The enemy tanks struggled to climb up the steep slopes, allowing a minenwerfer [short range mortar] to score a direct hit and set one on fire. The situation caused the defenders to curse the lack of German armor, as a few of their own tanks could have easily destroyed the French ones below.[209] As the French infantry closed in, the Germans ran out of hand grenades and resorted to hand-to-hand combat. The 3rd Battalion took heavy losses in this fight. 11th Company lost all three of its officers; Lieutenants Wesch and Jack killed, and Lt Straub severely wounded. Only 20 men in the company were left alive and unwounded at the battle's end.

A few kilometers to the east, IR 169's 2nd Battalion, commanded by Captain Schellig, made its stand in the high ground above the forest. There was a large gap on 2nd Battalion's left flank connection to the 1st Battalion, IR 57. As the French assault was nearing this sector, a panicked messenger from the IR 57 reported to Captain Schellig that his unit was being overrun and needed immediate assistance. Schellig calmly asked the courier for more information and then ordered his 7th Company to support the beleaguered 57th. The company donned its assault packs and then sprinted off through the gorge to east and into the battle. Midway to their objective, the 7th was received a direct hit from an artillery barrage. Half the company was killed or wounded, including its commander, whose arm was nearly torn off. The remaining men connected with the 57th and tried to patch the gap between the two units. Leutnant Lehmann, a platoon commander in 8th Company, was ordered to absorb the fragments of the 7th company and reinforce the line. Moments later, the 5th Company launched a counterattack that threw the French in retreat.

Off to the southwest, 2nd Battalion observed a mass of colonial infantry advancing from the Allemant heights in preparation to attack another unit on their right flank. The enemy was advancing in an open field that was just within the maximum range of the 2nd Battalion's machine guns. The gunners watched in great frustration as this target passed unmolested, for their last few belts of remaining ammunition was needed for their own immediate defense.

While the crisis on 2nd Battalion's left flank was momentarily checked, the French shattered the lines between IR 57 and IR 56. Lt Lehmann was ordered to stretch the battalion's left flank even further. Scouting to the east, he realized that both IR's 57 and 56 were in full retreat, leaving 2nd Battalion on its own. The battalion still continued to fight in position until all ammunition was gone, and then retreated towards the canal.[210]

The 52nd Division defense of the intermediary Pinon line on October 23-24 was stout enough to dissuade French ground forces from directly attacking the canal. While the Germans suffered terrible losses in the disastrous collapse of the Pinonriegel, the division's stand did enable a large quantity of men and guns to cross the canal to safety.

The retreat across the Ailette Canal was a sloppy affair. The lack of bridges resulted in great traffic jams of wagons, artillery batteries, horses and men piled up on the southern bank. German air squadrons did their best to provide protection, and overhead, trails of smoke from crashing planes marked the dog fights of French and German aircraft. The French air superiority trumped control of the skies, and the congested masses at the bridgeheads made inviting targets for staffing and bombing strikes. The Germans took severe losses from both the air and artillery strikes during the crossing.

As Lais recorded, "Everyone wanted to be the next person over the canal's train embankment." Most of the infantry were forced to jump in the chilly canal and swim to the north bank. Panic broke out among those who could not swim as NCOs swore and kicked at the men to get them to cross. Once across the canal, the only source of protection was the embankment, as the high water table made it impossible to dig any further type of cover. Lais wrote of the miserable situation faced by the disorganized, soaking wet troops:

> "First impression; massive quartering! The entire, almost straight train embankment close behind the canal is full of infantry... The infantry is tightly packed together, man to man, lying against the embankment. Eight infantry battalions, along with the rubble of the 13th and 14th Divisions, are squeezed into a sector width of hardly 800 meters. The heavy French artillery fire results in bitter losses." [211]

By the evening of October 25, the French continued to consolidate and appeared content to leave the two mile zone between the 52nd Division's recent stand and the canal as a no-man's-land. The Germans began to establish a permanent defense north of the canal. Part of this preparation included blowing up all of the remaining bridges spanning the canal.

No longer pressed by an imminent ground attack, German commanders realized a final opportunity to destroy some their artillery lying abandoned in the outpost zone. One deserted battery was reported to be at the edge of the forest at a site of the previous day's battle. Lais' MG platoon, along with a squad of infantry and a demolitions section from Pioneer Company 104, were selected for a mission to find and destroy the cannon before falling into French hands.

The detachment, now well supplied with ammunition, moved out after dark across one of the few wood-planked footbridges still standing. As far as Lais knew, there were no longer any friendly troops south of the canal and the disposition of enemy troops was entirely uncertain. The Germans moved as silently as possible towards the still-burning Pinon Forest. As they approached the reported destination, they found two intact German 10 cm field guns. To Lais' great surprise, they also found several German artillerymen who never received the orders to retreat and were waiting on a forsaken promise of ammunition resupply. The intrepid gunners still had ten rounds of high explosive shells remaining.

The machine gunners and infantry established a defensive position as demolitions crew prepared charges to destroy the cannon's breaches. It was soon determined there was a French infantry presence about 650 meters away and headed in their direction. The Germans set their machine gun and rifle sights at 500 meters and waited for the enemy to enter the kill zone. The French came within range and the Germans surprised them with a blistering fire. Those not hit were scattered in disarray.

No sooner had the firing ceased when the clanking of tank treads was heard. A French tank platoon appeared from behind a hill and advanced towards them. The machine gunners, infantrymen and engineers fell back to a better covered position while the artillerymen returned to their pieces and quickly placed them into action. The 10 cm cannon were high-velocity guns that proved to be excellent anti-tank weapons. The first shot landed short of the lead tank but the second scored a direct hit. The two guns continued firing and knocked out three more tanks with seven shells. The final tenth round proved a miss as the sole surviving tank lumbered safely back behind the hill.

The demolitions men returned to their work and set off the explosives that destroyed the guns. The detachment, now joined by the artillerymen, returned towards the canal through a deep forest path. As they emerged through the forest, an artillery barrage struck the marshy area between the woods and canal. Shrapnel from an incoming shells sent a lethal splinter through the throat of one of Lais' men. Lais wrote: "The blood stream swelled and I could do more to help him. He died in my arms."

The fire eventually paused and the detachment moved through the marsh to the footbridge. The last man had barely crossed over the span when Lais heard a yell of "Attention, explosion, head's down!" The bridge had been wired with explosives and the engineers were waiting the return of the patrol to blow it. Lais and his men dove for cover as an enormous blast came from behind and pieces of planking fell about them and clapped into the dark waters of the canal.[212]

The night of October 25-26 remained a nightmare for the masses of German soldiers huddling against the embankment. A heavy shelling began in the early morning hours. The embankment offered no protection from high-arched mortars and howitzers and several direct hits caused massive casualties. Lais' platoon was slightly more fortunate, as they occupied a somewhat better protected, over-watch position by the ruins of the main bridge to Pinon.

With dawn, the battle was over. The 52nd Division pulled out of line on October 26, marching 20 miles northeast through Laon and to the village of Richaumont.

The French La Malmaison offensive succeeded in finally taking the Chemin des Dames ridgeline. The collapse of the Pinonriegel convinced the German 7th Army commander that the Chemin des Dames was untenable. On the night of 1 November, 7th Army executed the Bunzelwitz maneuver, which involved the retreat of German forces over the Ailette River and canal, resulting in the abandonment of the Chemin des Dames heights. In terms of real estate, this resulted in the French gaining two miles of depth over a 12 mile length of line stretching east from Pinon, to near IR 169's initial deployment to Juvincourt.

IR 169's sacrifices before the Chemin des Dames – for 1917 at least – was finished. The IR 169 service journal described how "the battalions of the regiment again brought the repeated French attacks to a standstill and through determined counterattacks, forced the enemy into a partial retreat." The reality of the combat was much starker. The long hike to Richaumont gave the men time to reflect on the 12 days of battle in and around the Pinonriegel. Lais memoires speak to regiment's bitterness of being so incompetently mishandled by the commanding Army group. As the group's designated counterattack force, the 52nd Division should have remained intact to strike against a

French breakthrough, serving as the 'hammer, not the anvil.' The premature commitment of two thirds of the division's maneuver battalions to unfamiliar command structures was devastating to the units and eliminated any German capacity for a counterpunch.

German losses in the La Malmaison offensive were totaled as 38,000 Germans killed, wounded or missing and 12,000 prisoners, along with 200 guns and 720 machine guns, against 14,000 French casualties.[213] The 52nd Division's casualties were fearful. IR 169's reported losses included 14 officers (6 killed) and 831 men (with 133 recorded as missing, many of those were men forever entombed in the Pinon caverns.) Total losses for the combatants of the 1917 Aisne Campaign between April – October 1917 were 187,000 French and 167,000 German casualties. [214]

After a brief reassembly period at Richaumont, IR 169 took part in the 52nd Division's railway relocation from the Aisne battlefields to a 3rd Army controlled sector 60 miles southeast. This placed the regiment at the edge of the Meuse-Argonne Forest, 45 miles northwest of Verdun. The inbound trains arrived in the village of Savigny. From there, the regiment made a short hike past the Hindenburg Line stronghold at Falaise and into quarters at the villages of Monthois and Brieres.

The division was only allocated an eight day period of rest. It was a dreary time, with distinguishing quality of the lager camp remembered as being mired in ankle deep mud. Many new recruits were needed to beginning filling the vacancies left by the Aisne Campaign casualties. 52nd Division sought to rebalance the experience levels between the three regiments. To minimize complaints, the 52nd Division commander personally made the reassignment selections. The Pinon battlefield losses to IRs 111 and IR 170 were even worse than for IR 169. As a result, IR 169's remaining core infrastructure took an additional hit when it had to reassign 110 men to its two sister regiments. Lais recalled how tears flowed from weather-hardened faces as soldiers had to remove their 169 epaulets for that of the other regiments.[215]

Chapter 12
Transition to the 1918 Spring Offensives

IR 169 had only a week to recover from the Aisne Campaign when its battalions were rotated to the front to relieve IR 148 at the village of Ripont, eight miles south. [Ripont is another of the small French villages that were destroyed in the Great War and never repopulated – it exists today in name only.] From November 4 – December 15, the regiment manned the trenches three miles further south by the Mesnil Forest (Butte du Mesnil).

While in line, the regiment improved the defenses and conducted aggressive patrolling against the French. On 20 November, His Royal Highness the Archduke Friedrich II of Baden visited with the 2nd Battalion in the reserve area, with representatives of the other battalions attending.

The most notable event occurring during IR 169's service at Ripont was a large scale trench raid that 1st Battalion conducted on December 14. The raid was commanded by Leutnant d.R. Fritz Rombach, commanding officer of 1st Company. Rombach, who led the March 1917 raid from the Juvincourt trenches, was considered an expert in storm troop tactics. His organizational and leadership abilities were put to test in this far more complex operation.

Rombach's mission was to attack a 500 meter length of three enemy trench lines, designated on German maps (from west to east) as Points 74, 205, and 207. The assault group was tasked to destroy enemy positions and bring back prisoners. The targeted objective was embedded deep in the enemy's third trench-line. The attack required the storm troopers to first navigate the 200 meters of no-man's-land territory and breach the thick barbed wire obstacle field. The Germans then would assault into the first trench and continue 100 meters clear the second trench. The third, trench-line target objective was yet another 100 meters deeper in enemy territory.

Rombach's storm troop force included Leutnants Schwarz and Trefz, two Feldwebels, six Unteroffizieres and 51 volunteers from 1st Battalion. The force was augmented by an Unteroffizier and nine sappers (engineers) of the 52nd Division's Pioneer Company 104. Rombach prepared a thorough attack order that accounted for the smallest details. The plan's highlights included these components:

1. Assault Force Composition: The mission will be executed with five groups (storm troops) each consisting of: a leader, a second in command, nine men of the infantry and two sappers. Each of the five groups will also include two light machine gun sections consisting of one commander and four men.

2. Mission of the Storm Troops: Clearing of the French trenches [with Point 205 being the center-point of the third trench-line]:

-- Storm Troop 1: Points 74 to 205 [A 200 meter section of the western portion of the third trench-line target area.]
-- Storm Troop 2: Points 207 to 205 [A 150 meter section of the eastern portion of the third trench-line target area.]
-- Storm Troop 3: The 200 meter, western section of the second trench-line.
-- Storm Troop 4 : The 150 meter, eastern section of the second trench-line.
-- Storm Troop 5: Moves to the center position of the second trench-line. Using grenades, disrupt counterattacking enemy forces. The storm troop will destroy the large obstacle observed there and then advance to Point 205 in order to first reinforce Storm Troops 1 and 2 and cover the return of all the Storm Troops.

3. Withdrawal Phase Cover: Storm Troops 1-4 will designate three men at specific points to cover the withdrawal. Light MG Section (1) will cover the west flank and Light MG Section (2) will cover the east flank.

4. Assault Fire-cover:

-- Grenade Launchers: Two grenade launcher teams, each with two Granatenwerfers, will be positioned at forward saps and take specified enemy points under fire.

-- Indirect Machine gun Targets: [These four MG nests were located on elevated terrain, between 300-800 meters behind the third German trench line.]

Gun position Lahr with distance 1700m on point Z (southeast).

Gun position Freiburg with distance 1800m on point 203 (south).

Gun position Konstanz with distance 1600m on point 190 (southwest).

Gun position Mannheim with distance 2000m on point 91 (eastern flank of front enemy trench).

-- Direct Machine Gun fire: Two sections, each with two guns, in the German front line trench will suppress enemy to the left and right portions of the assault sector.

5. Reserve: The reserve force consists of one officer and 32 men in four groups (*Infanteriegruppen*). The reserve will stand ready near the tunnel exits of the first trench to assist where required.

6. Storm Group Starting Points: Each storm troop and two light MG teams are designated specific starting points in the sap trench to use as the launch point.

7. Storm Troop Battle Grouping: Storm troops will be led by two sappers with explosive loads. Immediately behind are the storm troop leader with four men, two designated as hand grenade throwers and two as hand grenade carriers. Half of this team will move outside the enemy trench while rest of maneuvers from the inside.

8. Weapons and Gear:

-- Every man on the assault teams carries eight stick-hand grenades and six egg-hand grenades and a sidearm, either Pistol 08 or Mauser C96 (9mm).

-- Gear: Three wire cutters for each storm troop. The leaders carry a stopwatch, luminous compass, signal whistle and signal lamp.

-- The cover troops will have one riflemen and two men with side arms. They will carry the same amount of hand grenades and have one wire cutter with them.

-- The MG groups will have 750 rounds in their drums. Every rifle man carries a signal-pistol with 20 rounds (will light up the raid from the flanks).

9. Equipment Issue: Gear and munitions will be handed out on December 14, at 0300 hours at the tunnel exit West.

10. Artillery and Mortar Preparations: Heavy artillery and mortars will fire a two minute barrage on the objective, then shift to flank and provide cover fire for remainder of the mission. Special mission for the heavy artillery is to target the French strongpoint, OUVRAGE, [one kilometer east of the central target zone.]

11. Start time for Storm Troop assault: 0 plus 120 Sec.

12. Return Time for Storm Troops: At 0 plus 30 min, storm troops will assemble in the first French trench-line. [Troop leaders had discretion on how to exfiltrate their units back to their own trenches based on the extent of enemy artillery fires.]

13. Reception Groups: The leaders of the reserve groups have a list of the names of the raid members. They will cross out the names as they return to the line.

14. Parole Codeword: L A H R.

15. Storm Troop Identification:

-- Storm Troops 1 and 2: White ribbon on left upper arm.
-- Storm Troops 3 und 4: White ribbon on right upper arm.
-- Storm Troop 5: White ribbon on left lower arm.
-- Light MG Troops: White ribbon on right lower arm.

16. Reassembly and Prisoner Collection: After return report to the West Tunnel exit. Take prisoners there!

17. Security: Nobody talks about this mission.

Rombach also added a postscript to the order that acknowledged the lack of flamethrowers: "This time the raid will be executed without flamethrowers (*Flammwerfers*) since we lost the entire Flammwerfertrupps in the last three missions. Requested replacements to flush out the enemy shelters did not arrive in time for the raid."

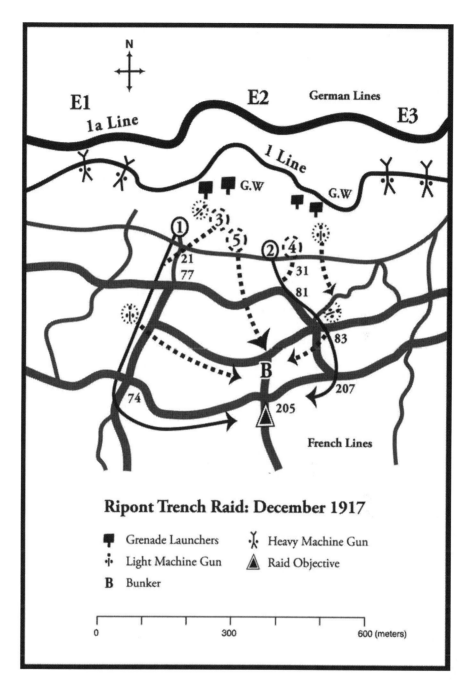

Ripont Trench Raid: December 1917

- ◼ Grenade Launchers
- ⁜ Light Machine Gun
- **B** Bunker
- 𝕏 Heavy Machine Gun
- ▲ Raid Objective

```
0                    300                600 (meters)
```

The Germans invested a great deal of effort in mission training. A full scale mock-up of the objective was constructed from aerial reconnaissance photographs. The entire assault group spent ten nights rehearsing the attack. Experiences of previous raids were extensively studied. In earlier missions, the assault troops launched into no-man's-land from their front-line trenches, causing an excessive delay in closing in on the objective. In this attack, the men would silently crawl as close to the enemy trenches as possible and await the assault order from the cover of shell craters. Sappers would blow up the obstacle fields during the preparatory barrage. As soon as the fires lifted, the assault squads would rush into the lead trench and roll up its defenders. While this advanced placement of the storm troops added speed for the assault, it risked exposing the attackers perilously close to friendly artillery fire.

Special attention was applied to trench clearing tactics. Storm troop maneuvering was choreographed so that half the teams attacked from inside the trench while the remaining members advanced from behind the rear edge of the parapets. Much emphasis was placed on hand grenade precision. Regimental doctrine stressed the quick, purposeful and accurate tossing of the grenades. Teams were trained to throw hand grenades in a sequenced, 'drum-fire' manner to increase the shock effect. Troopers practiced how to quickly and accurately fire their pistols in bursts that expended no more than half a magazine at a time. A core aspect of the storm trooper tactics focused on the smallest tactical element, the two-man buddy teams. It was essential that every combat action was a coordinated team effort, and the pairs would never intentionally be separated. The assault MG squads were issued captured French light machine guns, as the rate of fire was superior to German guns.

Three days before the raid, the teams rehearsed moving into their start positions by navigating with fluorescent compasses. After careful assessment of weather and lighting conditions, zero hour of the attack was set for 6:35 am on December 14.[216]

Assault group personnel were awoken at 2:00 am on the morning of the raid. An Unteroffizier walked from bunk to bunk and whispered to each raider "*Aufstehen, es ist Zeit*" (Get up, it is time). No word was spoken, and the men quietly moved into the tunnel leading to the front trench. Ammunition was issued and all hands were given sip of schnapps to warm up. From the tunnel the seventy-one men crawled out into their start positions. The sappers placed long rods with attached explosive loads into the enemy wire obstacles. Moments before the scheduled barrage, they lit the fuses and took cover in the bottom of shell craters.

The two-minute long artillery barrage opened right at zero hour. Disaster, however, struck at the onset when a short-ranged salvo exploded into the center of Storm Troop 2. When the fire shifted off the objective, it was realized that two men, one feldwebel and one unteroffizier, were killed and the most of the survivors left severely wounded. Lt. Schwarz, the Storm Troop 2 commander, received splinter wounds but was able to return under his own power to German lines. Storm Troop 4 diverted from its mission in order to help recover the dead and wounded. Other problems arose when some of the demolition explosions failed to clear obstacles, causing delays as the sappers scrambled to set off new charges. Despite these setbacks, enough men from the assault teams slipped through gaps in the wire and quickly cleared the first trench.

French defenders responded with a brisk automatic fire. At the western portion of the objective, enemy troops, pulled 'Spanish Rider' wire obstacles before the third trench. A wild hand grenade battle ensued. German sappers took advantage of the smoke from the exploding hand grenades and were able to blast open this new obstacle. French resistance started to break. Some of the defenders fled the trenches and ran towards the southwest, where they were cut down by plunging fire from covering machine guns. Other enemy troops took shelter in a large dugout and fired wildly from the bunker entrance. Leutnant Trefz, leader of Storm Troop 1 yelled for them to surrender. Whether or not they heard Trefz' command or understood their predicament, the trapped French soldiers continued to fire. The Germans regretted their lack of flamethrowers, as it would have been an ideal weapon for the circumstances. They instead rolled grenades down the bunker stairs. Screams could be heard from below, but no one escaped as bunker entrance collapsed from the detonations. With this strongpoint eliminated, Storm Troop 1 continued towards the primary object; Point 205, the center of the third trench.

The raiders battling in the French trenches had yet to learn of the shell strike on Storm Troop 2. The first indication of trouble was when Storm Troop 1 reached Point 205. There was no sign of Troop 2, which was supposed to link up and form the left flank. Soon after, two members of Storm Troop 4 arrived at the front to report on Troop 2's friendly fire calamity. Leutnant Rombach ordered Lt. Trefz to hold his position to ensure the right flank remained secure.

Back at the second French line, Storm Troop 3, led by Unteroffizier Kloh, united with Storm Troop 5 and finished clearing the trench. Five bunkers were found and destroyed with explosives, burying all enemy occupants. Kloh then led his party into a communications trench that connected the second and third trenches. At the middle of this section, the Germans encountered a large bunker the French used as a storage depot for construction materiel. A heavy fire came from the firing slots that blocked their advance. The bunker was especially well protected and topped with a one meter thick earthen roof. Unteroffizer Kloh, armed with a satchel charge, proceeded to crawl from outside the trench line and onto the bunker roof. Kloh pulled the fuse, counted two seconds and threw the charge down into the entrance port. The explosion blew three bodies out of the bunker, a severely wounded French officer and two mortally wounded enlisted men.

The raiding party had met its objectives. It cleared and controlled three enemy trenches inside a 400 meter wide and 300 meter deep intrusion point. There were no enemy troops left alive who were not already prisoners or were too severely wounded to transport back. Storm troop units exploited the area for anything of intelligence value as well as grabbing weapons and materiel for their own use. The spoils included steel shields, crates of hand grenades, grenade launchers and light machine guns. The raiding party still had three explosive charges remaining, which were used to blow up the communication trench between the second and third lines.

It was now time to exfiltrate back to their own trenches. In most cases, the men sprinted back the 150 meter distance to the designated rally point in the southwestern tunnel of the first trench. As they approached this position, the troopers called out the 'LAHR' password, jumped into the trench and checked in with the NCO's responsible for the accountability rosters.

At 7:15, the skies still remained dark, with a morning mist was rolling in. Leutnant Rombach queried the leader of one of reception groups and learned that a pioneer who was detailed to Storm Troop 2 could not be accounted for. Rombach gave the terse order to "*suche*" (search). Five minutes later the body of the sapper was returned to German lines. He was found in the vicinity of the first enemy trench, killed by a head shot. It was assessed he was hit by a lucky French round in the early stages of the attack. This was the only fatality resulting from enemy fire in the entire raid.

Major Berthold, the 1st Battalion Commander, was on hand to greet and praise the returning raiders. Initial results were promising. Prisoners were already being interrogated by an army group intelligence officer. Another intelligence windfall was a map, taken from the pocket of a dead French officer, which depicted the security outpost locations for the entire sector. Despite his command's accomplishment, Lt Rombach was displeased. He believed he had achieved more productive intelligence and materiel yields in previous raids and still bristled at the lack of flamethrowers for this mission. Major Berthold sought to reassure Rombach. "There is nothing you could have done better, even if you had the flamethrowers. Such are the fortunes of war." [217]

On December 16, two days following the raid, IR 169 was relieved in line by Reserve IR 236, of the 151st Reserve Division. IR 169's losses for the duration of the Ripont deployment included 1 officer and 50 men.

The regiment went into winter quarters in a cluster of villages six miles north of Monthois, which included the Toges, Vandy, Terron, Quatre-Champs, and Ballay. [This month-long posting placed the regiment just 10 miles west of the location where IR 169 would fight to its death 11 months later.] Training and field exercises were conducted at the battalion, regimental and brigade levels as well as with divisional artillery. The IR 169 field journal described a comprehensive, multi-echelon training programs that made a deliberate effort to integrate new recruits and focus on evolving, offensive trench warfare doctrine. Lais described this period: "In the foothills of the Ardennes Forest, we train day after day in offensive tactics – no defense. How this will be executed is not hidden from us; we have done everything to make us masters in these tactics." [218]

For the first time in three years, the regiment enjoyed quiet Christmas celebrations. On December 25, Major von der Becke Kluechssner was transferred from the regiment and command was passed on to Colonel Baron Schaeffer von Bernstein.

In its first operational deployment of 1918, IR 169 was called back to the front on January 9. The mission was to relieve Reserve IR 238, of the 52nd Reserve Division, located in trenches nine miles south of

Vouziers at the village of Somme-Py. The regiment was centered with IR 44, (2nd Infantry Division) on the right flank and IR 111 to the left. In this month-long posting, the regiment worked at expanding the defenses and conducting the usual assortment of trench raids and combat patrolling. IR 169 remained in line until February 14, when IR 238 was rotated back to the front and the regiment returned to the Vouziers' base camp complex. Losses in this month-long excursion to the trenches were 23 men, to include one killed.

When the regiment returned to Vouziers, the German Army was well underway in making preparations for the grand Spring 1918 Offensives. The late 1917 victory over Russia provided Germany with an enormous opportunity to go on the offensive in the west. In Petrograd, on November 7, 1917, the Bolsheviks seized control of the Provisional Russian government and quickly secured an armistice with the Kaiser, spelling the end of the war in the east. With this victory in hand, 50 German divisions were now free for transfer to the Western Front. Russia's elimination from the war left Germany as the single most dominant power in Europe. The resulting German troop strength on the Western Front increased by 30% at the same time that available British forces decreased by 25%.[219] For the first time since 1914, Germany had the opportunity to seize the initiative and launch an offensive so powerful that it could knock England and France out of the war. With America on the verge of deploying over a million troops to Europe, these offensives were Germany's last chance for victory.

The 1918 Spring Offensive, referred to as the *Kaiserschlacht* (Kaiser's Battle) or Ludendorff Offensive, was really a series of four major attacks intended to drive a fatal wedge between the British and French armies. Between March – August 1918, IR 169 would participate in three of these offensive pushes; Operation "Michael," the largest of the offenses aimed at retaking the Somme; the "Blucher-Yorck" Offensive on the Aisne's Chemin des Dames battlefields of 1917, and Operation "Georgette," the northernmost attack that returned the regiment to Flanders.

Upon its return to Vouziers, IR 169 began an intensive training program to prepare for the impending Kaiserschlacht. This included field exercises throughout the Argonne Forest at the company, battalion, regimental, brigade and divisional level. Storm troop doctrine was promulgated, tactics where specially trained shock troops infiltrated and bypassed enemy front line units, leaving these strong points to be mopped-up by follow-up troops. Armed with light submachine guns, flamethrowers and grenades, the storm troopers' tactic was to closely follow supporting barrages to attack and disrupt enemy headquarters, artillery units and supply depots in the rear areas, as well as to rapidly occupy territory.[220]

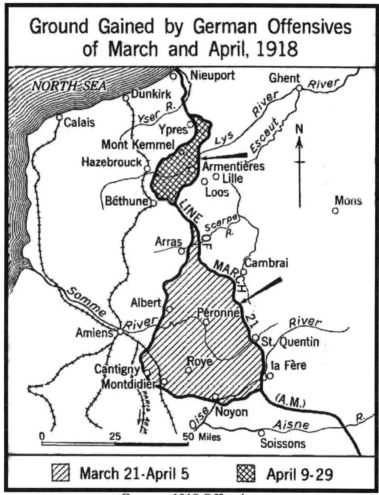

German 1918 Offensives

The Germans made significant gains in the Spring 1918 offensives. IR 169 entered the front lines of the Somme (Michael) Offensive near Montdidier on 26 March where it fought through 10 April. Later that summer, the regiment deployed north to the serve in the Arras sector from 14 July – 3 August, and in Flanders, near Hazebrouck, 10 – 18 August.

(AABE)

Dr. Bull, in *Trench*, illustrates how history's dramatic legend of German storm troop units has discounted small unit developments occurring within all combatant armies. Infantry tactics, learning from disastrous frontal attacks, evolved to stress platoon and squad level units using cover, light machine guns and large quantities of grenades to work around enemy strong points. The German *Nahkampfmittle* field manual prescribed close combat tactics emphasizing the role of grenades, pistols and movement from shell hole to shell hole. The German doctrine provided wide latitude to small unit leaders to use their discretion in maneuvering their troops.[221]

Core storm unit composition were the assault detachments (*Stosstrupps*) and groups (*Gruppen*). The groups were squad-sized units made up of riflemen and a light machine gun, with detachments combining a collection of groups and specialized elements. The composition of storm units were task organized based on the mission requirements, ranging from trench raids to major offensive attacks. Storm detachments could often range from one to five storm companies, one to two MG companies, a flamethrower section, a minenwerfer company and dedicated artillery batteries.

Storm troop employment in a division-level attack could begin with an infantry probe to expose enemy defenders. A second wave of elite storm companies with flamethrower units penetrated the weakest portions of the front enemy zones. The third wave, following 150 meters behind, were the storm battalion's heavy weapon sections that would support the assault of the forward storm companies and protect the flanks from counterattacks. Conventional infantry units came from further behind to eliminate bypassed pockets of resistance and maintain the momentum of the attack.[222]

Artillery tactics were refined to better support the initial breakthrough. The *Feuerwalze* rolling barrage doctrine created a three phased bombardment scheme. The first was a brief attack on the enemy's command and communications, the second, the destruction of their artillery, and finally, an attack upon the enemy front-line infantry defenses. To increase the shock, bombardments were carefully planned to be short and intensive.[223]

As demonstrated in 1st Battalion's December 14 trench raid at the Mesnil Forest, IR 169 was well on the way of mastering storm troop tactics. In the Spring 1918 offensives, IR 169 often adopted an ad hoc approach this doctrine, with several companies operating in storm troop capacity, followed by other companies in more traditional formations. During this transition phase Otto Lais was promoted to the rank of lieutenant and continued serve in IR 169's 2nd MG Company. Lais described the decentralized command structure of 1918 that leveraged the combat experience of junior officers and NCOs:

> "The year 1918 demanded particular measures. The war had taken on a new form, for which the tactics of the static war up to that point and the normal war of maneuver were insufficient. The Englishmen searched for a new style of fighting, and cleverly evaluated the experiences of earlier failures and defeats. We ourselves found a new method of warfare, which we built ourselves and was based on the combat experiences of the group, the company, the regiment, perhaps even of the division: lighting fast repositioning, don't wait for orders but instead rely on the trench warfare experience of the NCO's, the lieutenants and the commanders of smaller units. The great structure of orders of earlier defensive battles largely simply disappeared at the incalculable pace of summer 1918.
>
> The combat actions of the German front of 1918 showed splendid individual actions of single company commanders, single battalion and regimental commanders, individual division commanders accomplishments which punched through and carried supporting troops along with them." [224]

As the 52nd Division trained and readied their equipment for the offensive, there was also some brief time set aside for recreation. Troops were afforded the opportunity to attend the theater in Vouziers, and on March 6, the 52nd Division staged celebratory events to mark its third anniversary. Back in active service, the regiment took part in an operation in support of the deception plan for the coming offensive. From March 7-13, IR 169's three battalions were temporarily attached to different divisions to make diversionary movements and build decoy entrenchments in an area located 10 – 15 miles southwest of Vouziers. These assignments placed IR 169's 2nd Battalion with the 1st Reserve Division at St. Clement, 1st Battalion with the 2nd Infantry Division at Machault and the 3rd Battalion with the 52nd Reserve Division at Meday-Ferme. The regiment reassembled at Vouziers to make final preparations to include the transfer of nonessential baggage to the storage depot at Sedan, 25 miles north. Another change of command took place on March 18, when Colonel Baron Schaeffer von Bernstein was replaced as regimental commander by Lieutenant Colonel Woellwarth.

The Michael Offensive, named for Germany's patron saint, was launched on March 21, 1918 across a 60-mile front that centered on the old Somme battlefield. This attack pitted the German 2nd, 17th and 18th Armies (with 32 assault divisions and another 39 in reserve) in the Somme sector against the British 3rd and 5th Armies. To support a decisive breakthrough, Ludendorff had assembled 6,473 guns, half the number of all artillery pieces on the entire Western Front, and over 3,500 mortars and 730 aircraft. In a five-hour barrage, the Germans fired one million artillery shells, over 3000 shells per minute, at the British 5th Army lines. Storm trooper formations swarmed over the battered British positions, and by midday, the 5th Army was thrown back in retreat. In the first day of advance, the Germans took over 20,000 British prisoners and recaptured all the territory it had lost in the 7 month Allied Somme Offensive of 1916. British troops, long accustomed to the static nature of trench warfare, were unable to cope with the unparalleled German onslaught. 5th Army was flung in retreat, and by March 23, had lost up to 30 miles of ground.

On March 22, the 52nd Division was called forward to join the offensive with orders to serve as the 18th Army's XXV Corps reserves, centered in St Quentin, 70 miles northwest of Vouziers. On March 23, IR 169 departed Vouziers by train and disembarked on the western outskirts of St. Quentin. The 52nd Division was ordered onto the line in the southern portion of the breakthrough and tasked to relieve the 110th Grenadier Reserves (28th Infantry Division) engaged at Boussicourt, 30 miles to the southwest. It was a hard march, with the division arriving at the front at Davenscourt on March 25.

IR 169 had entered the battle in the last stages of the Michael Offensive and confronted stabilized French defenses. IR 169 first went into action by attacking French forces at the villages of Pierrepont and Hargicourt. The Germans were able to push the French back and continued attacks against the next series of defenses, two miles further west at the village of Malpart. The regimental field journal described heavy fighting occurring around the chapel and cemetery of St. Aignan-Eglise in Malpart. By March 26, this position marked the far limit in the southern portion of the Michael Offensive.

The following excerpt from *Baden in World War* described the experiences of an unnamed machine gunner assigned to IR 169's 3rd Machine Gun Company in this fighting:

With the IR 169 at Pierrepont

On Good Friday, the 52nd Infantry Division entered the 'great battle in France,' replacing the IR 28, which we had followed for days on their victorious campaign. It was an unaccustomed scene for us trench warriors, when the infantry lines, which included the 3rd Machine Gun Company, were forming up for the attack. The order came to the 169th: 'Fire at will.'

As evening was falling I followed along with the ammunition unit of our company into the village Pierrepont, which had been captured shortly before. The town was strangely still as it lay there, and we were nearly startled as the clock in the steeple of the village church struck the hour, a home-like sound, but strange to our ears! A sound from far-off times!

We reported to the battalion staff at the edge of town. Our orders: 'Stay here. A double guard for the ammunition supply. Make everything ready to move out. In addition...'We required no further instructions.

Up to now, there had not been many worthwhile items remaining for us in towns we had taken except broken wine bottles, chicken feathers, and more of the same. Now we were among the first to move in. In a roomy cellar we soon discovered a veritable butcher shop with all sorts of small animals. In addition there were wide shelves stacked high with the best red wine. For the exhausted bellies of us soldiers, it was almost too good.

A few hundred meters west of the town, wild small arms and machine gun fire erupted, which was soon joined by mortars located on the village street. Using doors and other items that we removed, we built gangways over the water that was flowing by the houses. At dawn the battle subsided; there were considerable losses. We moved away to the left.

During the days of Easter we were in reserve and were moved about here and there. The streets and the towns were frequently under heavy artillery fire. The advance had come to a standstill. Then we received orders to relieve the 1st Battalion that was in position on the high ground between Malpart and Grivesnes. Gun crews were reinforced as much as possible. I was assigned as lead machine gunner. Good! It had been a long time since those days of May 1915 when, from the blocking position at the sugar factory in Souchez [near Arras], I had shot at the French. An injury and a long 'veteran's benefit' had kept me from the front and the firing line for almost a year. So, back at it again! And also with the classification, "g.v." (fit for garrison duty).

In Malpart the guides were awaiting us. Through sodden fields, shell craters, and all sorts of other obstacles in the pitch-black night, it's necessary to stay on one's toes so that no one loses his way. A few bales of hay and a road just behind our position serve as markers for our path. Sweating and exhausted, we arrived at our objective. Our comrades from the 1st Machine Gun Company quickly briefed us on the most essential items. More than anything else, exposing one's head by daylight means sure death. They know this from bitter experience. Two of their people still lie dead behind the trench and will now be taken back with them.

But the losses are not all the troubles that were at this position. The outlook was not at all favorable. The trench is barely one meter deep. To the front, the piled-up earth provides protection against small arms fire. At our machine gun position, the trench bends sharply back to the right behind the cemetery of the St. Aignau-Eglise Chapel that lies diagonally behind us. This cemetery, surrounded by a strong wall, presents a major threat. The 1st Battalion had engaged in heavy fighting to possess it until it finally had to be given over to the French, who occupied it in force and fortified it. From the cemetery they can partially outflank our trench for 150 to 200 meters, and fire into our exposed corner. Maybe they had already set up a machine gun there or behind the pile of earth to the right, because they fired with uncanny accuracy whenever there was any movement. They also showed their alertness with rifle grenades and similar deviltry. Of course we weren't very keen on these, and we avoided any action that would unnecessarily draw fire to us and make our position untenable. We couldn't even properly handle and inspect our machine gun, as it was covered with a brown tarpaulin that was carefully covered with clay, and could not be moved during daylight without betraying our presence. Therefore the weapon was heavily lubricated.

The dismal, rainy April weather really didn't make our stay there very pleasant as we gradually took on the color of the soil. In the course of the day we tried to shift into all possible body positions. Only with the fall of darkness could one move their stiff limbs and, with effort, somewhat improve the trench in the rocky subsoil.

It was very modest even after the improvements. The final leftovers from the past "fat days" disappeared from our bread sacks. One morning there was a bit of excitement. A small group of Frenchmen suddenly appeared in the fog. An attack? No - they let it be understood they are calling for a mutual ceasefire because of the wounded. It takes place, and we do not fire. But doesn't it look as if the French are digging? Are they burying their dead? It's taking place to the right of the cemetery; from where we are, we can't really determine the location. Then, on the path to the cemetery, a form is coming toward us. Is it someone bringing rations or ammunition? He's heavily laden. All considered, it's a sin against one's blood and life to let the rascal stay on his feet. If supplies get tight for those people over there, maybe they will withdraw. I take aim at him with a rifle, but after I missed him, he disappears instantly behind a corner of the wall. But more of them are coming. The one in the lead crumples to the ground; the others withdraw as quickly as they can.

In the afternoon the enemy artillery became more active than usual. We responded powerfully in kind. We couldn't see the enemy trenches directly in front of us because after a level surface of about 200 meters there was a depression. The area around the windmill to the front was often the target of our shells. Suddenly alert was sounded. Heads up! To the left in the direction of Cantigny, we had a good view of the entire landscape. And there, the waves of enemy storm troops suddenly grew from the earth! We counted three, four, five! Are they really coming to us? There they are already! Off came the covering over the machine gun. The sudden excitement drives the blood through our cramped limbs all the way to our fingertips. My machine gun starts to hammer heavily.

From the damned nest of Frenchmen on our right flank they come sweeping over our trenches; our fire weakens. I have just let loose a burst of fire on the first wave of attackers when my weapon jammed. Pull the bolt; press it through - an obstacle in the barrel! Now, in this decisive moment I tear open the covering of the weapon case. In the excitement my comrade Himbert, who was feeding the ammunition belt, stood up a bit in order to look into the gun's action. At the same instant he fell to the ground at my side without a single sound. Dead! There was a hole in his helmet over his right eye. The weapon commander stepped up in his place. We pry our dead comrade's hands from the cartridge belt that he was gripping tightly and lay him to the side. This effort took place in seconds, because there was not one to lose. A blast from a grenade took out of action our team's second machine gun which was mounted in a highly elevated position behind us in the vegetation along the street. The same blast fatally wounded Under-Sergeant Mohr.

Shells come hissing over our heads and strike violently, one after the other, against the trench. Is our own artillery shooting us down? And there in front of us, one after the other, comes the waves of enemy attackers. The first of them are only a jump from us, with no kind of barrier between us, other than the sodden soil that clings to their feet. The wet weather that had caused the machine gun to jam because of the swelling of the cartridge belt. We opened a new box of ammunition and fed in a dry belt. An artillery battery located behind our defensive position has a direct view of the attackers, and finds the range of the first wave. They stumble and come to a halt. Now my weapon is again able to fire and it rattles away. We are saved. It wasn't long until everything in front of us was quiet once again. But a few '21s' rolled over into the cemetery and tore everything up, with shreds of debris flying over us. Everything depended on holding this position.

After we were relieved a few days later we wanted to convey our truly hearty thanks to the stout artillerymen back in the patch of woods for their loyal fire support at the decisive moment, but unfortunately we discovered they were no longer there." [225]

A large Allied counterattack, combined the overextension of the German logistical system, caused General Ludendorff to suspend offensive operations on April 5. The German's substantial gain in ground came at a cost of 239,000 casualties, with the Allies losing 255,000 men, 1,300 artillery pieces and 200 tanks. [226]

IR 169 remained at the front until April 10 when it was relieved by units of the 30th Infantry Division. Regimental losses in the Michael Offensive were 22 officers (5 killed) and 561 men.

On April 10, IR 169 was pulled back 20 miles east and quartered in a trio of hamlets; Cremery, Guny and Sept Fours. The next day, the regiment continued its journey by rail, eventually reaching the town of Sedan, 75 miles to the east. The regiment was billeted in the village of Douzy, five miles southeast of Sedan. For the next month and a half, the 52nd Division's movements were part of a larger German strategy to train, shift and stack reinforcements to support the next phases the Spring Offensive pushes. [227]

Sedan was rich in German military lore, with a historic battlefield that marked Prussia's seminal victory over France in the 1870 Franco-Prussian War. In 1918, the Sedan area served as a major German field training center, where a cadre of experienced soldiers instructed entire units on advanced storm troop and weapon systems tactics.

The base, established in March 1917, was on the northeast edge of the Ardennes Forest and located about 10 miles northeast of the regiment's winter 1917-18 billeting area. The facilities centerpiece was a large field training ground that was transformed into a full-scale mock-up of opposing trench systems, complete with earthworks, barbed wire obstacle fields, machine gun nests, crater fields and supporting artillery batteries. Transiting infantry and artillery units tested fire integration tactics and incorporated student feedback to advance doctrine. Unit-level training began with basic maneuvering skills that built to complex, live fire exercises that incorporated feurwaltz-based rolling artillery barrages. Officers received cross-training on various weapon systems and select machine-gun companies received specialized MG marksmanship training. Despite theater-wide munition shortages on the front lines, the center received ample quantities of ammunition for live fire and marksmanship training.[228]

The Sedan training period provided IR 169 with its first experience in operating alongside German tanks. In early 1918, the fledgling German tank corps assembled in Sedan for pre-deployment combat training. The tank force was a mix of German-manufactured A7Vs and captured British Mark IVs. The clunky A7V tanks, with a mass of 30 tons, were armed with a 5.7 cm Maxim-Nordenfelt cannon mounted at the front and six 7.92 mm machine guns on the sides and rear. The A7Vs were powered by two engines, protected by 30mm armor that could stop bullets but not high caliber shells, and was manned by a 16 man crew. The German Army only fielded about 20 A7Vs in the course of the war, as the tanks were too costly to manufacture and lacked the mobility needed to maneuver across the shell-churned terrain.

In addition to the A7Vs, the balance of the tank companies were made of a few dozen captured and rebuilt British Mark IV tanks, many of them recovered from the Cambrai battlegrounds. The Mark IV's came in male models, a cannon and three machine guns, and female version, with five machine guns. The Germans modified the engines by boring out the cylinders, making them faster than the original versions.[229]

The introduction of the IR 169 men to the panzer battalion was a memorable occasion. The crews, in gray, asbestos-lined suits, stood in contrast alongside the yellow-gold, green and reddish camouflage patterns of the tank hulls. The objective of the live-fire exercise was for the combined infantry and armor assault force to storm an enemy trench-line on the other side of the no-man's-land. The fire support program was designed to be a realistic as possible, with two artillery batteries and a minenwerfer section firing a rolling artillery barrage 45 meters ahead of the assault force.

The infantry and tank force commanders gathered to plot out the attack. The attack configuration, in a wedge formation, was based on three separate tank elements. *Abteilung* 1, codenamed *Blucher*, led the attack with a unit consisting of two tanks and a detachment of two machine gun platoons. The MG detachment, commanded by Leutnant Lais, was armed with four heavy machine guns. Lais carried a signal light for communicating with the Blucher tank commander. Groups II and III, with four tanks each, were to follow in a second wave. A loose line of storm troop infantry squads connected the two flanking tank groups.

With the planning completed, the officers returned to their units and disseminated the attack orders. Tank engines revved up and officer pulled out their watches to await the exact moment for the artillery barrage to begin. Right on schedule, the shells screamed overhead and the mock attack began.

Assaulting alongside the noisy, clanking tanks was not for the faint of heart. The tanks slid in and around the shell craters as their crews recklessly fired their cannons and machine guns just past the noses of accompanying infantrymen. In addition to the danger of the tank fire, shrapnel and debris from rolling barrage whizzed by the heads of the troops. Midway through the field, the lead element past a blinking yellow light, which simulated incoming anti-tank fire. Lais signaled to the tank commander and the final assault phase began. Lais' heavy machine guns laid a covering fire as the tank engines pitched to the highest speeds and raced for the objective. Then, at the climax of the attack, the tanks became mired in a ditch just before the front enemy trench. The follow-on infantry squads were diverted from their attack to help dislodge the tanks.

The tank assault exercise continued for a second day. Modifications were made the assault force structure, with a third tank and two light machine guns being added to the lead team and two additional tanks to each of the flank units.

The conclusion of the exercises left several of the IR 169 men wounded from the spray of artillery shrapnel, tank fire and hand grenade fragments. Lais speculated the losses would have been greater had not the tank cannons been of such small caliber. Still, the fact that men shed blood spoke to the realism of the training and battlefield conditions. While offensive use of German tanks in WW I was extremely rare, the greatest value of this training was to expose infantrymen to the vulnerability of tanks and techniques that could be used to defend against them. IR 169 would have occasion to put such skills to use in the months to come.[230]

The Sedan training schedule allowed the men to enjoy some downtime. The Douzy billeting area was only three miles east of the village of Bazeilles, which was a legendary landmark of the September 1, 1870 Battle of Sedan. During that battle, a small detachment of French marines established a strong point inside the inn of Auberge Bourgerie. Holding out for hours against an overwhelming force of Bavarians, the French commander, Captain Arsene Lambert, famously ordered to his men to hold out the last cartridge. When the Bavarian's finally took the building, they spared the French survivors, whom they respected for their display of great courage. [In 1899, the French government opened the Auberge Bourgerie as a museum, where it still remains a shrine to the French Troupes de marine.][231]

During one of their off-duty days, Lais and some of his comrades paid a visit to the Auberge Bourgerie, where they were kindly welcomed by the madame of the estate, who was a young girl at the time of the great battle. She gave the visitors a tour of the inn and old battlefield and recounted a touching story of a pair of French and German veterans of the fight who later became close friends. For many years, the men had a reunion at the village during each anniversary of the battle. One of the veterans died not long before the start of the Great War, with the other passing only two days later.[232]

The Sedan training program continued through early May. On May 9, the regiment relocated by rail 90 miles northwest to join the 18th Army Reserve in the vicinity of German initial breakthrough in the March 1918 Michael Offensive. The regiment was then billeted in a cluster of villages around Epenaucourt, Pargny, and Pertain, and continued to train and prepare for Germany's next great offensive.

Chapter 13
The 1918 Aisne Offensive and Flanders

The third week of May, the 52nd Division was called to participate in the next major phase of the greater Spring Campaign; the Blucher-Yorck Offensive [named after two Prussian generals from the Napoleonic era], also referred to as the Third Battle of the Aisne or May 1918 Offensive. The offensive was predicated on a decisive German breakthrough along the Chemin des Dames ridgeline – the same ground where IR 169 had shed so much blood in 1917. A breakout attack could quickly put the Germans on the banks of the Marne River, where, and for the first time since September 1914, place them within striking distance of Paris. Even if a direct attack on Paris wasn't feasible, this thrust would draw off British troops defending Flanders, making that long-contested region more vulnerable to a corresponding German attack.

The French 6th Army commander, General Duchne, was responsible for defending the Aisne region. The eastern portion of the Chemin des Dames was manned by four British divisions that had been badly mauled in Flanders. Seven French divisions held the remainder of the ridgeline. The quiet Aisne sector seemed a logical location to assign recently shattered units that needed time to recover. The natural strength of the Chemin des Dames positions further resulted in the overextension of the French and British divisions far beyond what otherwise would have been a normal frontage. Available reserve forces were negligible. Duchne, who had yet to embrace the concept of defense in depth, concentrated much of his combat power in the forward trenches, making those unfortunate troops more vulnerable to heavy artillery concentrations.

Throughout mid-May, the German 1st and 7th Armies, commanded by Crown Prince Wilhelm, the eldest son of Kaiser Wilhelm II, discreetly massed 41 divisions and over 4000 guns to execute one of the greatest surprise attacks of the war. Troop deployments included the tank battalion from Sedan, which transported 15 of its A7Vs, virtually all of Germany's entire fleet of these tanks, and several more of the reconverted British Mark IVs.German Major General Von Unruh, 4th Reserve Corps Chief of Staff, described the assembly process:

"The 7th Army, led by Lieutenant General von Boehn, was entrusted with the responsibility for carrying out the attack.

Headquarters staffs and reliable attacking divisions which had already distinguished themselves on the Somme were now withdrawn, made up to strength with reserves and gradually placed in the rear of the 7th Army. Here they enjoyed a well-earned rest in the quiet French villages, and soon recovered from their experiences in earlier battles." [233]

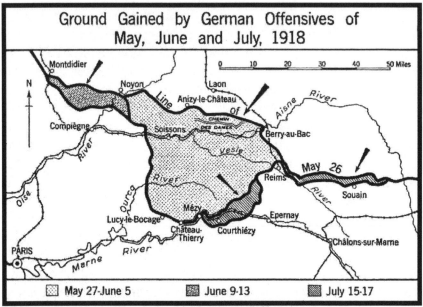

German 1918 Aisne Offensive

On 27 May 1918, IR 169 took part in the German storming of Chemin des Dames, entering the battle at Juvincourt (near the top middle arrow). The advance continued to the Marne River, 25 miles south, where French forces halted the regiment 5 miles NE of Courthiezy on 1 June.
(AABE)

On 23 May, the 52nd Division traveled 60 miles southeast by rail to join the 7th Army, Sissonne Group. IR 169 assembled in the village of La Malmaison, seven miles northeast of where it would go into battle. With Lt. Colonel Woellwarth transferred to the position as the senior 18th Army Quartermaster, Major Shiller was named the new, and what would become final commander of IR 169. The 52nd Division, along with the 50th Division and 7th Reserve Divisions, were assigned to

Corps von Schmettow. German corps were organized to cover a six mile-wide front, with three divisions in the first line, two divisions in the second, and one division in the third. Along with their three assigned regiments, each division was supported with two heavy artillery regiments, trench-mortars, engineers with bridging equipment as well as assorted signal, medical and other logistical support units.[234]

On the night of 26-27 May, IR 169 moved into the center of the 52nd Division attack formation, with IR 111 to its left and IR 170 to the right. IR 169's designated launch point was from just behind the same Juvincourt trenches it defended the previous spring.

Corps von Schmettow's objective was to first break-through the Juvincourt sector trenches held by the British 8th Division. Next, it was to execute a crossing of the Aisne River two and half miles beyond the British front lines. A large stone bridge spanned across the Aisne, and its parallel canal, at the village of Pontavert. The Germans needed to capture the bridge intact in order to keep their ambitious timeline. If they could secure an Aisne crossing in the opening hours of the attack, their chances for reaching the Marne River, 22 miles further south, were greatly increased.

The most prominent terrain feature in the 52nd Division immediate attack sector was the La Ville aus Bois [to the British, the Boise des Buttes], a forested hill mass by the hamlet of La Ville. IR 169 veterans remembered this hill well, as it dominated the battlefield when controlled by the French in the spring of 1917. A British veteran wrote: "On our own Divisional front the ground was uniformly flat, only broken by the Bois des Buttes, which rose like a giant mole hill from the plain. An ideal aiming mark for the German gunner." [235] On the eve of the attack, this position was newly occupied by the 2nd Battalion of the Devonshire Regiment. Its heroic May 27 defense of Boise des Buttes remains heralded in the annals of British Army history.

German commanders continued to refine their 1918 Feuerwalze artillery and ground support tactics. The Germans extensive knowledge of the defenses around Juvincourt and the Chemin des Dames allowed them to employ these tactics with uniquely devastating effect. In the weeks before the attack, German batteries silently registered their guns based on mathematical map surveys rather than actual ranging fires. The Germans were also careful to not increase the patterns of normal aerial reconnaissance. Every defensive position was plotted and allocated for coordinated fires that supported the ground assault with 80 pieces of ordnance dispersed over every thousand yards. The specific timing of the Feurewalze plan dictated every movement, from the assault of the storm troops at the forward edge of the battle to the advance of engineer and logistical units in the rear. Its execution in the early morning of May 27 reflected the best attributes of German military planning, efficiency and discipline.

IR 169 entered this battle at the peak of its wartime combat power. While the regiment suffered heavy losses in the closing days of the Michael Offensive, it had otherwise experienced relatively light front-line service for the past seven months. From November 1917 through early May 1918, IR 169 had gone through rigorous storm troop training programs, virtually all focused on offensive operations. It was now armed and equipped with best material that the German Army could offer. The regiment's cadre of battle-hardened NCO's and officers had time and resources to train and integrate its new recruits into a skilled and cohesive fighting unit.

Throughout the Aisne Offensive, Leutnant Lais commanded the 2nd Machine Gun Company support train consisting of two machine gun wagons, ammunition wagon and reserve cart. Lais, an experienced rider, was provided his own horse. Given the need for mobility and speed, IR 169's forward deployed machine gunners carried light MGs with limited ammunition in the initial stages of the attack. The heavy gun accessories and main ammunition stocks were to follow with the machine gun wagons. Accompanying Lais was the 2nd MGC's Sergeant Major and senior NCO, Feldwebel Nitz. Lais provided this description of Nitz: "What kind of a soldier was Feldwebel Nitz? Two days of rest in the filthiest position, and the company, including vehicles, would be fresh and brand new, as if just hatched from an egg. And for that, every company commander would learn to deal with Nitz's quirks." [236] Another faithful soldier in this command, one who would be at Lais' side for nearly the rest of the war's duration, was his personal orderly/courier, Dirksen. Lais spoke highly of this especially loyal and dependable young soldier in many passages of his memoirs.

IR 169 forward deployed on the night of May 25-26 to a railway embankment of Amifontaine, near Juvincourt. The front line trenches were filled with storm troop units pegged for the first attack groups. The follow-on attack waves, tens of thousands of troops, artillery formations and even tanks had to be assembled, stacked and hidden a short distance from the front. Exceptional measures were made to camouflage the troops and their equipment from enemy aerial reconnaissance. Infantry and storm troop companies were positioned six-eight kilometers behind the front. All wagons, carts and guns were extensively camouflaged and hid among the forests.

The German intelligence confirmed that the British divisions before them had been extensively bloodied in the recent Flanders offensive. It was assessed these forces were unlikely to provoke their foes in this seemingly quiet portion of the Western Front. Indeed, the British 8th Division opposing IR 169 in the coming fight lost 8,513 men in March and April, with its ranks backfilled by barely trained recruits. Every sign indicated that the British were completely unaware of the grave threat massing before them. The Germans were correct in their analysis that the British were considering this posting as a 'rest cure.' Sidney Rogerson, a subaltern serving in the British 8th Division's 2nd West Yorkshire Regiment, recorded the sentiments of the Tommies as they approached the quiet Aisne trenches:

> To the battered, battle-weary troops, whose only knowledge of France was based upon their experience of the northern front, the Champagne country in the full glory of spring was a revelation... Here all was peace. The countryside basked contentedly in the blazing sunshine. Trim villages nestled in quiet hollows beside lazy streams, and tired eyes were refreshed by the sight of rolling hills, clad with great woods golden with laburnum blossom; by the soft greenery of lush meadowland, shrubby vineyards and fields of growing corn. Right up to within two miles of the line civilians were living, going about their business of husbandry as if ignorant of the imminence of war.[237]

Lais commented on the prevailing German thoughts towards their unsuspecting foes: "' The poor devils! If they could only guess what would blossom in the next 24 hours. It would come at them in torrents." [238]

German soldiers took their last drags of cigarettes at twilight, as there could be no lighting of matches during the remainder of darkness. A hot meal was provided just before the troops set out for their attack positions. The field kitchen movement adhered to the

German attention to strict noise discipline. Kitchen wagon wheels were wrapped in straw and even horses wore straw boots. When the company cooks whispered 'ready,' mess kits and cups were carefully pulled out of cloth wrappings from their haversacks. The men ate silently. Rifles and entrenching tools were wrapped in sand bag covers and gas masks were tightly secured. Everything that could potentially rattle or make noise were covered. The infantry began their advance to the forward assembly positions at 10:00 pm, with the machine gun and support wagons trailing slightly behind. The forward-most deployed field artillery batteries also took part in this movement.[239] Howitzer and heavy mortar gunners removed camouflage from their guns and make them ready for the barrage.

Off to the north, a thunderstorm was brewing and lightning flashed. The large mass of men, horses and wagons necessitated that the columns remained closely packed together. All the men knew the peril they would face should the British guns open up first. The German artillery bombardment was scheduled for 2:00 am. Lais gazed at his watch constantly, time never seemed to move so slowly. It was 1:15. He heard the low rumble of two distant shots from enemy lines, followed by two more. Seconds later came the howl of the incoming shells; it just time enough for the sheer horror to register to before the moment of impact. Four shells exploded among an entire infantry company, instantly killing 15 infantrymen, five medics, eight machine gun wagon personnel and two horses. Many more were wounded and the surviving horses began to panic. Lais wrote of the endless moments before the German barrage fired:

"Each shell scores a direct hit. If they shoot again, it is the end of a fine march, if not the collapse of the offensive. Our nerves are frayed – where will the next strike land? However, they don't shoot again. Perhaps they have heard us somewhere, the night air can bear the smallest noise very far. The thunderstorm comes closer, small drops of rain fall. The hand of my watch approaches 2:00. The horses dance restlessly in agitation. Enemy guns flash again, this time not for us, the howl is in the direction of Amifontaine. A minute before 2:00, the watch seems frozen in time. Lightning flashes in the horizon, the explosion of the guns shortly afterward and is music to our ears. The Sabbath of Hell has begun. 4600

German artillery pieces and mortars of all calibers lead the May Offensive. The rumble shakes the air and unsurpassed lighting illuminates the night." [240]

Rogerson, on the receiving end of the barrage, recorded this experience:

"Suddenly, whizz – plop! Whizz – plop! Two German gas shells burst close at hand, punctual heralds of the storm. Within a second a thousand guns roared out their iron hurricane. The night was rent with sheets of flame. The earth shuddered under the avalanche of missiles leapt skywards in dust and tumult. Ever above the din screamed the fierce crescendo of approaching shells, ear splitting crashes as they burst ......all the time the dull, thud, thud, thud of detonations ... drumfire .... Inferno raged and whirled round the Bois des Buttes. The dugouts rocked and filled with the acrid fumes of cordite and the sickly sweet tang of gas. Timbers started; earth showered from the roof; men rushed for shelter, seizing kits, weapons, gas masks, message pads as they dived to safety. It was a descent into hell. Crowded with jostling, sweating humanity, the dugouts reeked, and to make matters worse, Headquarters had no sooner got below than gas began to filter down. Gas masks were hurriedly donned and anti–gas precautions taken – the entrances by saturated blankets, braziers lighted on the stairs. If gas could not enter, neither could air. As a fact both did in small quantities, and the long night was spent forty foot underground, at the hottest time of the year." [241]

Following the intensive high explosive shelling, the Germans subjected the entire enemy line with a ten minute barrage of gas shells. Some of these munitions included a special mixture of chemicals that compromised British gas masks. These were targeted against more distant command posts and artillery positions, as the Germans were not entirely confident their own gas masks were effective against this most horrible of weapons.

British artillery replied with a weak return fire that was soon entirely silenced. Given evidence to the accuracy of the German artillery registration efforts, the only one gun of the entire 45th Royal Artillery Brigade remained in action 30 minutes into the barrage.[242]

German commanders designed 4:40 am (x+160) as the moment for the ground attack. In the 20 minutes before the attack, engineers placed special bridging over the trenches so that the tanks could pass over. Other engineer squads ventured out to no-man's-land to clear passages through the obstacle fields. At 4:39 am, storm troop commanders raised their hands as a signal for their men to ready their weapons. Hand grenade squads pulled out their grenades and communications wiremen prepared their bulky cargos of rolled field phone wires. Tank engines were started and pitched to high levels of torque. Precisely at 4:40, the commanders' arms were lowered and the stormtrooper climbed out of their trenches for the 200 meter race to the British trenches. Trust in the Feurewalze was absolute, as supporting artillery fire did not lift from the lead trenches until seconds before the storm troopers reached their objectives.[243]

Opposing British troops, including 1st Battalion, 2nd West Yorkshire Regiment, were stunned. The ferocity of the bombardment blew in trenches, collapsed bunkers and destroyed defensive obstacle fields. The German storm units wasted no time to fully clear the trenches, as this was the job for the follow-on waves of conventional infantry. In moments, the first and second trenchlines were in German hands. The British put up a more determined stand in the third trenches, causing heavy losses on both sides. IR 169's 9th and 10th Companies participated in this segment of the struggle. Even as the fighting for the third trench raged, German engineers were already putting up bridging over the first trenches to make passage for the tanks, artillery and support wagons soon to follow. The West Yorks attempted a resolute defense, but stood little chance to slow the avalanche pouring over them. For the commander and staff at the British 8th Division's Headquarters, the indications of the disaster at the front unfolded with terrible speed:

"The 24th Brigade on the right reported "Enemy advancing up the Miette stream close to Brigade headquarters. Cannot hold out without reinforcements." Such news was startling in the extreme. But worse was yet to come, and at about 5:30 a.m. the left Brigade, 149th reported "enemy has broken our battle – line and are advancing on Ville au Bois." Thus before word had come of the front being assaulted, the

enemy had turned both flanks and was closing on the Bois des Butts."
244

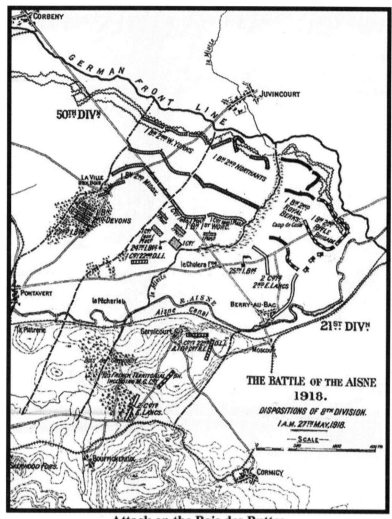

Attack on the Bois des Buttes

On 27 May 1918, IR 169 used Storm Troop tactics to assault from the Juvincourt trenches and overrun a British forces making a heroic stand at the Bois des Buttes. The regiment went on to assault across the Aisne River and canal between Pontavert and the la Pecherie fish farm. German artillery, using special chemical weapons, launched a deadly strike against the British in the Gernicourt Woods. By the day's end, IR 169 troops reached Bouffignereux. (Note; this map also depicts IR 169's Juvincourt position of Spring, 1917.)

(PD)

With the front three trenches in German hands, the only remaining form of organized British resistance before the Aisne was the 2nd Devonshire's Battalion. The Devonshire's sector comprised the Bois des Buttes, a twin crested hillock about thirty meters high and 500 meters across to the immediate south of the La Villa village. The hill was laced with underground quarries, with deep galleries that were dry and naturally protective to shellfire. The extensive underground network, fortified by both German and French troops over the years, was large enough to protect a brigade headquarters and three infantry battalions. Passages connected the complex to another fortified bunker system for the 5th Field Battery of the Royal Artillery. Of this later feature observed the 8th Division historian "This was at once a tactical and a social convenience – not only were we in close touch with our guns but we never lacked a fourth at bridge o `nights!" [245] The Devonshires, under the command of Lt Col Anderson-Morshead, only rotated into the forest the evening of the attack, having just spent the past week in reserve status training new replacements.

The protection of the quarries enabled the battalion to withstand the German bombardment relatively intact, but with little awareness of the situation outside. Once the shelling lifted, the troops raced to positions in trenches and bunkers with Companies B, C and D forward, with Company A in the reserve. The heavy early morning mist enabled the first groups of Germans, led by storm troops of the 50th Division, to close in at close range. German rifle-fired and hand thrown grenades flew into the trenches. The British repelled three separate attacks, leaving many dead and wounded on both sides. The sun started to burn off the early fog, exposing arriving German formations to Lewis machine gun fire at longer ranges. In one of many instances of heroism, 20 year old Private Borne fired his Lewis gun at 'German hordes' while all his comrades were shot down around him. As the Germans close in to 100 yards, he withdrew back a short distance and resumed his fire before falling mortally wounded.

German commanders began to appreciate the extent of the determined resistance, and briefly paused the ground attack to resume artillery fires. Aircraft flew into machine gun, bomb and mark the British positions for artillery strikes. Observations balloons, some tethered to tanks, added to the precision of the artillery fire. The Germans resumed the infantry attacks in such overwhelming numbers that it seemed nearly impossible for the British riflemen to miss a target. Trenches were taken, counterattacked, and taken again. The overpowering weight of the infantry attacks and artillery fires devastated the Devonshire ranks. The few survivors of three front line companies were knocked off the summit of the hill by 7:00 am.

Although Lt. Col. Anderson-Morshead's command was reduced to a handful of troops, he organized A Company and the battalion headquarters into a last stand defense on the reverse slope of the hill. From this position, they were still able to bring fire on German troops advancing towards the Aisne bridgehead at Pontavert.

IR 169's recent experience in training with tanks came of use when a pair of German converted Mark IV's joined the battle. In concert with other German units, IR 169 squads accompanied the tanks in the final series of assaults that wiped out the Devonshires. The British, with no anti-tank weapons available, were powerless to stop the armor. The tanks lumbered forward, firing machine guns and cannons to dislodge the British at the edge of the forest. These tanks were only stopped when they proved unable to climb the steep berms of the last artillery positions. [While the role of the tanks at the Bois des Buttes can hardly be qualified as decisive, it did provide IR 169 with the rare distinction as being one of the few German infantry units in the war to attack alongside their own armor.[246]]

IR 169 squads, augmented by machine gun teams, closed in on the last remaining positions. A newly assigned replacement officer began to direct machine gun fire into a bunker when he was torn to pieces by a hand grenade. A pioneer squad then maneuvered behind the bunker and destroyed it with an explosive charge. Leutnant Spies led a storm troop platoon, supported by machine guns of the 1st and 3rd MG Company, into the bunker complex to wipe out remaining defenders. In another trench, a group of British soldiers raised their hands in surrender. Leutnant D.R. Barth entered the position to take them as prisoners. As Lais described:

> "A fanatical scoundrel pulled a Browning pistol and shot Barth in the stomach, leaving him with a grievous wound. The Englishman paid for his treacherous act with his life. The remaining prisoners stood still, with snow white faces as they raised their arms as far as can be stretched. All were evacuated with an audible breath of air from their lungs."

By 9:30 am, the Bois des Buttes was fully in German possession and the path to the Aisne River was clear of organized resistance. Lt. Col Anderson-Morshead, last observed with pistol in one hand and riding crop in the other, was among the many British dead. The 2nd Battalion, Devonshire Regiment was practically annihilated, with 552 members killed or captured and less than 80 survivors left to regroup with the retreating British forces. The British Army recognized 2nd Devonshire Battalion's heroism by listing the Battle of Bois des Buttes with an exclusive unit battle honor.[247]

Captain D.R. Knapp, commanded IR 169's 2nd Battalion in this action. Lais described Knapp, who was a public prosecutor in Constance before the war, as being respected as a capable leader who possessed a deep sense of intellectual curiosity. A captured British colonel, who was being moved to the rear, took notice of the 2nd Battalion staff and asked if he could speak to their commanding officer. After being presented, he addressed Knapp in perfect German: *"Herr Hauptmann, ich begluckwunsche sie zu einer solchen Leistung Ihrer Truppe"* ("Captain, I congratulate you for the performance of your troops.")[248]

When the fighting subsided, Lais remembered pausing to reflect on the stunning battlefield landscape that left such significant milestones to his wartime service. Two miles to the southeast were the ruins of Berry-au-Bac. In the April 1917 battle, the fields beyond the town witnessed the destruction of 24 French tanks, one of which explored on a rainy night from the Juvincourt trenches. Another two miles to the southwest was the village of Pontavert and its stone bridge that crossed the Aisne. A few miles further to his right was the desolate Winterberg, which after so much bloodshed in the summer of 1917 was finally again under German control.

With the Bois des Buttes finally taken, the next objective was to cross over the Aisne River and canal, just a mile to the south past the forest.

The Devonshires stoic defense allowed British engineers time to blow up five small, wartime bridges that spanned the river between Berry-au-Bac and Pontavert. However, they did not have time destroy the main stone bridge at Pontavert. By 9:00 am, German storm troop and infantry units were soon on the near bank of the river, making prisoners of those British troops not able to swim across the river and canal.

A mile to the east of Pontavert and just off the river was a substantial fishery complex, recorded by the combatants as the 'La Pecherie Ferne.' On the south bank of the Aisne, disorganized British troops attempted to rally to defend the stone bridge. French reserve forces, described by Lais as 'grey-bearded elderly men' took up positions in a wood line across the river from the Pecherie. Another quarter mile south of the river began the Gernicourt Woods, a thick forest one mile wide and a half mile deep. The Gernicourt Woods was still shrouded with traces of the deadly light-green poisonous gas that the Germans used to target the British rear positions. IR 169 assembled for its role in the river assault between the Pecherie and Pontavert.

Lais arrived at the front leading 2nd MG Company's gun and ammunition wagons. It was a difficult journey, with the wagon convoy having been trapped within an obstacle field for over an hour before it could finally be untangled. Nearing the forward lines, Lais took note of large groups of British prisoners awaiting evacuation to the rear. The faces of the POWs reflected amazement as endless formations of Germans infantry and artillery followed behind the storm troop units.

Lais led the MG wagons behind the courtyard structure of the La Pecherie outbuildings. A large graveyard, filled with dead from the past three years of combat, covered much of the grounds. French troops from directly across the river and British machine guns from Pontavert peppered the Germans with gunfire. The MG Company support troops distributed ammunition and from the wagons and broke out the hardware to set up the heavy machine guns. Leutnant Fahr placed one section of machine guns at a nearby point where the river and canal ran directly alongside each other and opened fire.

With his ammunition supply duties fulfilled, Lais took a few moments to explore the farm buildings. He found one of the rooms being used as a dressing station, still staffed by captured British medical personnel: Lais wrote: "English doctors and medics treat friends and foes. All have respect for these people, who selflessly attend all while the battle rages nearby." [249] In another building, Lais' men came across a large pile of bedding material. They gladly took whatever blankets they could carry, leaving stacks of bed posts and frames alone, but noted for future use.

The Germans hurried to improvise ways to cross over the river and canal before the enemy could regroup. As a start, an infantry company found two abandoned barges. Lais wrote how someone from the 2nd MG Company came up the 'brilliant idea' to use the abandoned stores of bed frames and posts as framework to construct improvised footbridges. The pioneers quickly got work, lashing together the posts with wires and using wooden planks for the bridging. Within an hour, they had constructed footbridges sufficiently long enough to cross the 40 meter-wide river and canal at this uniquely narrow point.

A collection of IR 169 storm troopers and 6th Company were tasked to lead the river assault. The 9th Company, commanded by Leutnant D.R. Kastner, took position along the north bank to join the machine guns in providing covering fires. One of the 9th Company NCOs, Vice Master Sergeant Howe, was severely wounded but still stayed in line to fire his light machine gun. The enemy marksmanship proved sound, as several others nearby were killed with headshots.

At 10:00 am, the crude foot bridges were complete, and dragged up to the river. A number of the pioneers were shot as they swam into the river to set up the far side of the bridge. A squad of stormtroopers, led by Leutnant Selle, were the first to charge across. Selle and his entire unit were killed within a short distance of the crossing. Lais, who considered Selle a 'dear comrade,' was branded with the image of his friend's corpse lying face down in the mud. Other troops continued on. Crossing the shaky bridge was a perilous affair. Not only did the attackers face a deadly fire from the front and flanks, but they were heavily laden with rifles, assault packs, hand grenades and entrenching tools. A fall into the river would likely result in drowning.[250]

Squad-by-squad, enough Germans made it across the river and canal so that they could maneuver against the French troops immediately before them. One of the German leaders was the red-haired Leutnant Ries, described by Lais as being completely unflappable. Filthy dirty, and with a long stubble of a red beard, he attacked with great fury. Nearing the French position, he yelled with his rich tenor voice *'a' bas les armes!* (Down with your weapons!) Lais, somewhat sympathetically, recorded the plight of these French reservists:

"Scared of this red devil, the French landstrum commander could not raise his hands fast enough. It was a bad situation for the elderly men, accustomed to the beer and comforts of guarding the depots of Jonchery and Fimes [large French army depots 8 miles south], to be fetched up early in the morning by lorries and thrust into a frenzied battle against this God of Thunder, roaring devil-fire." [251]

Directly ahead was the ominously silent Gernicourt Woods. Due to the large concentration of the special 'yellow cross' gas targeted there, most German units bypassed the woods to open fields on either end. A small storm troop group, wearing well-inspected gas masks, was ordered to scout the center of the woods. There they found that the yellow cross gas indeed functioned as billed. The crews of an entire British artillery battery lay dead. Elsewhere, others were found dying or suffering in horrible agony. Lais reflected: "The Gernicourt Woods was a great cemetery. Gas is a cruel weapon and does not distinguish commands or victims. We were the victors in this murderous location because we had better gas masks." Foreshadowing the destruction of IR 169 five months later, Lais noted how "we also had to experience our own gas masks failing in a very insidious American gas attack in late October, 1918." [252]

German small units breached in the Aisne in greater numbers, forcing the British to abandon their defense of the southern end of the Pontavert Bridge. German pioneers quickly set up more substantial bridges across the river and canal that could support wagons and vehicles. The Aisne River was now fully under German control.

The next line of British resistance stood at the small village of Bouffignereux, one mile further south of Gernicourt Woods. At 10:30 am, the 1st Battalion, Wiltshire Regiment, came up from reserve positions in an attempt to slow the German advance. The Wiltshire's established a line in front of the village, with Companies D, B, and A forward, and two platoons of C Company in reserve. The ground between Bouffignereux and the Gernicourt Woods were open fields. To the east was a forest where a mounted British artillery battery paused along path in the midst of a copse of alder bushes.

In addition to the battery, the confused British retreat left a collection of supply, medical and munitions wagons becoming tangled in the small forested pathways. In early afternoon, a squadron of four German planes attacked into the woodlands, sending the some of the wagons crashing into the cover of the undergrowth. Shortly after, salvos of well-aimed artillery exploded on top of the British wagons and artillery sections, panicking men and horses. A section of the hidden artillery battery, with caissons, limbers and guns colliding together, dashed out to the road only to run in to the advancing German infantry. The battery commander and other section leaders were killed in the initial German volley and the remaining artillerymen taken prisoner. Two battery horses were killed and two others badly wounded and shot out of mercy.Nearby, a group of supply wagons tried to make an escape from the woods. The lead crews were also shot down and the rest of the personnel captured.

Lais noted how the English horses, of strong Norman breed, were well fed, had shiny coats and were in excellent condition. The first order of business was to unlimber the newly captured horses to replace the more worn-down German mounts. Some of the horses were unruly, leading the Germans to press the British farriers to assist in getting them under control. Lais wrote that while the Germans would never seek to harm their prisoners, they also did not appreciate the rather 'insolent attitude' displayed by this particular batch of POWs.

The main assault on Bouffignereux line took place at 5:30. The Wiltshire Regimental diary records that the attack struck with overwhelming artillery and machine gun fire, compelling the Wiltshire troops to retreat in small groups through the village to fight trailing, rear guard actions. [253]

Lais arrived in Bouffignereux just after the village was stormed. The intensity of the fighting was evidenced by the many dead British soldiers lying throughout the village streets. Still-warm corpses were dragged to the sides of houses so wagons would have free passage. At dusk, a large group of prisoners, described by Lais as having a more polite demeanor than those taken in the forest, gathered unguarded in the village center, waiting for evacuation to the rear. Artillery units entered the village with a heavy battery taking position in the church courtyard. Lais' MG wagons also set up near the church's high walls and occupied a house after feeding and watering their horses.

Elsewhere in IR 169's advance that day, infantry companies reached the high ground near Bouvancourt, two miles further south. Leutnant Spies, after leading his storm troopers in clearing British bunkers in the Bois des Buttes that morning, captured a unique prize – a functioning British tank. The popular Spies recounted his tale with great relish. It began with his leading a reconnaissance patrol two kilometers past the forward-most German lines. The patrol came across the lone tank and surprised its crew, killing two men and capturing the rest. Realizing the opportunity at hand, Spies man-handled the driver back into the tank and through a combination of gestures and sharp pokes to his ribs, guided him back to German lines. As he neared German forward positions, he realized that tank would likely be perceived as vanguard of a British counterattack, and risk drawing friendly fire. With his heart pounding furiously, Spies ordered one of his men take off his shirt and wave it wildly above the tank hatch. The ploy worked and Spies and his men returned to a jubilant welcome as all explored the four-man tank with great interest.[254]

That evening, the Germans in Bouffignereux feasted on British rations. They had not had the opportunity to sample British food since taking prisoners in the 1916 Somme Campaign. With great delight, Lais' orderly, Dirksen, filled any extra space in the wagon limbers with such delicacies' as white bread, butter, peach jam and corned beef. The best of these gourmet items were the dark coffee beans. Lais remembered how their mouths had longed for coffee that didn't taste like it was a by-product of German acorns.

It was a remarkable moment in IR 169's wartime journey. For the first time since September 1914, the regiment was attacking on a front with no enemy trenches, entanglements of barbed wire obstacles or clouds of poisonous gases immediately before them.[255]

By any measure, the German's May 27 storming of the Chemin des Dames was a major victory. In less than six hours, the German Army had reversed the French Army's entire 1917 gains that had cost the French six months of time, nearly 200,000 casualties and sparked a catastrophic mutiny. Thousands of British troops were killed or captured in the first day of fighting. The IR 169 field journal credited the regiment with the capture of over 470 prisoners, 37 machine guns, 100 pieces of artillery, one battery flag, and many horses, automobiles, bicycles and storage depots. Across the greater front, the Germans had taken 50,000 Allied soldiers prisoner and over 800 guns in the first three days of the offensive. The Kaiser and Field Marshal von Hindenburg were on hand to observe the battle, and on May 28, arrived at the Winterberg position where they interviewed captured British Brigadier-General Hubert Rees, commander of the 150th Brigade, 50th Division.[256]

German operations on May 28 was again orchestrated in accordance with the Feurwaltz. The artillery preparatory fires began at 6:50 am and the ground attack was set for 7:06. In Bouffignereux, the heavy artillery battery by the church shook the walls of the small village. At the appointed time, Lais' men hitched up their horses to the gun and ammunition wagons and followed the infantry advance southward. Cresting the high ground by Bouvancourt, Lais was met with one of the most dramatic scenes he recalled of the war. Through his field glasses, he saw advancing German battalions 400 meters down the valley, perfectly maneuvering as if it was a grand field maneuver. At 600 meters was the retreating enemy infantry, withdrawing in good order. 800 meters distant was a British artillery battery, its crews firing in a composed manner, despite the oncoming tide of German forces. Lais marveled at the discipline of the British gunners, who fought on until they had to withdraw their pieces at the very last minute.

What Lais witnessed was the assault on British forces around the village of Prouilly. Leutnant Kastner, who commanded IR 169's 9th Company in the attack, had a much closer optic. His description in the action was recorded in the 9th Company field journal. The attack first dispersed enemy troops in Bouvancourt, who retreated two miles south to Prouilly. Kastner led two platoons in pursuit. The British defended Prouilly by placing machine guns in the church bell tower and hardening houses into strong points, sending their enemy a lively fire. Germans pressed the attack into the village, and after a hard street battle, took the village along with 30 prisoners. The determined British battery described by Lais was forced to withdrew, but had to leave behind four munitions wagons that were taken under fire by the German's light machine guns. Some of the British units were able to establish a defensive line in the woods south of Prouilly. IR 169's line companies regrouped during the afternoon, and with the assistance of IR 66's 3rd Machine Gun Company, took the Prouilly woods. In addition to the munitions wagons and prisoners taken, Leutnant Kastner proudly reported the capture of ammo-bearing mules and a field kitchen.Since crossing the Aisne the previous morning, IR 169 had advanced eight miles, with 14 miles more to reach the Marne.

The Germans attacks across this portion of the front would doubtlessly been more costly had the British not lost so much of their artillery on the north bank of the Aisne. Rogerson recorded the state of their artillery in the wake of the German main attack:

"What a target the whole scene presented and what havoc even a few eighteen pounders would have worked on those crowded roads! But not a gun of either the 8th or 50th Divisional Artillery had been got across the river; while of the 25th Division, the 110th Artillery Brigade which had taken up positions on the low ground south of the Aisne, was practically wiped out by 9.a.m. and the 112th Brigade, though more fortunate, was only able to keep a few guns in action until the afternoon. Consequently, not only was it impossible to engage the enemy until he had come within rifle range, but he was enabled to move his guns and transport across the river without let or hindrance... It was a sight given to gunners only in dreams, but not a gun was available." [257]

Rogerson also recalled the boldness of German observation balloons: "They had come much nearer and against the clear sky looked startlingly close – a heated Cockney even guaranteeing that "*e could spit into the barsket from 'ere – easy!*" [258]

The next topographic obstacle before the Germans was the Vesle River. The Vesle flowed seven miles northwest to Reims. Two miles further southwest was the large town of Jonchery. Jonchery was an important prize, as it stood over a large stone bridge crossing and housed a large Allied supply depot.[259]

Jonchery initially appeared to be a tough objective. English troops had established defenses around the bridgehead over the Vesle and gave every indication they would put up a tenacious fight. Once again, it was Leutnant Spies who came up with a solution to carry the objective. Spies set out on a reconnaissance of the river and stumbled across a jetty that the British had left undefended. He immediately crossed with his small, patrol-sized unit and was promptly set upon by a much larger enemy force. Although outnumbered, Spies was able to hold his ground until enough IR 169 line companies were able to cross over and drive off the British attack. With the Germans now is strength on the south bank of the Vesle, the British retreated, leaving behind the bridge an enormous mass of supplies for the Germans to plunder.[260]

For the past three years, Jonchery was sufficiently back far enough from front that it had remained populated with civilians. With the German offensive suddenly at their doorstep, most of the remaining residents fled, leaving all possessions behind. This was the heart of the Champagne region, and Lais marveled at the resplendent wine and champagne cellars before them. Cattle, swine, and poultry were in abundance, and the ravenous German soldiers lost little time in pulling out bayonets to slaughter their next meal.

Lais' unit occupied a farm on the edge of town owned by an elderly Swiss couple named Irval, who unlike most other residents, remained in Jonchery. While old man Irval made no secret to his aversion to the Germans, he and his wife remained courteous and cooperative. Lais and his men set about to hold a great feast. As the commanding officer, Leutnant Lais felt compelled to don an apron and take up meat skewers to lord over the stove as the grill-meister. With a hearty '*Prost Mahlzeit!*' the men dug into the menu that included roasted pork loins in a red wine sauce, white rice and plenty of champagne. The company chief rounded out the meal with fine, dark coffee.

As the Germans feasted in Jonchery, serious trouble was mounting around them. Battered English divisions were pulled of the battlefield to regroup and were replaced by fresh French regiments. Eight miles east was the outskirts of the French fortress city of Reims. The city was ringed with massive underground forts that mounted large caliber artillery. The German division that was supposed to comprise the 52nd Division's left flank was delayed, making the 52nd the front-most left wing of the entire German offensive. With Allied troops having abandoned Jonchery, it became a prime target for the big guns of Reims.

Lais, along with their Irval hosts, were drinking their after-dinner coffee when the first salvo of illumination rounds struck the town. The Germans raced to recover whatever spoils of war they could carry off. Many of the supply wagons were in the vicinity of the town center, which was under the fire of incendiary projectiles. It was a hellacious scene, with artillery limbers and fuel tanks exploding and houses set on fire. The Germans braved the incoming fire to fill up enormous British supply wagons to capacity with war material, victuals and more than a few luxury items, including large quantities of sugar, flour, cases of white wine, butter milk, corned beef, sides of bacon, thousands of cigarettes and bars of chocolate and even writing stationery. The shelling wounded a few men and killed several horses. Lais recorded how the MG company supply personnel hoarded over the booty "like a dragon guards a gold treasure." Some of these supplies, such as lard, lasted the company all the way through mid-October.[261]

The offensive continued at 2:30 am the morning of May 29. IR 169's 3rd Battalion led the attack, which set of the northwest of Jonchery. 9th Company was on point and by 3:00 am encountered strong resistance just beyond the start point in thick woods north of Crugny. A 12 hour battle ensued, with the French only withdrawing after being blasted out by intense artillery fire late that afternoon. There were also elements of the shattered British divisions about the area, some groups still in fighting condition, others who all but given up the fight. IR 169 rounded up one squad of highly intoxicated British soldiers. They drunkenly explained to their captors that they thought it their duty to drink up a large cache of champagne rather than let it fall into German hands. [262]

The fluid nature of the offensive created confusion on both sides. The French defensive front really wasn't a line at all, but rather a random series of small units, strong points and artillery batteries scattered among villages, houses and forests. Some of these troops were placed by design, others simply forgotten about in the fog of battle. This situation made it impossible for the increasingly dispersed Germans to keep track of their foe's location.

In the early morning hours, Lais was leading his support wagons to 2nd MG Company's forward position, in the direction of Sarcy, five miles south of Jonchery. Lais' column was separated from the preceding unit and was traveling alone. Lais grew increasingly uneasy of the absence of friendly troops. The train came up to a crossroad where two German sentries were posted as guides. Lais approached the duo and asked which road to take. The sentries, who were apparently poorly briefed, merely shrugged in the direction of one of the roads. Lais recalled "It was one of those cursed situations where no one knows where the enemy is or where our lines end." It was midnight, and Lais continued on the designated road in a high state of vigilance. Lais halted the column and rode ahead alone. "Damn it, am I going the wrong way?" Lais returned and consulted with Feldwebel

Nitz, who was sitting on the limber of the ammunition wagon. They agreed it best to travel along a path to a clearing at the edge of a nearby forest, and await dawn.

"This decision was our disaster." Lais led the way with Nitz and the ammunition wagon directly behind him. As he neared the woods, he could make out dim shapes in the field directly ahead, an image blurred in the darkness. In instant later there was an enormous flash and explosions. Lais had led his men directly in front of a French artillery battery, in full firing position, not more than 80 – 100 meters ahead. Lais' horse reared up, throwing him to the ground. The horses of the ammunition wagon also panicked, and instantly turned around 180 degrees as they galloped to the rear. In the process, a wheel ran over Lais leg and injured his foot. The wagon continued a short distance before it broke into pieces. Lais lay stunned on the ground as the French cannon continued to blast away. Most of the rounds exploded about 50 meters behind him, he later realized that if the gun sights were set a few centimeters lower he would have been killed.

When the barrage finally ceased, Lais took stock of his surroundings. The contents of the ammunition wagon were strewn about, and he then saw a body on ground. He crawled over to see who it was:

"And on the slope of the hillside moans a man. I hasten to him; who is it? The face is very distorted. My God, that is Feldwebel Nitz. "Nitz! Nitz!" I call. He gives no answer and only moans. He no longer recognizes me. I swiftly run my hands over his body to investigate for wounds. No blood. I call to my troops, finally, there is a distant reply. "Come, help me carry him." Together we carry him 300 meters further in where the remaining wagons have gathered. One of the soldiers has an English tent canvas and we place it over him while another shines a flashlight. The result of the examination is that he has a splinter in the back, but more seriously, has been badly crushed by the wagons and horses in their mad dash. I immediately ordered him placed in the light pack wagon to be hurried back to a medical station in Jonchery."

The rest of the wagon column was badly shaken by the artillery ambush. The machine gun wagon was destroyed beyond repair with broken axels and yoke. In addition to Nitz, one driver was severely wounded and two other men injured when trampled by the panicked horses. One horse had two broken legs and had to be shot.

The column spent the remainder of the night in place and awaited for the word of Feldwebel Nitz's condition. The driver returned at daybreak with grim news. Nitz was taken into an operating tent within five minutes of arriving in Jonchery, but died later that night. The driver also relayed an account of the terrible scene in the field hospital. He described how hundreds of severely wounded troops were being treated, the smell of chloroform and blood, and stacks of amputated limbs. German and captured British doctors worked to the point of physical collapse as the operated together on patients. All the while the village was under heavy shell fire.[263]

By the end of May 28, the 52nd Division was spread across a six mile front that stretched from the villages of Bouilly, Sarcy and Lagery, six miles south of Jonchery. The tactical situation facing the 52nd Division was not getting better. The division to the east that was supposed to cover their left flank was still lagging far behind, stalled by heavy forested terrain and the heavy guns fired from Fortress Reims.

IR 169 continued its advance on the morning of May 29. One of its objectives was to reach the estate village of Villers-Agron-Aiguizy, five miles south of the regiment's center. The terrain was hilly, and again enemy forces fought from scattered villages and woods. The advancing Germans were faced with sporadic and distantly fired shelling. For the most part, the shellfire and spotty resistance did little to slow their rapid movement. Lais, whose wagons provided a lift to some of the foot-sore infantrymen, recalled it as the "picture of a proper tactical march."

Groups of British survivors of the initial attack continued to resist with great determination, time and again fighting a series of delaying actions. Rogerson described the 8th Division Commander, General Grogan's ever shrinking force:

"By this time the force under his command had become pitifully thin – a ragged army of Falstaffian dimensions. And what a collection! The General himself; his brigade staff – officers; Smythe, the G.S.O. III 8th Division, Major Cope of the 2nd Devons:

Colonel Moore of the 1st Sherwood Foresters, the only infantry C.O. of the 8th Division not already a casualty; two colonels of the 50th Division without a single man of the units they once commanded; a knot of machine gunners from the same division whose gun refused to function from lack of water; a woeful sprinkling of all units of the 8th and most of the 25th and 50th Divisions; in all about two hundred – all hungry, sleepless, dirty; many bleeding from wounds of greater or less severity. A number of French colonial troops, part of a division which had just come up as reinforcements, completed the tale of men." [264]

In mid-afternoon reports came that a collection of British forces were observed probing in the vicinity of Romigny Heights, three miles south of IR 169's front lines. This turned out to be a composite company-sized unit from the 151st Brigade of the 50th Northubrian Division. This element was comprised of survivors from a variety of fragmented battalions that including the 6th and 8th Durham Light Infantry and Northumberland Fusiliers. Other British units fighting in this area that day were the 5th South Wales Borderers. The British had little idea of the German dispositions as the 151st Brigade Company was ordered to act as advance guard and seize the high ground north and east of Romigny.[265]

The British advance was detected in time for the Germans to set up a hasty, but deadly ambush. The British formation suggested that its commanders had little appreciation for just how close their enemy was. Lais wrote how the British troops, observed at one mile to the south, emerged from the Romigny Heights and into the Aougny Valley as in "rows upon rows of khaki" and with the officers leading prominently from the front, perched high on horses - "a lovely attack."

IR 169 deployed rifle companies in a steep escarpment north of the small hamlet of Berthenay. Two heavy machine guns augmented the infantry's light machine guns. Further back, a platoon of four additional machine guns mounted long range sights. The British infantry were only supported by a weak, ineffectual artillery barrage that did little to disturb the defenders. At about 650 meters the German machine guns first opened fire, targeting the officers. The infantry and light machine guns joined in with a concentrated fire. Most of the British troops were cut down where they stood, and the few survivors scattered for the woods to the south. Lais recalled that it all happened with lightning speed. While the Germans had suffered hardly any losses, many British dead laid in thick rows on the sloping field of attack. Not long after, the Germans could hear the distant rumbling of lorries as other British troops moved off in retreat.[266]

By the end of May 29, most of the last British forces moved off the battlefield. Rogerson summarized the losses of the 8th Division:

> The Division was wiped out in the strict sense of the word. While it is always unsafe to generalize, it is extremely doubtful whether any other British division on the Western Front, certainly after early 1915, suffered such obliteration. Not an infantry C.O. or adjutant survived. Two out of the three Brigade Commanders were casualties, the third won the V.C. Among the infantry rank and file, the casualties mounted in almost every battalion to over 600. The total ration strength of the division during the time that the transport [off the battlefield] was about 1500 out of 12,000![267]

The 52nd Division was now only five miles north of the Marne. Before them, the French were establishing a strong defense of the bridge spanning the river south of the Verneuil Village. In a hard night battle, the French were driven back as the 52nd Division's IR's 170 and 111 took Passy-Grigny and IR 169 troops, reinforced by the brigade's reserve company stormed Pareuil. The Germans massed heavy field artillery, 21 cm mortars and 14 cm howitzers, in the village of Villers-Agron-Aiguizy to support the next series of assaults. The French also brought up large artillery reserves and pounded the Germans from both flanks. The most lethal threat came from the French batteries shooting directly down from steep vineyards on the Marne's southern bank to either side of the village of Troissy. The bridge was also defended by a series of machine gun nests.

Dawn of May 30 brought the Germans a long awaited view of the Marne. German artillery opened with a lethal shelling that shattered the exposed batteries on the south bank vineyards and slammed the defenders at the bridgeheads. Fires set by incendiary rounds blanketed the valley with plums of black smoke. A few bold German squads advanced on the bridge, but were cut down by the machine gun fire. This brief repulse aside, the ever-encroaching German infantry and artillery strikes were sufficient to convince the French that the bridge was in peril of capture. With a mighty blast that lifted portions of the bridge "as high as a church steeple," the French engineers blew it into the Marne.

With the capture of the Verneuil Bridge no longer an option, IR 169's mission changed from that of a river assault to connect with the 52nd ID's long separated left flank division. IR 169's 2nd and 3rd Battalions moved out of entrenchments before Verneuil by way of Pareuil, 1.5 miles to the northeast. Lais foreshadowed the next events as "a death storm for IR 169."

It was a terrible march. Long range artillery and masses of French planes pounded the German columns. Lais' gun-wagon detachment could barely pass through the rubble on the streets of Passy. A short distance ahead, between the villages of Passy and Aiguizy, the IR 169 Regimental Staff met with catastrophe. An artillery barrage scored a direct hit on the command group. Although its commander, Major Schiller, was left miraculously unhurt, virtually the entire rest of the staff group were killed or wounded. The dead included Adjutant Leutnant Seufert, Oberleutnant Kaiper and Leutnant Giehne. Most of the other enlisted orderlies and messages were also either killed or wounded, as were many of their horses. In an instant, IR 169's highly effective command and control infrastructure was wiped out.

Soon after, the 52nd Division's Brigade Commander, along with his staff, passed the 2nd MG Company train in Passy and took notice of Leutnant Lais' fine horse. The commander ordered Lais to assume the most pressing demand on the decimated IR 169 staff and by himself, ride to the northeast and establish contact with the separated left wing division. Lais, who learned to ride in 1914, prided himself as a fine horseman. Although Lais' new British mount was a powerful war horse, it was also skittish and was reacting badly to the constant incoming artillery. Lais exchanged it with another saddle horse, described as long-legged, skinny but devoted and reliable. It was a perilous ride as shells seemed to chase him throughout the route. Rounds screamed past his steel helmet, striking in the trees and road around him and sending shards of wood and shattered rocks through the air. He first learned of the nearby enemy infantry presence when French machine guns in a woodland to his right took him under fire. He could continue no further and turned back. Lais heartily cursed the absence of any brigade staff officers, as he was left alone for this mission. [268]

IR 169's journey in the Blucher-Yorek offensive came to climatic, crashing conclusion in the Battle of the Naverre Woods, a forest between the villages of Verneuil and Vandiers, barely one mile north of the Marne River.

The Germans had only the vaguest understanding of French formations on the north bank of the Marne. What was certain was gap that existed on the left flank, left vacant by the long overdue forces that were to link up with the 52nd Division. To force this connection, IR 169 was ordered to attack to the east in the direction of Vandiers. The regiment's immediate task was to clear the Naverre Woods, a densely wooded forest about a mile in circumference. Speed was essential, leaving no time for reconnaissance. Artillery ammunition stocks were so low that no shells could be wasted on unobserved targets. There were no opportunities to employ storm troop and Feurwaltz tactics. This attack would be made blind and with no artillery support.

The odds facing the attack was much worse than the German commanders could have understood. Well-camouflaged enemy machine gun nests already filled the woods. French trucks unloaded fresh infantry battalions near the Trotte woods, only another mile northeast of the Naverre Woods. These forces were poised to make a powerful counterattack at any moment.

IR 169, led by 2nd Battalion, made a straight on attack in two columns, one coming from the south from the direction of Verneuil and the other from the north through Pareuil. Lais' detailed this June 1 attack:

"With terrible losses, the 169th Regiment threw the French back to the eastern edge of the woods. Tree by tree, hedge by hedge, each had to be conquered. A few hours later the 2nd Battalion's 5th Company, complete with officers and almost to the last man, was wiped out. The battalion's other companies counted losses of 20 to 25 dead, leaving only 8, 12, and 15 men unwounded.

Wounded soldiers came out of the woods in rows. Many had been hit by machine gun fire, often two or three times. Lieutenant d.R. Leibold, an old machine gunner, emerged from the woods wounded. A company horse was quickly brought up and he was taken to the rear. Lieutenant d.R.

Schulze, also an experienced warrior, died with a shot to the head, along with his two messengers.

Other companies swarmed in. The French snipers were shot down from the beech trees. Close-in fighting raged in the bushes, and the newly arrived companies, with superhuman accomplishment, themselves half bleeding to death, threw the opponents back through the whole woods onto the eastern edge, and onto the vineyard slope of Vandieres. The French, with many times superior numbers, made four separate counterattacks. A mighty wrestling match started up.

Wherever you looked, there was a horizon of sky-blue uniforms. They sprang up from the vineyards. No lines, no waves. There were masses of them, thick, wide rows! The reaper of death raged among them. Our exhausted companies were even more decimated and had to give up a part of the territory of the conquered woods. They dug in in the middle of the woods in a forest glade and there they waited for the enemy. The enemy, in the meantime had suffered such losses that their spirit for attacking was gone.

The woods of Navarre and Pareuil became a large graveyard for the 169th regiment." [269]

French artillery and air supremacy made the situation hopeless. Artillery barrages badly damaged the regiment's baggage trains in Villers-Agron. The firing forced other German wagons and artillery reserves further to the rear, reducing their capabilities to support the infantry when they were needed most. Reconnaissance capabilities were crippled when French aircraft shot down an observation balloon.

The German machine guns and anti-aircraft weapons took measures to repel both the enemy air and ground assaults. Lais told of his experience on his brief detached service with an AA battery.

"I was deployed again with an antiaircraft battery against Verneuil, to fight against low flying planes that were attacking our infantry there. We traveled at a gallop over the badly shot up streets, in the direction of Verneuil, and stopped on the northern edge of the town. We brought down two planes in the first minutes with our antiaircraft guns. The first one crashed, burning, into the Marne, and the second hit the roofs of

Verneuil, and the third was forced to make an emergency landing on the other side of the Marne, close to the river bank. The rest departed hastily.

The MG section and the AA battery proceeded to Bunot Ferme and from there shot across river, with a distance of 1500 to 1800 meters into the thick rows of French infantry who were climbing down from Tryhohe and Boucquignyberg. It swarmed with troops over there. The direct fire of the two AA guns, and the two machineguns with telescopic sites hit with destructive effect. Then we went back at a gallop pace on the defile between Passy and Pareuil.[270]

The regiment held its tenuous grip in Naverre Woods throughout June 2, fending off seemingly endless counterattacks. The dead fell so thickly that they were stacked and used as ramparts. While the Germans were able keep their ground, it was clear the offensive was over.

In the night of 2 to 3 June IR 169 was relieved by IR 54 of the 50th Infantry Division. The regiment returned back towards the Aisne with a collection of prisoners captured from the 408th regiment. Lais recalled it being an "evil night." Night-configured aircraft attacked the streets as shells from heavy artillery bombardments howled by. As Lais' column passed Villers-Argon, they could hear calls from wounded inside a barracks, begging to be carried away. Just then, the building received a direct hit from a high explosive shell, killing several and adding to the injuries of other wounded men. Two of the division chaplains, a Catholic and a Protestant, ran into the debris to try to extract the moaning and helpless wounded. Another shell broke through the roof and exploded, killing Father Eisele and other men, but leaving Father Kortheuer miraculously uninjured.

Lais himself had a close call later that night during a roadside break north of Villers-Argon. He was standing with a tight cluster of seven soldiers when an explosion went off very close by. After picking himself up, Lais realized he was the only one in the group uninjured. Later in night, the 2nd MG Company, with Lt Fahr commanding, assembled together. Lightly wounded men were placed on the MG wagons and those more seriously wounded were placed into passing motor-ambulances. The convoy was frequently bombed by aircraft as it continued north. The 50 mile march eventually took the battalion over the Chemin des Demes near the Hurtebise battlefield, through Laon and finally to Voyenne.

From May 27 – 30, the German offensive had captured over 60,000 Allied soldiers and 800 guns and had advanced within 35 miles of Paris. As in the other major 1918 offenses, the German tactical gains were unsustainable. The Germans were overwhelmed by severe supply shortages, fatigue, lack of reserves and the loss of too many good soldiers that could no longer be replaced.

Major General Von Unruh described the end of the offensive:

> "It became all too clear that actions so stubbornly contested and involving us in such formidable losses would never enable us to capture Paris. In truth the brilliant offensive had petered out. This unpleasant fact was quickly realized by the High Command and the order came from General Ludendorff for us to consolidate the positions we had reached. The tremendous effect of modern fire is such that attack is only certain of success when made as a surprise against inferior forces unsupported by reserves, as was the position of the English in the Champagne. As soon as fresh and strong reserves arrive, the momentum of the attack must slow down, until a fresh blow is organized and delivered. Given equality in troops, it is ultimately the number of weapons and the way they are employed that is the decisive factor." [271]

The regiment's casualties were among the most severe it experienced in the war, with 38 officers (14 killed) and 952 men lost in seven days of fighting. Total French losses for the campaign were 98,000 casualties with the British losing 29,000. Estimated German losses were 130,000.

The regiment was allotted two weeks to recover and train in Voyenne. In mid-June, the 52nd Division was ordered north to return to Flanders. The division would be part of the general reserve in support the third major portion of the 1918 Spring Campaign, the Georgette Offensive, also referred to as the Fourth Battle of Ypres.

The Georgette Offensive, lasting April 9-30, began with the German 6th and 4th Armies launching a nine division attack against four Portuguese brigades in the area just north of IR 169's 1914–1915 La Bassee battleground. At the points of the deepest penetration, the Germans had pushed the Allies back 12 miles. British, Australian and French troops surged into Flanders and forced the Germans to suspend major offensive actions on April 29. After refitting, the 52nd Division was to be prepared to shore up the now threatened Georgette Offensive gains.

From 16-21 June, the 52nd Division began the departure from Voyenne by rail for the 70 mile trip north to Templeuve, on the southern outskirts of Lille. On arrival, the regiment took up quarters in the villages of Nomain and La Glanere, 16 miles west of the front lines. The Spanish Influenza outbreak of 1918 began to spread to the front lines and sickened more than half of IR 169's rolls, and killing at least four men. When Lais was struck down by the flu, orderly Dirksen made him a 'red cure,' consisting of 10 aspirins mixed into two liters of red wine. Lais' severe fever broke on the third day, and he was able to report back to duty on the fourth. Leutnant Fahr however, became so sick that he was evacuated to a rear area hospital. In what proved to be Fahr's extended absence, Lais assumed temporary command of the 2nd MG Company. The regiment resumed an individual soldier-level training program and on July 9, staged a sporting event in honor of Archduke Friedrich II's birthday. Soon after, orders came for the 52nd Division to report to the front for duty in the Arras sector with the 6th Army's northern corps.

IR 169's next posting were in the trenches before the village of Acheville, four miles southeast of Lens. The front battle lines migrated here a year earlier in the aftermath of the great Battle of Vimy Ridge. On July 13, IR 169 conducted its 20 mile march to Acheville. Four miles into the march, the regiment passed through the ruins of Orchies. In the course of the war, the regiment's veterans had witnessed a seemingly countless number of towns and villages that were destroyed in battle. The destruction of Orchies stood apart, as the village was deliberately burned by German forces in September of 1914 for retribution of French sniping on German ambulances. Lais wrote of this memory:

"Ruins of burned brick buildings lay at the entrance to the city. Glowing hatred flashes from the eyes of the residents as we march silently by. It seems as if the destruction occurred not four years ago, rather as it took place today. Nothing is forgotten, still less is forgiven." [272]

Arriving in Acheville, the regiment relieved Reserve IR 46th of the 19th Reserve Division, with IR 111 to its left and the 15th Reserve Division to the right. The initial stages of the Acheville deployment suggested it may be a relatively pleasant trench assignment. The weather was sunny and warm, artillery fire was infrequent and the British opponents across the no-man's-land provided no sign of offensive intentions. While there was always work to do to continuingly improve defenses, the men were able to replace their helmets with caps and enjoy the relaxed atmosphere.

The lack of combat activity was in part due to the lingering Spanish Flu that plagued both German and British forces. Lais was again stricken ill. Lais lay bedridden in his command post one night, incapacitated with a severe fever. Despite the warm climate, he profusely sweat and shivered under the cloak of his coat and several blankets. Even though Lais was too incapacitated to remain in command, the ethos of the unit leaders was such that reporting for sick call was out of the question. Besides, there was little threat of enemy attack, so Lais intended to ride out the fever in the trenches.

Bad news came from regimental headquarters; a senior officer arrived to conduct an unannounced inspection and would soon be at the 2nd MG command post. With Lais in no condition to appear fit for command, Dirksen came up with an idea. He fetched fellow soldier Ziegler, who was about Lais' size and had the persona needed to pull off an impersonation of an officer. Ziegler was a good choice for the charade, as he had previously stolen a piano from a nearby village without anyone suspecting him. Ziegler hastily donned Lais' uniform and moments later, stood ready to greet the senior commander with his authoritative Mannheim accent. Ziegler then gave a highly professional presentation of the company's machine gun positions. The VIP came away impressed, but members of the unit who were unaware of the ruse wondered who was this 'phantom Lieutenant' in place of their commander.

Lais was also presented with a more serious leadership challenge during the Acheville posting. The recent death of Feldwebel Nitz left a deep gap in the 2nd MG Company's leadership team. The new company sergeant major, described by Lais as Feldwebel X, proved a great disappointment. Feldwebel X, who was old enough to be a father to most of the men, gained his rank as a prewar reservist. Illness prevented him from front line service earlier in the war, and his posting with IR 169 at Acheville was his first combat assignment. In the best of circumstances, veterans of long-established combat units hold high expectations - and suspicions - of newly arrived leaders. Feldwebel X got off to a bad start when it soon evident he had no prior experience in serving in a machine gun company, let alone hold the import position of the company's senior noncommissioned officer. In addition to possessing deep tactical knowledge of MG operations, a credible company sergeant major also needed to master logistics and the handling of the wagons and horses. In comparison, IR 169's other two MG company sergeant majors, Feldwebels Koppe of the 1st MGC and Winkler of the 3rd MGC, stood out as excellent leaders and professional soldiers. Feldwebel X's alienation from these two strong role models further exasperated his isolation. Lais was put in a difficult situation; the soldiers of the 2nd MG Company had no respect for the man that should have been his right-hand leader.

Soon into the Acheville deployment, a ceremony was held for the presentation of Iron Cross awards earned during the Aisne-Marne campaign. Feldwebel X approached Lais afterwards, and noted his regret in how his lack of combat service made him ineligible for such recognition. He further speculated that his credibility as leader would be enhanced if he had a combat decoration to display. Feldwebel X went on to suggest he be given command of one of the company's machine-gun platoons for a two month period to provide an opportunity to prove himself.

Lais pondered the suggestion. There were some merits to X's request. For one thing, it would get him out of the 2nd MGC command post, where he was more of a nuisance than resource. He also agreed that Feldwebel X was indeed in need of front line experience, and that the quiet battlefield conditions at Acheville were conducive to this experiment. To reduce the risk to the platoon X was to lead, Lais secretly called over its current commander, a highly experienced and competent corporal. Lais explained his intentions that Feldwebel X's nominal command was to be in effect only for quiet circumstances. In the event an emergency would occur, the corporal would then resume command. Lais then wrote orders to that effect, and handed them the corporal to display as he deemed necessary.

Feldwebel X's new platoon command post was in the Acheville cemetery at the western edge of the village. Soon into his command, Feldwebel X appeared at the 2nd MGC command post, located behind an anti-aircraft machine gun bunker. The Feldwebel was wearing full battle kit, including steel helmet, assault pack, gas mask in the ready position, field glasses, and two grenades hanging from his belt. The men, all comfortably dressed on this hot day, looked on with amusement at this bizarre display of this 'wild warrior.' Feldwebel X formally reported to his commander, and then stepped up on the AA bunker's firing platform to gaze through his binoculars at the quiet British trenches, 700 meters distant.

One of the company NCO's had a remarkable talent to perfectly mimic the whistling sound of an incoming artillery shell. The opportunity was too much for the wag to resist, as he positioned himself behind X and let loose his best impersonation of an inbound, whistling artillery strike. Feldwebel X suddenly turned his gaze left, right, and then raced down into a bunker. The men around the CP burst in to hysterical laughter. Lais turned on the jokester with a firm rebuke and reprimanded him on how it was inappropriate to make fun of the feldwebel. Lais then tried to console Feldwebel X by saying he himself had earlier fallen victim to the rascal's prank. X returned to his platoon where he continued to 'compensate with enthusiasm for what he lacked in experience.'

A few days later, the battlefront had become more restless. The British began aggressive probing patrols and incoming artillery fire became more frequent. *Feldmutze* caps were stowed in ration bags and replaced by helmets. One night, an especially severe artillery barrage targeted the MG platoon position located in cemetery. Exploding shells blew caskets to surface as pieces of skeletons and rotting corpses were flung into the air. A rations-bearing squad received a direct hit, leaving one dead and two severely injured men to be found by a MG bunker entrance the following morning.

Lais' conscious could no longer bear the thought of having Feldwebel X remain in command of this platoon, and he directed his return to rear and take over the company's vehicles. Feldwebel X remained with the company for the next month, and in the campaign to follow eventually earned the combat decoration he so deeply desired.

He became seriously ill in early September, and left the regiment never to return. Lais came away from this experience respecting this old soldier, who did not lack for courage or noble intent. Feldwebel X was simply a pure infantryman from a by-gone era, with little capacity to master the machine gun apparatus and doctrine that evolved to the warfare of 1918.

IR 169's service at Acheville concluded on August 3 when it was relieved by Reserve IR 98 (207th Infantry Division) and was placed under the command of the XIX Corps Artillery Regiment. The regimental field journal recorded that between July 14 and August 3, the regiment took part in "lively" patrol activity and improved its defensive works. Losses included 1 officer and 38 men, with 1 officer and six men listed as killed in action.

IR 169's next deployment was 25 miles north, to the village of Vieur Berquin. Lais provided this account of the regiment's movement from Acheville to Vieur Berquin:

"We arrive from Lille, pass by Armentieres and arrive at Sailly on the Lys River. On the left side of the street is a soldier's cemetery. Wooden cross after wooden cross. There is no end to the cemetery. More than 17,000 fallen comrades are resting here, close to the approach route to the front." [273]

The march took the regiment just to the east of the La Bassee battlefield and ended at the village of Vieur Berquin, 25 miles southwest of Ypres. This location was the German's deepest penetration point of the Georgette Offensive and for past three months had become part the new front line. The 52nd Infantry Division's IR 111 was on the regiment's left, with IR 14 of the 4th Infantry Division to the immediate north.

On the British side of the trenches, IR 169 again faced off with an opponent from the Somme, the 11th East Lancashire (the Accrington Pals), which had been so badly torn apart in the July 1, 1916 attack on Serre. The Pals moved into line at Vieur Berquin during the second week of August from a reserve position at Morbecque, seven miles to the rear. Unlike the desolate no-man's-battlefields of the past three years, this battleground was relatively fresh with tall fields of wheat growing between the opposing trenches. There was a notable increase of British activity from the period August 15-19, when they exploited the cover of the wheat to capture several German outposts and advance their lines by 200 yards. In return, the Germans hit the Pals with a heavy artillery bombardment of gas shells on the evening of August 15, which contributed to the battalion's August 1918 casualties of 96 men killed, wounded or missing.[274]

Like most of the ground in Flanders, there was a high water table that made it impossible to dig deep trenches. Lais described the nature of the fighting in this sector:

> "The position is a simple base. There is no cover, and one can hardly dig in because a hole deeper than 40 cm immediately fills in with water. Everyone builds pieces of turf up around them to be protected against shrapnel. The front line ends in a ripe, almost too ripe field of wheat. Hour after hour there is bitter close combat. The Englishmen are incredibly active. During the day they constantly make local attacks; the nights are horrible. From dusk until dawn, our positions up to 10 kilometers deep are under intensive artillery fire.
>
> The enemy fears a new advance on our side and conducts a preventative heavy fire on the entire approach areas. The regiment is set in echelon in a narrow front width; the so-called 'rubber front.' (In case of attack the front line gives way, machine gun nests provide support; the rear reserve battalions then absorb the power of the enemy attack through their counterattack.)
>
> My 2nd Machine Gun Company is engaged on a nearly 4 km deep front. Each MG platoon composes one MG nest. It is the duty of a MG company commander to ensure his platoons report on a daily basis." [275]

The high ground to the northwest provided the British with excellent visibility deep into German lines. During daylight hours, British forward observers were able to call fire on individual men and forced German artillery batteries to reposition every evening. The German machine gun platoons were widely dispersed across the regimental front, with each platoon forming a nest of guns.

On August 18, the British conducted a major attack towards the village of Outtersteene, two miles to the east of Vieur Berquin. The

British attack coincided with the scheduled relief of the regiment by IR 14 the same day. While the IR 169 infantry companies were able to pull back, the machine gun companies were compelled to remain in line an extra day. Lais' machine guns received the brunt of the English attack:

"Around 7:00 pm, the English attacked; which we stopped in front of our machine guns. The infantry of the relief regiments, which were ahead of us in a grain field, were overrun to the last man. 400 meters to our right, dense formations of English troops are advancing, and enter an enfilading fire coming from my two furthest MG platoons. My platoon leaders, Zoerner and Schaefer, are shooting as gunners. Zoerner is the very personification of a peaceful soul, and Schaefer is a roughneck with a droopy mustache. These are old active duty MG soldiers, whose machine guns had not allowed one Englishman and not one Frenchman to pass. If they ever pulled out, it was only because they were ordered to. The idea that my always laughing comrade Zoerner and my grumpy roughneck Schaefer would ever show their back to the enemy is absurd.

In the morning dawn, around 3:00 am, the infantry's quick reaction force counterattacks and retakes all the terrain. We machine gunners of IR 169 were forgotten in the drama of events. After three quarters of an hour, the commander of the relief regiment comes to my fighting position.

'So, you're still here?' He is astounded to still find someone from the 169th here. The new MG company, which was supposed to have relieved us, has already been engaged elsewhere, without us having gotten the slightest notification. That's the way it was in a big battle!

Orders came for the company to assemble at the Ins bridge. At the dot of 4:00 am we take off. It is a great feeling, to turn one's back on the shooting and head into the rear areas." [276]

While in the Vieur Berquin lines, IR 169 lost 7 officers and 187 enlisted men, (including 35 killed in action). IR 169's most severe loss in the 1918 Flanders campaign cannot be quantified nor replaced in terms of numbers. It was in fighting during this period that the highly respected Leutnant Spies was killed. Spies would not live enough to receive the modest annuity he earned when awarded the Baden Gold Order for Gallantry.Lais speculated that the modest Spies went to his death believing that a lowly lieutenant like he was hardly worthy of such lofty recognition anyways.[277]

Soon after IR 169 departed, the British advance took Outtersteene Village. By the end of August, the Allies had reclaimed all of the ground throughout Flanders that the Germans had seized in the March Georgette Offensive.

By mid-August 1918, a series of major Allied pushes – the Hundred Days Offensive - were forming all across the Western Front. The Germans were learning that their big gains of ground in the Spring offensives were only pyrrhic victories. They simply did not have the troops or logistical resources required to hold the vast territory acquired in the preceding three months. The Allies, now reinforced with hundreds of thousands of fresh American troops, were staging for an attack intended to sweep back the German advances across the entire Western Front. Supported by over 500 tanks, the Allied attack began on August 8 at the city of Amiens, south of the Somme River and 30 miles southwest of Bapaume. In the first day alone, the Allies gained seven miles – an enormous amount of territory in terms of World War I breakouts. Tens of thousands of German troops surrendered as British forces raced to recover the lost Somme battlefields and retake the communication hub of Bapaume. The 52nd Division's role in responding to this disaster was to relocate from Flanders to reinforce the German effort to protect Bapaume.[278]

After leaving Vieur Berquin on August 19, IR 169 marched eight miles west to the village of Sailly where the men were treated to a feast of coffee, butter and sausage. The growing crisis in the Somme demanded a sense of urgency, and the regiment was pushed into a hard, 25-mile forced-march to the train depot at Templeuve, on the southern outskirts of Lille. It was a blistering hot day, and the men, having just withdrawn in the midst of a pitched battle, were exhausted before the grueling hike had even started. The machine gun companies mounted their guns on horse-drawn, anti-aircraft wagons, while the infantry companies were forced to run for the first several miles. The six-mile route from Sailly to Armentieres was along an elegant boulevard, with full trees that covered the troops from both the sun and enemy planes. As they neared the edge of Armentieres, the columns met a much starker, battle-scarred landscape, devoid of trees and littered with ruined buildings. Lais wrote of the approach into the city:

"All around craters, nothing but craters, trench ruins and wire obstacles. Somewhere there were corrugated tin huts, erected quickly with a minimum of effort for our engineers and for prisoners who were building streets here. On to the well-worn unpaved streets which led through the field of craters, there was dust centimeters deep; keep right, keep right; cursing, one keeps himself to the right of the road. On the other side are columns of freight trucks, motorized howitzers pressing forward; and in between are staff cars, ambulance, and so on, all heading towards Lille. We are marching in a cloud of dust, our tongues stick to the roof of our mouths, the collar of our tunics is left open and the sun is beating down on us.

'Airplane - take cover!' There doesn't seem to be any flak guns, or are our brothers sleeping in the heat? No, it can't be; so close to the city Lille there should be flak guns. The columns of vehicles stand still. My NCOs hang on to their three guns and fire. The soldiers take cover left and right of the street in craters and trench remnants. That's how it continues on towards close to Lille, where finally the flak guns can effectively engage.

Until then we are constantly harassed, and constantly the NCOs and gun commanders are attending to the guns. We have a total of 6 guns mounted on AA carriages; we have fired 4000 rounds on the march. We were struck by attack and reconnaissance aircraft. Aircraft bombs and MG strafing attacks ensure that the march doesn't get boring. Casualty list: one driver, one horse wounded by an aircraft dart bomb and one horse received two MG wounds in the rump. Deathly tired, we arrive exhausted in the suburbs of Lille." [279]

At 7:00 pm, several miles south of Lille, elements of the regiment loaded trains at the stations of Loos and Templeuve. Thirty minutes later, the trains rolled south on a 70 mile journey, travelling past

Cambrai. Some of the trains arrived at Fremicourt, just outside Bapaume, at midnight. Other trains stopped much further from Bapaume, forcing the men to make another difficult road march to their destination. Ultimately, most of the regiment assembled in the village of Beuguy, a few miles to the east of Bapaume, where they bedded down for the night in abandoned British barracks.

Another voice from the IR 169 history emerges at this point in the narrative. *Baden in the World War* contains an account credited to a machine gunner named "Kuebler," which details IR 169's departure from Flanders and operations through late August 1918. Kuebler's chapter is titled *In Picardy and Artois; With the 3rd Machine Gun Company of IR 169 at Bapaume (August 1918).* Kuebler wrote of his company's travel from Flanders to Bapaume:

> "On 19 August we were relieved in our position on the bow of Armentieres and were supposed to head to the lovely R&R quarters on the French-Belgian border that we had already gotten familiar with in June, to get some rest from the recent grueling weeks. With a small part of the regiment, the 3rd MG Company had already arrived at their destination where comfortable stand-by transportation from Germany was awaiting us. However, at the same time rumors arose that the regiment was going to be deployed in another direction. On the second day we marched in the direction of Lille, through a suburb of the city, and in the evening we boarded a train at the La Madeleine train station.
>
> As dawn broke, we recognized from our train several features from a region well-known to us from 1916. Soon afterwards we stopped at the Cambrai train station for several hours. Somewhere ahead of us the station platforms were said to have been destroyed by air attacks. We were fortunate that they weren't looking for us here. The mid-day meal was distributed, and finally we got moving again; but only for a short distance. At Rumilly we disembarked. We found there a small cemetery where we read the names of many of our countrymen from the 28th Infantry Division who died during the tank battle of the previous autumn.
>
> And now we marched on in the midday heat. It was tough on the young lads from the reserve who were marching with

us. For us veterans, the constant marches over paved roads made themselves uncomfortably apparent to our feet, especially after several weeks in our positions with no significant hiking to be made. In addition, there was the heat, which in the comfortless region of the 'Somme Desert,' was twice as severe. But we kept going, through the evening and into the night.

Enemy aircraft fired illumination rockets over our march route, using their light to spot targets. This caused some bottlenecks. Finally, after midnight we arrived at Beugny, our destination. After some back-and-forth, we found shelter in the English barracks that had corrugated roofs. Exhausted and completely soaked with sweat, we lay down on the floor and fell asleep." [280]

Infantry Regiment 169 had returned to the Somme.

Chapter 14
Return to the Somme:

The Battle of Bapaume and the Fight for Grevillers Forest

The House is crammed: tier beyond tier they grin
And cackle at the Show, while prancing ranks
Of harlots shrill the chorus, drunk with din;
'We're sure the Kaiser loves our dear old Tanks!'

I'd like to see a Tank come down the stalls,
Lurching to rag-time tunes, or 'Home, sweet Home',
And there'd be no more jokes in Music-halls
To mock the riddled corpses round Bapaume.

Sigfried Sasson, "Blighters"

The British Third Army, following its dramatic August 8 breakout at Amiens, took an operational pause from August 11-20 to build up reserves and prepare to retake the towns of Albert and Bapaume, the respective Allied and German bastions of the Somme 1916 campaign. The ten-mile wide offensive, with Commonwealth divisions from Great Britain, Australia, New Zealand and Canada, began on August 21 and supported by 200 tanks.[281] By the end of the first day, the Third Army had taken Albert and were within five miles of reaching Bapaume. A German counterattack on August 22 briefly halted the English advance.

As IR 169 assembled outside Bapaume, the 52nd Division was assigned under the command of the 2nd Army, XIV Reserve Corps. On the night of August 21-22, IR 169 unit commanders were issued 1:25,000 scale maps while wagons and trucks were loaded with supplies and munitions. Engineers readied rolls of barbed wire and other implements required for constructing defensive positions. With artillery booming in the near distance, many of the troops were still able to catch a few hours of sleep on cots in the abandoned British barracks complex. Shortly before 5:00 am, the battalions assembled in marching columns in preparation for the movement through Bapaume and then on to the front.

As Lais describes, the return to the Somme battlefields was an emotional experience for the veterans of the 1916 campaign:

"The company prepares assault packs as sergeant major inspects the gas masks, assigns new duties while other NCOs inspect the munitions boxes. March departure is scheduled for 4:45 am. At 4:30, with his watch in his hand, Dirksen shakes me awake. I put on my steel helmet, hang my binoculars around my head, gas mask to the front and we're ready to go! Where is my assault pack? 'I have taken the Leutnant's coat rolled up in mine' Dirksen responds! From the door of the barracks, I command 'Corporals, form a march column!' 'Company and vehicles ready for march!' comes the response. 'Good morning, company!' 'Good morning, Herr Leutnant!' 'At Ease!' There is laughter and the mood isn't bad. 'Are you still tired,' I ask the ranks? A soldier, speaking with a heavy accent from central Germany responds, 'Nooo, Herr Leutnant, but the feet are a bit soooore.' More laughter. My senior NCO, who has only been with the company for just less than two months, is getting a bit anxious. 'Herr Leutnant, we have to march!' 'My dear X.,' I reassure him, 'we will be right on time to die a hero's death.'

A courier comes from battalion. The company is to stand at 5:00 am on the street to Bapaume, direction of march, Miraumont [to the southwest]. 'OK then, lots of time. Drivers, take your places.' Hanging around, and then - march. Up ahead it's thundering unceasingly. The dead land of Artois must once again drink the blood of thousands of brave soldiers. The battalion marches.

We are marching through the ruins of the city of Bapaume, the Market Place, 'Place Fai d'Herbe' we see off to our right, the street is broad. Onward, onward! How often we marched in the Battle of the Somme 1916 in column formation through many villages of a prosperous population. How often we sang our marching songs on the broad army street Valenciennes - Bapaume - Albert - Amiens *Three Lillies, Three Lillies*', '*In the Field of an Early Morning,*' '*The Most Beautiful Land...,*' '*O Germany, we Honor You.*' For marches at night we preferred more sentimental songs: '*In Hamburg, where I was covered in Silk and Satin....*' It's an endless song, in which a girl is seduced by a leutnant, and then turns into a mouse. Our Leutnant S., a trainee officer, made the comment during the line 'covered in Silk and Satin .... it must have been a nice sock,' which was cynical, and of course kills the mood." [282]

Kuebler recorded the advance of the 3rd Machine gun Company to the front:

"Into the mad dreams and fantasies of our over-stressed nerves, there intruded the notorious order 'Fall out!' Was it a dream? It can't be for real, can it? But it is nevertheless our sergeant's voice. A gentle reminder at first, then gradually becoming more pressing. It takes some energy to get the whole company on their feet. The gun crews were organized, the equipment already made ready, and we go forward with a few vehicles. A hellish firefight was raging along the entire front. Apparently an attack is underway. As the sun was rising we reached the small town Bapaume, the ruins of Bapaume! Now, how that once so pretty country town appears!

In Grevillers the vehicles have to stop. Also, 'lock and load!' Still, we were able to rest a bit on the far edge of town. This land is familiar. In September 1916, our battalion spent a day on alert before its deployment at the farm of Mouquet. Will things turn out as well this time, too? Now we have taken an alert posture. But the road there was under observation and under fire. From there we move onward through the open field across the hill. Each machine gun acts independently with wide spacing between each other. But the English have already caught sight of us. They take us under heavy shelling. We leap from one shell crater to another, and making our way through very heavy fire. Exhausted, we finally come to the place where we were ordered, a cut in the deep valley of the Ancre.

But it appears to be an appropriate place for a field kitchen. Shot-up vehicles of all kinds lie all around. Despite our exhaustion, we look around for anything worth having, but we have come too late. Only a pile of cabbage heads is still lying there. So after some time in the pot, our lunch is ready. Even this tastes delicious, because since yesterday morning at the Cambrai train station, we have eaten just about nothing. Of course there was lots of complaining about our making a fire. But under any circumstances, the English firing would still be active. At the entrance of one of the few tunnels there we found provisional shelter. The wildest kind of rumors circulated. Attack? Counterattack? Relief? In any event, the situation was highly unclear. The earth was continually trembling because of the impact of the heavy shells, such that the underground bunkers were cracking. If one of the shells were to impact directly on us, we would be lost." [283]

In the late morning of August 22, the 52nd Division joined in the German counterattack. IR 169's 1st and 2nd Battalions were part of the main attack, with 3rd Battalion serving as the divisional reserve. The attack was aimed against British forces at Miraumont, just over two miles southeast of the Regiment's 1916 position in Serre.
Lais:

"After five miles, we are behind Pys Creek at the village of Irles, and before us is the downhill slope to the valley Miraumont. The rest of Irles is under fire. 'Company - halt! To the vehicles, get the guns ready!' We also take the sleds/skids with us. The Sergeant Major takes the combat baggage up to a position on the edge of the village of Grevillers, half way back to Bapaume. We were already in this sector of the front a long time in 1916, one felt at home there and yet still foreign.

Our battalion was serving as the ready reserve. While we marched down in open order to the valley of Miraumont, the 52nd Division's IR's 170 and 111, as well as two battalions of the 169th were already preparing for a counterattack. The street to Miraumont is now under sharp fire. 'Double-time, march! Lay yourself flat!' Now come huge chunks of shrapnel. The act of taking cover is quite a thing for the poor guy who is carrying the gun skid apparatus on his back. The skids dig painfully into his back and his upper thigh whenever he throws himself down. 'Faaace to the side! Further! Run, man!' It's particularly bad at that corner. With sweat dripping and panting lungs and heaving sides, we throw ourselves on the high embankment of the rail line of Miraumont. 'Everyone there?' 'Yes, sir!' 'Casualties?' ' No, sir!' The embankment is under moderate fire of quite heavy caliber. One can avoid it. Much of the shrapnel is absorbed by the muddy ground, which has been transformed into a swamp by the Somme-Ancre Battle of 1916.

'Get ready! Secure the guns.' 'Sir, we have a report from battalion. The company is to take up positions in a northwest direction towards the Serre - Puissieux Road and occupy first the quadrants of the map 3225, 3226 of the ridgeline towards Miraumont.'

'I congratulate you, gentlemen! Today we are certainly going to end up in L6, or in the former "Swinging Boat" in Serre. First and Second platoon each go 50m left and right of me, ahead, third platoon with me, fourth platoon follows in 100m distance.'

The guns go first over the embankment. Up and over onto the embankment! Sctch...Stsch... Sctch.. Four long strides and on the other side we let ourselves slip down on the seats of our pants. The company goes ahead. The village terrain of Miraumont offers good cover: crater by crater, remnants of walls and shot in cellars, covered with green overgrowth, now being hit by shells from the current barrage.

With us, the infantry of the 3rd Battalion is advancing against the heights. One sees nothing of the enemy, but now we begin to receive heavy small arms fire. The commander of the 9th Company falls dead. The enemy fire pauses, and we stand erect in the terrain and sweep the horizon with our eyes through the binoculars. Infantry advances in thin lines by group and platoons all the way to the horizon!

On order, I deploy my guns in echelon along the terrain and inspect their fields of fire. The battle is silent, and it's hardly noon. The artillery fire has pretty much stopped, and in our minds it appears to clear up, and we feel ourselves to be part of a big success, a rare opportunity for troops in a larger war of maneuver to be able to experience. And that's the way it is, too. The English breakthrough failed, and my humble 'lieutenant's military mind' understands, that the German

Army has been given a grandiose chance on the blood-soaked ground between Miraumont and Sommecourt to turn the page.

We send the couriers on their way. The heights in front of us are free! Why are we not attacking?

Our division was engaged with other regiments for a counterattack, and threw the opponent even further back from his kick-off positions. Our opponent had to leave behind heavy cannon, which he had already brought forward, or in some cases, destroy them in place. These guns stood in the middle of the most forward line, which we advanced over. The retreating British field artillery came under a terrible crossfire of machine guns. The majority of their cannons were lying tipped over in a field of craters.The exhausted horses fell and died under our MG or rifle fire. The British infantry fell back in their trenches as the enemy brought up more artillery.

By the afternoon of the first day of our counteroffensive, the British attack was decimated and brought to disorder. An entire afternoon, an entire evening passed. In the sector I controlled, there wasn't a single shot; the infantry battle had ceased.

In the evening I got the order to take my entire MG company behind the embankment and be prepared for further action. A ready reserve element of the 9th Company was already there.

So, no attack order was issued from the Army Group. Everyone, from the most junior lieutenant up to the commanders, had the feeling that an immediate further push, supported by another division, would mean a catastrophe for the entire English attack front. Were there no reserves available? I don't know: our casualties were limited up to then, and our division was still one of the best Storm Divisions; our people still preferred to attack, rather than let ourselves be slowly barraged to death in the craters.

Was this a result of two large of the physical distance of the Corps staffs and the Army Group leadership to the fighting troops? I don't know!" [284]

Lais' almost nostalgic prediction to his men that they would soon arrive in Serre never came to pass. The Allies reinforced the front with large amounts of infantry artillery and their aircraft controlled the sky. The Germans, with scant protective cover, were caught in a massive artillery bombardment and took heavy losses. At the embankment of Miraumont, three 9th Company commanders were killed within 24 hours. Lais, in addition to his duties as the 2nd Machine Gun Company Commander, also assumed temporary command of the decimated 9th Company. Lais:

"In the evening and into the night the English reinforcements rolled in, division after division. Artillery was thrown into gaps, regiment after regiment. In the clear light of the moon in the night English aircraft pilots flew up, dived down low and attacked individual couriers as well as platoon and company commanders. I was attacked for a quarter of an hour as I was ducking into a field of craters with a courier, until I found a shot-up cellar as cover.

The great opportunity was missed! The embankment of Miraumont was under heavy fire since the break of dawn. I had already emplaced my guns in echelon. One MG platoon was with me on the embankment for special reserve engagement. The more the sun rose into midday, the worse it became behind the embankment. It's apparent that the opponent fears a German advance and assumes that the reserves are at the embankment. At the foot of the dike, lying 1-2 meter deep in the earth, remain hand grenade depots left over from the time of the 1916 Battle of the Somme. For the most part, the sheeting/packaging has been ripped off. We press our bodies to the wet earth, we dig holes with our hands and press our steel helmets, our heads into the ground rrumm....rrrum...rum...rum.

Spot by spot, heavy caliber shells tear holes in the powerful levee, rip it apart, like one would tear down a wall, flatten it. How is it possible, there is so much heavy artillery? Heavy clumps of earth are thrown onto our legs, which hang out of the holes as railroad ties are thrown through the air. Suddenly someone throws himself down next to me, groans, yells, can only get a few broken words out. 'Herr Leutnant... we have been buried...' 'Who is buried,' I yell. 'The 9th Company Commander with all couriers' he reports, swallowing. Up and over! His location is 50 meters distant.Dirksen says: 'I will come with you, Herr Leutnant!' 'No, stay there!' Dirksen follows me anyway. I.... Ssscchhh.... take cover...rrumm! Further, up and at them - For God's sake man, stand up!

What is happening! He only makes a gurgling moan, turns his eyes up, I try to bring him to... it's all over. It is the third company courier of the 9th, shot through his neck. I hasten on, and ask if someone is here from the 9th. 'Yes' 'Come with me, then Corporal.' 'Jawohl, Herr Leutnant.' 'Take cover!' yells Dirksen, and all three of us throw ourselves into a narrow hole. It's blazing, there is smoke, stink, and then we are almost entirely covered. The crackling lasts for seconds, the clumps of earth and stones on our backs and steel helmets – 'That was almost a one-way ticket to St. Peter,' says Dirksen.

'Your company commander is buried!' I yell into the corporal's ear; because in the same second in which the clumps are landing around us, another shell explodes close enough to deafen us.

Finally we arrive. The hole has been covered up, boots and a lower thigh can be seen sticking out. Pathetic, dead legs. We constantly have to take cover, but we get them out. Their faces are yellow-white, and covered with blood; skulls are shattered.

We lay the bodies down behind the embankment and call over members of the company. From the battalion headquarters, word comes that a lieutenant of the 10th company will certainly be named as the new company commander of the 9th. In an hour his deputy comes tumbling over to me, with a chalk white face, and reports that this new company commander has just been killed; 'It was a direct hit, we can't find anything left of him.'

In the evening of this heavy day my soldiers and the soldiers of the 9th Company take eleven dead to the street of Pys, so the engineers can pick them up. That was the Embankment of Miraumont." [285]

The intensive British artillery fire continued unabated. In preparation of the inevitable infantry attack, the Germans tried to build a series of strong point defenses, but machine gun squads were getting blown to pieces as they came into line. British planes joined the attack.

The overburdened 2nd Machine Gun Company was finally pushed beyond the limits of human endurance. Lais:

> "My soldiers have to drag the heavy guns on skids through fields of craters. Constantly we are attacked by low flying airplanes. Flying at an elevation of 20 and 10 meters above the earth, they fire bursts from their double-barreled machine guns into the open shell holes and remnants of trenches.
>
> The gun crew is constantly getting smaller; one dies, another one gets a shot in the belly and another takes three shots through the upper thigh from an aircraft strafing attack, and then bleeds to death in a minute. Instead of two munitions cases, which are plenty heavy enough, my soldiers of my heavily decimated company are struggling under the weight of four and five cases of belted MG munitions. Every time they change position or take cover, the heavy, sharp-edged ammo cases painfully dig into their backs.
>
> My company is exhausted. It has been engaged the longest of all companies. In Flanders they shot the English attack waves to pieces, and fought, for a day and night, with an entirely different regiment out of a sense of duty. It is now at the end of its physical strength.
>
> My couriers have joined the guns. My boy Dirksen and I run ourselves to carry messages and pass on instructions. With care, and out of necessity, I can still find enough men to serve the machine guns. The crews, which have shrunk down from 7 or 8 men, down to 3 and 4 men, are breaking down under the double ammunition load. There's nothing to be done for it, they have to! For without enough ammunition, they could send the whole MG company home again, because with only dozen carbines of the riflemen and pistols of the gunners, you can't keep the enemy back for very long.
>
> My soldiers stumbled and fell from exhaustion. Their eyes shut while feeding in the belts. In the craters, they fall asleep during the heaviest bombardment out of sheer exhaustion. While being shelled, they stagger while shifting positions and are too tired and indifferent to take cover. And then comes the most extreme warning sign! The platoon leader of the platoon which is the furthest to the front comes to me in the night:

'Herr Leutnant, we ate the iron rations (which are supposed to be preserved for emergencies), my platoon is so tired that I can't send anyone else to fetch rations!'

In the same hour I take a report form and write the following words on it: 'I request to pull back the company for a day, since I am no longer in the situation to be responsible for the fighting power of the company.' I gave the exact reasons and the length of time of our engagement in the Lys and then brought the report myself to battalion headquarters. The captain and battalion commander, an officer whom we honored for his goodness and deep sense of duty, is appalled when I request that he send the report further to the regimental headquarters. The report is sent to the regiment.

The IR 169 Regimental Commander, Major Schilling, a soldier's soldier, who was always in the thick of things among his fighting regiment, and always as far to the front as possible, determined that the company should immediately come back to the rear trains/baggage at the edge of Grevillers (three miles to the rear). There is located an intact barracks with cots. In the same night, the regiment is to be relieved and put on reserve duty in and around the Grevillers forest. Naval infantry, which comes out of Kurland in the East, takes over our positions.

For one day and night my company rests. Some wounded return from the hospital, and 10 new recruits arrive from the recruit depot. A young, recruit full of himself, reported to me that some of the men had been to the front to dig trenches, and that one of them had even been killed. 'So, you've already smelled gunpowder?' 'Jawohl, Herr Leutnant!' they roar back. I respond, 'So then, be careful you don't catch a cold, if you experience it just a tad heavier here!'

There are shatterproof bunkers inside the barracks. During the night, at 1:00 am, gas rounds land in and around the camp. 'Everyone into cover, let the motor vehicles stay, bring the horses up to the heights of Avesnes.' A direct hit lands on one of the bunkers. A rifleman, who had just returned from hospital yesterday as healed, is dead. Another rifleman of the most recent recruit group had his thigh torn off by the round, and a third one had his jaw destroyed. 'Medic!' they are calling anxiously, medic! We are lucky that a few minutes later an ambulance stops at the entrance to the village Grevillers-Avesnes-Bapaume." [286]

On August 23, 3rd Battalion/169 took up positions on the edge of the Grevillers Forest [referred to in Allied accounts as the Loupart Woods], which was situated on the high ground southwest of the village. The woods, which had been badly shot up in 1916, had returned to life with new trees and growth emerging above the underbrush. The rolling terrain offered cover to both the defenders and attackers. All considered, the gunners were well pleased with the fields of fire, which covered the exit from the Ancre valley below. While old trench systems crisscrossed the area, threats from multiple directions required new works to be established at the edge of the woodline. The Germans began to dig in as random artillery fire began to land nearby.[287]

Keubler described how the 3rd Machine Gun Company took up position at the Grevillers Forest on the evening of August 23:

"As it grew dark, we received orders to occupy the heights lying behind us. We are joyous. Up there it is significantly calmer. Of course we are lying under the open sky up there. A few tent panels tied together and stretched over a shell crater provide some protection against the night air. The next day was fairly quiet. We have a good view of our former front and staging area. Back in November 1916 our front faced the south; now it is almost the opposite. In the afternoon we received orders to occupy an old stretch of the trench at the northern cliff of the hill in order to safeguard our right flank. Our front was on the Grevillers - Irles road, therefore, to the north. Towards evening the platoon leader and the NCO from the other machine gun went looking for a bunker to spend the night. While this was going on, a very heavy barrage came rolling in on us - to the front, to the rear. So, away from that place!

We executed a change of position exactly according to regulations, with rifles to the left. We crept through an old barbed wire entanglement, and there we found a few quite large shell craters. Into the deepest one! If we don't get a direct hit, we are safer here than in the level trenches. We are fortunate. The heavy artillery keeps pounding away over there. Suddenly it got very lively. If we only knew for sure where our front-most line really was."[288]

IR 169's position was designated the secondary line of defense. A battalion of German naval infantry passed through the forest to take up new positions at the very front edge of the line of battle. This unit, made up largely of new recruits, had only recently joined the Western Front and was unprepared for the intensity of combat they now faced. [Throughout the war, the German Navy fielded security forces designated as naval infantry. These units were made up of surplus sailors and new recruits from Germany's port cities. Earlier in the war, especially in Flanders, the naval infantry had performed well. Their quality declined as the war went on, as reflected with the sailors being armed with captured Russian Mosin-Nagant rifles instead of standard-issue Mausers. By 1918, the German Army, desperate for manpower, inserted some of these Fourth Class-rated units into the Western Front, with predictable results.] [289]

Allied aircraft continued to torment Germans both day and night. Lais described the rage of the infantrymen against the pilots who fought far above the mud:

"The night is unpleasant as airplanes arrive! They fly down low, these rude dogs, and roar above our heads - one would like to have a word with them! They fire flares, which fall slowly down under a parachute and light up the terrain. They hunt everything which can be seen in the light, everything which curses and crawls. They have a special eye out for the roads/paths which the convoys use. Hand bombs and machine gun bursts. My lord, that was a night! Everywhere these flares above the landscape, swinging on their parachutes and seeming like they never want to extinguish. It's rattling and spitting and hissing over us and doesn't give us a minute of peace. They drop a hail of bombs on our occupied craters and trenches.

Inside of us is a terrible anger. Not one of these daredevil pilots collides with another during this night attack. On the next day, one of them has to make a crash landing in the no-man's-land, and the plane flips onto a trench. Both of the crewmen, the pilot and machine gunner, jump out unwounded and run to the English forward lines, only 50 meters away. They are both seized by a patrol of our infantry (which were already in no-man's-land) and stupidly attempt to defend themselves with their pistols.

The anger that has been boiling inside erupts as the infantrymen lose their temper. In a few seconds the crewmen are beaten into formless lumps with shovels and spades. We have a rage, a hate towards these pilots who have interfered in an infantryman's battle. We just have one wish, to get our hands on one of these smartasses; we who have never so much as touched a hair of a captured enemy." [290]

Regiments belonging to the New Zealand Division [although both Lais and Kuebler refer to them as British] were now facing IR 169. Throughout August 23, the New Zealanders were readying their attack. A German defensive line that stretched in front of the village of Grevillers, with the Grevillers Forest a mile southwest, was now among the final obstacles to Bapaume. IR 169's history recorded the 3rd Battalion's defense of the Grevillers Forest as one of regiment's most heroic and bitter struggles of the entire war.

The New Zealanders, forgoing the standard artillery prep, launched a surprise attack in the evening hours of August 23. The ferocity of the sudden attack smashed the naval infantry division to pieces. Racing towards Grevillers, the panicked sailors fled past the IR 169 positions and ignored all attempts to rally them. A grizzled, veteran NCO sailor tried in vain to stop the rout of his men. With tears in his eyes, he begged to join the ranks of the 3rd Battalion for the coming fight. IR 169's secondary position at the edge of the forest had suddenly become the front line.

Kuebler recalled the confused melee that lasted well into the night.

"Then, all at once it got very active in the woods in the direction of Bihucourt [one mile to the northwest]. Dense masses of men came rolling down into the valley hollow. At first we were doubtful whether they were actually English. Our machine gun, set up on the rim of the shell crater, was ready for action. Now we can recognize the plate-like helmets of the Tommies. Aiming point: 1200 meters into where the ranks were the densest. 'Continuous fire.' Some spread apart; some remain lying in place, but the bulk of the attackers surge onward. The ones in the front have reached the road. Don't our troops have a line somewhere out there? But it looks like the entire attack is fastening upon our lines on the flank. We are holding the front itself and are doing all that is humanly possible.

My gunner on my right, Ellermann, is shooting splendidly, a cigarette at the corner of his mouth. Our machine gun is hot; we've already fired half of our ammunition. The English close their ranks again and again, as if they were growing from the earth. Now the first ones have reached the hollow of the valley, from our view, in a dead corner. Therefore, we must get out of our hole in order to remain in contact with the others at the old position. Everything comes with us - empty boxes, cartridge belts. A few leaps and we are again in part of the trench. It's already been vacated. To the right the English have driven forward in the high point of this line and have captured our platoon leader and those accompanying him. We insert ourselves in the broad front and keep on firing.

The English attack gradually comes to a standstill, but our front is torn up. We have a tremendous feeling of uncertainty as night falls. The units get together and try to get back in contact with each other. This is difficult to achieve, as the division was not deployed as a whole but was divided up into different groups of other troop contingents. The din of battle from a while ago has now turned almost completely silent.

From the left flank, where we no longer have any contact at all, we hear continuous shouts whose meaning we can't understand. The English? The shouts come nearer and nearer. Finally we understand the strange sounding question, 'Is this the army?' Parts of a naval infantry division have swarmed into the left flank and are now trying to join up with their neighbors. In the course of the night a continuous line is reestablished, mainly by manning old trenches." [291]

At 4:15 am on August 24, the New Zealand 1st Brigade attacked towards the Grevillers Forest from its assembly area in the village of Achiet-le-Petit [IR 169's former rest area from the 1916 battle]. Two British Mark V and several newly fielded light Whippet tanks supported the attack.[292] Scattered fragments of naval infantry troops that had been trapped in no-man's-land were swept up in the renewed attack, and became intermingled with the surge of New Zealanders headed for Grevillers. The Germans in the wood line initially held their fire, hoping that the panicked sailors could somehow break away or take cover. When the mixed horde came within 150 meters, the German defenders had no choice; it was either shoot or risk being overrun. The concentrated fire of the six machine guns of the 2nd MG Company mowed down all before them, leaving a field full of dead Kiwis and German sailors.[293] The first New Zealand attack was stopped.

Allied planes joined the fight, diving down to strafe the German trenches. To the defenders' great relief, a German squadron of 18 Fokker DR 1 Triplanes arrived on the scene. Following a quick dogfight, the Allied aircraft were temporarily driven off. For the next few hours at least, the German squadron provided air cover over their trenches. In support of the next attacks, the New Zealanders more than made up for the lack of artillery used in the earlier assaults. A rolling barrage poured over the German trenches and then swept back again. The New Zealanders then launched multiple infantry attacks, with each being ripped apart by German machine gun and rifle fire.

Both Lais and Kuebler recalled the series of assaults:

Lais:

"Shortly after midday the steamroller of fire comes creeping up the valley, passes us over and goes further, then comes back again. Two hundred meters, a hundred meters in front of our guns, the English attack waves crest and ebb back. It doesn't even get to close combat. Our firing positions are excellent. It does become more unpleasant when the fire of trench mortars draws closer. We press ourselves against the edge of the trench. Schiiirack....rack! The second impact is directly on the edge of the trench, rips away 30 cm of cover and bounces off our steel helmets. The splinters fly sharp over our heads away into the rear wall of the narrow and shallow trench. We spit, sneeze, cough, and wipe the dust and dirt out of our mouths, nose, ears and eyes. 'My Lord! That was damn close to a hero's death! Two point five centimeters more and we could go collect our bones.' The battery fires only two salvos when one of my machine guns, equipped with a telescopic sight, is able to range the gunners at over 400 meters.

Again and again the English assault lines raise themselves up. Hour for hour the brown wall of earth, fire, iron and smoke comes closer, passes over us, fixes on our positions, tapers off, and then brings death and destruction; and always, enough defenders survive so our steady machine guns and rifle fire cut down the next waves of attackers.

The day is difficult and bitter. In our parched bodies, in our leached, burned out foreheads there is a mute rage. I seldom saw a more barbarous battle." [294]

Kuebler:

"Two of our company's machine guns had been lost. A detachment under the leadership of a vice-sergeant-major went to the rear to fetch ammunition and rations. Towards morning a few of the men came back, the cooking pots still half full of cold soup. Most of the others had fallen into the hands of the English somewhere in the Grevillers Forest while on their way back to the front. The English, who had already pushed already forward, advanced further the next morning with the help of tanks. Even though we lacked artillery support, the English had scant success. But our companies suffered heavy losses, and gradually the situation on our right flank became more and more threatening. Now our front was facing east. The English had moved in that direction in various groups to ready themselves." [295]

By early afternoon, the German air cover flew off and the Allied planes returned.

Kuebler:

"We had to show very good fire discipline because we had
not received any more ammunition. That afternoon an enemy
aircraft flew quite low over our position. Of course we had to
try to drive him off. He constantly flew circles and loops over
us, making whistle and horn signals in order to convey his
observations to the English deployed in front of us. We
mounted our machine gun on the lip of the trench and fired at
him whenever he made a pass over us. With our naked eyes
we could see our bullets impacting on his wings, but the
aircraft appeared to be well-armored. Then we would hug the
ground, dead still, as soon as we could be seen by the observer
in the aircraft, whom we could clearly recognize. From time to
time he, too, would fire his machine gun at our trenches. That
didn't give our nerves any relief." [296]

Lieutenant Koebele, one of 3rd Battalion's company commanders,
led his men in an especially intrepid defense of a portion of the
Grevillers Forest. Koebele was well-supported by a platoon of
machine guns from the 3rd MG Company led by Vice Corporal Mall,
Otto Lais' good friend and a hero from the 1916 battle of Somme.
Here, Lais told of the fierce fighting and the ultimate fate of Corporal
Mall:

"Whoever possesses this section of trenches also possesses
and controls the Grevillers Heights. And that's what the
opponent thinks, too!
I will now recount what the soldiers of the 3rd MG platoon
told me later of the heroic death of Vice Corporal Mall. The
opponents had gotten a foothold 30 – 50 fifty meters in front
of this section of trench and forced their way to the edge of the
woods. The first wave of their assault troops rose up, dashed
ahead and then took cover into the shell craters. New waves,
fresh rows of troops, pushed their way forward from behind.
The English artillery poured fire into this sector, regardless of
the danger to their own troops. The attackers suddenly appear
out of the smoke and swirled-up earth; they are only five
meters away. In a split second the defenders, who themselves

were just pressing their bodies against the protective earth, rise up and do their work. Machine gun bursts fire into the attacking troops. Here and there our infantrymen jump out of cover and go to work with rifle stocks, picks and spades.

The fight is one of cruel mercilessness. Stick hand grenades fly into the remnants of the enemy as they flounder towards a retreat.

Exhausted, our men sink back into the trenches to take cover. Already, the enemy aircraft come and dive down to ten and twenty meters altitude; dropping bombs and firing machine guns into the trenches and craters. Most of the rounds miss, but some bursts of 25 and 30 shots raise sparks as they strike the position. The tip of the opponent's' advance is within hand grenade throwing range.

Trench mortars fire and the opponent engages flame throwers on the right wing. This time they advance under the protection of the low flying aircraft, and are thrown back yet again.

Both of the MGs of Mall's platoon are engaged separately and relentlessly mow down the enemy. Without regard to death, individual English troops attempt to 'take care of" the MG that Mall is serving. Again and again they push forward in an assault; again and again they sink back into their craters. The MG in front of them isn't shooting anymore! - Misfire!

The main bolt spring has broken and the gun crew works feverishly to repair it. Within seconds, the English assault leader grasped the situation and orders his men to charge. In the same moment, Mall jumps up, looms over earthwork, and with amazing speed throws hand grenade after hand grenade. The only available rifleman unscrews the fuse and passes the grenades up to Mall. Already the English attack has come to a standstill all along the line.

The infantry and machine gunners all have their hands full as they engage in the close combat. Two men frantically continue to work on the MG as they try to clear the blockage. Mall's grenade throwing has forced the Englishmen to take cover until all available hand grenades have been thrown. The two infantrymen fire clip after clip from their rifles, as one is quickly shot down. English hand grenades clatter around the defenders. Again, the English captain jumps up and calls for his men to follow him. Vice Corporal Mall jumps entirely out of cover, pulls out his Luger pistol and fires half his magazine into the body of the English officer. While collapsing, the mortally wounded Englishmen fires at Mall and hits his neck vein. The hero quickly bleeds to death.

The English troops hesitated, and for 2 or 3 seconds went down into cover. Howling from rage, they rise up again, while our MG is already loading. Ducking, two riflemen crouch behind the MG.

The gunners' hands do not tremble. Forward and back, forward and back; press it through, raise the nose of the gun high, ratatatata.... it strikes into the Englishmen as they rush forward with their rifles - at least 30 men. At three steps, at 10 steps distance from the gun, they tumble all over one another. The rest of the work is done by the rifle butts and spades of the infantry. Since 8:00 am they have launched 11 attacks. Vice Corporal Mall is hauled back into the trench. He is dead.

The German trenches, craters, and cover around him are filled with our own dead. The day brings terrible losses. In the morning, as the battle just began, came an officers' call for the battalion. Of these, there are ten officers who are older than the rest. These men had been called up as reserve NCO's in 1914 and were wounded in the first battles of the war. They then carried out garrison duty and have now arrived at a front line troop again. They are not familiar with the customs and habits of trench fighting, of a battle of attrition. Through some happenstance, they were not distributed among the companies and fought as a group in the heavy fighting around the trench sector at Grevillers Heights.

By the arrival of the evening, nine of the ten are dead." [297]

3rd Battalion's situation in the Grevillers Forest became dire. To the immediate south, the 2nd Auckland Battalion seized the village of Grevillers while other New Zealand forces surged to the north. 3rd Battalion was at risk of being cut off and surrounded. In the following passage, Kuebler recounted the collapse of the Grevillers Forest position and his harrowing escape:

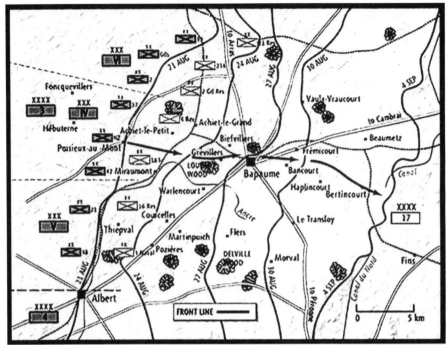

Battle of Bapaume

In defending Bapaume in late August 1918, IR 169 fought in fierce engagements against UK forces at Miraumont, Grevillers Forest (Loupart Forest in English accounts) and Le Transloy. The 3rd Battalion's 23-24 August defense against the New Zealand Division at Grevillers Forest marked some of the regiment's most intensive fighting of the war.

(NZH)

"Despite all our requests, we received no kind of artillery support. We seemed to have been abandoned altogether. Reports of losses constantly ran through the trenches...mainly from deadly headshots. This was no wonder in the enlarged trenches where one could be fired upon from three sides and at such short distances. It was enough to make us despair, especially as the pilot was flying tighter and tighter circles above us. Already we could see the stalks of grass in front of us waving back and forth whenever a Tommy would leap or creep into another shell crater...and we were almost out of ammunition. Then, directly in front of us, an Englishman got up on his knees and observes through the grass. Could he be estimating the distance for a hand grenade? In front of me a corporal from an infantry regiment takes aim at him.I look over his shoulder at his target and then - a resounding blow on the helmet of the man in front of me; he lies dead at my feet.

At the same instant, about 50 meters further to the left, a whole row of English suddenly stand up on the edge of the trench, while the few of our troops who are still able, raise their weapons out of the trench. That picture will remain in my heart forever. Now the end is coming, one way or another. With the help of a loyal comrade, I set the machine gun with the last cartridge belt on the edge of the trench and let fly. The whole belt feeds through. That should give us a little time. Back into the trench and along the trail. With the gun mount gone, and the machine gun on my back, we head out through the trenches to the right. Apart from the dead and wounded, there are very few people to be seen.

An elevated road cuts diagonally across our old trench. The English have set up a machine gun near this location which has cut off the way back. A few men have tried to escape by leaping over the road and to reach the trench on the other side. Most were shot down. But we nevertheless want to escape with our machine gun. In short bursts the English machine gun sweeps over the road with well-aimed fire. We lie still and observe for a few moments. Can a jump between life and death save us? I grab the machine gun by the muzzle and burn my hand in the process because of the recent firing. My comrade, Corporal Zenkert, grabs the grip. We tighten the hook, just like on the exercise field. I calculate the timing of enemy bursts. "Jump! Up! Go! Go!" In seconds we are over. I feel nothing and thank God I am still alive. But when I turn around, I see that part of my brave comrade's jaw is hanging down. He is bleeding heavily. We bind his wound and help him back in the trench. A few medics were there, and there was enough work for them. But it was impossible to evacuate the wounded. Another comrade from my gun crew is leaning on the edge of the trench, struck by a shot in the hip and appears pale as death. I never again hear anything about the third comrade, the sharpshooter, who was with us.

While here, we also hear that the front has pulled back to the rear and to the left, and also that our battalion was supposed to have evacuated the high ground that morning. For this reason, there was no artillery support for the whole day. Therefore, any resistance is futile; there are no longer any means available. So the wounded had to be left to their fate. I bade farewell to my comrades. The trench ran parallel to the tree line and was only a short distance from it. The forest was full of the English. Above, in an old observation tower, stands a Tommy as big as a tree. One could almost take him down with a pistol. But it's not worth drawing their attention to us. The trench had caved in at several points, and one had to cross the blockages either by jumping or by crawling. Suddenly the man in front stops. Now what? With me are a comrade from our company and a lieutenant from IR 170. We realized that if we could get down to the path in the trench, we would again have cover. So we try it. But we had to get rid of our combat packs to keep from having a target on our backs. I also have to leave my machine gun. With a heavy heart, I remove the action and feeder to take with me. Should I now destroy it? Maybe the current situation would change once again? Now we slide along on our stomachs, heads down, up to the precipice. We're going to make it.

A little regret comes over me. Maybe I could still have dragged the machine gun out next to me? But finally one has reached one's limit. We realize this as soon as the excitement has subsided. Over there is a freshly dug trench. A rallying point? Nearby, there are a few large and recent shell craters. You could still smell the powder from their detonation. This segment of the trench was altogether empty, but to the side were lying all the packs of the engineers who had dug in here and who had apparently been driven off by the shelling. Everything was brand new, issued a few days ago at a garrison in northern Germany. It's placed right in our hands. Quickly, we are again equipped, better than with the assault packs we had thrown away. The valley floor shows no sign of life, but there is great disorder further to the rear at Ligny-Thilloy. Artillery and columns of troops are bombed by a squadron of aircraft. Just then an American pilot was led to the rear. He was the one who had previously shot us to pieces, but subsequently crashed behind our lines.

We finally learn where our regiment is to assemble. With the strength we still had left we dragged ourselves back.

When it got dark, the field kitchens were there. More than enough food was available. There were no longer quite so many coming to get it. Our stomachs full for the first time in days; we were overcome by lead-like sleep. My comrade, Unteroffizier Wolf, had remained somewhere to the front, come what may, until dark. Then he stumbled upon a machine gun, after he had lost his own, and brought it back. My machine gun! The only one of the company's! With the occupation of the high ground just about all the way down to the road, the English had stopped their advance so that the wounded could return during the night.

Soon we got the command, '3rd Battalion, 169th, Fall in! Count off!;' 'One, two three...seventeen, end!' the left file leader reported. With the NCOs and two lieutenants, we barely muster a 40-man fighting strength for the entire battalion. 'We're moving into a support position west of the town. Right face, route step, march!'[298]

The final struggle in Grevillers Forest tapered off after twilight. IR 169's 3rd Battalion had suffered terrific casualties, was nearly out of ammunition and was virtually surrounded. At 10:00 pm, those still left in the forest received orders to retreat. It was almost too late to escape and those most seriously wounded were left behind. Assisted by the near pitch black darkness, Lt. Koebele was finally able to slip his small force through a narrow gap in the enemy lines at 1:00 am on August 25.

The New Zealand Division also took heavy losses in the battle they would later refer to as 'Bloody Bapaume.' In the fighting around Grevillers, the 2nd Otago Battalion suffered particularly heavy casualties, to including having their commander and adjutant killed by sniper fire while reconnoitering enemy positions. The losses to this battalion were such that the unit was rendered unfit for further operations until September 2. In total, three of New Zealand's four leading battalions had lost their commanders in the approaches to Bapaume. In the period between August 22 – September 2, the New Zealand Division's losses totaled 2,283, with 411 killed in action.[299]

As the 3rd Battalion made its dramatic stand at Grevillers Forest, other elements of IR 169 also had a hard fight on the days that followed August 24. The IR 169 line ran two miles southeast from the Grevillers Forest to the village of Thilloy.

The British 63rd Naval Division was responsible for taking the twin villages of Thilloy and La Bricoche was. The three brigades of the 63rd Division were a compilation of Royal Marine, Naval Infantry (surplus sailors mobilized as infantry) and conventional British Army battalions. Unlike the fourth rate German Naval Infantry Division, the 63rd Naval Division was considered a high quality unit.

Among the 63rd Division units attacking Thilloy was the 4th Battalion/Bedfordshire Regiment, of the 190th Brigade. The war diary of the 4/Bedforshire's from August 25 – August 28 revealed the strength and intensity of the German defenses. Throughout a series of attacks, the battalion was continually hampered by an exposed right flank, which was stuck both by under-ranged British artillery and intense German machine gun fire. The 4/Bedforshire commander also complained of a lack of tank support. In an ill-fated attack on August 27, a section of C Company was able to make its way into Thilloy, only to be pinned down by heavy machine gun fire striking from both flanks. British veterans described how the Germans had 'a perfect defensive position which commanded the approach from in front and on the right flank.' With all their officers either killed or wounded, the C Company survivors fell back through the village to the sunken road from where the attack had originated. With their ranks decimated, the 4/Bedforshire withdrew back to Miraumont later that night after being relieved by the 8th Manchester Regiment." [300]

Chapter 15
Bapaume and the Retreat from Le Transloy

The battle for Bapaume continued through the first days of September. The heavy fighting of late August left many of the IR 169 line companies, especially those from 3rd Battalion, in tatters. After a brief reassembly, IR 169 went back into line, taking position around the village of Le Transoly, two miles south of Bapaume. The 52nd Division was assigned to defend the southern approaches to Bapaume, with IR 169 making up the division's left flank. While the New Zealand Division continued to invest Bapaume, the rest of the British 3rd Army push aimed at breaking the northern and southern flanks. The southern portion of this effort struck at Le Transoly.

IR 169 veterans from the 1916 Battle of the Somme remembered this ground well. Le Transloy was the scene of terrific fighting earlier in the war. The village was now reduced to piles of bricks, with the exception of a rubble-cleared path that marked what had once been the main street. An imposing sugar factory stood on the northwest exit to the village, providing IR 169 with some measure of a redoubt for their right flank. The ground before the German line was a sea of large shell craters, which provided the advancing British with convenient cover.

The 2nd Battalion established a defense along an abandoned trench line in the southeastern portion of the village. Lieutenant Lais set up the four remaining guns of the 2nd Machine Gun Company on a small, rather exposed ridge 30 meters behind the infantry position. Here, the gunners were forced to make a tradeoff for less cover in order to get better fields of fire.

The British 17th Division came into line before Le Transoly on the evening of August 29, with their 52nd and 31st Brigades at the front and the 50th Brigade in reserve. On August 30, the 51st Brigade launched a series of failed attacks. The British regrouped for a more determined push on September 1. The plan was designed to have the 50th and 52nd Brigades work around each side of Le Transoly, with artillery suppressing the German strong points within the ruins of the village. The 21st Division was assigned the task of clearing the Sugar Factory.[301]

September 1 was a scorching hot day. The British artillery preparation was less intense than others that IR 169 had endured, but it was remarkably accurate. Two hours into the barrage, high-caliber howitzer rounds began impacting among the 8th Company, posted in a reserve location. The Germans immediately realized the fire was coming from one of their own batteries, located five miles to the rear at Rocquigny. A courier raced back to the battery to order a cease fire. Meanwhile, the mortally wounded 8th Company commander was among the many casualties resulting from the fratricide.

The 17th Division infantry attack came from three directions. German machine guns began their fire when the British troops came within 700 meters. The rolling ground and abundance of large shell holes made the terrain favorable for the attackers. Small groups of soldiers leaped from hole to hole, closing the distance to the German positions while absorbing only a minimum of losses. Regimental commander, Major Schiller, observed the progression of the battle from the 2nd Machine Gun Company position. In order to get a clear glimpse of the situation, Schiller had to stand exposed on open ground. With shells and bullets flying around him, Schiller saw a grim vision.[302] Lais:

> "More and more new waves of British troops come over the height; they come like ants now, and spread out over the terrain. We, just a few lines of infantry with four machine guns firing at excessive rates, stand or lie against an overwhelming superiority. A real infantry battle rages. Our infantry in front of us takes terrible casualties. My four guns rattle nonstop. More and more Englishmen come over the heights. The pressure becomes terrible." [303]

The waves of British infantry began to mass 400 meters to the front of the German main line. In an instant, the British infantry line opened fire, blanketing the Germans with a terrific volume of rifle fire.

Directly to the 2nd Battalion's left, a hard-fighting but under-strength German Landwehr regiment was barely hanging on. In small groups, the reservists were launching vigorous counterattacks that resulted in fearful losses. Soon there would be no one left to secure IR 169's left flank. The IR 169 machine guns directed fire to the half-left in order to give the Landwehr men some level of fire support. It was nearly too little, too late. The British were able to establish a wedge between the 2nd Battalion and the reserve regiment. Two Lewis machine guns took up an enfilading fire along the length of the German trenches. The 2nd MG Company was hit hard and lost nine men in less than 15 minutes. Four of these were killed instantly with another three falling mortally wounded with gut shots.

The German ranks began to break. A crazed infantryman ran screaming out of the trenches and had to be physically subdued by a medic. Just as some of the machine guns began to run out of ammunition and all seemed lost, a German field artillery battery galloped up and unlimbered their guns only 300 meters from the surging British. The guns rapidly went into action and blasted shells into the British at point-blank range. Many of the British troops began to panic and raced for their own lines. With their last few belts of ammunition, the German machine guns began a blocking fire along the British line of retreat. Lais described the carnage:

> "In a mass, the Englishmen climb out of the pass and attempt to get over the heights and away to Le Transoly. They have a deathly fear, you can see it from their backs; they aren't thinking any more on taking cover, they run and run and stumble and fall. Instead of spreading out from one another, they run clumped up together in their anger and confusion. A shell hits right in the middle of one of these groups. Those few who can run away as individuals fall under our MG fire. Our left flank is cleared. With a cruel precision and distribution of shots, the battery works over the terrain. The deadly urgency of the last quarter hour is forgotten.
>
> The German front attacks without an order. Out of their mouths comes a hoarse roaring, from deep in the breast; it is not a Hurrah, it is the dull thunderous groan of a mortally wounded lion, who with his last strength gathers himself to leap. With steel helmets on at an angle on top of the emaciated faces, our infantry advances. They don't jump, they don't run, they don't duck down into cover. With long, wide, and heavy steps they advance towards the enemy. Something implacable is in this counterattack. The opponent gives up the slope." [304]

On September 2, IR 169 pulled back two miles and took up a new position around Rocquigny. The veterans were disappointed to see that very few of the replacements sent to replenish the infantry companies had any combat experience. Lais, although having lost two thirds of his MG crews strength, was hesitant to trust untested recruits in manning his guns. Instead, Lais reassigned the 2nd MG Company's complement of drivers, clerks, armorers and other support personnel to service the four machine guns.

That night, Lt. Lais was summoned to Major Shiller where he received orders to take permanent command of the 9th Rifle Company. Command of the 2nd MG Company reverted to Vice Corporal Zoerner. Lais' loyal striker, Dirksen, insisted on accompanying him. The new replacements swelled 9th Company's strength up to 80 men. In addition, the company was issued two light machine guns. Inspecting his new command, Lais could only recognize a handful of familiar faces who remained from earlier in the war. While the new light machine gunners demonstrated that they could load and fire their weapons well enough, Lais was frustrated to learn they lacked the expertise for such basic skills as adjusting the bolt mechanism.

IR 169's withdrawal to Rocquigny left a large gap with the neighboring German regiment to its left. To cover his vulnerability, 9th Company was detached for independent duty and temporary control under the regiment directly to the south. The former German line between Le Transloy and Sailly-Sallisel was now the new no-man's-land and the British were concentrating for their next round of attacks near the villages of Les Boeufs and Morval. The brigade commander was on hand to send off the 9th Company with cigarettes and an obviously heavy heart. The company moved out with the men carrying only their weapons, assault packs (with spades) and sandbags full of hand grenades.

After taking sporadic artillery fire, Lais was able to maneuver his company to a position that had good fields of fire into Le Transloy and the fields to the east. Up to the north, IR 169 retained strong control over the ground to their front. Signs of the impending British attack were becoming apparent, as battery after battery of unmolested English heavy guns were observed coming into position less than two miles away near Les Boeufs.

Lais received instructions to report to the battalion commander of the regiment to the south. He entered the command post to see the battalion commander, a cavalry captain with little infantry experience, completely befuddled by conflicting instructions from his higher headquarters. The battalion adjutant ordered 9th Company to move from its current strong position and into the valley now swelling with a horde of British troops. Lais' protests were rejected and the order to attack stood.[305] Rather than sacrifice his entire company with an order he knew to be suicidal, Lais chose to lead a reconnaissance patrol of five men towards the valley. The patrol met with a storm of artillery and small arms fire which killed three of the men. Lais and two others, including Dirksen, barely made it back to 9th Company when the entire German front began to collapse.

The greater German position had become untenable. The methodical 3rd Army advance was finally achieving its objectives. Further to the south, the 2nd Australian Division captured the village of Péronne, while to the north a Canadian Division broke through German lines near Arras. Bapaume was no longer defensible and Ludendorff ordered a general retreat back to the Hindenburg Line, abandoning all of the territory won earlier in 1918.[306]

By the time Lais was aware of any pull back, IR 169 had already departed from its position at Rocquigny, leaving 9th Company to make its own way back to friendly lines. Lais:

"A breathless courier comes running: The position is immediately to be cleared/vacated in direction of the slope of Sailly-Sallisel. The enemy is through on the right and the flank has been surrounded. A wild mishmash of orders follows. I was just supposed to attack, and a few minutes later everyone is to be cleared out. Questioning, I search the area to my right with the field glasses and I cannot see any advancing Englishmen at all. 'Dirksen, run fast to battalion and report that our right flank is free for a long line of sight.' Dirksen runs back a few minutes later; 'they are already all gone' he reports.

The regiment on whose right flank 9th Company was attached to, still had up to strength companies. They however, were now all gone by way of the field of craters, behind the heights, and were pushing past the ground to the west of Sailly. The platoons and companies were jammed up behind one another. The men from the other regiment didn't have any assault packs and were instead carrying heavy backpacks. The entire readjustment to the left has gotten bogged down. For several minutes we can't get a step forward, and then everyone rushes further in dense groups; all in the light of day and only a few hundred meters away from the enemy. Can that end well?

We advance, bent over, go down deep on our knees, with only the hope that the enemy doesn't notice. And then it all breaks loose above us. We are the last of the retreat, and far in front of us, almost at Sailly-Sallisel, English machine guns hammer against the heights that slope down there. Somewhere the companies must have become visible. A few seconds later entire batteries of the enemy pull into line. Piles of humanity, yelling and swearing, run into each other. Shells impact into the masses; yelling, crying wailing and cursing. All of the ground stands under black smoke and a brown curtain of blown up clay earth. Our only advantage was that we could swing around to the right. Back to the old position! I yell, and my NCO's yell. A part of the company, the young replacements, lose their heads and run to the protective overhang of Sailly where they are swept up in this terrible flight. I saw little more of them. I estimate I have fourteen dead since the morning.

With the remnants of my company and a few veterans from the attached regiment, we run, stumbling and falling, taking cover and rising up again, and make the short distance to our former position in the nick of time. The enemy has secured the heights around us and is carefully pushing beyond it, with some of them only 20-30 meters before us. A little more speed on the Englishmen's part and we would have been at a distinct disadvantage against six times our number.

My light machine gun fires up the enemy's assault troops as our hand grenades fly down the hill. Around the slope the puffs of smoke from the explosions of the hand grenades are thick on top of each other. The enemy is overwhelmed and withdraws down to the floor of the valley with casualties.

So there we are sitting there isolated. Should we attempt to fight our way through to the northeast in the direction of my regiment? No, it won't work; we would be pushed off into the depression like rabbits. To the south and southwest of us, the slope and low ground are under heavy fire. The high-lying terrain of Sailly disappears under black billowing clouds of smoke. Shells burst close behind us. I still have 21 men, including a medical NCO, and two NCO's and seven men of the other regiment. Medical NCO Kratzer tears off his red cross armband, rips up his *Soldbuch* (paybook and ID record) and takes an infantry rifle in his hand. Exactly east of here on the North-South Rocquigny-Sailly line, 800 meters in front of Mesnil, is an artillery defensive position with attached trenches marked on the map.

So, let's go; as long as we can, on the high ridgeline which is under less fire than the hollows north and northeast of Sailly! Somewhere we must be able to break through the blocking force. As the crow flies it must be between 600-700 meters.

We have to travel into a hollow 200 meters before the destination. Exhausted as we are, we are indifferent to the situation. Our lungs simply can't absorb any more air. The enemy has naturally kept up the pressure behind us and his machine guns are firing after us. We stagger entirely mixed up through the shell impacts and the curtain of dust and smoke. My light machine gunner, Katzer, Dirksen and I make the decision. The hollow is a smoking, billowing, raging witches' cauldron; ahead of us to the right they are shooting. If one should stagger to the left, they would sink up to their heads in the thick mud! Ahead of us, behind us, geysers of earth are ripped up by artillery fire.

'How many are missing?' 'Seven, Herr Leutnant!' is the answer. It is a salvation that fewer shells are landing here. Fifty meters ahead of us it is just as crazy as before. Sight is limited due to the undulating black curtain of fire. The hollow, through which we just had to go through, had previously served as a convoy route. The loose clay earth formation of the road, which has been ground to powder by convoys lessens the impact of the barrage. Three of my men, and four of those who attached themselves to us, are missing; apparently ripped into atoms by a direct hit. Later I learn that the cavalry captain and the battalion commander to whom I was subordinated met the same fate.

Here we are quite alone on a broad sector in front of Le Mesnil, almost in the middle between Sailly and Rocquigny (as the crow flies 2.5 kilometers). We aim our rifle sights towards the heights on which we were still fighting less than an hour ago and determine it is 700 meters distant.

Half to the right, 20 meters in front of us, is an abandoned gun position that is reinforced in concrete. In a bunker behind it we find 5000 rounds of machine gun ammunition and recover a brand new, heavy machine gun with a carriage bearing lightly bent skids and torn off hand wheel. We take the gun back to the trench and set it in an enclave directly above the bunker. I load and fire a few shots towards the heights. It works!

Artillery fire is now only directed on Sailly itself. To our left we still observe friendly troops at Le Mesnil, while others near Sailly retreat in broad rows under the black smoke. Le Mesnil is under a heavy barrage by naval guns.

I spread out my people along a 100 meter line and order them to immediately take cover into the bunker should we take heavy fire. With Dirksen serving as a guide, I fire the heavy machine gun to establish a range at 700 meters directly to the west. The light machine gun is ranged 500 meters to the northwest. We have 22 others serving as riflemen. In the late afternoon, a heavy bombardment sweeps over us like a steamroller, and then concentrates 300 meters beyond on some unoccupied trenches in front of Le Mesnil. Apparently they think that is where the front line is. The first English assault troops come over the heights. We immediately open fire with all rifles and the two machine guns, halting the enemy advance. It's getting dark, night is coming. Along with the twilight, a new German infantry unit pushes its way through the narrow (and at most a meter deep) trenches and advance beyond us. They are creeping on their bellies and sliding on their knees so they won't be seen. As far as I can remember, it was a Silesian regiment. [The Silesians were from the German/Prussian province of Silesia - Schlesien in German - which is now part of Poland.]

The commander of the Silesian regiment himself comes and shakes my hand and my peoples' hands and gives us a few words of highest recognition for our actions. He wants to know our names so that he can report up to higher.

I orient the new company commander on the fields of fire and then lay myself down to sleep in the only bunker. We set out only two sentries to watch over our machine guns. Everyone else who belongs to me is already sleeping soundly on the bare wood. The trench above is occupied by the Silesians." [307]

The extent of the German retreat had yet to be communicated to all the front-line troops. After only a few hours of sleep, Lais was woken to the news that the Silesian Regiment was withdrawing and that 9th Company was no longer connected to other friendly forces on either flank. Throughout the remainder of the night, Lais sent out patrols and beat off several British probes. 9th Company continued to be depleted, with two more men killed, one seriously wounded and two others missing after trying to link with German forces still in Sailly. At dawn, Lais pulled his men out of the defenses and made for the village of Le Mesnil.[308]

Lais described the trials of 9th Company's final journey back to German lines:[309]

There is a heavy barrage from Sailly to Rocquigny. The trenches, which we held during the evening, are ablaze. The tree ruins of Le Mesnil disappear under the dense smoke of the heavy impacts. A few hundred meters behind us, artillery thunders and smashes. The enemy allowed himself to be deceived throughout the whole night by a handful of forgotten soldiers and they are pounding away with immense resources against an empty, deserted field.

With hastening steps, supporting our wounded between us, we march east into the breaking morning.

The measure of our misfortune is not yet full. Shortly before we reach Lechelle [one and half miles northeast of Le Mesnil] we are caught in the strafing machine gun attack of a low flying English reconnaissance squadron, which surprises us while we are in open terrain with hardly any cover. A severely wounded man, along with the two stretcher-bearers, lie in the street, full of holes. Both the NCO's from the other regiment are mortally wounded; one of them dies in a few minutes, the other after being carried a short distance in his shelter half. Of those men

~ 347 ~

who joined us from that other regiment, only one is still alive. My Company has 13 men left

There are no German soldiers anywhere. The region is devastated. Overhead rounds from the German level-trajectory artillery howl past. Behind, the English artillery barrage impacts onto empty land. We are withdrawing to the north. The day is sunny; the barrage behind us has stopped. A giant, yellow sausage glimmers in the sunlight ahead of us and to the left. Thank God, it is a German observation balloon.

But that really can't be! We should have met up with our own infantry some time ago. The observation balloon moves slowly to the north, in the same direction we are going. Then it stops and goes lower. Now we are about the same elevation as the balloon, and we confirm laconically, 'The Tommies!' Our field glasses confirm this. The last two days were so intense that this English observation balloon just doesn't bother us anymore. We turn to the northeast a bit and soon resume our northerly direction.

We have delayed the English advance along a 1.5 mile stretch for several hours. We have caused the enemy to waste his artillery to an unimaginable extent.

Tired but alert, we double-time along our route of retreat. We are often reminded of the need for caution: the September sun is hot, and our stomachs are growling. My heart is heavy because of the state of our company, now patched together out of so many diverse elements. The company's magnificent accomplishment are overshadowed by its losses.

We are challenged! The first of our men calls, 'Where are you coming from?' We are at the edge of the new German advanced position. Their forward position's tactical use of terrain is splendid. We recognize the camouflaged anti-tank rifles only when the crews emerge from their holes to stare at us. We unload our rifles!

The constant question is when the Tommies will get here. To our left the enemy has already come in contact with our thin line of pickets. Our answer is resoundingly clear: 'This evening you can expect the Tommies!" We ask, 'Have you heard anything about the 169th Regiment?' We are answered 'No, not a trace.' We come to our field artillery, to our howitzers. Here they have prepared a good reception for the enemy. The gun crews give us our first warm meal.

'Have you seen the 169th?'

'Yes, there's one of them with us, In fact, there he is'

It turns out to be one of my young people who was lost in the confusion at Sailly. He was wounded in the cheek by shrapnel and was wearing a thick gauze bandage around his head. He didn't want to go to the field hospital; he was happy to be back with us. When we asked him, he said he had no idea where the regiment was forming up. An artillery major and his adjutant came up to inspect the guns and batteries of his sector. I gave him my report. He replied, 'Boys, you've had a tough time of it!' He gave my troops and I cigarettes and a light.

To my question of where our regiment was, he said, 'Over on the other side of Belu and Hermies (10 miles southwest of Cambrai) a severely shot up division is supposed to be forming up.'

Just past Belu, in the direction of Cambrai, I met people from our division. I asked. 'Do you have any idea of where my regiment is forming up?'

They told me, 'Yes, right over there, by the hedgerow to the left of the road.'

At the entrance to a small meadow, surrounded by a hedge in a manner typical of the Cambrai landscape, stood the brave commander of our regiment.

'Ninth Company! One Officer, 14 Men Returning.'

He extended his hand and said, 'I was just about to give up all hope of your getting back.' Then he turned around and pointing into the hedge-encircled field, said, 'Here the regiment is forming up.'

'My God!' I thought, 'This company-and-a-half should be a regiment.....'

The field kitchen was there; we spent the night in bivouac and in the morning we marched to our base.[310]

On September 8, IR 169's retreat carried 30 miles northeast of Cambrai and across the Belgium border to the village of Blaton. The 52nd Division loaded on trains and returned back to Flanders, traveling 30 miles north to arrive at Ingelmuenster, Belgium. The regiment went into quarters in the cluster of villages of Gulleghem, Moorsele and Ledegem, all on the outskirts of Rousselare. Although the front was only 15 miles to the west, near Ypres, the regiment saw no action on this final deployment to Flanders.

The terrible of fighting of August pushed IR 169 to near its breaking point; a major refit and reorganization was desperately needed. New coats, blouses and trousers were issued to all the men and each of the line companies received two of the new German anti-tank rifles; the Mauser 1918 T-Geweher. Weighing 41 pounds and operated by a two-man crew, these monstrous rifles fired a powerful 13.2mm, armor-piercing round that inflicted a violent recoil upon the gunner. In the course of the R&R, Crown Prince Rupprecht inspected the regiment.

In addition to the usual practice of filling the ranks with individual replacements, an entire veteran unit, Replacement (*Ersatz*) Infantry Regiment 29, consisting of Badeners and Westphalians, was absorbed into the three existing 52nd Infantry regiments, IRs 111, 169 and 170. Each regiment disbanded three infantry and one machine gun companies and dispersed those soldiers into the remaining units. Entire IR 29 companies were then integrated into the existing regiments to backfill those disbanded. This provided a welcome addition of combat-seasoned soldiers who came with an established chain of command and were already equipped with their own weapons, horses, wagons and other essentials. By the time reorganization was complete, the average 52nd Infantry Division infantry company had approximately 140-150 NCOs and enlisted, with the three machine gun companies standing at just under 100 enlisted men.[311] Regimental strength averaged 1,500 men. During this period, Lais departed the 9th Company and went on to command IR 169's 3rd Machine Gun Company, now reconstituted with 92 men. 32 new replacements blended with the 60 IR 169 veterans.[312]

On September 21, the 52nd Division was transferred from Flanders to a general reserve position near Metz. IR 169's portion of the journey took them from Blaton and Ville Perumerille, Belgium for the 230-mile train journey south. On September 22-23 the regiment then went into quarters in the villages of Colligny and then Remilly, 15 miles southeast of Metz, and assigned to Army Group Gallwitz to serve as the General Headquarters Group Reserve under Gruppe Metz. Lais remarked how pleased the men were to return to the German Lorraine and of the attractive qualities of the young women there. This pleasant respite lasted less than three days.

Chapter 16
Meuse-Argonne Forest (Part I): The Kriemhilde Stellung

In late September 1918, the Allies launched the last great offensive of the war. A core part of this attack involved 1.2 million troops of the American Expeditionary Forces (AEF), with many of its units recently bloodied in such places as Chateau-Thierry, Belleau Wood and the St. Mihiel Salient. The resulting month-long Meuse-Argonne Campaign was one of the bloodiest battlegrounds in the U.S. Army's history. For IR 169, this battle spelled its annihilation.

The U.S. First Army positioned 22 American divisions along a 25-mile line that centered 12 miles northwest of Verdun. The terrain was dominated by the Meuse River running on a northwest to southeast axis above the thick Argonne forest. The attack's objective was to sever the all-important German rail-link between Flanders and Metz at Sedan.

The Americans assembled three full strength corps to confront five depleted German divisions. Thirteen of the First Army-controlled divisions (nine U.S. and three French) were lined up along the front, with nine more divisions available in ready reserve. The Germans identified the build-up and alerted reinforcements to counter the coming onslaught.[313]

While the Germans assigned to the Meuse-Argonne were vastly outnumbered, they occupied some of the strongest positions in the entire Western Front. The German defenses were anchored on a segment of the Hindenburg Line that ran east-west along the center of the Argonne Forest. The killing ground actually began ten miles south of the Hindenburg Line trenches with a deadly series of defensive belts. The particular sector of the line that the 52nd Division came to defend was centered around the *Kriemhilde Stellung*. The defensive works blended well into the deep, shell-shattered forests and integrated numerous barbed wire entanglements, minefields, concrete machine gun bunkers and fields of fire covered by abundant artillery reserves. American military historian SLA Marshall described the terrain as "so repellent as to suggest that nature had designed it to serve as a barrier," and as "among the thickest and most elaborately ramified earthworks zone ever assaulted by U.S. troops." [314] Lt. Gen. Robert Lee Bullard described the approach to this section:

"The way out is forward, through the Kriemhilde Stellung, eastern section of the Hindenburg Line.... It is not a line, but a net, four kilometers deep. Knee-high wire is interlaced in the grass, and tangled devilishly in forests.... Pillboxes are in succession, with one covering another. There are no 'fox holes', but rather concrete positions. There are more bits of trenches and wire with a few light guns. It is a defense in depth until it leads to the main trenches. Many of them are in baffling irregularity, so that the attacker cannot know when he has mopped up.... Farther back, there is also a defense in depth with a wide band of artillery emplacements." [315]

First Army's early morning attack on September 26 was preceded by a three hour bombardment from 2,700 guns firing 250,000 rounds. Eight hundred Allied aircraft supported the attack. At 5:30 am, the infantry advanced under cover of a rolling artillery barrage.[316] The center-left of the American attack was assigned to the 35th Infantry Division, a unit facing its first battle. A National Guard unit, the 35th Division was made up of men from Missouri and Kansas. Among its ranks was Captain Harry S. Truman, commanding officer of D Battery, 129th Field Artillery, and his brother, Captain Ralph E. Truman, who served as a divisional intelligence officer. The 35th Division was further supported by a battalion of light tanks from the 344th Tank Battalion, personally led in this battle by Regimental Commander Colonel George S. Patton III. In this fight, the 32 year old Patton, armed with a hiking stick, walked behind his two-man Renault FT tanks. The tanks had a turret- mounted 37-mm gun and had a road speed of approximately 4.5 mph.

Spread across a two-mile front, the 35th Division attack kicked off before the village of Vauquois. Its mission was to reach the village of Exermont, six miles north and just over halfway to the core Hindenburg line defenses. Covered by dense fog and smoke rounds, the attack started well enough and soon carried past the village of Varennes, a mile and half towards the objective. [Varennes' other claim to history was as the location where Louis XVI and Marie Antoinette were captured at the beginning of the French Revolution.[317]]

The fog lifted as the Americans approached the Montfaucon Heights, leaving the infantry and tanks exposed in open fields. The

Germans made devilish use of the choppy terrain to mass machine guns and cover multiple fields of fire. When the shooting started, the stunned Americans were hit with fire came from the front, flanks, and in some cases, even the rear. Near Cheppy, barbed wire entanglements and heavy fire from 25 German machine gun nests stalled the lead infantry companies and a section of Patton's tanks. The arrival of additional tanks only contributed to a bottleneck as German planes directed artillery against the increasingly muddled American troops. In an attempt to get the attack moving, Patton led a small force forward when he received a severe hip wound. Eventually, a combined infantry-tank force flanked the German line and allowed the advance to resume.[318]

The Germans moved to stem this breach by scrambling the reinforcement of five additional divisions into the Argonne. The 52nd Division, serving as the theater reserve, was placed on ready alert the evening of September 26. IR 111, augmented by IR 169's 2nd and 3rd Machine Gun companies, assembled by the nearby railhead within an hour after receiving the alert orders. The only information available was that American forces had overrun a German guards division and was breaking through the Ardennes defenses. Lais recalled of how the locomotive engines were fully steamed as the men loaded onto the cars and of the insane rate of speed that carried them through Metz and into the dark Argonne Forest in the early hours of September 27. The first elements of the IR 111 task force arrived at the St. Juvin Station on September 28, and unloaded to the sounds of the battle for Exermont, just five miles to the south.

The American's effort to take Exermont, and subsequent German counterattacks, drove this early phase of the campaign. Randal Gaulk described the key terrain features that shaped this battle:

"Exermont is a small rural village nestled in a hollow just a few kilometers east of the Aire River Valley and about 10 kilometers north of the AEF jump-off line. The town is flanked by two hills: Montrebeau (elevation 224 meters) to the south, and Montrefange (240 meters), to the north. A small stream runs through the town, close to Montrefange. Northeast of Montrefange is the German-named Lichtenauer Heights (272 meters), noted for its long, narrow crest. To the east of that is the Marian/Romange Heights (269 meters). A vast network of hollows and ravines connects throughout the hills.[319]

The fresh troops from 52nd Division and 5th Guards Division were ordered to counterattack through Exermont to reclaim the ground recently lost. IR 111, as the 52nd Division's lead regiment, raced to the Lichtenauer Heights to spearhead the assault. Moving out of the St. Juvin railhead, the IR 169 machine gun companies lugged their heavy machine guns and ammunition by hand, as their support wagons could not traverse through the rubble covered streets. Once of out of town, the infantry dispersed in tactical formations and the MG wagons came up to help relieve the gunner's back-breaking loads. It was a clear, mild day, but the recent rain caused mud to cling to boots, horse legs and wagon axles. The movement took them past well-established defensive positions and over undulating, forested ground scarred by years of combat. Elsewhere, Lais observed deep forested valleys and described how the hill mass of Montrebeau "stood as if a guard in the middle of a battle-zone, lying in the dark shadow and recumbent on the forest slope."

On the morning of September 29, the 111/169 force winded up the back slopes of the Lichtenauer Heights, the steep ridgeline that ran east from the top of Montrebeau. Lais hiked to an elevated point and spied the terrain ahead with his field glasses. Directly below and to his left was a large forested area. 2000 meters to the south, the forest ended and open fields led to the village of Exermont. Lais estimated the distances, and calculated that the open ground was just outside the effective 2000 meter range of conventional machine gun ammunition. The 2nd and 3rd IR 169 MG companies deployed their total of 16 guns into firing positions along the ridgeline and waited. Lais wrote of the moment, "our lips grew tighter and tighter." [320]

A weakened, final American surge on the morning of September 29 pushed lead elements of the 140th Infantry Regiment into Exermont. Retreating before them were hard pressed German defenders of the 3rd Foot Guard Regiment, men exhausted from three days of intensive combat. The Germans were pushed back one more kilometer, allowing the Americans to take possession of Exermont and the heights to the east. The 140th Infantry Regiment suffered heavy losses and only had a fragile hold Exermont and the ground 300 meters north of the village.

The three days of fighting left the 35th Division as badly chewed up as the Germans they had just driven away. The U.S. resupply operations were crippled when retreating Germans pioneers blasted huge craters in the only road available, delaying movement of artillery, food and ammunition. The American's had barely entered Exermont when disastrous instructions called for them to continue the attack. Devoid of supporting artillery fires and ignorant of the great enemy strength the before them, the attack orders ensured their destruction.

Meuse-Argonne Campaign

From 29 September – 1 November 1918, IR 169 engaged US forces in the Meuse-Argonne Offensive. Map highlights include a counterattack against the 35th Division at Exermont on 29 September; defending against the 1st and 42nd Divisions between Exermont and Romange, 30 September – 14 October; Recuperation near Mouzon, 15-21 October; Ready Reserve by Buzancy, 22 October – 31 October; and destruction by 2nd Division at Landres St Georges, 1 November.

(PD)

Lais received his first glimpse of U.S. soldiers as they emerged out of the clearing between Exermont and entered the forward edge of the Montrefange Woods. The extreme range of the targets kept his machine guns silent. Lais watched as the unsuspecting American infantry advanced in wave after wave. Next came a squadron of 14 light tanks. Two batteries of German artillery, which had just deployed on the rear slope of the Lichtenauer Heights, opened fire on the tanks. Two tanks received direct hits; Lais likened them to burning like bright lamps. The remaining tanks continued their advance, but in a seemingly more confused condition.

The doughboys advanced deeper into the woods and eventually stumbled into the waiting IR 111 fire sacks. The IR 169 machine gunners on the crest of the Lichtenauer could only listen to the sounds of the battle, as they had no visible targets in the forest below them. The howitzers firing behind the ridge sent rounds directly over the machine gunners, with the rounds exploding 1500 meters ahead into the forest. Lais' men, especially the younger replacement troops, grew anxious at the noise of the unseen battle below, but were kept occupied by camouflaging their positions and support wagons.

Lais was also impatient at the prospect of enemy tanks wandering unmolested through the forest floor. He ordered one of his section chiefs, Sergeant Mussolf, to take three gun crews armed with anti-tank grenades to hunt for exposed tanks. The grenades were manufactured by the company armorer, who created incendiary devices by inserting a mixture of phosphorus and benzoyl into the explosive casings. The weapons were detonated by a timed fuses. Using these improvised explosives was a dangerous task that required good timing, precise throwing skills and a steady nerve. Mussolf's section entered the forest and soon enough came across two light tanks driving on a forest path. Moments later, this pair was joined a third tank following at distance of 30 meters. The trio of tanks were separated from supporting infantry, making them easy bait for Mussolf's patrol. The Germans moved in and skillfully tossed the grenades so they exploded on the tanks' fuel containers. In seconds, all three tanks were engulfed in blazing flames that incinerated their crews.

Up on the ridge, the commander of the howitzer battery behind the 169 MG companies conferred with Lais, where it was assessed that the Americans would soon be retreating out of the forest, and through the clearing from where they came from. They concocted trap to cover the escape zone with a deadly combination of coordinated machine gun and artillery fires. Down in the forest, the repulse of the American advance was never in question. After suffering heavy losses, the U.S. infantry fell back in disarray through the woods and began to exit into the clearing towards Exermont. Lais ordered the gunners to mount sighting scopes and load their guns with long-range ammunition that extended the maximum effective ranges out to 2500 meters. Both 169 MG companies opened fire and created a 'fearful ring of steel' for those caught in the field. The artillery, which had precisely registered the target area, fired salvo after salvo. Entire groups of American soldiers were cut down and blown apart by the fire. Lais appraised that few of the Americans who entered the Montrefange Woods managed to escape. The 140th U.S. Infantry Regiment, which went into the battle three days earlier with 4,000 men, was practically destroyed.

The German counterattack launched at 2:00 pm. Major Wulff, the acting IR 111 commander, personally led his 2nd and 3rd Battalions of IR 111 in the vanguard of the assault. The attack advanced quickly, facing only minor delays resulting from the difficult terrain and scattered pockets of American resistance. Several American machine gun nests fired at a distance with some effect, but were quickly silenced by the well-directed fire of IR 111's 2nd MG Company. The German attack plowed through Exermont and crossed the Gotteberg Hollow creek to the south of the village.

The IR 169 MG companies took position on the right flank of the IR 111 attack. Lais recalled with great pride how his machine gun sections advanced as if on field maneuvers. A Guards Division staff officer, who remained on the battlefield after his battered unit was relieved the previous day, approached Lais with tears in his eyes. The major rhetorically questioned that after four years of war, what more was left to be done. Lais reassured him that the remaining two regiments of the 52nd Division would soon be in line.[321]

By 3:00 pm, IR 111 had reached the Montrebeau Woods, erasing all of the American gains of the previous day. The Americans would have likely been pushed all the way back to the offensive's initial starting point had not it not been for the courageous deployment of the 35th Division's 110th Engineers Regiment. The 1,200 men of the two engineer battalions held a strong line of defense near Baulny, two miles south of Exermont. A large concentration of divisional, corps and army-level artillery, totaling 31 batteries of guns, put up a wall of fire protecting the new defensive line. The new American line held.

The guard's regiment that was supposed to be adjacent to IR 111's right was delayed, leaving this flank exposed. As the enemy situation stabilized, American assaults began to strike with localized counterattacks. The fighting in the Montrebeau Woods went back and forth through night and morning 29-30 September. Recorded IR 111 losses for September 29 was 53 killed, 14 wounded [a likely under-reported statistic] and 15 missing.

At daylight, IR 111 held a tenuous grip on the northern edge of the woods. American aircraft appeared over the battlefield and directed a tremendous artillery barrage that resulted in heavy casualties and pushed some of the Germans back towards Gottberg Hollow. American tanks and infantry attacked as the fighting see-sawed through the woods. IR 111's losses for September 30 were 22 killed, 74 wounded and 5 missing.

The remainder of the 52nd Division came into line on October 1 to replace the two Guards Divisions on either flank of IR 111. IR 169 took up position on the 52nd Division's right flank, IR 111 remained in the center with IR 170 on the left. Regimental leadership changes also took place, with IR 111's assigned commander, Oberstleutnant Weerth returning from leave. Acting commander Major Wulff receiving decoration for his leadership of September 29 attack.[322] Lais' Third MG Company was reunited with IR 169's Third Battalion, commanded by Captain Meier. Before the war, the diminutive Meier was an attorney from Ludwigshafen. Lais was very fond of Meier and their close friendship transcended the more conventional relationship expected of a battalion and company-level commander. The 3rd MG Company remained attached to the Third Battalion for the remainder of the campaign.[323]

The opposing U.S. 35th Division lost 7,000 men in three days. The division disintegrated as command and control broke down at all levels. Many of the survivors wandered leaderless through the rear lines as thousands of wounded lay in squalid conditions. The 35th Division's collapse was considered as one the greatest AEF debacles of the First World War. At the request of its divisional commander, the remnants of the 35th Division was pulled off the line and replaced by the 1st Infantry Division on October 1.[324]

For the rest of October, fighting in this general local involved German troops from 52nd Division, along with units that included the 37th and 5th Guards Divisions, defending against the oncoming American 1st, 42nd and 2nd Divisions. This battle zone was no more than three miles wide and six miles deep. The most significant terrain in this zone was the Aire River, which ran on a north-to-south axis and served as the left boundary for the advancing American units. German artillery, dug in on the high ground to the west of the Aire, blasted the oncoming Americans through a catacomb of ravines on their exposed left flank.[325] Efforts to silence this unremitting fire was a major American objective in the next phase of the struggle for the Argonne Forest.

The Germans did their best to leverage the tangled forested areas and rugged ravines to stop the Americans before they could threaten the hardened Kriemhilde Stellung defenses. A breakthrough of that line would be catastrophic.

Nearby, two of the great dramas of the American World War I experience took place near the vicinity of IR 169's early October operations.

A few miles to the west, the saga of the American 'Lost Battalion' was played out during the first week of October. The Lost Battalion is the sobriquet given to nine companies of the U.S. 77th Division that were trapped and besieged by German forces from 2 – 7 October. The 554 man battalion, under the command of Major Charles Whittlesey, began isolated in deep Charlevaux Ravine and surrounded by German troops. For the next six days, the Germans poured in fired from the lip of the ravine and conducted multiple attacks, some employing flamethrowers. The Americans, critically short on ammunition, food and medical supplies, suffered enormous deprivations as they fought among their many unburied dead. Despite overwhelming odds and nearly 300 casualties, Major Whittlesey rejected offers to surrender and continued to fight until rescued on October 7. Whittlesey and two others received the Medal of Honor.[326]

A second epic U.S. Army legend remembered from the Meuse-Argonne Campaign was that of Corporal (later Sergeant) Alvin York of the 82nd Infantry Division. This action occurred on October 8 to the immediate west of the 52nd Division's zone. In the 82nd Division assault across the Aire, Corporal York was part of 16-man unit ordered to silence a cluster of German machine gun nests. After taking command from his wounded squad leader, York personally killed 15 German soldiers and led efforts to capture 132 more, resulting in his being awarded the Medal of Honor.[327] The action of York's squad were a microcosm of the 82nd and 1st Division's efforts to push German artillery from its sanctuary across the Aire.[328]

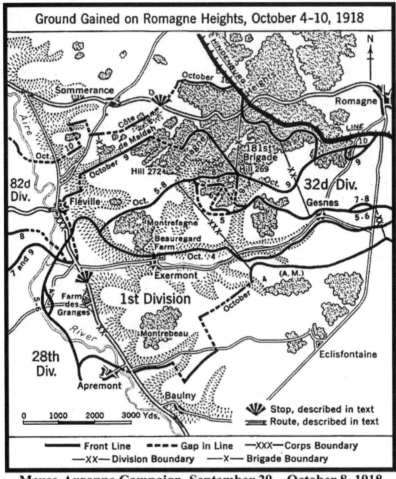

Ground Gained on Romagne Heights, October 4-10, 1918

Meuse-Argonne Campaign, September 29 – October 8, 1918

On 29 September, two IR 169 MG companies supported IR 111's counterattack against the 35th Division at Exermont from the Montrefange Heights and reaching the Montrebeau Woods. From 30 September – 8 October, IR 169 defended the Montrebeau Woods against the 1st Division, when it was forced to retreat across the Exermont Valley to the Romange Heights.

(AABE)

October 1 was the last relatively quiet day as both fresh German and American troops deployed for the next act of the Meuse-Argonne Campaign.

The U.S. 1st Infantry Division, which arrived at the front September 30 – October 1, was an experienced, regular Army unit that had fought well at Cantigny, Soissons and St Mihiel. In its journey to the front, 1st Division troops were taken aback by the stream of 35th Division dead and wounded being evacuated to the rear. The division went into line where the 35th Division's 110th Engineers made their stand by Baulny.[329]

The 1st Division set out with three objectives; reclaim the northern edge of the Montrebeau Woods; advance to the northwest to take the village of Fleville and continue northeast to capture the Montrefange (Hill 240) and adjoining Lichtenauer Heights. Accomplishing these goals would put the Americans halfway to the Kriemhilde Stellung.[330]

The 52nd Division defense of the Montrebeau Woods placed IR 169 on the division's left flank, IR 170 in the center and IR 111 on the right. To the east of IR 169 stood the 115th Division, with its IR's 171, 172 serving as the 52nd Division's left flanking counterpart. The back and forth fighting of September 30 left most of the northern portions of woods in German hands, while Americans held the center.

The chaotic state of the 35th Division's withdrawal made the 1st Division's transition to the front a dicey task. The 1st Division's immediate priority was to fix the location of the German defensive positions across its new front. The lead battalions sent out reconnaissance patrols to confirm what would prove false rumors of a German retreat. On the division's right flank, the 26th Infantry Regiment sent out a 70-man patrol commanded by two officers. The battalion commander, worried about what the patrol might encounter, ordered a signal squad with a field telephone and breast wire reel to accompany it.

The patrol set out one hour before dawn and advanced in two waves, the first consisting of skirmishers, the second wave of squad columns that were about 50 feet in the rear. The fog was thick. The patrol made it 500 meters into forest when they ambushed of network of machine gun nests firing from multiple directions. Of the 70 troops that departed on the patrol, only one officer and 12 men returned.[331] Such was the cost of surveying a small portion the German line hidden inside the Montrebeau Woods.

October 2 opened with a distinct increase of American artillery fire that intensified by the hour. A frantic battalion messenger reported to Lais with orders to meet impending enemy attack in another portion of the forest. The rain had turned the lower portions of the forest floor into a swampy muck. The deep mud and thick bramble made it impossible to bring in the gun wagons to transport the machine guns and ammunition, so it all had to be lugged by hand. High explosive artillery shells split apart trees, mixing lethal wood splinters with the steel shrapnel. Other shells landed with a thud, followed by a puff that released smoke, and possibly poison gas. The already arduous hike now had to be made with the burden of wearing gas masks. The company finally arrived at the designated position and the men immediately set to work digging primitive protective positions. The exhausted men and buried their faces into shallow holes as artillery burst among them.[332]

The Meuse-Argonne Campaign's second phase lasted from October 4-28, with the 1st Army's renewed effort to breach the Hindenburg Line. The 52nd and neighboring German divisions began this phase by blocking the American 1st Division's attempt drive six miles north to the Landres-et- St. Georges portion of the Kriemhilde Stellung.

The main attack began the morning of October 4. 1st Division infantry battalions charged forward under the cover of a rolling artillery barrage with the American guns firing at a rate of 10 rounds per minute. The Germans defense of the Montrebeau Woods inflicted heavy losses on the Americans with snipers, machine guns and aircraft-directed artillery fire. The Americans seemed to be constantly on the move, probing or attacking into every ravine. Lais counted the Germans as repelling seven distinct American attacks, several supported by tanks. The 52nd Division artillery zeroed in on a section of seven tanks, destroying five and sending the surviving two to turn in retreat.[333]

A heavy fog descended that evening, which served to cover a German counterattack to regain a lost position. The men of IR 169 never received a formal attack order, but in conjunction with IR's 171 and 172 moving to their left, and IR 170 to the right, arose from their positions and began to creep towards the American lines, 200 meters distant. There were no German preparatory fires, leaving the Americans unaware of the looming strike. Nearing enemy lines, Lais could make out the silhouettes of the flat American helmets. As rifle fire exploded, Lais could hear the terrified cries of the enemy shouting 'The Germans! The Germans!' In a flash they closed into the American position. Those Yanks who were not able to flee were shot down or captured. Lais believed an opportunity was lost in not pursuing the routed enemy, but there was nothing left for it. The Germans ravenously consumed the food and water left by their vanquished foes. The Americans also abandoned large quantities of weapons and ammunition.[334]

October 5 was a seminal day in the battle of Montrebeau Woods. The confused nature of the woodland fighting was reflective of an instance occurring midday, when regimental messenger, Private First Class Mener, reported to Lais. Lais remembered Mener as a rather jovial sort of person who, before the war, served as the head bartender of a prestigious Frankfurt nightclub. Rather than wearing the required steel helmet, Mener appeared before him with his cap worn at a rakish angle. Also in tow were two American prisoners. With a degree of flourish, Mener described how he single-handed had ambushed a six-man patrol in the thick underbrush. He killed four of the unsuspecting Americans and took the other two as prisoners to Lais' position.[335]

The fighting that day left the 3rd Machine Gun Company with severe losses, and by day's end, only six guns were left serviceable. In the following passage from his memoir, Lais reflected on the toll taken among his most trusted and beloved men. The loss of two of these men were especially painful; Dirksen, his loyal orderly and Ziegler, the skilled con artist who 'stood ranks' as commander that night in Acheville when Lais was bedridden with fever:

> "The devil comes again. The Americans press with all of their combat power across the entire German front. Our resources grow thinner and thinner all the while the area we have to defend grows longer... Deadly American artillery fire reverberates through the forest. The explosions of the dreaded heavy 18 cm [155 mm] guns are hideous blasts." ...It becomes lonelier and lonelier for me.... My company is ever smaller. My old comrades fall one after the other. On October 5 I lost my dear and devoted lad Dirksen, as well as my messenger Ziegler, my new armorer Fuchs, and section leader Margarthe."
> [336]

The western portion of the 52nd Division's right flank collapsed and American forces surged towards Exermont, and leaving IR 111 exposed from the rear of the forest. IR 111's 2nd Battalion was wiped out. One officer and 100 men of the battalion were captured unwounded. Most of the remainder were killed in the fighting.[337]

Slowly, the Germans were forced to give ground in the Montrebeau Woods, leaving the 52nd Division to be pushed back in a scattered line across the eastern portion of the Exermont Valley. American troops exploited the break of the German right flank and attacked into Exermont. As the battle moved into the shattered village, new bodies of the 1st Division soldiers became intermingled with the decaying corpses of 35th Division men who were killed several days earlier. All five of the light Renault tanks supporting the attack into the village were disabled by German anti-tank weapons.

IR 169 withdrew two kilometers northeast of the Montrebeau Woods to a forested area east of Exermont. For the next three days the 1st Division continued their attack to secure Exermont and take Montrefange and the Lichtenauer Heights one mile to the north.

The U.S. 3rd Battalion of the 26th Infantry Regiment led the attack after coming from the reserve, moving past Exermont as it thrust towards Montrefange. American forward observers, aided by field phones, had become highly adept at directing their artillery fires. In this attack, one field artillery officer with exclusive control of two cannons was credited with destroying multiple machine gun positions and two enemy field guns. For the next two days, German and American assaults and counterattacks raged between the Montrebeau and Montrefange Woods. On October 6, a fierce German attack dissolved the 3rd Battalion's right flank swept up a forward communications network of 70 American signalmen. A handful of NCO's averted a larger crisis when they halted the rout and rallied a stand. Another powerful German counterattack then pounced from the north, but was driven back by a promptly delivered artillery barrage.
[338]

The 52nd Division suffered terrible losses. By October 5, IR 111, now down to two battalions, could barely count 180 men still in fighting condition. On October 6, replacements arrived in the midst of the battle, bringing IR 111 up to 300 men; still a shadow of the 1,500 man force that entered the Argonne nine days earlier. The new men were of marginal use. The following portion from the IR 111 history is equally applicable to the state of affairs for 52nd Division's IR 169 and IR 170.

"The troops were in position or heavy combat for months on end no significant break. They were psychologically worn down; physically exhausted by their efforts and bad nutrition; and they barely knew one another anymore. The new replacement troops had no, or little experience in being under fire. They were poorly trained and no one could depend on them. As a result, they would run away from any artillery fire in spite of the vigorous efforts of the leaders. The whole weight of the battle was carried on the few leaders and old Badeners (Zahn 1936)." [339]

The American artillery fire continued without pause and how the pressure became worse each day. Ammunition became scarce and the men went 24 hours at a time with no food and little sleep. It all came to a breaking point on October 8. Lais:

"We insufferably remain in the forest. Explosions crash in the forest and 18 cm shells smashes into the ground. The valley is gassed. A large attack is to be expected. The mighty American force has vast quantities of ammunition while we have little. We lay in narrow holes and wait. Artillery smashes us in a two hour barrage. Mentally and physically exhausted, I fall into a deathly sleep. The racket suddenly stops and I am jolted awake. My poor company, in the radius of 100 square meters, lies practically buried. Four men are killed and three severely wounded. Now I only have 25 men left... New shells howl but land with a puff. Gas! The severely wounded can be heard groaning under their masks. Wagons come from the rear and are filled with dead and severely wounded – a path of suffering." [340]

The 52nd Division could no longer hold its position in the Exermont Valley. The next defensible terrain was two kilometers to the north; the Romange Heights, which ran adjacent from the Liechenacer Heights up to the northeast, and ending in hill known to the Germans as the Marienberg. The retreat from the valley up to the Marienberg was made under great duress and was poorly executed. Lais' command did not receive the movement order and his shell-shocked 3rd MG Company was nearly left behind. The men of the small company jumped from crater to crater as they dodged a bombardment of high explosive and gas shells. Exhausted, with lungs starving for air under the burden of gas masks, the 3rd MGC finally made it up the Marienberg slopes to rejoin the 3rd Battalion hours later.[341]

The 52nd Division's new defensive line was manned by a disjointed collection of units. IR 169 held the division's left flank, Pioneer Companies 103 and 104 were in the center and IR 170 on the right. The division's IR 111 was separated to the west by two battalions from two different regiments. The 52nd Division's top priority for the following morning was sort out its troop displacements by repositioning IR 111 to replace the two pioneer companies. An American pre-assault bombardment targeted command posts at the battalion, regimental and divisional levels. Command and control fell apart as the fire cut telephone wires and killed messengers.

The early morning hours of October 9 were especially foggy as the Americans set loose a powerful rolling artillery barrage. The fog and incoming smoke rounds made it difficult to discern if gas shells were being fired. The subsequent American ground attack caught the 52nd Division in the worst possible situation. A large section of front line trenches were left vacant when the pioneer units displaced before IR 111 could replace them. U.S. infantry units, led by elements of the 1st Infantry Division's 16th Infantry Regiment, poured through the gap and penetrated well behind the German lines.[342] The American's ambushed IR 111's newly arriving 3rd Battalion from behind, cutting it off from battalion and regimental command elements. A counterattack from IR 111's 2nd Battalion paused the American fire long enough for some of the 3rd Battalion survivors to flee and fall under IR 169 command. German units on the 52nd Division's right flank collapsed, allowing waves of American infantry units to swarm past the IR 111 regimental command bunker. IR 111 Commander Obersleunant aus dem Weerth and his staff were trapped inside the bunker for 20 hours before finally surrendering. While the surviving IR 111 elements continued to fight under IR 169 and IR 170 command in coming days, this proud Baden regiment was finished as a cohesive fighting unit.[343]

For a time, the IR 169 line held firm, with the line and MG companies firing every weapon at their disposal and throwing scores of grenades. With the visibility at less than 100 meters, there was great confusion on both sides. A localized German counterattack captured over 100 American prisoners, who were hurried to the rear with hands held high.

IR 169 commanders received a glimmer of good news when they learned that the nearby IR 109, its sister regiment from Baden, was preparing an attack to relieve them. The 169ers had reason to be optimistic, as IR 109 was entering the battle fresh, and with a field manning strength that was larger than the entire 52nd Division. The help never arrived, as IR 109 was hit with such a severe artillery strike that it was taken out of action before it could even enter the battle. The Marienberg and Romange Heights were lost. On October 10, IR 169 began their retreat to the last German bastion of prepared defenses in the Argonne – the Kriemhilde Stellung.

The opposing 1st Division were left with less than 2,500 effectives. 1st Division's casualties, which totaled over 7,500 men in 10 days of combat, were the highest of any American division in the entire Meuse-Argonne Campaign.[344] On October 11-12, the shattered 1st Division was pulled out of line and replaced with IR 169's next adversary, the 42nd 'Rainbow Division.'

A U.S. National Guard unit, the 42nd Division saw combat in the Champagne-Marne, the Aisne-Marne and the Battle of Saint-Mihiel before entering the Meuse-Argonne. The division came into battle at the Meuse-Argonne with its share of future American military legends. Brigadier General Douglas MacArthur commanded the division's 84th Brigade. 35 year old Major (later Colonel) "Wild Bill" Donovan, a prominent Wall Street lawyer, commanded the 1st Battalion, 165th Regiment, a New York City based unit. Donovan became one of the most decorated U.S. soldiers of the war and, during World War II, led the Office of Strategic Services, the forerunner of the Central Intelligence Agency. Also assigned to the 165th Regiment was the famed chaplain, Father Francis Duffy. Duffy's inspiration on the battlefield was such that he was later commemorated with a major motion picture and statue that now lords over Times Square.

By mid-October, American senior commanders realized that the front-wide offensive was stalled. The core German defenses, although stressed, remained intact and American losses were in the tens of thousands. General John 'Blackjack' Pershing, the AEF commander, ordered another offensive to begin on October 14. Opposite IR 169, the 42nd Division was ordered to break the Kriemhilde Stellung at Landres St. George and then push on through to the third segment of German lines at the Barricourt Heights, another 10 miles north. The transition time needed for the 42nd Division to enter the front provided IR 169 with a rare respite and an unfettered movement into the Kriemhilde Stellung.

The 42nd Division's attack objective was divided in two sectors. To the American's east (left) side, stood the villages of St. Georges and Landres-et-St. Georges. The villages themselves were converted into defensive strongpoints. Between the villages was an open 1.5 kilometer field with three lines of barbed wire defended by interlocking machine gun positions and mines. The Germans loosely connected the wire strands to their posts, making them more resilient to artillery fire. The region on the 42nd Division's right flank was dominated by the Cote de Chatillon, a long and hilly ridgeline.[345] Newly arrived 42nd Division units conducted reconnaissance operations as they prepared for the October 14 offensive.

IR 169 completed the movement into its Cote de Chatillon sector at 4:00 in the morning of October 11. The men had been led to believe that they would be inheriting a well-prepared and highly fortified position. While most American accounts of the battle speak to the great strength of Kriemhilde Stellung, Lais and his comrades had a profoundly different perception. As the dawn broke, it became clear the renowned strength of the Kriemhilde was but a myth. Lais was dismayed at the state of neglect of the position, which had been constructed the year before. The defenses were not much more than a shallow trench on either side of an existing street. Captain Meier, the IR 169 3rd battalion commander, was rendered speechless as he wordlessly pointed to the locations he wanted Lais to deploy his machine guns. Later that day, Meier was inspired to compose a silly song about how the Kriemhilde Stellung was nothing but a death trap. Lais marveled that these works were from an era of what the men's grandfathers would have built back in 1864. How could a defensive system, designed in 1917, not account for anti-tank trenches? Lais was especially incensed at the elaborate craftsmanship went into the woodwork by entrance points; not only was it a waste of effort, but the planking actually restricted quick access. There were no bunkers and the complete absence of camouflage made the position a convenient bulls-eye for enemy aircraft. Lais concluded his lengthy complaints of the shoddy state of the defenses as: "Dear readers: This horrible description about the Kriemhilde Stellung is the naked truth." [346]

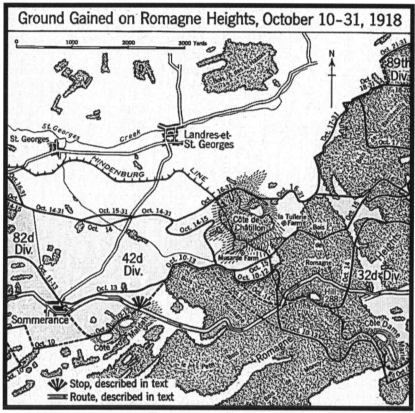

Meuse-Argonne Campaign, The Kriemhilde Stellung

After being pushed of the Romange Heights on 10 October, IR 169 took up position in the Cote de Chatillon portion of the Kriemhilde Stellung line. The regiment faced troops from the 42nd Infantry Division until relieved on October 14 for a five day refit period. IR 169 returned to the Kriemhilde Stellung in the early morning hours of 1 November between St, Georges and Landres-et-St. Georges.

(AABE)

Once the Germans got over their shock the men worked like 'those possessed' to improve the trenches. Within the space of hours, trenches were deepened, firing platforms constructed and enfiladed fields of fire established. Although the positions remained far short of 1918 doctrinal standards, the last minute renovations at least provided a more credible obstacle against the American attack.[347]

On the afternoon of October 11, orders came down from regimental headquarters for Captain Meier to send the 3rd Battalion machine guns deep into no-man's-land. The intent was to position the guns well beyond the anticipated enemy artillery barrage zone, leaving them intact cut down the main infantry assault. The gunners would then somehow have to escape back to friendly lines with an enemy attack still at their heels. Lais, along with his men, were horrified at the prospect of this suicide mission. For the first time in the war, Lais was afraid that command would refuse to obey orders. Lais recalled: "I am at the end of my strength, and my men are not much better. It is ridiculous to think that that anyone of us will come back should the Americans launch a major attack." Captain Meier was also appalled at the orders. Resigned to definitive tone of the orders, Meier reluctantly directed Lais to prepare for the mission.

The Third MG Company had taken so many losses that it could only man four machine guns. A fifth gun was damaged by a shrapnel strike and was abandoned in the trench. The patrol readied their ammunition and equipment, to include a supply of incendiary grenades for Sergeant Mussolf to throw should tanks be encountered. Just prior to departure time, an infantry patrol returned to trenches and reported no visible enemy activity ahead. The machine gunners set out at dusk, and silently advanced several hundred meters along a steep forest path. They came to a point where they had 300 meters of open ground before them and set up an ambush position. Lais speculated that the Americans, still inexperienced in tactical operations, were liable to advance along a road leading to the German trenches. The machine guns were laid-in and the men settled into wait. Lais wrote of the evening:

> "Mussolf observes straight and towards the right, I watch the steep slope in the flank and the forest path. An hour passes, nothing. Two hours go by, nothing. The fog in the evening time grows much thicker, and our restlessness sets in as we lay in the damp grass. Mussolf gazes tensely... The fog gets heavier! My God, when the fog gets thicker, our fields of fire

disappears. I watch through my binoculars as my blood pressure rises. Another hour passes. 150 meters out something seems to stir. Mussolf quietly hisses 'Alarm.' Figures begin to emerge from the fog. Two, four, and entire group. The fog blurs them again. I'm not sure if they are coming from road. Two appear again, with rifles at hand. They are traveling on the left and right sides of the road. In a slight distance behind, two groups of eight men walk on both shoulders of the road. Fifty meters behind them comes a main column of Americans. When the lead group is 50 meters ahead I quietly whisper commands. Three machine guns are to fire into the main group in the distance, the remainder of the patrol, along with the fourth MG, will attack the advance party.

The Americans pause, and then advance more hesitantly. The advance party is directly before us, then 10 meters, 5 meters. Our weapons are ready to fire. A sharp blow of my whistle; a fraction of a second later we explode death and the devil into the Americans. Four machine guns spew destruction. Their advance party, rather than taking cover in the woods on the opposite side of the street, panic in horror and run in a tight group back along the road. After a few meters they are all cut down. 50-80 meters out, the main column is hit with the fire of three machine guns. They are dreadfully clustered and roar of the guns brings a giant reap of death. The battle is finished in less than three minutes." [348]

The MG patrol, with the ambush complete and the screams of the wounded enemy behind them, returned back to German lines to receive a warm welcome from a mix of their IR 169 and 170 comrades. Lais took a moment to speculate what would have been outcome had the Americans conducted a major attack that night, or had the ill-fated reconnaissance force been less careless.

The quality of troop replacements had reached a new low, with the German Army now relying on the older extremes of the Landstrum reserve system, with men as old as 60 years of age sent to fill front line gaps. The IR 169's 3rd Battalion adjutant led a group of these Landstrum replacements into the Cote de Chatillon trenches. Not long after their arrival, the trench came under small arms fire from an enemy force hidden deep into the fog. As German machine guns opened in response, the new Landstrum men went into a crazed panic, described by Lais as 'having the maturity of the devil.' Some stacked their knapsacks into stepping platforms to leap out of the trenches and flee to the rear. Enraged at their cowardice, Lais grabbed the rifle out of one of old gray-bearded Landstrumer's hands. With a pocketful of cartridges, he rose on a firing platform and shot madly at the unseen enemy. When his rifle jammed, he still stood exposed to incoming fire as he tried to clear the chamber. From his right side, Sergeant Mussolf reached up and threw Lais back onto the trench floor. "Herr Leutnant" he calmly explained, "How can you stand there and not expect to be shot? Besides, this would leave your commander, Captain Meier, without his one true friend." Lais, upon regaining his senses, realized that his mad display of fury had at least snapped the remaining Landstrumers out of their panic.

The brief firefight ended as suddenly as it began. The fire appeared to have come from a reconnaissance patrol testing the German defenses in prelude to the main attack. Lais wrote of the toil of enduring 16 days of unrelenting combat and how their tormented state of their minds caused them to 'see ghosts and play events two and three times over... The burning eyes of the sentries stare into the darkness; where is the enemy?'[349]

The Germans made more substantial use of gas munitions in the early phases of the campaign, with the Americans more than catching up in its later days. The frequent fog and forest conditions carpeted vast stretches of the battlefield with toxic residue, making all combatants ill and fatigued from the omnipresent, poisonous vapors. Fully one quarter of the U.S. 1st and 42nd Divisions losses were recorded as chemical-related casualties.[350] One of those temporarily disabled included BG MacArthur, who was caught in a poisonous gas barrage on October 12 while on a reconnaissance of German positions.

The 42nd Division completed preparations for the October 14 main assault. The division's 83rd Brigade formed on the left and targeted the German lines between the villages of St. Georges and Landres-et-St. George. The open terrain and strong German lines made the 83rd Brigade's mission extremely difficult. While Lais' account tells of the Kriemhilde Stellung's deficiencies, it remained plenty formidable for those having to attack it. The indomitable Father Duffy described the German defenses in his autobiography: "The wire consisted of three thick lines, each reinforced in places 20 feet thick, bound in small squares by iron supports. In back of it was a four-foot trench for machine guns, wide enough to allow gunners to swivel. The next two lines were at 30 yard intervals, giving gunners fields of fire." [351] The 83rd Brigade had to charge over an open one-mile field just to reach the German trenches.

The sector that IR 169 defended was to be attacked by MacArthur's 84th Brigade, which comprised the 42nd Division's right flank. This objective was only slightly less onerous, as attackers were afforded at least some semblance of cover provided by the Bois de Romange. Attacking from the woods, the 84th Brigade was to pass through the Musarde Farm and penetrate the trench system along the hill mass on the Cote de Chatillon. The Americans later estimated that the Germans defended this area with over 200 machine guns. German artillery, firing from the east side of the Meuse River covered the avenues of approach.[352]

The three day pause in battle allowed the Americans to mass a large concentration of artillery. The U.S. artillery barrage slammed into the German defenses in the early hours of October 14, with much of the fires were targeting the barbed wire entanglements. Lais' company was fortunate to only lose one man dead while an adjacent unit suffered two officers and a number of enlisted men killed.[353]

The 83rd Brigade's attack on St. Georges and Landres-et-St. George was a disaster. The biggest problem was that the artillery fires failed to destroy of the obstacle fields. While the Americans planned to use tanks to cut through the remaining barbed wire, few of them actually made it to the front. The torrent of machine gun fire left many American engineers dead across the entanglements as infantrymen tried to take cover in shell holes. Major Donovan's leadership of the 165th's 1st Battalion's first assault wave resulted in his award of the Medal of Honor. The award citation noted how Donovan "Moved among his men in exposed positions, reorganizing decimated platoons and accompanying them forward in assaults. When he was wounded in the leg by a machine gun bullet, he refused to be evacuated and continued with his unit until it withdrew to a less exposed position." [354] No amount of personal heroism could penetrate these defenses and the 83rd Brigade was thrown back with severe losses.

On the American right, MacArthur's 84th Brigade advanced against the Cote de Chatillon. Although the Americans made a few small gains, the Germans handily repulsed the main attacks. That night, AEF Headquarters ordered the 42nd Division to hold whatever ground was captured and to maintain contact with the enemy.

For IR 169, the night of 14-15 October finally brought escape from the trenches when they were relieved by IR 152. Lais recorded of event:

> "It was high time. My soldiers were fully exhausted and fell asleep leaning against their weapons. ...The battalion adjutant arranged to have the more severely wounded assisted. We leave behind 18 days of uninterrupted heavy combat, 18 days of wearing soaking wet uniforms and boots, 18 days with little sleep and often no food to eat.[355]

IR 169's field journal puts its losses from September 29 – October 14 as 20 officers (four killed) and 659 enlisted men. The losses of those American troops that fought in the 52nd Divison's sector during this period, which included the 35th, 1st and 42nd Divisions, totaled over 16,000 men.

The timing of the 52nd Division's departure from the Cote de Chatillon allowed the IR 169 to barely escape the main American ground assault. On the evening of October 15, MacArthur, perhaps inspired with the spirit of his father, a Union hero of the Civil War, gave orders for his brigade to make a midnight bayonet attack against German works. Fortunately for the doughboys of the 84th Brigade, staff officers talked MacArthur out of the scheme and instead devised plans to use terrain and overwhelming firepower their advantage. On October 16, the brigade's 168th Regiment, under the cover of a 30 minute, one million round machine gun barrage, assaulted through a lightly defended ravine and took the Cote de Chatillon. The Germans quickly established a new defensive line to the north of the ridge, halting any further 42nd Division gains.[356] Although the net gain of ground was minimal, the American's capture of the Cote de Chatillon was the first fracture of the Kriemhilde Stellung. To the northwest, the Landres-et-St. George strong-points remained firmly in German hands.

Chapter 17
Meuse-Argonne Forest (Part II): A Regiment Dies a Hero's Death

The battered 52nd Division departed the front in the midst of a driving rainstorm, with a 17 mile march across the Meuse River to the village of Mouzon. IR 169 went into quarters in the nearby villages of Mairy and Brevilly, the same vicinity where it was billeted during the Sedan training period of April 1918. The 52nd Division's rest and refit period lasted only five days, with troops remaining on alert status during the entire time.

On October 19, the 52nd Division formed for an inspection and motivational speech by the Army Gruppenfuher. Any inspirational value was lost when the men had to wait in formation for three hours in the pouring rain before the General spoke. He concluded his address with a 'hurrah' for the Kaiser. Lais reflected that after four years of war, the men had become apathetic towards the Emperor. It wasn't that the soldiers were either loyal or disloyal to the Kaiser – they simply no longer cared.[357]

The tone of Lais' writings at this point in his 1936 book, *A Regiment Dies a Hero's Death*, takes a darker and more cynical tone. He describes letters from home that presented a bleak existence of suffering families and hungry children. The deadly Spanish Influenza plague was raging, both at home and in army ranks. The men were becoming increasingly demoralized. In one passage, Lais tells of how, in the process of writing his memoir, he had two wartime photographs displayed on his desk. One was of the NCOs of the 3rd Machine Gun Company taken in Laon in summer 1917. The other was of the 2nd Battalion officer corps taken in the forests of the Champagne region on the eve of the May 1918 Offensive. The pictures are marked with crosses over the images of those killed and stars above those who were wounded. Of his many comrades depicted in both photographs, only two or three were left unmarked.

All the German divisions across the entire 5th Army zone were now in a badly depleted state. In its final configuration, it is likely that IR 169 had less than 1000 men in line, with the three battalions averaging 250 soldiers, former company-level strength, and companies now the size of what should have qualified as platoons.

Despite the short period refit period and poor quality of replacements, Lais was amazed that the regiment was still capable of rebuilding itself. He described how the 52nd Division ranks were patched together by a collection of veterans returning from field hospitals, new men arriving from replacement depots and converted clerks and farriers – anyone who could carry a rifle. The Third MG Company arrived at the rest area with about 20 men, and received replacements that brought the final strength up to 38 soldiers. In quality and quantity, this unit was far less capable than the 92 man company Lais led into the Argonne a month earlier. Lais concluded: "The troop is now complete and ready to die once again – for us 169ers, to its last death." [358]

Hours after the Gruppenfuher's October 19 speech, the 52nd Division was alerted and prepared for frontline redeployment. The drill turned out be false alarm and the men returned to quarters. At 3:00 am on October 21, IR 169 received new alert orders. This time it was the real thing as the 52nd Division was called forward to serve as a ready reserve unit for the 5th Army's western flank.

The regiment marched the railhead at Mouzon and immediately loaded on the waiting trains. Lais deployed four machine guns on the top of a car and the weapons were loaded with anti-aircraft ammunition. This precaution aside, the Germans were not expecting much of an American aircraft threat, as the weather was rainy, the fog was thick and German pursuit planes were supposed to patrol at higher altitudes. Soon after departure, the Germans were taken by surprise when a flight of seven American planes came zooming at the train from 50 meters above. Although their hand-dropped bombs missed, bullets from the machine gun strafing ripped into personnel compartments, seriously wounding a number of men. Lais sarcastically recalled 'it was not a pleasant journey.'

The trains' traveled 20 miles south and reached their destination point of Harrincourt at 3:00 pm. Harrincourt was seven miles northwest of the 52nd Division's recent defense of the Kriemhilde Stellung the previous week. IR 169 veterans were already familiar with the area, as it was only six miles west of the villages where the regiment spent the winter of 1917-1918 in training and operational rotations.

IR 169 detrained while Harrincourt was under artillery fire. A barrage was striking the far edge of the village, causing a traffic jam of troops and a munitions supply column. The 3rd MGC took advantage of a brief pause in fire to race through the rubble and into the open fields south of the village. The weather had turned much colder and the skies continued to pour rain for yet another day. Most of the soldiers spent the night exposed to the elements, envying the MG company's horse farriers, as they were able to take shelter with their horses in a small stable.

IR 169 took up position in prepared defenses situated along a two mile line that linked the villages of Verpel to the west, Erdochern in the center and Imecourt on the east. Three miles southeast of Imecourt was the embattled village of St George on the Kriemhilde Stellung, which remained under attack by the U.S. 42nd Division. The Third Battalion took up position in a lush forest near Erdochern. To IR 169's direct front, and in the first line of battle, stood the 24th Baden Division, comprised of IR's 469, 470 and 471.

IR 169's status as the ready reserve placed them only two miles back from the front line. The regiment was in prime artillery range from the heavier caliber American guns seeking targets in rear areas. Lais wrote of the perpetual cycle of the firing of guns, shells exploding in the trees, endless rain, and little to eat.[359] German artillery munition stocks had become so depleted that they could seldom return counterbattery fire. The frugal Germans were astounded at the copious amounts of artillery shells being fired by the Americans and considered this blanket targeting to be a wasteful expenditure of ammunition.

The sunny weather of October 23-24 brought the return of U.S. airpower. First Army's Air Corps, with 821 aircraft at its disposal, swarmed over German front lines and rear support areas. Lais described how the American planes flew over by the hundreds. The air attacks had limited consequences to those German troops in well protected, camouflaged trenchlines. It was a different story for units exposed in marching columns and in vehicle convoys, as they suffered heavy losses.

The First Army underwent a major reorganization in the last two weeks of October. Pershing, frustrated at the lack of progress of the October 14-15 offensive, ordered a major overhaul across the entire front. Poor performing commanders were relieved, exhausted troops rested and fresh divisions moved forward. There were many dead to be buried and wounded to care for. The logistical infrastructure was improved and roadways were fixed. 1,500 artillery pieces, including 38 super-heavy railway guns that fired battleship-sized projectiles, moved into position. The new offensive was planned for November 1, with the objective being a breakthrough of the German center. Pershing was determined that this third offensive phase would bring a definitive conclusion to the campaign.[360]

The epicenter of the First Army's last great effort was focused on the Kriemhilde Stellung villages of St. Georges and Landres-et-St. George.

In the previous month of fighting, most American commanders were hesitant for using large concentrations of poison gas, fearing a direct retribution from the Germans. [It was an odd tactical decision, as the Germans had already been firing large amounts of gas against the Americans without such concern.] In this final offensive, the new corps and army-level commanders had no such reservations about chemical warfare and planned for extensive concentration of phosgene gas, mixed with high explosive fires, as a core component of its fire plans. The Americans began to incorporate gas attacks to soften up the breakthrough target areas in the week before the 1 November offensive.[361]

On the evening of October 25, a messenger came to the 3rd MG Company with orders for Lais to report to IR 169 Regimental Headquarters. The command post was located in the cellar of a mill by small brook. There, Lais was delighted to be reunited with his old friend, Hanne, now serving as the adjutant for the Fifth Army Artillery Group. The German artillery corps had amassed sufficient munition reserves to launch a powerful, army-wide strike on a specific target. In this time-on-target fire mission, every German heavy artillery piece within range would fire a specified number of rounds at the exact same moment. Hanne was at the IR 169 command post to coordinate the targeting.

The following afternoon, Lais, along with Captain Meier and a battalion commander from IR 470, led a patrol into the forested no-man's-land to reconnoiter a potential target for the artillery strike. They spied a forward American position that appeared to be a suitable target. On their return trip, ranging shells began to fall around them - they had been spotted. The party took shelter in a steep vale in the moment before a battery-level barrage zeroed in on them. Lais recalled how he and Meier grimaced under their helmets as the ground around them shook with exploding shells. There was a brief pause in the fire, and the patrol party raced along the forest path as fast as their legs could take them until they reached friendly lines.

The time-on-target mission was slated to strike the American position at 9:00 am on October 27. Lais, along with four machine guns, advanced to a point where they could observe the target. Lais anxiously gazed at his watch. Precisely on time, the ground behind rumbled as every available cannon over the entire Fifth Army front let loose. The American outpost, which become complacent at the lack of German firing in recent days, was taken by complete surprise. The targeted area exploded in smoke and shrapnel. The survivors of the initial barrage ran to the rear in panic, with many of those being blown apart by subsequent salvos. The position was abandoned and the Americans in this sector were pushed back 500 meters. While the tactical value of the surprise artillery attack was negligible, this display of impressive firepower gave the much beleaguered German infantrymen a temporary morale boost.[362]

October 27 was also the day that Lt Otto Lais gave up his temporary command of the 3rd Machine Gun Company to Lt. D.R. Wahl. Wahl returned back to his company after an extended convalescence leave to recover from wounds. Lais was now slotted to take over permanent command of an infantry company. Lais also received orders for a long overdue home leave, which had to be suspended due to the crisis at the front. Before he assumed his new command, Lais was placed on a special staff assignment. In his memoirs, Lais credited this transfer for saving him from being present in the catastrophe that destroyed his regiment three days later.[363]

On October 28, squadrons of American aircraft circled over German lines. The planes, in a synchronized movement, dropped bombs and flew off. Few of the bombs seem to explode, leaving many of the Germans to assume they were duds. Perhaps the Americans were relegated to using expired French munition stocks? There were none of the tell-tail signatures of a typical gas strike; the unusual odors and white and green colored plumes of smoke that the Germans had become accustomed to watch out for. As the winds shifted, cries of Gas! Gas! Gas! screamed out as the men tousled to don their masks. For some it was too late, as soldiers writhed on the ground gasping for air as blood sprayed from their mouths and noses. The Americans had struck with a phosgene attack, a chemical agent that was odorless and colorless.

IR 169's 2nd and 3rd Battalion were fortunate to be located on higher ground, where the gas quickly blew away and casualties were light. This was not the case with 1st Battalion, which had taken position in a hollow near Verpel. The 1st Battalion was commanded by Major Berthold, an officer who was badly wounded in the 27 May 1918 attack of the Chemin des Dames and who was recognized for holding his battalion to a high state of preparedness. For the next 48 hours, large concentrations of American heavy artillery specifically blanketed the battalion with a ring of explosive and phosgene shells. Lais wrote of the massacre: "The inferno lasted two days and nights. Few were able to jump through the ring of fire and gas. The majority of the companies lay suffocated, the ravine was their grave…The death of the regiment had begun." [364]

Only 35 men from the entire 1st Battalion contingent remained able to able to return to ranks. A post-war U.S. Army Chemical Corps study of the use of gas in the Meuse-Argonne Campaign recorded that the 1st Battalion, IR 169 suffered over 200 casualties in the Verpel gas barrage.[365] When the 1st Battalion, IR 169 marched off to war August 1914, it carried an elite '*Leib Guards*' designation. It was destroyed just prior to the war's last great offensive without having fired shot.

Lais, in his new assignment, passed a field train at Imecourt that was filled with chemical attack casualties being evacuated to the rear. A young NCO grabbed Lais by the arm, and spitting blood, begged "*Herr Leutnant, can you help me?*" The man's shaking fingers were futilely trying to unholster his pistol in an effort to end his misery. Lais could not muster the fortitude to assist in the man's suicide, but did his best to comfort him in the next half hour before he died in his arms.[366]

In the last days of October, the 52nd Division was ordered to move from the group-reserve position and replace the 42nd Division in their Kriemhilde Stellung trenches. IR 169 drew the task to defend the front lines between St. Georges and Landres-et-St. George, about a three and a half mile march southeast of their current posting. While the Landres' positions had proven to be effective strong points against the initial American attacks, its defenses were badly smashed from weeks of sustained artillery targeting. The area was also devoid of forest cover, making any form of natural cover nonexistent. As the division prepared its movement, Lais was detailed to guide in the incoming regiments that would occupy the 52nd Division's vacated positions.

American units were also in movement. Back at the 52nd Division's former battleground in the Kriemhilde Stellung, the U.S. 42nd Division was finally being pulled out after two weeks of combat that cost the division 3,679 men.[367] The replacing unit was the battle-tested 2nd Infantry Division, whose two brigades comprised a unique mix of Army and Marine Corps regiments. Although it was a U.S. Army division, it was commanded by the highly competent Marine Major General John A. Lejeune. [Following the war, Lejeune went on to be the 13th Commandant of the Marine Corps, and earned the reputation as 'the Greatest Leatherneck of all Time.' The unit's courageous performance at Belleau Wood in June 1918 remains a cornerstone in U.S. Marine Corps' lore.] The 2nd Division came into line the night of October 30/31.

Advancing on a 2.5 mile wide front, the 2nd Division's objective for the November 1 attack was to smash through the Kriemhilde Stellung at Landres-et-St. Georges and then advance six miles north to the next German defensive system, the Freya Stellung, atop the Barricourt Ridge. The German defense at Landres-et-St. Georges was the center-point of the entire 1st Army attack, which pegged it to receive a colossal volume of artillery fire in the coming attack. In addition to its substantial organic artillery capabilities, the 2nd Division was augmented by no less than three army and corps level artillery brigades as well as the artillery brigades of the 1st and 42nd Divisions. Altogether, this amounted to over 300 guns. 2nd Division was also reinforced with one of the largest concentration of American heavy and light tanks ever to be deployed in the war.[368]

Lais, along with a group of four NCOs, hiked to the Harrincourt train station at 1:00 am on October 31 to link-up with the regiment that would replace IR 169. The inbound train carrying the new troops was delayed due the long-range artillery targeting Harrincourt. Lais party's trek into Harrincourt was only made possible by moving during 20 minute breaks in the fire. Just as the group arrived at 3:00 am, a large nighttime air raid struck the town, sending the men into a filthy drain pipe for cover. When that attack concluded, Lais and his comrades enjoyed a blessed few hours' sleep in a warm hut by the station.

The trains carrying the new regiment arrived at 11:00 am. The fresh battalions were well manned at 80-100 troops per company. A single aircraft, thought to be German, circled lazily overhead. Suddenly, the plane screamed down in an attack dive as it was recognized to be an American fighter. Anti-aircraft guns barked as the plane flew over at 20 meters. The pilot's guns must have had jammed as it flew off without having fired a shot. With that close call behind them, Lais and his NCOs guided the new troops towards IR 169's soon to be vacated position. Always on the alert of a sudden air attack, the men dashed whenever they had to traverse through open ground. The units began arriving at their destination at twilight. Lais found the sudden absence of enemy artillery fire to be oddly disconcerting – as if a quiet before a large storm. As the new replacement battalions moved into position, the departing IR 169 companies scurried off to their next posting in the Landres sectors. IR 169's maneuver units now consisted only of the 2nd and 3rd Battalions, with the few survivors of the 1st Battalion dispersed between them. Lais and his collection of NCOs finished guiding in the newly arrived troops at 2:00 am, November 1. They intended to rejoin the now displaced IR 169 at daybreak.

Grim whispers were passed throughout the night; recent aerial reconnaissance reports identified scores of American tanks massing near Landres-et-St. Georges. *"Watch out – tanks"* was warned over and over. The men lacked confidence in the few battalion-level weapons available to defend against a serious armored assault. The new giant anti-tank rifle, the Mauser 1918 T-Geweher, referred to by Lais as ancient 'blunder-buss,' were unpopular. At 41 pounds, they were cumbersome to carry and its punishing recoil left the gunner's shoulder badly bruised. A rare hit that could disable a tank was considered more a chance of luck than skill. Incendiary grenades were in short supply, forcing the infantrymen to beg gasoline and diesel from the drivers so they could fashion Molotov cocktails from thin-walled bottles. In the preceding battles, 52nd Division troops had proved effective in repelling attacks by isolated tanks or small armored squadrons. They feared that this meager arsenal of anti-tank weapons would leave them helpless if confronted by massed armor columns that were well-supported by infantry.[369]

The IR 169 formations began to arrive in Landres in the early hours of November 1. The night was rainy and sky pitch-black. Commanders, attempting to reduce confusion from a simultaneous transfer of troops, delayed the trench entry of some companies until dawn. These men were had to scrape temporary, shallow fighting positions behind the main trenches. This digging had barely begun when a storm of heavy artillery fire descended at 3:30 am.

This was one of the most powerful artillery bombardments conducted by the AEF in the entire war. With field pieces shooting at a rate of 12 shells per minute, the firing was so concentrated that one marine officer noted "that scarcely a square foot of ground in the enemy's front line area was left unturned by bursting shells." [370] In addition to the sheer volume and speed of shells fired, the lethality of this barrage was augmented by a large blend of phosgene gas rounds. An American unit history recorded: "the sky was alight from then until daybreak with the constant flashes seeming to come from every ravine for miles to the rear. The ground shook with explosions." [371]

The German Fifth Army artillery batteries were able to strike some of the American assembly areas, costing the 1st Battalion, 6th Marines a hundred casualties before H-hour began. The German counter-fire did not last long as the overwhelming power of the American artillery silenced many of the German guns, including those more forward deployed pieces that could have been used in anti-tank roles.

Lais endured the barrage from the shelter of the sturdy Verpel-Imecourt trenches. His telling of IR 169's annihilation came largely from accounts of survivors who were taken prisoner and returned to Germany after the war.

"The riflemen and machine gunners of the 8th Baden Infantry Regiment dug in. Suddenly they hear the noise of artillery fire, and see the flashes of firing from thousands of enemy batteries over a huge front on the horizon. It is a big attack. Three hours of continual bombardment land on the infantry that is unprotected in the fields ahead. The enemy is using a huge quantity of munitions.

Our men, as well as the close-range batteries of the division artillery, have to experience this hell from 4:00 to 7:00. They keep their noses pushed tight into the mud of their foxholes. Three hours of bursting shells kill, wound, and blow men to pieces. Then the tanks come. Tanks, tanks, and more tanks. Row after row. The 11th row comes. It seems to never end." [372]

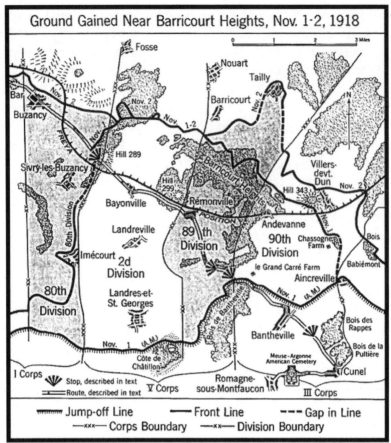

Ground Gained Near Barricourt Heights, Nov. 1-2, 1918

Legend: Jump-off Line · Front Line · Gap in Line · Corps Boundary · Division Boundary · Stop, described in text · Route, described in text

Last Stand at Landres-et-St. Georges, November 1, 1918

In the early morning hours of 1 November, IR 169 was entering the Kriemhilde Stellung just west of Landres-et-St. Georges when struck by a massive artillery barrage. The Marine Brigade and tanks from the 2nd Infantry Division overran and destroyed all IR 169 front line positions. 52nd Division survivors assembled that night at Bayonville, as remaining IR 169 and IR 111 fragments were merged into a detachment for the retreat across the Meuse River.

(AABE)

The Americans went over the top at 5:30 am. The 2nd Division troops that attacked the IR 169 positions came from its Marine Brigade. Heavy Mark V tanks led the way and easily chewed through the barbed wire entanglements that had stymied previous American assaults. Light Renault tanks, trailed by infantry squads, closely followed. The rolling barrage, carefully programmed for an attack over the broken terrain, was perfectly executed.

The lead waves of marines were met by scores of dead Germans who appeared to have been killed by the gas. The marines stormed over the trench lines and soon were deep into the defensive zone. Although hopelessly outnumbered, many of the Germans still put up a vigorous defense. In a wood-line south of St. Georges, a series of German machine gun nests initially sustained a heavy rate of fire. Marine Captain Macon Overton guided his men in knocking out five German machine guns and was killed when directing a tank against the sixth.[373]

The Germans stood little chance against the descending wave of armor. Survivors later told of how soldiers threw hand grenades against the tanks with no effect. Some used the tactic of allowing tanks to roll over them so they attack from the rear, only to be cut down by grapeshot rounds fired by other tanks. Machine gunners fired armor-piercing SmK rounds at tank viewing slots, which set a handful of tanks ablaze. Several more tanks were knocked out by the few forward deployed artillery guns still serviceable.

In the attack on 2nd Battalion's positions, a dozen tanks surrounded a 2nd MG Company platoon, first killing the senior NCO and then wiping out its remaining troops. The tanks rolled on and flattened the reserve companies. The 2nd Battalion command staff manned mortars that had been brought up from the rear. They also were quickly overrun. Whoever was not killed became a prisoner. Those captured here included 2nd Battalion Commander Hauptmann Knapp and Leutnant Fahr, the 2nd MG Company Commander.

Lais chronicled the destruction of the 3rd Battalion:

> "It is even worse for the 3rd Battalion of the 169th. Trapped in a tight semicircle of the enemy, they used up their mortar rounds. The mortar leader, Leutnant d. R. Kretzschmann, from Pforzheim, who is usually very calm, lies flat on the ground after putting round after round into the enemy advance. Schnuerer, a medical NCO who was taken prisoner, told us after his release that it was a wonder that Kretzschmann was not shot dead by the Americans. My dear commander and friend, Captain Meier, could not bear the thought of being taken into captivity and tried to break through the ring of hundreds of Americans that encircled him. Seven of his people

were killed within a few meters. He was shot in the abdomen and died three days later in an American aid station." [374]

Lais concluded:

"The Iron Regiment is no more. In the gray dawn of November 1, 1918, the month of Germany's calamity, the 8th Baden Infantry, Regiment 169, named the Iron Regiment, died a hero's death." [375]

IR 169's regimental command post was located far enough to the rear to avoid the catastrophe. Lais described the tragic story how Major Schilling waited for hours and then days, as not a soul from his regiment returned from the front. Finally after three and a half days of waiting, a lieutenant who had been at front came back with his courier and three NCO's. The small party was somehow able to escape, but had no further details on fate of the two missing line battalions. These few men, along with the regimental staff, was all that could be found of IR 169.[376]

While a few additional soldiers continued to straggle back to the ranks, IR 169 was finished a regimental fighting force. In this last battle, the regiment lost 19 officers and 548 enlisted men. The 52nd Division was also practically destroyed, losing 4,000 men since arriving in the Meuse-Argonne in late September, with 1,000 alone being captured on 1 November.

By noon, the 2nd Battalion, 5th Marines had already reached beyond Bayonville, four miles past the Hindenburg Line, and by the end of the day, had penetrated 10 miles deep.

That evening, on a hillside outside of Bayonville, the 52nd Infantry Division attempted to gather the remaining elements of its infantry regiments. All that could be accounted for were 35 officers and 242 enlisted men.[377] Those fragments, as well as other scattered forces, took part in the 5th Army's 16 mile retreat across the Meuse River on November 3.

Once across the Meuse, IR 169 reassembled on the north bank village of Moulins, four miles northeast of the town of Beaumont and the site of their mid-October rest. Here, on November 3, Lais finally was able to rejoin what was left of IR 169. Major Schiller, emotionally grabbed Lais' hand and said "You are the only one from your company that I have seen again!" In addition to the regimental staff, only 20 rifleman and two machine guns could be counted.[378] With so few troops remaining, IR 169 was merged with the survivors of IR 111 to form an ad hoc security detachment on the banks of the Meuse at the forest of Alma-Gisors. The Germans destroyed the remaining bridges over the Meuse and prepared defenses on the northern bank against the expected American river-crossing operations.

The U.S. 2nd Infantry Division continued its drive to the Meuse following its November 1 breakout. After overcoming significant German resistance at Beaumont on November 5-6, the vanguard of 2nd Division finally reached the river by November 8. Despite its shattering losses, the German Fifth Army was still able to regroup on the north bank of the Meuse and establish a credible defensive line. As part of this effort, the IR 169/111 Detachment was briefly posted in a wooded area that joined the Bois Alma-Gisors and de l'Hospice forests and was centered in a sharp loop of the Meuse.

Imperial Germany was deep into its death spiral. Battlefield defeats, severe food shortages, the spread of the Spanish influenza pandemic and labor strikes exhausted Germany's ability to continue the war. Austrian and Turkish allies surrendered, leaving Germany to stand on its own. On October 30, the sailors of the German Navy mutinied when ordered to launch a final, suicidal sortie against the British fleet. In Berlin, a swelling socialist uprising was threatening to engulf Germany in civil war. The German Chancellor, Prince Max of Baden, reluctantly sent an armistice commission to Rethondes, France on November 8. With no hope for continuing either the war or his empire, the Kaiser fled to Holland on November 10 and abdicated shortly thereafter. The final details of the armistice was not finalized until November 10, and the fighting continued until 11:00 am, November 11, 1918.

The outbreak of revolution resulted in 52nd Division's redeployment back to Germany just before the war's formal end. Even in Germany's collapse, the 52nd Division still attempted to regenerate once again. On November 8, the division received 100 new troops from a replacement depot. Lais wrote how in perfect column and with music playing, the small division marches to a loading rail station in Belgium for its return to south Baden. "The war with the foreign enemy is to end, with the war against the internal enemy begins to rise. The seeds of the

November revolution bears abundant fruits. The war of the brother against the soul of his brother begins." [379]

An act of final madness spread across the entire Western Front on the morning of November 11, as both sides spent the last few hours of the war locked in a frenzied artillery barrage. Thousands of men were killed and wounded for a cause no greater than the expenditure of prepositioned artillery stocks. At the Bois Alma-Gisors, which the IR 169/111 Detachment had recently departed, the war played out a tragic final chapter for the pursuing U.S. 2nd Division. Even though the American high command understood the war was likely to end within a matter of hours, the 5th Marine Regiment of the 2nd Infantry Division was still ordered to conduct a treacherous river assault across Meuse at the Bois Alama Gisors the night of November 10/11. Major General Lejeune's misgivings on the value of conducting the attack were well-placed. The losses for the two battalions of the 5th Marines for the November 10/11 night attack were 31 killed, 148 wounded, and 75 missing and presumed drowned.[380] When the fighting finally ended hours after the scheduled 11:00 am ceasefire, a marine recalled how German soldiers "swarmed over waving bottles of brandy, with drinks being quickly traded for American cigarettes. One would have thought they were long-lost brothers." [381]

IR 169's service continued after the fighting had ceased. The most immediate of the Armistice terms demanded that all German military forces depart from French and Belgian soil within 15 days. Allied divisions would then march into Germany's Rhineland to become an occupation force. With the establishment of the Provisional German Republic, some of the existing German units, to include the 52nd Division, were called to serve as security forces in the neutral zones in western Baden.

IR 169's 100 mile journey back to Germany took it through northern Luxembourg and across the German border at Wintersdorf. The regiment sorted out stragglers from other units and continued 200 miles by train to the designated neutral zone in southwestern Germany, just across the Rhine from the 1914 Mulhouse area battlefields.

The revolution movement, sparked by the revolt of naval forces, quickly spread throughout the Germany as the working classes joined the military insurgents. The dynastic rulers of all the German states followed the Kaiser in abdication, with Frederick of Baden relinquishing his throne on November 22. Workers and soldiers councils, under the umbrella of the Social Democratic Party, emerged to lead the revolution and assume political and military powers. Lais' account of the period provides a glimpse of how close Germany came to falling under a Bolshevik form of revolutionary government.

Once in Germany, Lais took his long overdue leave before reporting to IR 169's new Regimental Headquarters in Kandern. Kandern, at the southwestern corner of Germany, was 15 miles across the Rhine River from Mulhouse. Lais arrived with few possessions, due to the regiment's officer baggage holdings being looted in Luxembourg during the withdrawal from France. Lais wrote how his fine officer's overcoat, uniforms, underwear and good field glasses were all 'socialized' by the Soldier Counsel's redistribution program. "The baggage that I will take to the regiment I wear on my body. With difficulty I scratch some underwear together. In the totally impoverished Germany of 1918 there is nothing left."

Arriving in Kandern by train, Lais was confronted with the stark impact of the revolutionaries' control. Soldiers no longer saluted officers, as such honorifics were considered as anti-socialist practices. Lais, who was wearing his sidearm, was accosted by a checkpoint guard who commanded; "Halt! Entering the platform with a weapon is not allowed!" In a test of wills, Lais ignored the guard and continued on. A senior cavalry corporal, a large heavy man with an ice gray mustache and wearing a broad saber, observed the exchange. The corporal was veteran of the old school and respected Lais' act of defiance. As Lais passed, the corporal clicked together his spurs and presented a perfect salute. Lais quietly thanked the man who remarked, "That was a sensitive situation just now, Leutnant, I was preparing to draw my sword."

All that remained of IR 169's wartime core was the small collection of officers and men who had been posted far enough to the rear during the November 1 calamity. Along with Lais, this amounted to Major Schiller, an adjutant, a regimental doctor, an administrative section, a handful of men from the intelligence detail and some truck drivers. The few officers remaining were allowed to retain their rank, but had no authority. The regiment was now controlled by the Soldier's Council, who scorned the imperial officers and referred to them as comrades. After reporting to Major Schiller, Lais was given superficial command of the 9th Company. On his way out of the office, Lais was pulled aside by an administrative clerk who warned: "My condolences, Leutnant. It is the worst company that we have. The chairman of the Soldiers' Council, Corporal W., was detailed to the 9th Company, and the bloke is supposed to have the whole regiment in hand."

The Soldier's Council ruled all functions, to include reclassification of the old 169er cadre. One such man was Trumpeter Lindecke, who had been shot through is lung and could no longer play a bugle. A Soldier's Council session was conducted in a manner that ridiculed Lindecke for his combat service before reassigning him as a typist.

The regiment's ostensible mission was for border protection of the Upper Rhine region. To the east, the nearby Alsace Province had returned to French control. To the south, the Swiss closed its border with Germany in an attempt to halt the spread of the communist movement. In reality, the assigned security function was a farce at the regiment no mission capacity other than demobilization. Still, IR 169 ranks swelled, but not with fighting troops, but rather displaced ethnic German 'comrades' of Swiss and Alsatian citizenship who were blocked from returning home. These men, already discharged from their former units, had to be put back in uniform and administratively cared for. Adding to this burden, IR 169's home garrison at Lahr sent forward recruits from year-group 1900 who had been inducted for service but were still in trainee status when the war ended.

If there was bright spot for Lais during this period, it was the personal connection he had with the town of Kandern. Lais' parents and grandparents had once lived in the town and he had fond memories of visiting there as a boy. It was a sad homecoming however, as his relatives suffered greatly from impoverishment and wartime losses. One such tragedy was the fate of Lais' cousin, a young man who was killed in the war and left his parents without their only son and heir to the farm.[382]

For the next six months, the regiment conducted a systematic demobilization process that led to its full disbanding. On December 11, the regiment relocated ten miles further east to the towns of Schoenau, Schopfheim and Rheinfelden. The regiment was now focused on full demobilization. Before Christmas, year groups 1880-1895 were discharged, soon followed by those in the 1896-1899 classes. On February 7, 1919, the remaining elements of the regiment were transferred 60 miles north to the Freiburg area villages of Emmendingen, Malterdingen and Teningen. The active regiment merged with the 169th Replacement Battalion and completed the turn-in of all remaining equipment and horses. Battalions and companies were disbanded and an office for the liquidation of the regiment was established. In mid-May, this dwindling group moved 20 miles north to the regiment's original Lahr headquarters. All remaining components of the IR 169 were merged into the liquidation detachment of XIV Corps Headquarters. The official end came on May 19, 1919, when Infantry Regiment 169 was fully deactivated. The Iron Regiment truly was no more.

The IR 169 Regimental History summarized the cost of the war: Between August 1914 – November 1918, 440 Officers and 22,100 enlisted men were listed as having served with the regiment. Of these, the regiment suffered the following losses. [Factoring in the men missing who never returned, those who later died of wounds and replacements who were killed before they could be placed on the rolls, the mortality rate was likely significantly higher.]

	Officers	Enlisted men
Killed in action:	105	2,555
Missing	25	1,041
Wounded multiple times	25	203
Wounded twice	60	967
Wounded once	103	5,883
Captured	19	916
Total	337	11,565

(AABE)

Postscript

Two of the primary German narratives came from Albert Rieth and Otto Lais. The following passages summarize their experiences after the war:

After recovering from his wounds in the battle of La Bassee, Albert Rieth was discharged from the army in spring 1915. He returned to Pforzheim where he resumed his trade as a toolsmith. While Pforzheim escaped the direct physical ravages of the war, 1,500 of the town's young men died in the conflict; a substantial portion of the military-aged men from a total population of 70,000 residents. In 1922, Albert married Helene Feiler, daughter of the owner of a local lumber mill. A year later, Albert and Helene celebrated the birth of their only child, Kurt Albert Rieth (the author's father).

The postwar destruction of Germany's economy made it a hard place to raise a family. With Pforzheim's once prosperous jewelry industry in shambles, Albert, at age 35, followed the path of many other skilled German tradesmen and immigrated to the United States in 1926. Albert established residence in Providence, Rhode Island and joined a large community of German immigrants working in the city's burgeoning jewelry industry. Helene and young Kurt followed Albert to America 17 months later.

Soon after his arrival, Albert gained life-long employment with the Speidel Jewelry Company in Providence. Kurt, after graduating high school in 1942, also joined his father at Speidel. Albert again experienced the trauma of world war when Kurt was drafted into the U.S. Army in February 1944. Kurt was assigned to an artillery observation unit in Patton's Third Army and saw heavy combat in France and Germany. In letters home, Kurt would sometimes hint at his location with references to some of Albert's World War One battles in the Lorraine. [In 2004, the author published a history of Kurt Rieth's unit, titled *Patton's Forward Observers; The History of the 7th Field Artillery Observation Battalion, XX Corps, Third Army*, Brandylane Publishing Inc, Richmond, VA.] While Kurt returned safely home, Pforzheim was fated for complete destruction. After almost escaping the war unscathed, Pforzheim was the target of a large Royal Air Force fire-bombing raid on February 23, 1945. The city center was entirely destroyed and 17,000 people, 30 percent of the population, were killed. All that Albert and Helene knew of their hometown and many of their loved-ones was gone.

Speidel prospered in the postwar years, and became one of the world's leading watch band manufacturers. Albert rose to become the company's senior toolmaker, with Kurt eventually becoming the chief designer. Together, they helped design and produce Speidel's famous "Twist-O-Flex" watch band. Kurt's marriage to Marian Talley provided Albert and Helene three grandchildren. Albert was still employed by Speidel at the time of his death on May 28, 1970, at age 79.

Otto Lais survived the war to become an accomplished artist. In 1981, the Apple Tree Gallery of Karlsruhe published a book that showcased a collection of his works, titled *Otto Lais, The Graphic work of Symbolic Realism in the 20th Century*. The book contained a biographic sketch of Lais' life and work, much of which is summarized below.

Following World War I, Lais returned to the Karlsruhe area where he attended the Baden Art School to study art, composition, violin and piano. His interests led him to sketching and caricatures, and by 1922, a local paper published a series of his political cartoons, many depicting the relationship between Germany and France. Lais worked as an elementary school art teacher while also establishing a career as a portrait artist.

Throughout the 1920's, Lais became a fixture in Karlsruhe's bohemian, cabaret-sub culture. This period influenced his artwork, and Lais became well-known for his specialization in the *Aktkunst* (erotic art) realm of etchings, a style which had become popular in the 1920's. Between 1921 and 1933, he was known to have produced 100 etchings. Many of Lais' pieces took on dark themes of gritty city streets, prostitutes and satanic images, often with his self-portrait in the background.

With the rise of Nazism in the early 1930's, Reich Minister Joseph Goebbels established the *Reichskulturkammer (RKK)* (Reich Chamber of Culture). The RKK was intended to gain control over the entire cultural life in Germany and promote Aryan art consistent with Nazi ideals. Lais refused to join the RKK, which, in 1936, led to the Nazis banning public exhibition of his work. From that point on, Lais ceased commercial art efforts.

In 1935, Lais published a pamphlet of his World War I experiences in the 1916 and 1918 Battles of the Somme titled *"A Machine Gunner in Iron Regiment 169."* Two other books followed that included his 1936 work, *A Regiment Dies a Hero's Death [1918]*, and *The Battle in the Limestone Chalk [1917],* published in 1942. In all of these publications, Lais accompanied the text with a series of sketches that depicted his combat experiences.

In addressing Lais' World War II experiences, the 1981 biographic sketch only informs us that he was called back to active German Army service and was discharged in 1945. Further research indicates he had remarkably distinguished war record in the Wehrmacht. Lais eventually rose the rank of Lieutenant Colonel and commanded the 858th Grenadier Regiment of 346th Infantry Division. The 346th Infantry Division was formed in September 1942 and for nearly two years served as an occupation, security and fortification defense unit along the French coast.

Lais' regiment was stationed in Le Havre when the Allies invaded Normandy on June, 6 1944. By June 10, most of the 346th Division was fighting in the German counterattack against British and Canadian forces around the Caen perimeter. The 346th took heavy losses in the Normandy campaign, losing over half its personnel and most of its artillery after the retreat from Falaise in late August. The division reformed in Holland and fought against Canadian forces in the September – November 1944 Battle of the Scheldt.

Lais prowess as a combat leader in World War II was evident in his being decorated with the highly distinguished Knight's Cross of the Iron Cross Award on September 30, 1944. Lais was one of only four soldiers in the 346th Division who won this honor in the entire war. Lt. Colonel Lais was captured on April 15, 1945 when Canadian forces overran the 858th Grenadier Regiment in Holland. The remainder of the 346th Division surrendered to the British north of Arnhem at the war's end a few weeks later.[383]

After the Second World War, Lais returned home and became a headmaster at a secondary school as he devoted his time to watercolor paintings. Today, pieces of Lais' artwork can be found in fine private collections and museums.

A summary of Lais' work in a German *Who's Who* website article describes a theme of 'world-weariness and disaffection,' a title of one of his etchings. Lais' bio also suggests he displayed traits of a manic personality, where "his sometimes exuberant joy of life mingled with a deep melancholy." [384] It would be an interesting study to examine to what extent the darker themes of Lais art may have been influenced by an accumulation of wartime horrors. His entire life considered, one has to assume that Lais regarded his teaching and artistic accomplishments, rather than military service, to have been his legacy.

Lais died on March 5, 1988 in Wegbert-Merbeck, Germany, at the age of 89.

Acknowledgements

The production of this book was very much a team effort, and I am indebted to many good friends who made this publication possible.

The project began with Walther Mueller's translation of my grandfather's 1915 journal. Our family owes a huge debt of gratitude to Walt, who spent many hours in this painstaking undertaking.

All of the German source material, most printed in the difficult-to-read, old Fraktur script, required translation into English. I was blessed by a cadre of excellent German speaking friends who devoted a great deal of effort in the translations. In the first addition, Tom Bierchenk, with the assistance of his father, Ulrich Bierchenk, translated much of Otto Lais *A Machine Gunner in the Iron Regiment.* M. Allen Saunders, whose vast intellect ranges from that of a German language scholar to a hillbilly banjo picker, translated lengthy passages from *Baden in World War* as well as much of the IR 169 Field Journal. Two other good friends, Crad Kennedy and Lisa Narkiewicz, also contributed their German language skills to the project.

For the second edition, another close friend and superb German linguist, Will Hirama translated important passages of Lais' *A Regiment Dies a Hero's Death.* Crad Kennedy again helped out in translations, with Kathleen Etter assisting in editing. Megan Moore, a talented graphic artist, created the topographic representation of the 1917 trench raids.

Andrew Jackson is the author of the *Accrington's Pals, The Full Story,* which is the excellent history of the British unit that opposed IR 169 at the Somme on July 1, 1916. Andrew was an enormous assistance to me by providing me with copies of Lais' first book as well as IR 169's Field Journal. I used Andrew's translation for Lais' account of the first day of the Battle of the Somme. [At the request of G. Braun, I fully cited all segments used from Otto Lais.] Andrew also generously let me use maps and photographs [some originally sourced to Hardy Huber] from his book.

In September 2015, Ray Merkler reached out to let me know his father, Karl Merkler, served as a machine gunner in IR 169 in the later portions of the war. Like my grandfather, Karl emigrated to the U.S. in the 1920s. Karl raised his family in New Jersey, where Ray resides today. Ray was kind enough to share photographs and records of his father's IR 169 service, which included Karl being awarded the Iron Cross (2nd Class) and the Silver Baden Merit medal. Karl was wounded at least one in the war, and his son recalls watching him pull shrapnel splinters from his knee years later. Ray also provided me with a copy of Lais *Hero's Death* book, which was an important spark in my starting the second edition. I've greatly enjoyed my communication with Ray and value our connection of having IR 169 forefathers who started new lives in the United States. Wartime pictures of Karl Merkler can be found in this book and at the website: www.ironregiment169.com.

My membership in the Western Front Association has been a great resource to connect with World War I enthusiasts as to leverage its vast repository of information. One contact I particularly value is with Jonathan Vernon, a true scholar on the study of the First World War and the Digital Editor of the WFA's monthly eNewsletter. In 2015 I asked WFA to review the first edition of the book, a task that Jonathan took on with gusto (to the extent that he read the book three times). Jonathan's review of the book was very kind, but he fairly noted the book would have been well served with more content on 1917-1918. My dialogue with Jonathan was another inspiration for me to start the second edition.

Another virtual friend I made with WFA was with member Andy McGoldrick. Andy provided me with a number of great photographs of IR 169 soldiers as well as the War Diary for the 2nd West Yorkshire Regiment, which brilliantly details the British side of the trenches in the May 27 1918 German Aisne Offensive.

I appreciate a number of World War One authors who reached out to me with assistance. Included in this group are Ralph Whitehead, who authored Volumes I and II of *The Other Side of the Wire, With the German XIV Reserve Corps on the Somme,* Helion & Company Ltd, UK, 2013. The XIV Reserve Corps served in the same sector as IR 169 in much of the Somme Campaign, and his exhaustively researched books were a great resource. Ralph also sent me a number of IR 169 photographs. I value the outreach by Frank Robinson, who along with his wife Janet and Frank Bucholz, wrote *The Great War Dawning; Germany and its Army at the Start of World War I,* Verlag Militaria, Vienna, Austria, 2013. *Great War Dawning* is a beautifully illustrated book and a superb resource for understanding the training, tactics and composition of the Imperial German Army at the beginning of the war. Much of the new content in the opening chapter on the training of a German infantry regiment came from this resource. I was fortunate to have brief exchanges with Dr Jack Sheldon and Dr. Stephen Bull, two preeminent authorities of the subject of World War One, and appreciated their words of encouragement.

Over in Germany, I need to thank Karl Dellears, an expert on Baden World War I units who, in 1996, connected me with the initial information I needed to get started. The help of my German cousin, Peter Richert, was also instrumental in my gaining access to important source information for both the first and second editions.

I'm grateful for the invaluable editing assistance of several good friends who share a passion for history. Dr. Les Cullen, with a PhD in History from Texas Tech, is a brilliant military historian and writer. Together, we have tromped through many battlefields, ranging from Little Big Horn, to Vicksburg and Antietam. His depth of knowledge on any number of historical-related subjects are unparalleled to anyone I know. Les spent many hours poring over the text, and made invaluable suggestions on the content and style of the final product. Two other good friends and colleagues from my own Army days, Colonel Patrick K. Keough (U.S. Army, Ret.) and Lieutenant Colonel Dave Moore (U.S. Army, Ret.), also loaned their expertise and writing skills to this work.

My former U.S. Army colleague, Colonel Gerald York (U.S. Army, ret.), graciously provided an endorsement for the book. Col. York is the grandson of one of America's most distinguished World War I soldiers, Sergeant Alvin York. Col. York has done much to promote the legacy of World War I history in the United States, and it is an honor to have his support for this work. I found it interesting to learn that Sergeant York's actions that resulted in his receiving the Medal of Honor in October 1918 occurred a short distance away from IR 169's position in the Meuse-Argonne Campaign.

I would like to give deep thanks for the encouragement and efforts of my publisher C. Stephen Badgley, who made this project possible. Stephen is responsible for the cover artwork and put great personal effort into the editing process. Badgley Publishing Company is a terrific small publishing house and I couldn't be more pleased with his support.

Finally, I want to thank my wife Joanna, whose encouragement and patience was essential.

Photographs

Albert G. Rieth, the author's grandfather, joined the 1st Battalion, 109th Leib Grenadier Regiment in Karlsruhe during the fall of 1912. In early 1913, this unit was re-designated as the 3rd Battalion, Infantry Regiment 169 and re-based in Villingen. (Author's Collection)

Pre-war post card depiction of IR 169 troops in training exercise.

In the summer months of 1913, IR 169 conducted field training in the Heuberg Stetten Training Camp. Albert Rieth is kneeling 2nd from the right. (Author's Collection)

3rd Battalion IR 169's arrival in Villingen, March 1913
(Author's Collection)

3rd Battalion, IR 169 presenting colors, Villingen Barracks, January, 1914
(Author's Collection)

A photograph of the ruined train station at Napoleonsinsel just after the battle.

A fanciful rendering of the Battle of Sarrebourg.

Massengräber in Hochwa'sch b. Saarburg i. L.
Nach der Schlacht v. 18.—21. Aug 1914

German cemetery at Hochwalsch, where IR 169 attacked on August 20, 1918, during the Battle of Sarrebourg.

The Battle of Baccarat: This bridge over the Meurthe River was filled with scores of dead French soldiers on August 25, 1914. The church in the background shows the damage from German shelling during the battle.
(This photograph was taken one week after the battle.)

The canal where much of IR 169's fighting took place during the La Bassee Campaign, October 1914 - March 1915. (BPC Collection)

German dead near the La Bassee Canal
(BPC Collection)

Left: Musketier Friedrich Strauch, 2nd Co, IR 169. Killed in action at Auchy-La Bassee, 31 December 1914. Age 21.

Right: Albert Rieth was wounded during the La Bassee Campaign in early 1915 and was sent to recover at a military hospital at Schweinfurt. In this photograph, he is standing in the doorway of the hospital.

This sketch, dated February 16, 1915, was drawn by Gustav, Albert's father, and shows a nurse dressing his injured foot at the military hospital in Schweinfurt. (Author's Collection)

Gallery of IR 169 Soldiers, circa 1914-1915

Photo courtesy of the Drake Goodman Collection

Photo courtesy of the Drake Goodman Collection

Photo courtesy of the Drake Goodman Collection

Photo courtesy of Ralph Whitehead

Photo courtesy of Ralph Whitehead

5th Company Group at Lahr, Germany 1915
Photo courtesy of Andrew Jackson, Hardy Huber Collection

5th Company, IR 169 in a rest area of the Somme, 1916.
Photo Courtesy of Andrew Jackson, Hardy Huber Collection

The British 11th Battalion, East Lancashire Regiment, the *"Accrington Pals,"* suffered over 80% casualties in its July 1, 1916 attack against IR 169 trenches in the Battle of the Somme. The Battalion is pictured here in 1914, preparing to depart England for the war.

(Courtesy of Andrew Jackson)

IR 169 took nearly 600 casualties on the British attack at Serre on 1 July 1916. This is death notice of one of those men, 20 year old Johann Schmid, who was assigned to the 3rd Company.

Courtesy of Ralph Whitehead

Trench held by 5th Company, 2nd Battalion, IR 169, at Serre
Photo courtesy of Andrew Jackson, Hardy Huber Collection

IR 169 Troops by a gas alarm bell at The Somme
Photo from the Drake Goodman Collection

IR 169, 2nd Battalion Command Post, Serre.
Photo courtesy of Andrew Jackson, Hardy Huber Collection

This French Schneider tank was knocked out in the April 16, 1917 attack at Juvincourt. IR 169 moved into this vicinity days later. Otto Lais wrote of harrowing experience in inspecting one of these tanks during a brief, nighttime break in shell fire.

Photo from the Drake Goodman Collection

A German Machine Gun Crew
Photo courtesy of Bruce Jarvis

"The Winterberg"
The Germans called the steep plateau above Craonne as the Winterberg,
as its shell-blasted, chalk landscape resembled an Alpine Mountain. IR
169 suffered extreme casualties here in late July 1917.
Photo from Hardy Huber Collection

**German 52nd Division soldiers atop the
Winterberg in 1917.**
Photo from Hardy Huber Collection

On May 27, 1918, IR 169 took part in a massive German assault that pushed the Allies from their Aisne River defenses, 25 miles south to the Marne. In this photograph, German infantry advances across the Chemin des Dames launch point.

By Spring 1918, IR 169 mastered the Storm Troop tactics that were employed in the German Spring Offensives. (This photo, most likely of troops in training, provides an image of how a German assault of that era would appear.)

In 1916, Karl Merkler, (left) from the village of Mörsch [present day Rhinstetten, a suburb of Karlsruhe], went through IR 169's training pipeline before being diverted for service on the Eastern Front. He returned to active service with IR 169 in Spring/Summer of 1918. He was wounded twice in the war and immigrated to the United States in the 1920's, where he settled and raised a family in New Jersey.

He served in an IR 169 Machine Gun Company. In the photo below he is pictured lying at the bottom, 2nd man on the left.

Photos courtesy of Ray Merkler.

This classic image personifies the German infantryman of 1918.

One of IR 169's most desperate struggles of the entire war was its defense of the Grevillers Forest on August 24, 1918. Here, New Zealand infantry, supported by British Mark V tanks, move past Grevillers. Note captured German 4.2 inch field artillery pieces in the distant right.

Otto Lais / Self-portrait

Otto Lais, who was born near Karlsruhe, served as an IR 169 machine gun squad leader in the 1916 Battle of the Somme. He was promoted through the enlisted ranks to lieutenant and commanded both machine gun and rifle companies in some of fiercest combat of the war. Only 21 years old at the war's end, Lais returned to Karlsruhe to become a noted, if controversial artist. He was recalled to the German Army in World War II and commanded a Grenadier regiment on the Western Front. Following the war, Lais resumed a quiet life as an art teacher.

Bibliography, Sources, and Research

Books

Anon (1914–1921). *The Times History of the War Vol XII*. London: The Times.

"*Battle of Mouquet Farm, France, 5 August – 5 September 1916*". Department of Defence (Australia). Archived from the original on 15 April 2011.

American Armies and Battlefields in Europe, Washington, D.C., Government Printing Office, 1938.

Banks, Arthur, *A Military Atlas of the First World War*, Trowbridge (UK), Redwood Books, 1997.

Balck, W. (1922). *Entwickelung der Taktik im Weltkrige*. Translated *as Development of Tactics, World War by the General Service Schools* Press 1922 (Kessinger 2008 ed.). Berlin: Eisenschmidt.

Bennighof, Michael, Ph.D, *German Naval Infantry in the Defense of Berlin*, Avalanche Press, 2013.

Bucholz, Frank; Robinson Janet; Robinson Frank *The Great War Dawning; Germany and its Army at the Start of World War I*, Verlag Militaria, Vienna, Austria, 2013.

Bull, Stephen, *Trench: A History of Trench Warfare on the Western Front*, Osprey Publishing, UK, 2010.

Collier & Son, *The Story of the Great War*, NY, NY, Collier & Son, 1916.

Collier & Son, *Collier's Photographic History of the European War*, NY, NY, Collier & Son, 1917.

Commemorative Publication for the 1ˢᵗ Regimental Day of the former 8ᵗʰ Baden Infantry Regiment 169 on 30 and 31 August 1924. (Provided by Andrew Jackson, and credited "courtesy of Verlag Mortitz Schauenburg GmbH.)

David, Daniel, *The 1914 Campaign, August - October, 1914*, NY,NY, Military Press, 1987.

Department of the United States Army, *American Military History, 1607-1953*, Washington, D.C, U.S. Government Printing Office, 1956.

Doyal, Arthur Conan, *The British Campaign in France and Flanders, Vol. VI*, Chapter IV.

Attack of Byng's Third Army, August 21, 1918, to September 29, 1918. First published by Hodder & Stoughton, London, 1920; taken from a Project Gutenberg of Australia eBook format.)

Duffy, Francis P., *Father Duffy's Story; A Tale of Honor and Heroism, of Life and Death with the Fighting 69ᵗʰ (Garden City, NY, 1918).*

Deutshe Verlust Listen 1914-1917. (German World War One Casualty Listing).

Falls, C. (1940). *Military Operations France and Belgium, 1917 Vol I, The German Retreat to the Hindenburg Line and the Battles of Arras* (IWM & Battery Press 1992 ed.). London.

Farrar-Hockley, Anthony, *Death of an Army*, NY, NY, Morrow Inc, 1968.

Farrar-Hockley, *The Somme*, Pan Books, London, 1983.

Ferrell, Robert H., *America's Deadliest Battle, Meuse-Argonne, 1918, University Press of Kansas, Lawrence, KS, 2007.*

Fosten, D.S.V, Marrion, R.J., Embeleton, G.A., *The German Army 1914-1918*, Osprey Military, UK, 1999 Edition.

Graves, Robert, *Goodbye to All That*, First Edition, Jonathan Cape 1929.

Hart, Peter, *1918: A Very British Victory*, Phoenix Books, 2008, London.

Hastings, Max, *Catastrophe 1914: Europe Goes to War*, Knopf, NY, 2013.

Horne, Charles, *The Great Events of the Great War, Volume II*, National Alumni, 1920.

Horne, A. *The Price of Victory*, London, 1962.

Infantry in Battle, The Infantry Journal Inc, Washington, D.C., 1939.

Jackson, Andrew, *Accrington's Pals; The Full Story*, Pen & Sword, South Yorkshire, United Kingdom, 2013.

Keegan, John, *Opening Moves*: 1914, NY, NY, Ballentine Books, 1971.

Keegan, John, *The First World War*, London, Knopf, 1998.

Lais, Otto, *Machinegewehre im Eisernen Regiment (Machine Gunner in the Iron Regiment), 8 Badisches Infanterie Regiment Nr. 169*, G. Braun, Karlsruhe, Germany, circa 1935.

Lais, Otto, *Ein Regiment Stirbt den Heldentod (A Regiment Dies a Hero's Death)* Gutsch Verlag, Karlsruhe, Germany, 1936.

Lais, Otto, *Die Schlacht im Kreidekalk (The Battle in the Limestone Chalk)*, Verlag G. Braun, Karlsruhe, Germany, 1942.

Langenfeld, Ludwin, Otto Lais; Das graphische Werk Eines symbolischen Realisten der zwanziger Jahre. (*Otto Lais, The Graphic work of Symbolic Realism in the 20th Century*), Verlag Karl Schillinger, Freiburg i. Br., 1981.

Lensel, Edward G. *A Companion to the Meuse Argonne Campaign*; Chapter on *The 111th German Infantrerie Regiment by Exermont*, John Wiley and Sons, UK, 2014.

Lomas, David. *First Ypres 1914*, Osprey Publishing, Oxford, UK, 1998.

London Stamp Exchange, *The Histories of Two Hundred and Fifty-one Divisions of the German Army Which Participated in the War (1914-1918),* London, London Stamp Exchange, 1920.

Marix Evans, Martin (2002) *1918: The Year of Victories*, Arcturus Military History Series, London: Arcturus.

Marshall, SLA, *The American Heritage History of World War I*, NY, NY, Simon and Shuster, Inc, 1964.

Middlebrook, *The First Day on the Somme*, Penguin Books, London, 1971.

McCarthy, C (1993). *The Somme: The Day-by-Day Account* (Arms & Armour Press 1995 ed.).
London: Weidenfeld Military.

Miles, W. (1938). *Military Operations, France and Belgium, 1916. 2nd July 1916 to the End of the Battles of the Somme* (IWM & Battery Press 1992 ed.). London.

Muller-Loebnitz, *Die Badener im Weltkrieg*, G. Braun, Karlsruhe, Germany, 1936.

Philpott, W. (2009). *Bloody Victory: The Sacrifice on the Somme and the Making of the Twentieth Century* (1st ed.). London: Little, Brown.

Reichsarchiv, *Der Weltkreig 1914/1918*, Berlin, 1925-1939.

Review of Reviews, *Europe at War, NY, NY*, Doubleday, 1914.

Rogerson, Sidney. *The Last of the Ebb; The Battle of the Aisne, 1918*, Greenhill Books, 1937 (2007 edition), London.

Rogerson, Sidney. Supplement to *War Diary for the 2nd West Yorkshire Regiment*; titled. *A Narrative of Events Between the Aisne & the Marne Between May & June, 1918*

Sheldon, Jack, *The German Army on the Somme*, Pen & Sword, South Yorkshire, United Kingdom, 2005.

Sheldon, Jack, *The German Army at Ypres 1914*, Pen and Sword, UK, 2010.

Sheldon, Jack, *The German Army in the Spring Offensives 1917; Arras, Aisne & Champagne*, Pen and Sword Military, 2015

Edwin Simmons and Joseph H. Alexander, *Through the Wheat; The U.S. Marines in World War I*, Naval Institute Press, Annapolis, MD, 2008.

Simpson, Andy. *The Evolution of Victory: British Battles of the Western Front, 1914–1918*. Tom Donovan, 1995.

Tyng, Sewell, *Campaign of the Marne*, 1914, NY, Longsmen's Green, 1935.

Use of Gas in the Meuse-Argonne Campaign; September – October 1918, Washington, D.C., U.S. Chemical Corps, 1958.

Terraine, John, *The Great War*, London, Wordsworth, 1965.

The Times, *The Times History of the War*, London, The Times, 1920.

Tuchman, Barbara, *The Guns of August*, NY, NY, Ballantine Books, 1962.

Willmott, H.P. *World War I*, Dorling Kindersly (DK) LTD, NY, NY, 2009.

Whitehead, Ralph J., *The Other Side of the Wire, Volume 1, With the German Reserve XIV Corps on the Somme, September 1914-June 1916*. Helion & Company Ltd, UK, 2009.

Whitehead, Ralph J. *The Other Side of the Wire, Volume 2, The Battle of the Somme, With the German Reserve XIV Corps, 1 July 1916*. Helion & Company Ltd, UK, 2013.

Wren, Jack, *The Great Battles of World War I*, NY. NY, Madison Square Press, 1971.

Zabecki, D. T., *The German 1918 Offensives: A Case Study of The Operational Level of War*, Taylor & Francis, 2005.

Zaloga, Steven J. *German Panzers 1914-18*, Osprey Publishing, UK, 2006.

Professional Journal, Newspaper, Magazine, and Internet Articles

4th Battalion Bedfordshire Regiment Report on Operations August 20-28, 1918. (This report was accessed via the website: "The Befordshire Regiment in the Great War, edited by Steven Fuller.)

Gray, Jack, *The New Zealand Division in France and Flanders, May 1916-November 1918,* Internet posting, Christchurch, NZ, 2005.

Keep Military Museum website, info@keepmilitarymuseum.org, Bois des Buttes page.
The Long, Long Trail; The British Army in the Great War of 1914-1918. www.1914-1918.net/army.htm.

Laudan, Sebastian, *The Evolution of Trench Warfare; La Bassee-Auch-Loos 1915: A German Perspective*. STAND TO! The Journal of the Western Front Association, Special Edition, September 2015.

Lupfer, Timothy T, *The Dynamics of Doctrine: The Changes in German Tactical Doctrine during the First World War*, from the Leavenworth Papers Series, Combat Studies Institute, U.S. Army

Command and General Staff College, Fort Leavenworth, Kansas, July 1981.

Reicharchive 1942 *Der Weltkrieg 1914 bis 1918: Die militärischen Operationen zu Lande [The World War 1914–1918: Military Operations on Land]. XIII (Die digitale landesbibliotek Oberösterreich 2012 ed.). Potsdam: Mittler. 1942. OCLC 257129831.*

Rickard, J. *Battle of La Bassée, 10 October-2 November 1914*, (25 August 2007) http://www.historyofwar.org/articles/battles_la_bassee.html

Rickard, J, *Second Battle of Bapaume, 21 August-1 September 1918*, (5 September 2007) http://www.historyofwar.org/articles/battles_bapaumeII.html.

Sass, Erik credited to article appearing mentalfloss.co,/article/61283, titled *WW I Centennial, Germans repulsed at Givenchy*. January 25, 2015.

The Western Front Association Website, "www.westernfrontassociation.com" Land War tab; '*This Month in February 1915, the Coldstream Guards and Irish Guards at Cuinchy*'article (also cited as *Commonwealth War Graves Commission Newsletter February 2013 www.cwgc.org*) http://www.cwgc.org/media/86973/wfa_feb_newsletter.pdf . Footnotes Includes cited works by Kipling and passages from *Deeds that thrill the Empire, True Stories of the Most Glorious Acts of Heroism of the Empire's Soldiers and Sailors during the Great War. Hutchinson & Co, Year of Publication: circa 1919 As cited in* WFA '*This Month in February 1915, the Coldstream Guards and Irish Guards at Cuinchy*'article, online edition.

86ᵉ Regiment d' Infanterie, Historique de la Bataille du 25 Aout 1914 A Baccarat, zogotounga.free.fr/galerie/divers/baccarat.pd.

Yves Le Maner, Director of La Coupole, History and Remembrance Centre of Northern France. Article titled *The Battle of Givenchy, 18-22 December 1914*. http://www.remembrancetrails-northernfrance.com/history/battles/the-battle-of-givenchy-18-22-december-1914.html.

Eyewitness Accounts – Unpublished

Rieth, Albert, *Kriegserinnerungen: 1914, Von A. Rieth, Hornist im Regt 169*, Schweinfurt, 1915.

Rieth, Albert, *World War I Era Photo Journal*, Pforzheim, (assembled circa 1925.)

Rieth-Taffel, Ursula, *Letter on the Background of Pforzheim during World War I*, Puch/Hallein (Austria) 1999.

Notes on Map Sources

Primary Maps included are from Baden in World War, (G Braun, Karlsruhe, Germany, 1936) (referenced as BIWW), American Armies and Battlefields in Europe (Washington D.C. U.S. Government Printing Office, 1938) (referenced as AABE), Accrington's Pals; The Full Story, (Andrew Jackson, Pen & Sword, South Yorkshire, United Kingdom, 2013) (referenced as AP) and the Infantry Regiment 169 Field Journal and Unit History, written 1922 (referenced as IR 169 History or IR).

New Zealand History net; URL:
http://www.nzhistory.net.nz/media/photo/battle-bapaume-map 9, (Ministry for Culture and Heritage), updated 14-Aug-2014 (referenced as NZH), and Collier's New Encyclopedia, v. 10, 1921 (CNE). Map 15, Battle of Pinon, sourced to Story of the Great War, Volume VII, Published by PF Collier, NY, found on internet from http://www.archieve.org/details/storyofgreatwar07/churuoft[Date=1920. Maps of the Juvincourt and Ripont Trench Raids were based on representations found in *The Battle in the Limestone Chalk* (Referenced as LC), and prepared for this publication by Megan Moore.

Maps found in the Public Domain where orginal sourcing cannot be confirmed are listed as PD.

[Note: American Armies and Battlefields in Europe is the U.S. Army's official guide to World War One battlefields. The version used was reprinted by the U.S. Army Center of Military History in 1995 and contains annotations for stops that are described in the text of the book. First Published in 1938, it was intended as a travel guide for tourists visiting the American battlefields, While oriented from the U.S. Army perspective, many these maps provide an excellent representation of the ground where IR 169 fought upon.]

Map Sources

1. Baden Pre-War Garrisons   BIWW
2. Southern Portion of Western Front   AABE
3. Central and Northern Portions of Western Front   PD
4. IR 169 at Battle of Mulhouse   BIWW
5. Routes of Invading German Armies, 1914   AABE
6. Battle of Sarrebourg; Opening Movements   BIWW
7. IR 169 at Battle of Sarrebourg   BIWW
8. IR 169 in St. Mihiel Sector   BIWW
9. IR 169 at La Bassee   BIWW
10. Battle of the Somme; Serre Defenses, 1 July 1916   RH
11. Battle of the Somme; British Attack, 1 July 1916   AP
12. Battle of the Somme; Serre Besieged, July – Dec 1916   PD
13. Juvincourt Sector; Spring 1917 and May 1918   AABE
14. Juvincourt Trench Raid, May 1917   LC
15. Battle of Pinon   PD
16. Ripont Trench Raid, December 1917   LC
17. German 1918 Offensives   AABE
18. German 1918 Aisne Offensive   AABE
19. Attack on the Bois des Buttes   PD
20. Battle of Bapaume   NZH
21. Meuse-Argonne Campaign   PD
22. Meuse-Argonne Campaign, Sep 29-Oct 8, 1918   AABE
23. Meuse-Argonne Campaign, The Krimhilde Stellung   AABE
24. Last Stand at Landres-et-St. Georges, Nov 1, 1918   AABE

Notes

Prologue

[1]Jack Sheldon, *The German Army at Ypres 1914*, Pen and Sword, UK, 2010. p. X.

Chapter 1. Prelude to War

[2] *Feltschrift zum Regimentastag des ehem. 8. Bad. Infantry Regiment NR 169 in Lahr, am 30.und 31. August 1924.* (For future notes, referred to as *IR 169 Field Journal/Regimental History*) Pages 3-4. This pamphlet, published in 1942, consists of a brief unit history, a field journal of operations in the war and a detailed account of the 1916 Battle of the Somme.

[3] John Keegan, *The First World War*, Knoff, New York, 1999, p. 12.

[4] Gerard DeGroot, Book review in the Washington Post's "Bookworld"Section, December 1, 2013.

[5] Frank Bucholz-Janet Robinson- Frank Robinson in *The Great War Dawning; Germany and its Army at the Start of World War I,*Verlag Militaria, Vienna, Austria, 2013. pp. 93-95.

[6] Ibid, p.99

[7] Ibid, p.201.

[8] Jack Sheldon, *The German Army On the Somme*, Pen and Sword, UK, 2010, Appendix II.

[9] Bucholz, J. Robinson, F. Robinson, pp 177-198 (references to this paragraph are taken from Chapter 9 'The Officers Corps,' from this source).

[10] Ibid. p. 199.

[11] Barbara W. Tuchman, *The Guns of August*, Ballantine Books, NY, 1994 edition, p. 172.

[12] Bucholz, J. Robinson, F. Robinson, p 197.

[13] Ibid.

[14] Leib Regiment 109 History website, viewed 15 June 2014, http://ka.stadtwiki.net/Leibgrenadierregiment.

[15] Bucholz, J. Robinson, F. Robinson, p 201.

[16] Ibid, pp. 202-205.

[17] Anthony Farrar-Hockley, *Death of an Army*, Wordsworth Editions, UK, 1998 edition, p. 11.

[18] Bucholz, J. Robinson, F. Robinson, pp 221-230.

[19] Alistair Horne, *The Price of Glory, Verdun 1916*, Penguin Books, UK, 1993 edition, p. 12.
[20] Ibid, p. 73.

Chapter 2. Opening Moves: The Battle of Mulhouse
[21] Tuchman, p. 74.
[22] *Die Badener im Weltkrieg*, (Baden in World War), G. Braun, Karlsruhe, Germany, 1935, p. 18.
[23] J. Terraine, *The Great War*, Wordsworth Editions, London, 1965, p. 31.
[24] Tuchman, pp. 29-30.
[25] Ibid, p. 185.
[26] *The World War, 1914-1918, Military Operations on Land, Volume I, The Frontier Battles in the West.*
[27] Keegan, *The First World War*, p. 74.
[28] Karl Dellers, personal account, August 1998.
[29] Tuchman, p. 172.
[30] *Baden in World War*, pp. 24-31. Unless otherwise noted, all remaining details of IR 169's operations during the Battle at Mulhouse are from this source.
[31] *The Times History of the War*, Published by "The Times,"Publishing House, London, England, 1919.
[32] Hastings, Max, *Catastrophe 1914: Europe Goes to War*, Knopf, NY, 2013, pp. 168-169.
[33] Keegan, *The First World War*, p. 88.

Chapter 3. The Battle of Frontiers: Into the Lorraine
[34] DeGroot, Washington Post, December 1, 2013.
[35] Keegan, *The First World War*, p. 88.
[36] Tuchman, p. 91.
[37] Hasting, p.172.
[38] John Keegan, *Opening Moves, August 1914*, Ballantine Books, NY, 1971, p. 62.
[39] J. Terraine, p. 34.
[40] Hastings, p. 174-175.
[41] Keegan, *Opening Moves, August 1914*, p. 67-70.
[42] Ibid.

[43] Ibid, pp. 71-72.

[44] One of the oral combat vignettes passed down by Albert Rieth to the author (circa the late 1960s) most likely happened here. An officer instructed Rieth to sound a bugle. An instant later, the officer had his head blown off.

[45] This ambush of the French artillery battery is another incident recalled by the author as being told by Albert Rieth. In his telling, Albert made the point of the horror of witnessing enemy troops and horses being cut down at close range. His recollection corresponded closely with the account in the Baden regimental history.

[46] *86ᵉ Regiment d' Infanterie, Historique de la Bataille du 25 Aout 1914 A Baccarat*, viewed 9 January 2017, www.zogotounga.free.fr/galerie/divers/baccarat.pd.

[47] *Baden in World War*, pages 37-42. Unless otherwise noted, all remaining details of IR 169's engagement in the August 20-21 Battle of Sarrebourg are from this source.

Chapter 4. The Meurthe Campaign and the Battle of Baccarat

[48] Hastings, p. 176.

[49] *The Times History of the War*, "The Times", p, 396.

[50] Tuchman, p. 234

[51] *Die Badener im Weltkrieg*, pages 43-45. Unless otherwise noted, all remaining details of IR 169's engagement in the Battles of Baccarat and St Barbe are from this source.

[52] *86ᵉ Regiment d' Infanterie, Historique de la Bataille du 25 Aout 1914 A Baccarat*. (All details from the 86th RI at the Battle of Baccarat and St. Barbe were taken from this source.)

[53] Hastings, p. 187.

[54] www.telegraph.co.uk › History › World War One. "WW1 German soldier recalls moment he bayoneted foe to death."

[55] *Histories of Two Hundred and Fifty-One Divisions of the German Army which Participated in the War (1914-1918)*, compiled from records of Intelligence section of the General Staff, American Expeditionary Forces, at General Headquarters, Chaumont, France 1919 (1920).

[56] Keegan, *The First World War*, p. 318.

[57] Bucholz, Robinson J., Robinson F. *The Great War Dawning*, p 330.

[58] *The Badener im Weltkrieg*, pages 72-74. Unless otherwise noted, all remaining details of IR 169's engagement in the St Mihiel Salient are from this source.

[59] Keegan, *The First World War*, p. 185.

Chapter 5. The Race for the Sea; The First Battle of Ypres

[60] Graves, Robert, *Goodbye to All That*. First published by Robert Graves in 1929, recent U.S. editions by Anchor Books. Use of quote here as inspired by Western Front Association's (WFA) '*This Month in February 1915, the Coldstream Guards and Irish Guards at Cuinchy*'article, online edition, also cited as *Commonwealth War Graves Commission Newsletter February 2013, viewed February 2016, www.cwgc.org.*, https://familysearch.org/patron/v2/TH-904-49979-248-5/dist.pdf?ctx=ArtCtxPublic&session=USYS5EC0C61D095E0D9FE C1B10F2E953A8D2_, with original source from Grave's *Goodbye to All That*, first edition published by Jonathan Cape, 1929.

[61] Keegan, *The First World War,* pp. 123-137. (Portions of this section on the Battle of Ypres, to include this direct passage, has been taken largely from Keegan's "The First World War", and is summarized with this single footnote.)

[62] WFA '*This Month in February 1915, the Coldstream Guards and Irish Guards at Cuinchy*'article, also cited as *Commonwealth War Graves Commission Newsletter February 2013 www.cwgc.org,* see footnote 63.

[63] *Baden in World War*, pp. 79-80.

[64] Lomas, David. *First Ypres 1914*, Osprey Publishing, Oxford, UK, 1998, p. 29-30.

[65] J. Rickard, *Battle of La Bassée, 10 October-2 November 1914*, (25 August 2007) cited as *Commonwealth War Graves Commission Newsletter February 2013 www.cwgc.org.*, https://familysearch.org/patron/v2/TH-904-49979-248-5/dist.pdf?ctx=ArtCtxPublic&session=USYS5EC0C61D095E0D9FE C1B10F2E953A8D2_idses-prod02.a.fsglobal.net, viewed January 9, 2017.

[66] Lomas, pp. 86-87 places the losses at over 135,000, while Sheldon, in the *Germany Army at Ypres*, page XIV lists German casualties at 80,000.

[67] Sebastian Laudan, *The Evolution of Trench Warfare; La Bassee-Auch-Loos 1915: A German Perspective.* STAND TO! The Journal of the Western Front Association, Special Edition, September 2015. pp 46-47. (For anyone interested in a detailed exploration of German trench construction in 1914-15, this article, rich with period illustrations, is highly recommended.)

[68] Laudan, p. 48.

[69] Ibid p. 49.

[70] Westmann, S, 1964, *WW1 German Soldier Recalls Moment he Bayoneted Foe to Death*, viewed 14 March 2014, The Telegraph, www.telegraph.co.uk › History › World War One "WW1 German soldier recalls moment he bayoneted foe to death."

[71] Article titled *The Battle of Givenchy, 18-22 December 1914.* credited to: Yves Le Maner, Director of La Coupole, History and Remembrance Centre of Northern France., viewed February 15, 2016, http://www.remembrancetrails-northernfrance.com/history/battles/the-battle-of-givenchy-18-22-december-1914.html.

[72] The *Long, Long Trail*; The British Army in the Great War of 1914-1918. www.1914-1918.net/army.htm.

[73] A number of postcards exist that depict Albert Rieth's stay at the hospital, which illustrate the medical treatment provided to wounded German troops once they reached their homeland. Included in this collection are two postcards that document the February 1915 visit of his father to the hospital. The cards, sent by Albert's father to his wife in Pforzheim, provide a brief description of his condition. One of these cards contains a sketch of Albert having his foot dressed by a nurse and speaks to the kindness of the hospital staff. Most of the other cards, dated in March 1915, contain pictures of Albert recovering with other patients and the medical staff. The facility appears clean and the patients well cared for (to include local excursions complete with beer drinking). It was during this period that he wrote his journal. The last photograph we see of Albert in uniform is dated April 1915.

[74] Sass, Erik credited to article appearing mentalfloss.co,/article/61283, titled *WW I Centennial, Germans repulsed at Givenchy*. January 25, 2015. viewed February 2016

[75] WFA '*This Month in February 1915, the Coldstream Guards and Irish Guards at Cuinchy*'article, online edition. Also cited as *Commonwealth War Graves Commission Newsletter February 2013* *www.cwgc.org*
All portions attributed to Kipling were cited to his '*Irish Guards of the Great War, Volume One.*'

[76] *Deeds that thrill the Empire, True Stories of the Most Glorious Acts of Heroism of the Empire's Soldiers and Sailors during the Great War*. Hutchinson & Co, Year of Publication: circa 1919 As cited in WFA '*This Month in February 1915, the Coldstream Guards and Irish Guards at Cuinchy*'article, online edition, viewed February 2016.

[77] Laudan, P.49.

[78] Ibid, p 53.

Chapter 6. The Battle of the Somme, Part I, Britain's Bloodiest Day

[79] Keegan, *The First World War*, p. 175.

[80] SLA Marshall, *The American Heritage History of World War* I, Simon and Schuster, NY, 1964, pp. 79-80.

[81] H.P. Willmott, H.P. *World War I*, Dorling Kindersly (DK) LTD, NY, 2009, p 105.

[82] Ralph J. Whitehead, *The Other Side of the Wire, Volume 1, With the German XIV Corps on the Somme, September 1914-June 1916*. Helion & Company Ltd, UK, 2009. pp 224-225.

[83] Sheldon, *The German Army On the Somme*, p. 76-78.

[84] Ibid, p.78.

[85] Martin Middlebrook, *The First Day on the Somme*, Penguin Books, London, 1971, p. 59.

[86] Sheldon *The German Army On the Somme* "At all levels of command"p. 71. "Detailed instructions were" pp. 100-106.

[87] Whitehead, Ralph, *The Other Side of the Wire, Volume 2, The Battle of the Somme, With the German XIV Corps, 1 July 1916*. Helion & Company Ltd, UK, 2013. p. 118-119.

[88] Sheldon, *The German Army On the Somme*, Appendix II

[89] Fosten, D.S.V, Marrion, R.J., Embeleton, G.A., *The German Army 1914-1918*, Osprey Military, UK, 1999 Edition. P. 33.

[90] Sheldon, *The German Army On the Somme,* p. 93-94.

[91] Whitehead, *The Other Side of the Wire, Volume I.* pp 275-279.

[92] *IR 169 Field Journal/Regimental History.* (All subsequent entries prefaced by Regimental History (RH) is from this source.)

[93] *Experiences of Baden Soldiers at the Front, Volume 1: Machine guns in the Iron Regiment (8th Baden Infantry Regiment No.169)".* Otto Lais, (G. Braun, Karlsruhe 1935) . P. 1. (Note, all subsequent passages in italics, *and annotated as "*Lais*, Iron Regiment",* come from this source.)

[94] Middlebrook, p. 78-79.

[95] Andrew Jackson website, *www.pals.org.uk/pals_e.htm*

[96] Jackson, Andrew, *Accrington's Pals; The Full Story*, Pen & Sword, South Yorkshire, United Kingdom, 2013, pp. 70, 79.

[97] Middlebrook, p. 87.

[98] Ibid, pp. 87-89.

[99] Lais, *Iron Regiment*, p. 2.

[100] Middlebrook, p. 95.

[101] Jackson, 94-114. This single footnote serves to reference all additional information related to the Accrington Pals and 94th Brigade operations at the Somme. Unless detailed elsewhere, this includes specific quotes as well as general gisting.

[102] Farrar-Hockley, *The Somme*, Pan Books, London, 1983, pp. 103-104.

[103] Middlebrook, p. 143.

[104] Ibid. p. 87.

[105] Ibid, p. 90.

[106] Jackson, pp. 100-101.

[107] Whitehead, Ralph, *The Other Side of the Wire, Volume 2,* p. 110

[108] Ibid, *The Other Side of the Wire, Volume 2,* pp. 115-116.

[109] Ibid p. 115. (Quoting Middlebrook, p.138)

[110] Middlebrook pp. 121-125.

[111] Jackson, www.pals.org.uk/pals_e.htm: [Note: As Andrew Jackson points out, Lais understates the effectiveness of the German artillery fire, which was actually very devastating to the British attack. Lais'

perspective however, can be easily understood – when facing a horde of enemy infantry, more supporting artillery fire was always desired

[112] Lais, *Iron Regiment*. p. 2

[113] Whitehead, *The Other Side of the Wire, Volume 2,* pp 115, 132.

[114] Ibid p. 3.

[115] Whitehead, *The Other Side of the Wire, Volume 2,* pp. 117-119.

[116] Middlebrook, p.151.

[117] A.H. Farrar-Hockly, *The Somme*, p. 114.

[118] Jackson, p. 110.

[119] Lais, *Iron Regiment*, pp. 3-4.

[120] Sheldon, *The German Army On the Somme,* pp. 144-145.

[121] Lais, *Iron Regiment*, p.4.

[122] A.H. Farrar-Hockly, *The Somme,* p. 114.

[123] Jackson, p. 113.

[124] Whitehead, *The Other Side of the Wire, Volume 2,* p. 132.

[125] Lais, *Iron Regiment*, p. 4

[126] Jackson, p. 215.

[127] Middlebrook, p. 219.

Chapter 7. The Somme, Part II: Serre Besieged

[128] A.H. Farrar-Hockley, *The Somme* p.197.

[129] Lais, *Iron Regiment*, p. 5.

[130] Ibid, pp. 5-6

[131] Ibid, p. 6.

[132] Willmott, pp. 188-190.

[133] Lais, *Iron Regiment*, pp. 6-7.

[134] *"Battle of Mouquet Farm, France, 5 August – 5 September 1916"*. Department of Defence (Australia). (Archived from the original on 15 April 2011. As taken from https://en.wikipedia.org/wiki/Battle_of_Mouquet_Farm on March, 10, 2014.

[135] Lais, *Iron Regiment*, pp. 8-9.

[136] Ibid. pp. 10-11.

[137] Miles. p. 428.

[138] Jackson, pp. 131-132.

[139] Lais, *Iron Regiment*, p. 9.

Chapter 8. The Somme, Part III; The Last Stand at Serre

[140] Lais, *Iron Regiment*, pp. 10-11.

[141] *IR 169 Field Journal/Regimental History*. The Battle of the Somme.

[142] Miles, W. (1938). *Military Operations, France and Belgium, 1916. 2nd July 1916 to the End of the Battles of the Somme* (IWM & Battery Press 1992 ed.). London: p. 478.

[143] Philpott, W. (2009). *Bloody Victory: The Sacrifice on the Somme and the Making of the Twentieth Century* (1st ed.). London: Little, Brown. pp. 414-415.

[144] McCarthy,, C (1993). *The Somme: The Day-by-Day Account* (Arms & Armour Press 1995 ed.). London: Weidenfeld Military. pp 155-156.

[145] Jackson, p. 132.

[146] Lais, *Iron Regiment*. pp. 11-12.

[147] Ibid, pp. 13-14.

[148] Ibid. p. 15.

[149] Ibid. p. 16.

[150] Ibid.

[151] Ibid. p. 17.

[152] Ibid. p. 18.

[153] McCarthy, pp. 155-156.

[154] Lais, *Iron Regiment*, pp. 18-19.

[155] Ibid. p. 18.

[156] Ibid.

[157] *IR 169 Field Journal/Regimental History*. The Battle of the Somme.

[158] Lais, *Iron Regiment*. p.19.

[159] Ibid, p. 20

[160] Ibid, p. 20.

[161] *IR 169 Field Journal/Regimental History*. The Battle of the Somme.

[162] Jackson, p. 136.

[163] Miles, p. 527. (Including 45,000 German losses.)

[164] Miles, p. 512.

[165] Philpott, pp. 414-415.

[166] Sheldon, *The German Army On the Somme,* p. 399.

Chapter 9. "This Terrible Bench;"Serre, December 1916 and a 1917 Return to the Alsace

[167] *IR 169 Field Journal/Regimental History*.

[168] Lais, *Iron Regiment*, p. 21.

[169] Ibid. pp. 22-23.

[170] Ibid. pp. 23-24.

[171] Ibid. p. 24.

[172] Ibid. pp. 24-25.

[173] Lais, Otto, *Ein Regiment Stirbt den Heldentod (A Regiment Dies a Hero's Death)* Gutsch Verlag, Karlsruhe, Germany, 1936. p. 115. All further references from this source listed as "Lais, *Hero's Death*).

[174] Lais, Otto, *Die Schlacht im Kreidekalk (The Battle in the Limestone Chalk)*, Verlag G. Braun, Karlsruhe, Germany, 1942. All information detailing IR 169's operations at Altkirch are taken from pages 25-36 from this source. Future references from this reference listed as "Lais, *Limestone Chalk*").

[175] Roads to the Great War Website, *100 Years Ago, the Coming of the Turnip Winter*. http://roadstothegreatwar-ww1.blogspot.com/2016/09/100-years-ago-coming-of-turnip-winter. Viewed, September 29, 2016.

[176] Author's interview of Ray Merkler (son of Karl Merkler), June 6, 2017. Ray recalled his father often commenting on the lack of rations during this period, and used the expression included in this text.

[177] Bull, Stephen, *Trench: A History of Trench Warfare on the Western Front*, Osprey Publishing, 2014, pp 180-182.

Chapter 10. The 1917 Aisne Campaign: Juvincourt and the Winterberg

[178] Willmott, pp. 204-208.

[179] Sheldon, *The German Army in the Spring Offensives 1917; Arras, Aisne & Champagne*, Pen and Sword Military, 2015, p. 145.

[180] Falls, C. (1940). *Military Operations France and Belgium, 1917 Vol I The German Retreat to the Hindenburg Line and the Battles of Arras* (IWM & Battery Press 1992 ed.). London. P. 495-496.

[181] Lais, *Limestone Chalk, pp.* 143-146.

[182] Ibid, pp. 147-149.

[183] Description of Granatenwerfer 16 provided from "Forgotten Weapons" website, viewed September 5, 2016. http://www.forgottenweapons.com/granatenwerfer-16.

[184] Lais, *Limestone Chalk*, p. 152-157

[185] Lais, *Limestone Chalk,* p. 151.

[186] Sheldon, Jack, *The Germany Army in the Spring Offensives 1917,* pp 237-238.

[187] Anon (1914–1921). *The Times History of the War Vol XII.* London: The Times, pp. 104-105.

[188] Lais, *Limestone Chalk,* pp. 158-160

[189] Ibid, pp. 117-121.

[190] Anon, p. 212

[191] Lais, *Limestone Chalk* pp. 161-165. IR's refitting at Lappion is taken from these pages.

[192] Ibid, p. 166.

[193] Rogerson, p. 124.

[194] Lais, *Limestone Chalk,* p. 168.

[195] Ibid p. 166-174. Lais descriptions of IR 169's first four days in fighting on the Winterberg are taken from these pages.

[196] Ibid, p. 174-187. Highlights of Lais account IR 169's fifth – six days of Winterberg fighting are from these pages.

[197] Ibid, p. 166.

[198] Ibid, pp. 190-194. Summary of casualties, burials and movement off the Winterberg.

[199] Ibid, pp. 195-200. Deployment to Bouconville sector.

Chapter 11. The Battle of Pinon

[200] This passage gives hint that Lais was frustrated that IR 169 never published an official regimental history. This was likely a strong motivation for his writing three books on the regiment's wartime service.

[201] Ibid, pp. 206-208. The 52nd Division's refit in La Selve.

[202] Reicharchive 1942 *Der Weltkrieg 1914 bis 1918: Die militärischen Operationen zu Lande [The World War 1914–1918: Military Operations on Land]. XIII (Die digitale landesbibliotek Oberösterreich 2012 ed.). Potsdam: Mittler. 1942. OCLC 257129831.* Descriptions on La Malmaison troop strength and planning information come this source, Page 114-118, retrieved 8 October 2016 from https://en.wikipedia.org/wiki/Battle_of_La_Malmaison, viewed December 2016.

[203] Lais, *Limestone Chalk* pp. 215-219. Deployment to the Pinon reserve positions.

[204] *The Times History of the War*, PDF version, XVI. London: The Times. 1914–1921. OCLC 70406275. Page 225. Retrieved 10 October 2016, from https://en.wikipedia.org/wiki/Battle_of_La_Malmaison.

[205] Lais, *Limestone Chalk,* pp 219-226. Description of entrapment inside Pinon Cave, 19-20 October 1917.

[206] Ibid,pp. 227-229. The opening of the French ground assault.

[207] Various sources on the launch of the offensive summarized from *Battle of La Malmaison Wikipedia* article, cited above, including Reicharchive 1942, pages 121. Retrieved November 25, 2016. Descriptions of 52nd Division efforts to organize the defensive line are from *Kreidekalk* pp 240-241.

[208] Lais, *Limestone Chalk* pp 232-236. The stand of the 2nd Bn, IR 111 on Oct 23.

[209] Lais published *Limestone Chalk* in 1942, at which time he was a reserve officer again serving the German Army in world war. His reflections on Germany's WW I armor deficiencies in comparison to its 1942 capabilities likely came to his mind in this passage.

[210] Ibid, pp 242-249. The defense of IR 169 battalions on 23-24 October.

[211] Ibid, pp 251-253. The retreat across the Ailette Canal.

[212] Ibid pp 253-256. Patrol to disable abandoned artillery and return to German lines.

[213] Philpott, W. *(2014). Attrition: Fighting the First World War. London: Little, Brown.* As cited from *Battle of La Malmaison Wikipedia* article, Retrieved December 6, 2016.

[214] Anon, pp. 210-211.

[215] Lais, *Limestone Chalk,* pp. 258-260. Aftermath of Battle of Pinon.

Chapter 12. Transition to the 1918 Spring Offensives

[216] Lais, *Limestone Chalk* pp. 284-289. The operations order and mission planning of the raid.

[217] Lais, *Limestone Chalk* pp 290-299. Execution of the raid.

[218] Ibid, p. 300.

[219] Banks, p. 180.

[220] Simpson, Andy. *The Evolution of Victory: British Battles of the Western Front, 1914–1918.* Tom Donovan, 1995. pp. 117-118.

[221] Bull, *Trench: A History of Trench Warfare on the Western Front*, p 240. p. 246.

[222] Lupfer, Timothy T, *The Dynamics of Doctrine: The Changes in German Tactical Doctrine during the First World War*, Combat Studies Institute, U.S. Army Command and General Staff College, Fort Leavenworth, Kansas, July 1981, pp 43-44.

[223] D T Zabecki, *The German 1918 Offensives: A Case Study of The Operational Level of War*, Taylor & Francis, 2005, p. 56.

[224] Lais, p. 31.

[225] *Die Badener im Weltkrieg*, pp. 326-328.

[226] Marix Evans, Martin (2002) *1918: The Year of Victories*, Arcturus Military History Series, London: Arcturus, p. 63.

[227] Willmott, p. 255.

Chapter 13. The 1918 Aisne Offensive and Flanders

[228] Lupfer, pp. 23-24.

[229] Zaloga, Steven J. *German Panzers 1914-18*, Opsrey Publishing, UK, 2006, pp 16-17.

[230] Lais, *Hero's Death*, pp. 75-80.

[231] *House of the Last Cartridge* website: Description of the museum and 1870 Battle of Bazeilles taken from website: https://translate.google.com/translate?hl=en&sl=fr&u=https://fr.wikipe dia.org/wiki/Maison_de_la_derni, as viewed on February 19, 2017.

[232] Lais, *Hero's Death*, p. 75.

[233] Rogerson, Sidney. *"The Last of the Ebb; The Battle of the Aisne, 1918*, Greenhill Books, 1937 (2007 edition), London, p. 122

[234] Ibid, p. 127. (All further references from this source listed "Rogerson, *The Last Ebb*.)

[235] Rogerson, Sidney. *Supplement to War Diary for the 2nd West Yorkshire Regiment*; titled. *A Narrative of Events Between the Aisne & the Marne Between May & June, 1918.* p.1. (All further references from this source listed "Rogerson, *An Narrative of Events*.")

[236] Lais, *Iron Regiment*, p. 29.

[237] Rogerson. p.1. 'Rest cure' quote from page 3.

[238] Lais, *Hero's Death*, p. 94.

[239] Ibid, p. 95

[240] Ibid, pp. 96-97.

[241] Rogerson, *An Narrative of Events*. p.6.

[242] Ibid. p.7.

[243] Lais, *Hero's Death* pp. 99.

[244] Rogerson, *An Narrative of Events,* p.7.

[245] Ibid. p.3.

[246] Lais, *Hero's Death* pp. 112. Lais sketch of the battle depicts German troops assaulting alongside a Mark IV tank.

[247] Keep Military Museum website: *The Battle of Bois des Buttes,* viewed 15 May 2016. http://www.keepmilitarymuseum.org/history/first+world+war/the+dev onshire+regiment/the+second+battalion/the+battle+of+bois+des+butte s. All details from the British perspective on the Devonshire's stand on 27 May 1918 originates from this source.

[248] Lais, *Hero's Death,* p. 99.

[249] Ibid, p. 104.

[250] Ibid, p. 108.

[251] Ibid, p. 109.

[252] Ibid, pp. 110-111.

[253] The Wardrobe, Home of the Wiltshire, (Duke of Edinburghs) Regiment website, viewed 2 July 2016, *First World War, 1918, 1ˢᵗ Battalion,* http://www.thewardrobe.org.uk/research/history-of-regiments/the-duke-of-edinburghs-wiltshire-regiment-1881-1920-the-wiltshire-regiment-duke-of-edinburghs-1920-1959; and memorial webpage for Corporal Harry George Hunt, killed in action on May 27, 1918.

[254] Lais, *Hero's Death,* p. 115.

[255] Ibid, pp. 112-113.

[256] Hart, Peter (2008). *1918: A Very British Victory,* Phoenix Books, London, p. 283.

[257] Rogerson, *An Narrative of Events,* p. 12."

[258] Ibid, pp. 9-10.

[259] Lais, *Hero's Death* pp. 118.

[260] Ibid, pp. 121.

[261] Ibid, pp. 123-125.

[262] Ibid, p. 141.

[263] Ibid, pp. 126-129 contains the account of the Lais' columns nighttime ambush by a French artillery battery.

[264] Rogerson, *An Narrative of Events,* pp. 14-15.

[265] Captain R. B. Ainsworth M.C., The Story of the 6th Battalion, Durham Light Infantry, as viewed July 16, 2016, https://archive.org/stream/6thbattaliondur00ainuoft/6thbattaliondur00a inuoft_djvu.txt. This account places the 151st Brigade Company at Romigny on May 29, 1918 in a description that matches Lais' narrative.

[266] Lais, *Hero's Death,* pp. 130-131.

[267] Rogerson. 21.

[268] Lais, *Hero's Death,* pp. 132-135.

[269] Ibid, pp. 136-137.

[270] Ibid, pp. 137-138.

[271] Rogerson, *The Last Ebb,* p. 146-147.

[272] Lais, *Hero's Death,* p. 142.

[273] Lais, *Iron Regiment,* 25.

[274] Jackson, p.195.

[275] Lais, *Iron Regiment.* p. 26.

[276] Ibid.

[277] Lais, *Hero's Death,* p. 115.

[278] Jackson, p.196

[279] Lais, *Iron Regiment,* p.27.

[280] *Baden in World War,* pp. 390-391.

Chapter 14. Return to the Somme; Battle of Bapaume

[281] Willmott, p. 264.

[282] Lais, *Iron Regiment,* p. 30.

[283] *Baden in World War,* p. 391.

[284] Lais, *Iron Regiment,* 30-31.

[285] Ibid, pp. 31-32.

[286] Ibid, pp. 32-33.

[287] Ibid, pp. 33.

[288] *Baden in World War,* p. 391

[289] Bennighof, Michael, Ph.D, *German Naval Infantry in the Defense of Berlin,* Avalanche Press, 2013 (portion on WW I taken from on-line

excerpt, retrieved May 2014,
http://www.avalanchepress.com/GermanNavalInf.php.)

[290] Lais, *Iron Regiment*, pp. 33-34.

[291] *Baden in World War*, p. 392.

[292] Gray, Jack, *The New Zealand Division in France and Flanders, May 1916-November 1918,* viewed in May 2014 from from 2005 Internet posting,
http://christchurchcitylibraries.com/Heritage/Publications/
NewZealandDivisionInFranceAndFlanders/NewZealandDivisionInFra
nceAndFlanders.pdf.

[293] Lais, *Iron Regiment*, p.34.

[294] Ibid, p.35.

[295] *Baden in World War*, p. 392.

[296] Ibid.

[297] Lais, *Iron Regiment,* pp. 36-37.

[298] *Baden in World War*, p. 392-394.

[299] Gray, Jack, *The New Zealand Division in France and Flanders.*

[300] *4th Battalion Bedfordshire Regiment Report on Operations August 20-28, 1918.* Report was viewed in April 2014 as viewed by the website: *The Befordfordshire Regiment in the Great War*, edited by Steven Fuller. http://www.bedfordregiment.org.uk/.

Chapter 15. Bapaume and the Retreat from Le Transloy

[301] Arthur Conan Doyle, *The British Campaign in France and Flanders, Vol. VI, Chapter IV*, the Attack of Byng's Third Army, August 21, 1918, to September 29, 1918. First published by Hodder & Stoughton, London, 1920; taken from a Project Gutenberg of Australia eBook format.)

[302] Lais, *Iron Regiment*, p. 37

[303] Ibid, p. 38

[304] Ibid.

[305] Ibid, pp. 39-41.

[306] Rickard, J (5 September 2007), *Second battle of Bapaume, 21 August-1 September 1918*, viewed April 2014 from website.
http://www.historyofwar.org/articles/battles_bapaumeII.html.

[307] Lais, *Iron Regiment*, pp.42-43.

[308] Ibid, p. 44.

[309] Ibid.

[310] Ibid pp. 45-46

[311] Gaulk, Randal S. *A Companion to the Meuse Argonne Campaign*; Chapter on *The 111th German Infantrerie Regiment by Exermont*, John Wiley and Sons, UK, 2014, p 235.

[312] Lais, *Hero's Death*, p. 170.

Chapter 16. Meuse-Argonne Forest (Part I) : The Kriemhilde Stellung

[313] SLA Marshall, pp.333-334.

[314] Ibid, 333.

[315] PBS, *The American Experience*, McArthur. From following website, viewed February 2014: http://www.pbs.org/wgbh/amex/macarthur/maps/chatelion02.html

[316] Robert H. Ferrell, *America's Deadliest Battle, Meuse-Argonne, 1918, University Press of Kansas, Lawrence, KS, 2007, p 43.*

[317] *American Armies and Battlefields in Europe*, Center of Military History, Washington D.C. 1992 edition (first published in 1938 by the American Battle Monuments Commission). p. 222.

[318] Carlo D'Este, *Patton; A Genius for War*, Harper Perennial, NY, 1995, pp. 254-258.

[319] Gaulk, p 235. Most of the information of IR 111's operations from Sep 28 – Oct 2 are from this source.

[320] Lais, *Hero's Death*, p. 155.

[321] Ibid, description of Sep 29 operations, p. 159-160.

[322] Gaulk, p 236-237. (Here, Gaulk records that Major Wulff was given command of IR 169 at this time, but Lais accounts in the later period of the Meuse-Argonne Campaign lists Major Schilling as the IR 169 commander. It is likely that Major Wulff may have briefly had command of IR 169, but for whatever reason, later reverted back to Schilling.)

[323] Lais, *Hero's Death*, p. 209.

[324] Ferrell, pp. 56-72.

[325] Ibid, p. 80.

[326] Ibid, p. 74-79.

[327] *American Armies and Battlefields in Europe*, pp. 229-230.

[328] Ferrell, p. 85.

[329] Ibid, p. 96.

[330] Ibid, p. 96.

[331] *Infantry in Battle*, The Infantry Journal Inc, Washington D.C., 1939. pp. 340-342.

[332] Lais, *Hero's Death*, pp. 166-169.

[333] Gaulk, p 239.

[334] Lais, *Hero's Death*, p. 170.

[335] Ibid, p. 172.

[336] Ibid, p. 171.

[337] Gaulk, p 240.

[338] *Infantry in Battle*, p. 271.

[339] Gaulk, p 236-240.

[340] Lais, *Hero's Death*, p. 174.

[341] Ibid, p. 175.

[342] *Infantry in Battle*, pp. 188-192.

[343] Gaulk, p 242.

[344] Ferrell. pp. 96-99.

[345] Jones, Nathan A. *A Companion to the Meuse Argonne Campaign*; Chapter on *Cracking the Kriemhilde Stellung,* John Wiley and Sons, UK, 2014, pp. 108-109.

[346] Lais, *Hero's Death,* pp. 186-189.

[347] Ibid, p. 190.

[348] Ibid, pp. 191-194.

[349] Ibid, pp. 195-196.

[350] *Use of Gas in the Meuse-Argonne Campaign; September – October 1918*, Washington, D.C., U.S. Chemical Corps, 1958.

[351] Francis P. Duffy, *Father Duffy's Story; A tale of Honor and Heroism, of Life and Death with the Fighting 69th (Garden City, NY, 1918),* p. 265-267_. (This citation came from Ferrell, p. 104.)

[352] Ferrell, pp. 56-72.

[353] Lais, *Hero's Death,* p. 196.

[354] *American Armies and Battlefields in Europe*, p. 243.

[355] Lais, *Hero's Death,* p. 197.

[356] Ferrell. P 107-108.

Chapter 17. Meuse-Argonne Forest (Part II) : A Regiment Dies a Hero's Death

[357] Lais, *Hero's Death,* p. 199.

[358] Ibid, p. 198.

[359] Ibid, p. 206.

[360] Ferrell, pp. 111-118.

[361] *Use of Gas in the Meuse-Argonne Campaign.*

[362] Lais, *Hero's Death,* pp. 208-210.

[363] Ibid, p. 213.

[364] Lais, *Hero's Death,* pp. 211-212.

[365] *Use of Gas in the Meuse-Argonne Campaign.*

[366] Lais, *Hero's Death,* p. 213.

[367] *American Armies and Battlefields in Europe*, p. 327.

[368] Edwin Simmons and Joseph H. Alexander, *Through the Wheat; The U.S. Marines in World War I,* Naval Institute Press, Annapolis, MD, 2008., p 224.

[369] Lais, *Hero's Death,* These pages describe the period Oct 27-early hours of Nov 1, 1918. pp. 214-219.

[370] Simmons/Alexander, p. 225.

[371] Ferrell, p. 232.

[372] Lais, *Hero's Death,* pp. 222-223.

[373] Simmons/Alexander, p. 227.

[374] Lais, *Hero's Death* p. 224

[375] Ibid, p. 47.

[376] Ibid, p. 225.

[377] Simmons/Alexander, p. 233.

[378] Lais, *Hero's Death,* pp. 231-232.

[379] Ibid, p. 235.

[380] Simmons/Alexander, pp. 234-237.

[381] Ibid, p. 239.

[382] Lais, *Hero's Death,* pp. 235-238. Lais on post-Armistice activities.

Postscript

[383] References to German World War II service of an Otto Lais come from the following sources: Lais capture by Canadian forces is per Mark, Zuehlke, *On to Victory, the Canadian Liberation of the Netherlands, March 23 – May 5, 1945.* Douglas & McIntyre, Canada, 2010. On-line reference to Lais' combat award from '*Feldgrau.com, Knights Cross Holders,*' found on http://www.feldgrau.com/KnightsCrossHolders2.

php?ID=3560, viewed December 17, 2016. Information on the service of the 346 Infantry Division taken from *www.axishistory.com*, viewed on http://www.axishistory.com/bookstore/150-germany-heer/heer-divisionen/3482-346-infanterie-division; viewed December 18, 2016. Additional details on the 346th Infantry Division is from the Canadian Soldiers website: http://www.canadiansoldiers.com/enemies/infanterie346.htm; viewed December 17, 2016.

[384]Langenfeld, Ludwin, Otto Lais; Das graphische Werk Eines symbolischen Realisten der zwanziger Jahre. (*Otto Lais, The Graphic work of Symbolic Realism in the 20th Century*), Verlag Karl Schillinger, Freiburg i. Br., 1981, pp 7-10.

A summary of the bio sketch is taken from this source, with the exception of the German "Who's Who" website article reference taken from: *de.wikipedia.org/wiki/Otto_Lais*. Viewed, December 16, 2016.

For more great stories visit our website @

www.BadgleyPublishingCompany.com

Printed in Great Britain
by Amazon

27729920R00267